Organizational Data Mining: Leveraging Enterprise Data Resources for Optimal Performance

Hamid R. Nemati
University of North Carolina at Greensboro, USA

Christopher D. Barko
University of North Carolina at Greensboro, USA

IDEA GROUP PUBLISHING

Hershey • London • Melbourne • Singapore

Acquisition Editor:	Mehdi Khosrow-Pour
Senior Managing Editor:	Jan Travers
Managing Editor:	Amanda Appicello
Development Editor:	Michele Rossi
Copy Editor:	Heidi J. Hormel
Typesetter:	Jennifer Wetzel
Cover Design:	Lisa Tosheff
Printed at:	Integrated Book Technology

Published in the United States of America by
  Idea Group Publishing (an imprint of Idea Group Inc.)
  701 E. Chocolate Avenue, Suite 200
  Hershey PA 17033
  Tel: 717-533-8845
  Fax: 717-533-8661
  E-mail: cust@idea-group.com
  Web site: http://www.idea-group.com

and in the United Kingdom by
  Idea Group Publishing (an imprint of Idea Group Inc.)
  3 Henrietta Street
  Covent Garden
  London WC2E 8LU
  Tel: 44 20 7240 0856
  Fax: 44 20 7379 3313
  Web site: http://www.eurospan.co.uk

Library of Congress Cataloging-in-Publication Data

Nemati, Hamid R., 1958-
  Organizational data mining : leveraging enterprise data resources for
optimal performance / Hamid R. Nemati and Christopher D. Barko.
      p. cm.
  ISBN 1-59140-134-8 (hardcover) -- ISBN 1-59140-135-6 (ebook)
  1. Knowledge management. 2. Data mining. 3. Business--Data
processing. I. Barko, Christopher D., 1968- II. Title.
  HD30.2.N46 2003
  658.4'038'028563
                                                          2003008882

paperback ISBN 1-59140-222-0

British Cataloguing in Publication Data
A Cataloguing in Publication record for this book is available from the British Library.

NEW from Idea Group Publishing

- **The Enterprise Resources Planning Decade: Lessons Learned and Issues for the Future**, Frederic Adam and David Sammon/ ISBN:1-59140-188-7; eISBN 1-59140-189-5, © 2004
- **Electronic Commerce in Small to Medium-Sized Enterprises**, Nabeel A. Y. Al-Qirim/ ISBN: 1-59140-146-1; eISBN 1-59140-147-X, © 2004
- **e-Business, e-Government & Small and Medium-Size Enterprises: Opportunities & Challenges**, Brian J. Corbitt & Nabeel A. Y. Al-Qirim/ ISBN: 1-59140-202-6; eISBN 1-59140-203-4, © 2004
- **Multimedia Systems and Content-Based Image Retrieval**, Sagarmay Deb ISBN: 1-59140-156-9; eISBN 1-59140-157-7, © 2004
- **Computer Graphics and Multimedia: Applications, Problems and Solutions**, John DiMarco/ ISBN: 1-59140-196-86; eISBN 1-59140-197-6, © 2004
- **Social and Economic Transformation in the Digital Era**, Georgios Doukidis, Nikolaos Mylonopoulos & Nancy Pouloudi/ ISBN: 1-59140-158-5; eISBN 1-59140-159-3, © 2004
- **Information Security Policies and Actions in Modern Integrated Systems**, Mariagrazia Fugini & Carlo Bellettini/ ISBN: 1-59140-186-0; eISBN 1-59140-187-9, © 2004
- **Digital Government: Principles and Best Practices**, Alexei Pavlichev & G. David Garson/ISBN: 1-59140-122-4; eISBN 1-59140-123-2, © 2004
- **Virtual and Collaborative Teams: Process, Technologies and Practice**, Susan H. Godar & Sharmila Pixy Ferris/ ISBN: 1-59140-204-2; eISBN 1-59140-205-0, © 2004
- **Intelligent Enterprises of the 21st Century**, Jatinder Gupta & Sushil Sharma/ ISBN: 1-59140-160-7; eISBN 1-59140-161-5, © 2004
- **Creating Knowledge Based Organizations**, Jatinder Gupta & Sushil Sharma/ ISBN: 1-59140-162-3; eISBN 1-59140-163-1, © 2004
- **Knowledge Networks: Innovation through Communities of Practice**, Paul Hildreth & Chris Kimble/ISBN: 1-59140-200-X; eISBN 1-59140-201-8, © 2004
- **Going Virtual: Distributed Communities of Practice**, Paul Hildreth/ISBN: 1-59140-164-X; eISBN 1-59140-165-8, © 2004
- **Trust in Knowledge Management and Systems in Organizations**, Maija-Leena Huotari & Mirja Iivonen/ ISBN: 1-59140-126-7; eISBN 1-59140-127-5, © 2004
- **Strategies for Managing IS/IT Personnel**, Magid Igbaria & Conrad Shayo/ISBN: 1-59140-128-3; eISBN 1-59140-129-1, © 2004
- **Information Technology and Customer Relationship Management Strategies**, Vince Kellen, Andy Drefahl & Susy Chan/ ISBN: 1-59140-170-4; eISBN 1-59140-171-2, © 2004
- **Beyond Knowledge Management**, Brian Lehaney, Steve Clarke, Elayne Coakes & Gillian Jack/ ISBN: 1-59140-180-1; eISBN 1-59140-181-X, © 2004
- **Multimedia Security: Steganography and Digital Watermarking Techniques for Protection of Intellectual Property**, Chun-Shien Lu/ ISBN: 1-59140-192-5; eISBN 1-59140-193-3, © 2004
- **eTransformation in Governance: New Directions in Government and Politics**, Matti Mälkiä, Ari Veikko Anttiroiko & Reijo Savolainen/ISBN: 1-59140-130-5; eISBN 1-59140-131-3, © 2004
- **Intelligent Agents for Data Mining and Information Retrieval**, Masoud Mohammadian/ISBN: 1-59140-194-1; eISBN 1-59140-195-X, © 2004
- **Using Community Informatics to Transform Regions**, Stewart Marshall, Wal Taylor & Xinghuo Yu/ISBN: 1-59140-132-1; eISBN 1-59140-133-X, © 2004
- **Wireless Communications and Mobile Commerce**, Nan Si Shi/ ISBN: 1-59140-184-4; eISBN 1-59140-185-2, © 2004
- **Organizational Data Mining: Leveraging Enterprise Data Resources for Optimal Performance**, Hamid R. Nemati & Christopher D. Barko/ ISBN: 1-59140-134-8; eISBN 1-59140-135-6, © 2004
- **Virtual Teams: Projects, Protocols and Processes**, David J. Pauleen/ISBN: 1-59140-166-6; eISBN 1-59140-167-4, © 2004
- **Business Intelligence in the Digital Economy: Opportunities, Limitations and Risks**, Mahesh Raisinghani/ ISBN: 1-59140-206-9; eISBN 1-59140-207-7, © 2004
- **E-Business Innovation and Change Management**, Mohini Singh & Di Waddell/ISBN: 1-59140-138-0; eISBN 1-59140-139-9, © 2004
- **Responsible Management of Information Systems**, Bernd Stahl/ISBN: 1-59140-172-0; eISBN 1-59140-173-9, © 2004
- **Web Information Systems**, David Taniar/ISBN: 1-59140-208-5; eISBN 1-59140-209-3, © 2004
- **Strategies for Information Technology Governance**, Wim van Grembergen/ISBN: 1-59140-140-2; eISBN 1-59140-141-0, © 2004
- **Information and Communication Technology for Competitive Intelligence**, Dirk Vriens/ISBN: 1-59140-142-9; eISBN 1-59140-143-7, © 2004
- **The Handbook of Information Systems Research**, Michael E. Whitman & Amy B. Woszczynski/ISBN: 1-59140-144-5; eISBN 1-59140-145-3, © 2004
- **Neural Networks in Business Forecasting**, G. Peter Zhang/ISBN: 1-59140-176-3; eISBN 1-59140-177-1, © 2004

Excellent additions to your institution's library! Recommend these titles to your Librarian!

**To receive a copy of the Idea Group Publishing catalog, please contact 1/717-533-8845,
fax 1/717-533-8661,or visit the IGP Online Bookstore at:
[http://www.idea-group.com]!
Note: All IGP books are also available as ebooks on netlibrary.com as well as other ebook sources.
Contact Ms. Carrie Skovrinskie at [cskovrinskie@idea-group.com] to receive a complete list of sources
where you can obtain ebook information or IGP titles.**

Dedication

Hamid R. Nemati --

This book is dedicated to the most wonderful people in my life about whom there can never be enough good things said. Try as I may, all my attempts fall short. To my wife, my best friend, my soul mate and the love of my life for her passion for free thinking and tolerance and for being a constant reminder of all good things that are possible. To my son, for his energy, enthusiasm and free spirit. Being your father has been the most fulfilling experience in my life. To my parents who have always been there for me with love and unwavering support from beginning and whose love has sustained me through it all. They both have encouraged me to develop a love for learning and have shown me the joys of discovery. You are all my greatest inspiration and have touched my life in so many wonderful ways and left me a better person because it.

Christopher D. Barko --

This book and research are dedicated to my wonderful and loving wife, Cindy, and my beautiful children, Matthew and Sarah, whose priceless smiles at the end of the day make it all worthwhile. Without your support, sacrifice and understanding this book would not have been possible.

I also want to dedicate this book and research to my magnificent and loving parents and grandparents who taught me the joys of computing, a love for nature and a disciplined work ethic that amply rewards those who diligently and meticulously search for the truth. Thanks Mom and Dad.

I also dedicate this book to my brother, Mike, and sisters, Lizzie and Katie, whose friendship and companionship over the years are immeasurable. Vigorously pursue your dreams and may happiness accompany you wherever you go.

To my friends, both new and old, a heartfelt thanks to you for your wonderful friendship that has made my life immeasurably richer and more fulfilling.

To all those readers who appreciate nature's beauty in its many facets while on the trails or trekking to the mountaintops, may you find solitude and inner peace in its captivating splendor and elegant perfection.

And lastly, I want to thank my friend and mentor Hamid Nemati whose guidance, friendship, dedication and encouragement for this book and research have made it all a success.

Organizational Data Mining: Leveraging Enterprise Data Resources for Optimal Performance

Table of Contents

Preface

Mountains of business data are piling up in organizations every day. These organizations collect data from multiple sources, both internal and external. These sources include legacy systems, customer relationship management and enterprise resource planning applications, online and e-commerce systems, government organizations and business suppliers and partners. A recent study from the University of California at Berkeley found the amount of data organizations collect and store in enterprise databases doubles every year, and slightly more than half of this data will consist of "reference information," which is the kind of information strategic business applications and decision support systems demand (Kestelyn, 2002). Terabyte-sized (1,000 megabytes) databases are commonplace in organizations today, and this enormous growth will make petabyte-sized databases (1,000 terabytes) a reality within the next few years (Whiting, 2002). By 2004 the Gartner Group estimates worldwide data volumes will be 30 times those of 1999, which translates into more data having been produced in the last 30 years than during the previous 5,000 (Wurman, 1989).

This proclamation about data volume growth is no longer surprising, but continues to astound. Although for businesses, more data isn't always better. Organizations must assess what data they need to collect and how best to leverage it. Collecting, storing and managing business data and associated databases can be costly, and expending scarce resources to acquire extraneous data fuels inefficiency and hinders optimal performance. Managers must thoroughly understand the factors driving their business in order to optimize their data management efforts.

In spite of this enormous growth in enterprise databases, research from IBM revealed that organizations use less than 1 percent of their data for analysis (Brown, 2002). This is the fundamental irony of the "Information Age" we live in: Organizations possess an enormous amount of business information, yet have so little real business knowledge. And, to magnify the problem further, a leading business intelligence firm recently surveyed executives at 450 companies and discovered that 90 percent of these organizations rely on gut instinct, rather than hard facts for most of their decisions, because they lack the necessary information when they need it (Brown, 2002).

The solution for these problems lies in a technology known as Organizational Data Mining (ODM). ODM is defined as leveraging data mining tools and technologies to enhance the decision-making process by transforming data into valuable and actionable knowledge to gain a competitive advantage (Nemati & Barko, 2001). ODM eliminates the guesswork that permeates so much of corporate decision-making. Advances in ODM technology have helped many organizations optimize internal resource allocations, while better understanding and responding to the needs of their customers.

ODM can analyze enormous volumes of data while determining the most pertinent data to focus on. The end result is optimal resource allocation and improved business performance.

This book is the result of numerous observations that data mining is gaining greater acceptance within organizations and delivering colossal benefits, yet there are few scholarly books devoted to the exploration of both the organizational and technical factors involved in leveraging enterprise data resources for optimal performance. Our objective is not to address all aspects of ODM — this would obviously require many more volumes. In addition, this book is not a data mining how-to manuscript — there are many of those available that adequately cover the technical aspects of data mining. Instead, we intend to explore and bring to light a number of interesting and practical domains within ODM, which integrates both data mining and organizational disciplines, such as organizational learning and behavior, business culture and ethics, business strategy and knowledge management. Practitioners, educators and members of the research and development community will each find relevant and enticing material in the following chapters.

ORGANIZATION OF THE BOOK

Chapter I begins with an introduction to ODM by explaining what it is, how ODM is distinctly different from simple data mining, and briefly elaborate on its significance in today's competitive organizations. In addition, we take a look at the current status of ODM research, examine the evolution of ODM to the present day and contemplate its challenging yet opportunistic future. The remaining sections of the book explore ODM from different organizational perspectives. These sections are the Strategic Implications of ODM, Business Process Innovations through ODM, ODM Analytics and Algorithms, Industrial ODM Applications, and ODM Challenges and Opportunities. These sections contain many insightful and cutting-edge chapters from some of the best and brightest practitioners and researchers in ODM. We will now elaborate on each section's contents in more detail.

The first section, Strategic Implications of ODM, contains Chapters I through V on ODM's supporting role in formulating and implementing corporate strategy. Chapter II looks at multinational corporate sustainability from a content-analysis approach. The authors argue that companies are no longer motivated by finances and that societal concerns are being recognized and addressed by corporate board members of Fortune's Global 500. This chapter employs the use of content analysis of corporate messages to quantify the frequency/presence of certain words and phrases related to corporate sustainability within the annual reports of 24 multinational firms. Chapter III utilizes Michael Porter's Five Forces Model to understand the potential strategic value of ODM within the Australian Banking industry. This chapter explores how ODM can affect industry structure and attractiveness by assisting businesses, such as banks, to defend themselves against forces, such as those asserted by buyers, substitute products, new entrants and suppliers. Chapter IV investigates the role of ODM in supporting strategic decision making by providing validation for Micro-Theories (MTs), which are beliefs regarding the organization's task environment, such as sales increasing in a certain segment or customers preferring a certain product. This chapter suggests a four-step process for identifying and verifying MTs and illustrates this with a hypothetical example of a bank. Chapter V focuses on the privacy implications of ODM. The authors look at ethical data management issues from both an organizational and governmental viewpoint.

Section Two, Business Process Innovations through ODM, contains chapters exploring how ODM enables business process innovation. Chapter VI looks at the potential of knowledge exchange in organizations and provides readers with an understanding of the human dynamics of expert knowledge exchange in the realm of virtual teams. The authors present research, theory and the methodologies now in professional use to assess information exchange potential for knowledge management (KM) related activities at the team level as well as from the perspective of organizational culture. Chapter VII introduces practical issues of information navigation and organizational knowledge management involved in delivering customer service via the Internet. This chapter presents an adaptive, organic approach to knowledge management and discusses a state-of-the-art application named RightNow eService Center that embodies this concept. Chapter VIII discusses formulating a successful purchasing negotiation strategy and proposes that the buyer's level of expertise and/or simulated negotiation experiences through the experiential learning process help him/her better prepare for the negotiation and, thereby, increase his/her bargaining strength. This chapter uses both statistical data analysis and data mining techniques to demonstrate their usefulness in the optimal performance of business-to-business negotiations. Chapter IX focuses on extracting value from virtual organizational discussions through textual data mining. This chapter proposes a method of recovering value from the text of virtual group discussions based on methods derived from the communication field.

The third section, ODM Analytics and Algorithms, includes chapters of a more technical flavor and investigates new methods in ODM analytics and algorithms. Chapter X presents an integrated model in which data mining and online analytical processing (OLAP) complement each other to support intelligent decision making for data-rich environments. Chapter XI presents knowledge mining in decision support system model analysis. The three stages of mathematical modeling include model formulation, solution and analysis, with the later being seldomly addressed and, thus, the focus of this chapter. Chapter XII discusses recent advances in the use of agent technology in Decision Support Systems (DSS) and introduces a model for an agent-based DSS. This chapter informs the readers about the state-of-the-art in agent-based DSS and illustrates an example of an agent-based DSS for investment decisions. Chapter XIII proposes a methodology to scan, analyze and classify the content of primarily text-based Web documents to aid an organization in gathering information. The purpose of this chapter is to develop and demonstrate a methodology used to aid an organization in its environmental scanning efforts in light of the vast quantities of information available via the Internet.

The fourth section, Industrial ODM Applications, contains case studies of commercial applications of ODM and demonstrates how leading organizations are leveraging this technology for optimal performance. Chapter XIV discusses the basic concepts of data warehousing and, then, illustrates them through a case study of the global enterprise data warehouse (GEDW) implemented at 3M. The lessons learned at 3M can help other companies with their data warehousing initiatives. Chapter XV addresses ODM in franchise organizations. This chapter describes a comprehensive franchise framework, identifies the most important aspects of a franchising business and describes the role OLAP and data mining play and the necessary data items to ensure success. Chapter XVI examines the use of fuzzy clustering and expert reasoning for the identification of firms whose financial statements are affected by fraudulent financial reporting. The authors use a combination of fuzzy logic, expert reasoning and a statistical tool as an innovative method to evaluate the risk of fraudulent financial reporting. Chapter XVII describes ways in which library and information managers can use data mining in their libraries, i.e., bibliomining, to understand patterns of behavior among library users and staff members, and patterns of information resource use throughout the institution. This chapter presents a global view of the data generated in libraries and the variety of decisions that those data can inform. Chapter XVIII discusses how advances in data mining translate into business context. This chapter focuses on the retail industry and highlights the art of business implementation rather than the science of knowledge discovery in databases (KDD).

The last section, ODM Challenges and Opportunities, investigates the current challenges and opportunities surrounding ODM and how organizations are leveraging it to build or sustain a competitive advantage. Chapter XIX discusses impediments to exploratory ODM success. These impediments are based on an expert's anecdotal observations from multiple projects, either reviewed or undertaken by the author. The intent of the chapter is to provide an organization with a structure to anticipate these problems and prevent their occurrence in ODM efforts. Chapter XX argues that knowledge resides in human minds and is created by the continuous action and interaction happening in specific social contexts. This chapter highlights the advantages of adopting a constructionist knowledge approach and presents some constructionist guidelines to assist in the definition of ODM practices that leverage knowledge creation in organizations. Chapter XXI discusses the three phases of Web mining (data gathering, analysis and reporting) and describes each of these phases in detail along with a discussion of Electronic Customer Relationship Management (eCRM). In addition, integration issues and challenges surrounding Web mining and eCRM are explored. And lastly, Chapter XXII introduces a framework for ODM suited for both data-driven and hypotheses-driven problems. This ODM framework includes a comprehensive processing scheme that aims at increasing the benefits of ODM and other data analysis approaches by allowing a wider range of business problems to be tackled and by providing the users with structured guidance for planning and running analyses.

In closing, we believe that all enterprises are slowly moving from the Information Age to the Knowledge Age, where organizations will use ODM and supporting technologies to augment intuition with the purpose of allocating scarce enterprise resources for optimal performance. Industry professionals have suggested that many corporations could maintain current revenues at half the current costs, if they optimized their use of corporate data. Whether this finding is true or not, it sheds light on an important issue. Leading corporations in the next decade will adopt and weave these ODM technologies into the fabric of their organizations at all levels, from upper management all the way down to the lowest organizational level. Once the first organization within an industry realizes a competitive advantage through ODM and assimilates it into its decision-making process, it is only a matter of time before one of three events transpires: its industry competitors either adopt ODM, change industries or vanish. By adopting ODM, an organization's managers and employees are able to act sooner rather than later, anticipate rather than react, know rather than guess and, ultimately, succeed rather than fail.

REFERENCES

Brown, E. (2002, April 1). Analyze this. *Forbes, 169*(8), 96-98.

Kestelyn, J. (2002, August 12). No longer an afterthought. *Intelligent Enterprise,* 5(13), 6.

Nemati, H. R., & Barko, C. D. (2001) Issues in organizational data mining: A survey of current practices. *Journal of Data Warehousing*, 6(1), 25-36.

Whiting, R. (2002, February 11). Tower of power. *InformationWeek,* (875), 40-43.

Wurman, R. (1989). *Information anxiety is produced by the ever-widening gap* between what we understand and what we think we should understand. New York: Doubleday.

Acknowledgments

We wish to thank all of the authors for their insightful and excellent contributions to this book. Many of these authors also served as referees for chapters written by other authors, and to those referees, we are very grateful for their constructive and comprehensive reviews. We also acknowledge and appreciate the support of the Department of Information Systems and Operations Management (ISOM) at the University of North Carolina at Greensboro for providing online resources and numerous supplies during the inception, promotion and creation of this book. Special thanks also go to the publishing team at Idea Group Publishing. In particular we want to express our gratitude to Amanda Appicello whose professional guidance, assistance and support enabled the successful and timely completion of this project.

In closing, we both want to thank our families for their love and support throughout this year-and-a-half long project.

Hamid R. Nemati and Christopher D. Barko
University of North Carolina at Greensboro, USA
December 2002

Section I

Strategic Implications of ODM

Chapter I

Organizational Data Mining (ODM): An Introduction

Hamid R. Nemati
University of North Carolina at Greensboro, USA

Christopher D. Barko
University of North Carolina at Greensboro, USA

ABSTRACT

An increasing number of organizations are struggling to overcome "information paralysis" — there is so much data available that it is difficult to understand what is and is not relevant. In addition, managerial intuition and instinct are more prevalent than hard facts in driving organizational decisions. Organizational Data Mining (ODM) is defined as leveraging data mining tools and technologies to enhance the decision-making process by transforming data into valuable and actionable knowledge to gain a competitive advantage (Nemati & Barko, 2001). The fundamentals of ODM can be categorized into three fields: Artificial Intelligence (AI), Information Technology (IT), and Organizational Theory (OT), with OT being the core differentiator between ODM and data mining. We take a brief look at the current status of ODM research and how a sample of organizations is benefiting. Next we examine the evolution of ODM and conclude our chapter by contemplating its challenging yet opportunistic future.

SETTING THE STAGE

The competitiveness of the new global economy requires immediate decision capability. A recent study of more than 800 U.S. business decision-makers found that most respondents are making more decisions in the same amount of time but are missing opportunities because their decisions are not made quickly enough. In addition, these decision makers are not fully utilizing available resources and are often unable to gather sufficient information to make a fact-based decision (Wessel, 2002). The amount of data available today is doubling every five years, and corporate America is able to utilize less than 7 percent of the information it manages (Anonymous, 2001). Research from IBM also revealed that organizations use less than 1 percent of their data for analysis (Brown, 2002). As noted in the preface, this is the fundamental irony of the Information Age we live in — organizations possess enormous business information, yet have so little real business knowledge.

In the past, companies have struggled to make decisions because of the lack of data. But in the current environment, more and more organizations are struggling to overcome "information paralysis" — there is so much data available that it is difficult to determine what is relevant. Organizations today routinely collect and manage terabytes of data in their databases, thereby making information paralysis a key challenge in enterprise decision-making. Once the essential data elements are identified, the data must be reformatted, processed and analyzed to generate knowledge. The resulting knowledge is then delivered to the decision makers for collaboration, review and action. Once decided upon, the final decision must be communicated to the appropriate parties in a rapid, efficient and cost-effective manner.

ORGANIZATIONAL DATA MINING

The manner in which organizations execute this intricate decision-making process is critical to their well-being and industry competitiveness. Those organizations making swift, fact-based decisions by optimally leveraging their data resources will outperform those organizations that do not. A robust technology that facilitates this process of optimal decision-making is ODM, which is defined as leveraging data mining tools and technologies to enhance the decision-making process by transforming data into valuable and actionable knowledge to gain a competitive advantage (Nemati & Barko, 2001). ODM eliminates the guesswork that permeates so much of corporate decision-making. By adopting ODM, an organization's managers and employees are able to act sooner rather than later, be proactive rather than reactive and know rather than guess.

ODM spans a wide array of technologies, including, but not limited to, e-business intelligence, data analysis, online analytical processing (OLAP), customer relationship management (CRM), electronic CRM (e-CRM), executive information systems (EIS), digital dashboards and information portals. ODM enables organizations to answer questions about the past (what has happened?), the present (what is happening?) and the future (what might happen?). Armed with this capability, organizations can generate valuable knowledge from their data, which in turn enhances enterprise decisions. This decision-enhancing technology enables many advantages in operations (faster product development, increased market share with quicker time to market, optimal supply chain management), marketing (higher profitability and increased customer loyalty through more effective marketing campaigns and customer profitability analyses), finance (improved performance through financial analytics and economic evaluation of business units and products) and strategy implementation (business performance management (BPM), the Balanced Scorecard and related strategy alignment and measurement systems). The result of this enhanced decision-making at all levels of the organization is optimal resource allocation and improved business performance.

Profitability in business today relies on speed, flexibility and efficiency at quality levels thought unobtainable just a few years ago. The slightest imbalance along the supply chain can increase costs, lengthen internal cycle times and delay new product introductions. These imbalances can eventually lead to a loss in both market share and competitive advantage. Meanwhile, organizations are also forging closer relationships with their customers and suppliers by defining tighter agreements in terms of shared processes and risks. As a result, many businesses are deeply immersed in continuously re-engineering their processes to improve quality. Six sigma and Balanced Scorecard type efforts are increasingly prevalent. ODM enables organizations to remove supply chain imbalances while improving the speed, flexibility and efficiency of their business processes. This leads to stronger customer and partner relationships and a sustainable competitive advantage.

ODM VERSUS DATA MINING

Data mining is the process of discovering and interpreting previously unknown patterns in databases. It is a powerful technology that converts data into information and potentially actionable knowledge. However, obtaining new knowledge in an organizational vacuum does not facilitate optimal decision-making in a business setting. The unique organizational challenge of understanding and leveraging ODM to engineer actionable knowledge requires assimilating insights from a variety of organizational and technical fields and developing a comprehensive framework that supports an organization's quest for a sustainable competitive advantage. These fields include data mining, business strategy, organizational learning and behavior, organizational culture, organizational politics, business ethics and privacy, knowledge management, information sciences and decision support systems. These fundamental ODM elements can be categorized into three main fields: AI, IT, and OT. Our research and industry experience suggest that successfully leveraging ODM requires integrating insights from all three categories in an organizational setting typically characterized by complexity and uncertainty. This is the essence of ODM. The core differentiator between ODM and straightforward data mining is OT.

OT AND ODM

Organizations are primarily concerned with studying how operating efficiencies and profitability can be achieved through the effective management of customers, suppliers, partners and employees. To achieve these goals, research in OT suggests that organizations use data in three vital knowledge-creation activities. This organizational knowledge creation and management is a learned ability that can only be achieved via an organized and deliberate methodology. This methodology is a foundation for successfully leveraging ODM within the organization. The three knowledge creation activities (Choo, 1997) are:

- **Sense making** is the ability to interpret and understand information about the environment and events happening both inside and outside the organization.
- **Knowledge making** is the ability to create new knowledge by combining the expertise of members to learn and innovate.
- **Decision-making** is the ability to process and analyze information and knowledge in order to select and implement the appropriate course of action.

First, organizations use data to make sense of changes and developments in the external environments — a process called sense making. This is a vital activity wherein managers discern the most significant changes, interpret their meanings, and develop appropriate responses. Second, organizations create, organize and process data to generate new knowledge through organizational learning. This knowledge creation activity enables the organization to develop new capabilities, design new products and services, enhance existing offerings, and improve organizational processes. Third, organizations search for and evaluate data in order to make decisions. This data is critical. Since all organizational actions are initiated by decisions and all decisions are commitments to actions, the consequences of which will, in turn, lead to the creation of new data. Adopting an OT methodology enables an enterprise to enhance the knowledge engineering and management process.

In another OT finding, researchers and academic scholars have observed that there is no direct correlation between IT investments and organizational performance. Research has confirmed that identical IT investments in two different companies may give a competitive advantage to one company but not the other. Therefore, a key factor for the competitive advantage in an organization is not the IT investment, but the effective utilization of information as it relates to organizational performance (Brynjoflsson & Hitt, 1996). This finding emphasizes the necessity of integrating OT practices with robust IT and AI techniques in successfully leveraging ODM.

ONGOING ODM RESEARCH

Given the scarcity of past research in ODM and its growing acceptance and importance in organizations, we have conducted empirical research over the past few years that explored the utilization of ODM in organizations along with project implementation factors critical for success. We surveyed ODM professionals from multiple industries in both domestic and international organizations. Our initial research examined the ODM industry status and best practices, identified both technical and business issues related to ODM projects, and elaborated on how organizations are benefiting through enhanced enterprise decision-making (Nemati & Barko, 2001). The results of our research suggest that ODM can improve the quality and accuracy of decisions for any organization willing to make the investment.

After exploring the status and utilization of ODM in organizations, we decided to focus subsequent research on how organizations implement ODM projects and the factors critical for its success. Similar to our initial research, this was pursued in response to the scarcity of empirical research investigating the implementation of ODM projects. To that end, we developed a new ODM Implementation Framework based on data, technology, organizations and the Iron Triangle (to be published in an upcoming issue of *Industrial Management and Data Systems*). Our research demonstrated that selected organizational data mining project factors, when modeled under this new framework, have a significant influence on the successful implementation of ODM projects.

Our latest research has focused on a specific ODM technology known as Electronic Customer Relationship Management (e-CRM) and its data integration role within organizations. We developed a new e-CRM Value Framework to better examine the significance of integrating data from all customer touch points with the goal of improving customer relationships and creating additional value for the firm. Our research findings suggest that despite the cost and complexity, data integration for e-CRM projects contributes to a better understanding of the customer and leads to higher return on investment (ROI), a greater number of benefits, improved user satisfaction and a higher probability of attaining a competitive advantage.

ODM ADVANTAGES

A 2002 Strategic Decision-making study conducted by Hackett Best Practices determined that "world-class" companies have adopted ODM technologies at more than twice the rate of "average" companies (Hoblitzell, 2002). ODM technologies provide these world-class organizations greater opportunities to understand their business and make informed decisions. ODM also enables world-class organizations to leverage their internal resources more efficiently and effectively than their "average" counterparts who have not fully embraced ODM.

Many of today's leading organizations credit their success to the development of an integrated, enterprise-level ODM system. For example, Harrah's Entertainment has saved over $20 million per year since implementing its Total Rewards CRM program. This ODM system has given Harrah's a better understanding of its customers and enabled the company to create targeted marketing campaigns that almost doubled the profit per customer and delivered same-store sales growth of 14 percent after only the first year. In another notable case, Travelocity.com, an Internet-based travel agency, implemented an ODM system and improved total bookings and earnings by 100 percent in 2000. Gross profit margins improved 150 percent, and booker conversion rates rose to 8.9 percent, the highest in the online travel services industry.

In another significant study, executives from 24 leading companies in customer-knowledge management, including FedEx, Frito-Lay, Harley-Davidson, Procter & Gamble and 3M, realized that in order to succeed, they must go beyond simply collecting customer data and translate it into meaningful knowledge about existing and potential customers (Davenport, Harris & Kohli, 2001). This study revealed that several objectives were common to all of the leading companies, and these objectives can be facilitated by ODM. A few of these objectives are segmenting the customer base, prioritizing customers, understanding your customer's Internet behaviors, engendering customer loyalty and increasing cross-selling opportunities.

ODM EVOLUTION

Past

Initially, IT systems were developed to automate expensive manual systems. This automation provided cost savings through labor reductions and more accurate, faster processes. Over the last three decades, the organizational role of IT has evolved from efficiently processing large amounts of batch transactions to providing information in support of tactical and strategic decision-making activities. This evolution from automating expensive manual systems to providing strategic organizational value led to the birth of Decision Support Systems (DSS), such as data warehousing and data mining. Operational and DSS are now a vital part of many organizations. The organizational need to combine data from multiple stand-alone systems (financial, manufacturing, distribution) grew as corporations began to acknowledge the power of combining these data sources for reporting. This spurred the growth of data warehousing, where multiple data sources were stored in a format that supported advanced data analysis.

The slowness in adoption of ODM techniques in the '90s was partly due to an organizational and cultural resistance. Business management has always been reluctant to trust something it does not fully understand. Until recently, most businesses were managed by instinct, intuition and "gut feel." The transition over the past 20 years to a method of managing by the numbers is both the result of technology advances, as well as a generational shift in the business world as younger managers arrive with IT and experience.

Present

Many current ODM techniques trace their origins to traditional statistics and AI research from the 1980s. Today, there are extensive vertical data-mining applications providing analysis in the domains of banking and credit, bioinformatics, CRM, e-CRM, health care, human resources, e-commerce, insurance, investment, manufacturing, marketing, retail, entertainment and telecommunications. Our latest survey findings indicate that the banking, accounting/financial, e-commerce and retail industries display the highest ODM maturity level to date. The need for service organizations (banking, financial, health care and insurance) to build a holistic view of their customers through a mass customization marketing strategy is critical to remaining competitive. And organizations in the e-commerce industry are continuing to improve online customer relationships and overall profitability via e-CRM technologies (Nemati & Barko, 2001).

Continuous technological innovations now enable the affordable exploration of enormous volumes of data. It is the combination of technological innovation, creation of new advanced pattern-recognition and data-analysis techniques, ongoing research in organizational theory and the availability of large quantities of data that have guided ODM to where it is today.

ENVISIONING THE FUTURE

The number of ODM projects is projected to grow more than 300 percent in the next decade (Linden, 1999). As the collection, organization, and storage of data rapidly increases, ODM will be the only means of extracting timely and relevant knowledge from large corporate databases. The growing mountains of business data coupled with recent advances in OT and technological innovations provides organizations with a framework to effectively use their data to gain a competitive advantage. An organization's future success will depend largely on whether or not they adopt and leverage this ODM framework. ODM will continue to expand and mature as the corporate demand for one-to-one marketing, CRM, e-CRM, Web personalization and related interactive media increases.

As IT advances, organizations are able to collect, store, process, analyze and distribute an ever-increasing amount of data. Data and information are rampant, but knowledge is scarce. As a result, most organizations today are governed by managerial intuition and historical reporting. This is the by-product of years of system automation. However, we believe organizations are slowly moving from the Information Age to the Knowledge Age, where decision makers will leverage ODM and Internet technologies to augment intuition in order to allocate scarce enterprise resources for optimal performance.

As organizations set a strategic course into the Knowledge Age, there are a number of difficulties awaiting them. As its name suggests, ODM is part technological and part organizational. Organizations are comprised of individuals, management, politics, culture, hierarchies, teams, processes, customers, partners, suppliers and shareholders. The never-ending challenge is to successfully integrate data mining technologies with organizations to enhance decision-making with the objective of optimally allocating scarce enterprise resources. As many consultants, professionals, industry leaders and the editors of this book can attest, this is not an easy task. The media can oversimplify the task, but successfully implementing ODM is not accomplished without political battles, project management struggles, cultural shocks, business process reengineering, personnel changes, short-term financial and budgetary shortages, and overall disarray. ODM is a journey, not a destination, so there must be a continual effort in revising existing knowledge bases and generating new ones. But the benefits far outweigh both the technical and organizational costs, and the enhanced decision-making capabilities can lead to a sustainable competitive advantage.

Recent ODM research revealed a number of industry predictions that are expected to be key ODM issues in the future (Nemati & Barko, 2001). About 80 percent of survey respondents expect Web farming/mining and consumer privacy to be significant issues, while more than 90 percent predict ODM integration with external data sources to be important. We also foresee the development of widely accepted standards for ODM processes and techniques to be an influential factor for knowledge seekers in the 21st century. One attempt at ODM standardization is the creation of the Cross Industry Standard Process for Data Mining (CRISP-DM) project that developed an industry and tool neutral data-mining process model to solve business problems. Another attempt at industry standardization is the work of the Data Mining Group in developing and advocating the Predictive Model Markup Language (PMML), which is an XML-based language that provides a quick and easy way for companies to define predictive models and share models between compliant vendors' applications. Lastly, Microsoft's OLE DB for Data Mining is a further attempt at industry standardization and integration. This specification offers a common interface for data mining that will enable developers to embed data-mining capabilities into their existing applications. One only has to consider Microsoft's industry-wide dominance of the office productivity (Microsoft Office), software development (Visual Basic) and database (SQL Server) markets to envision the potential impact this could have on the ODM market and its future direction.

Although many improvements have materialized over the last decade, the knowledge gap in many organizations is still prevalent. Enterprises that see the strategic value of evolving into knowledge organizations by leveraging ODM will benefit directly in the form of improved profitability, increased efficiency, and a strategic competitive advantage.

REFERENCES

Anonymous. (2001, February 17). The slow progress of fast wires. *The Economist, London, 358* (8209).

Brown, E. (2002, April 1). Analyze this. *Forbes, 169*(8), 96-98.

Brynjolfsson, E. & Hitt, L. (1996). The customer counts. *InformationWeek,* (September 9). Online at www.informationweek.com/596/96.mit.htm.

Choo, C. W. (1997*). The knowing organization: How organizations use information to construct meaning, create knowledge, and make decisions.* Retrieved from Oxford University Press website: http://www.choo.fis.utoronto.ca/fis/ko/default.html.

Davenport, T. H., Harris, J. G., & Kohli, A. K. (2001). How do they know their customers so well? *Sloan Management Review, 42*(2), 63-73.

Hoblitzell, T. (2002, July). Disconnects in today's BI systems. *DM Review, 12*(6), 56-59.

Linden, A. (1999, July 7). CIO update: Data mining applications of the next decade. Inside Gartner Group, Gartner Group Inc.

Nemati, H. R., & Barko, C. D. (2001). Issues in organizational data mining: A survey of current practices. *Journal of Data Warehousing, 6*(1), 25-36.

Wessel, D. K. (2002). Decision making in the digital age. *DM Review,* Resource Guide, 16-18.

Chapter II

Multinational Corporate Sustainability: A Content Analysis Approach

Riad A. Ajami
University of North Carolina at Greensboro, USA

Marca Marie Bear
University of Tampa, USA

Hanne Norreklit
Aarhus School of Business, Denmark

ABSTRACT

Multinational corporate sustainability is dependent upon factors other than short-term profit concerns and the capacity to generate wealth for shareholders. In the 21st century, a corporation's future prospects are also linked to issues related to social acceptance and corporate legitimacy and respectability. Moreover, corporate viability increasingly requires the participation of all corporate stakeholders in the corporation's decision-making process. Organizational Data Mining (ODM), in the form of content analysis, can be used to examine or "mine" documents such as corporate annual reports for important data or trends. In this context, content analysis becomes useful in determining both the financial and non-financial measures of a corporation's viability. In addition to providing a reflection of current corporate performance, content analysis of corporate annual reports allows internal and external stakeholders to better determine the corporation's future direction and strategic orientation.

INTRODUCTION

Multinational corporate activities in the 21st century are unquestionably driven by a multitude of factors, including globalization and technological capabilities resulting in unprecedented economic re-alignments of entire industries. Moreover, multinational corporate sustainability, namely survival and viability, is a matter of far greater urgency. Multinational corporations exist by responding to new economic trends and adapting to strategic factors and industry volatility. In the past, the corporation's bottom line drove and signified superior or inferior corporate performance. For example, the corporation's primary objective lay entirely with its ability to maximize shareholder wealth. It is no longer enough for companies to be solely financially motivated. More than ever, societal concerns are being recognized and addressed by corporate board members of Fortune's Global 500. Managing stakeholder concerns significant to overall corporate performance, decision making and strategic thinking are the hallmarks of today's most successful companies. Fortune's annual corporate reputation survey is a popular source for information on social performance (Griffin & Mahon, 1997). The Fortune rankings are based on the opinions of senior executives, directors and analysts who are asked to rate the 10 largest companies in their industries on eight different aspects of reputation, one of which is social performance. As it turns out, the social performance scale is highly correlated with overall corporate reputation (Fryxell & Wang, 1994). The Domini 400 Social Index, a socially screened counterpart to Standard and Poor's 500, outperformed its competition over a three year period from 1997-2000. Furthermore, the Social Investment Forum reports that, in the U.S., there is over $2 trillion in assets under management in portfolios that screen for ethical, environmental and corporate social responsibility concerns. This figure represents 13 percent of the estimated $16.3 trillion investment assets managed by professional investment groups. The social performance indicators of this index include community impact, diversity, employee relationships, environmental impact and product safety.

The definition of corporate existence is broadening to include active stakeholder engagement in addition to wealth creation for shareholders. Thus, the multinational corporate sustainability perspective takes into consideration two complimentary concerns: corporate legitimacy and respectability as well as shareholder wealth creation. In order to balance this dichotomy of stakeholder engagement and wealth maximization in an age of accelerated globalization, rapid growth in cross-border trade and investments, and unprecedented technological advancements, it is crucial for multinationals to properly manage "knowledge flow" in order to create learning organizations and knowledge-sustaining systems. Organizational Data Mining (ODM) is a tool that CEOs, managers and corporate board members are turning to in order to more adeptly and synergistically manage globally dispersed assets and capabilities and engage external constituents and global stakeholders in long-term value creation and enhanced legitimacy. ODM facilitates cross-border information categorization and supports the quest for creating global competitive advantages, thereby contributing to the creation of rational strategic corporate decision making that benefits a wide array of a corporation's internal and external stakeholders.

Specifically, ODM is the process of sifting through large volumes of data to spot patterns and trends that may be useful in improving a company's overall strategic plan as well as the day-to-day functions of the firm. Cohen (1999, p. 5) describes ODM as prospecting for profits in the depths of a company's database: "It's like looking for gold in your computer." Furthermore, Yoon (1999) describes ODM as the process of combining techniques from statistics, database management, machine learning and pattern recognition to automatically extract or "mine" concepts, concept interrelations and interesting patterns from large databases. ODM uses a discovery-based approach in which pattern matching and other algorithms are employed to determine key relationships in various data (Weir, 1998). Succinctly stated, ODM is the analysis of relying on existing data to seek out new or previously unknown or unrealized information. By analyzing existing data through ODM techniques, value is created for both the firm as well as external stakeholder groups, such as consumers, creditors, suppliers, retailers and communities.

In order for multinational corporations to support and optimize cross-border knowledge management and data control systems in today's complex global environments, various taxonomies, including ODM techniques, are being employed by cross-functional management teams, CEOs, board members, academicians and government officials. Moreover, taxonomies have been defined as the systematic classifications of conceptual space that allow information categorizations in order to map out and attain a better understanding of the confluence of corporate resource deployment options, priorities and future actions. Moreover, financial resource deployment and the use of metaphors and pronouncements by corporate decision makers are indicators of past performance and could provide insights for future corporate action and strategic options.

The approach to ODM and taxonomies that this study employs is a thorough and systematic content analysis of 24 annual reports of multinational corporations found on the Financial Times' "FT 500" list. The focus is to assess corporate activities and concerns regarding corporate sustainability. A corporation's annual report is its narrative regarding corporate performance and action plans. The financial statements not only explain and demonstrate the capabilities of the firm to an external audience, but they also serve as an internal road map for internal managers regarding the corporate priorities and options (Mouritsen, 2000). It is reasonable to assume that there is a certain degree of symmetry between the concepts that are expressed in the financial statement and the internal managerial control system.

STAKEHOLDER PERSPECTIVES AND A BALANCED SCORECARD APPROACH TO GLOBAL SUSTAINABILITY MANAGEMENT MODELS

Stakeholder Perspectives

The key to understanding corporate legitimacy and sustainability begins by mapping out and understanding stakeholders' priorities. In its Principles of Corporate Governance, the Organization for Economic Cooperation and Development (OECD)

(1999, p. 17) states that corporations should "encourage active cooperation between corporations and stakeholders in creating wealth, jobs and the sustainability of financially sound enterprises." For a multinational corporation, the relationship with stakeholders becomes even more complex. A multinational corporation has a broader and more diverse environment in which it operates and upon which it depends. Therefore, it must be concerned with its relationships with various stakeholders on multiple levels. Ajami and Khambata (1990) note that, by operating in several national environments, the multinational corporation must legitimize itself simultaneously to multiple societies and to multiple stakeholders. Furthermore, the "legitimating environment" that evaluates a multinational corporation's success in its stakeholder relationship consists of all of its home and host country institutional environments as well as supranational institutions (Kostova & Zaheer, 1999).

The ability to manage a variety of competing stakeholder interests has emerged as a significant topic in the management literature. Related issues are the relationship between stakeholder management, performance measures and the perception that a firm is, in fact, socially responsible (Harrison & Freeman, 1999). Stakeholder salience, the degree to which managers give priority to competing stakeholder claims, is also emerging in relevance. Additionally, using data provided by 80 CEOs of U.S. corporations, Agle, Mitchell and Sonnenfeld (1999) examined relationships among the stakeholder attributes of power, legitimacy, urgency and salience, CEO values and corporate performance. They found strong support for the power, legitimacy and urgency-stakeholder salience relationships, as well as some significant relationships among stakeholder salience, CEO values and corporate social performance. However, they found no support for the stakeholder salience-financial performance link.

In essence, there are two distinct stakeholder management models: the strategic stakeholder management model and the intrinsic stakeholder management model (Berman, Wicks, Koth & Jones, 1999). In the Strategic Management Model, the nature and extent of managerial concern for a stakeholder group is determined solely by stakeholders' ability to improve a firm's financial performance. Thus, management will attend to stakeholder interest to the extent that stakeholders can affect the firm's financial performance.

The Intrinsic Stakeholder Commitment Model contends that firms ought to have a moral commitment to treating stakeholders in a positive way. This commitment, in turn, shapes corporate strategy and ultimately impacts the firm's financial performance. In this model, achieving profitability without considering the impact on other stakeholders is considered unethical and dysfunctional. Some of the stakeholder areas important to firm operations include employees, customers, natural environment, workplace diversity, product safety and community relations. It should be noted that the results of the study by Berman et al. (1999) provide support for the Strategic Management Model but not for the Intrinsic Stakeholder Commitment Model.

Firms that create and sustain stakeholder relationships based on mutual trust and co-operation tend to have a competitive advantage over those that do not, because paying attention to these two factors helps firms to create a better reputation and more respectability, which ultimately provides an economic benefit (Jones, 1995; Barney & Hansen, 1994). Simply stated, managerial attention to multiple stakeholder interests can affect a firm's financial performance and add tremendous value to a multinational firm's overall performance (Freemann & Gilbert, 1988). Thus, corporate strategy and longevity depends, in part, on creating a "fit" between the values of the corporation, managers and employees and the values of the firm's primary stakeholders.

A Balanced Scorecard Approach to Global Sustainability

Mounting internal and external pressures on multinational corporations necessitate not only corporate profitability but also sustainability and social acceptance. This approach denies corporate decision makers the comfort of thinking of themselves as private, profit-seeking institutions without responsibilities to their stakeholders (Ajami & Khambata, 1990). The balance scorecard (BSC) developed by Kaplan and Norton in 1990 is a multidimensional framework that uses measurement to describe an organization's strategy (Kaplan & Norton, 1996a, b). This instrument is designed to measure both current operating performance and the drivers of future performance. Creating a BSC requires translating a company's strategy and mission into specific goals and measures; managers then track those measures as they work towards their goals.

Senior executives and managers of the 21st century must pay more attention to widely used business models in the hope of creating superior financial performance and strategic success including social responsibility. These business models are increasingly being relied upon and linked to corporate mission, vision, and long-term and short-term strategic and financial objectives. Proponents of these management models tend to agree that they do create global competitive advantages for the firms that employ them.

The following business models are increasingly being relied upon and linked to corporate mission, vision and long-term and short-term strategic and financial objectives: Deming's (1986) Total Quality Management (TQM) model; Kaplan and Norton's (1996) Balanced Scorecard (BSC) model; Business Process Reengineering (BPR), which was developed by Hammer and Champy (1993) and later revised by Hammer (2001); Argyris's (1977) Organizational Learning (OL) model, which appeared again in 1994 with Argyris and Kaplan; and Turney's (1992) Activity-Based Management model.

Of these models, the BSC approach is a comprehensive intertextual reference to modern management models. Furthermore, the model relies on strategic success (Porter, 1980, 1985; Kaplan & Norton, 1996b). Porter (1985) argues that the essence of formulating a competitive strategy lies in relating a company to the competitive forces in the industry in which it competes. Therefore, the strategy has to be based on the market segments to be served, and then followed by the identification of the internal business processes, which the firm needs to excel in, if it is to deliver value to the targeted customers in the market segments. Thus, the competitive strategy of a firm ought to be driven by its environment rather than by its core competencies or resources (Prahalad & Hamel, 1990; Collis & Montgomery, 1995).

Specifically, the BSC supplements a corporation's financial measurements with nonfinancial measurements. For example, it translates the vision and strategy of a business unit into objectives, and measures variables in four different areas: financial, customer knowledge, internal business process, and learning and growth. First, the financial perspective emphasizes wealth maximization for its shareholders. Second, the customer knowledge perspective determines how the company wishes to be viewed by its customers. Third, the internal business process perspective describes the business processes that the corporation has to be particularly adept in so as to satisfy its shareholders and customers. Fourth, the organizational learning and growth perspective involves the changes and improvements the company needs to realize if it is to make its vision come true (Kaplan & Norton, 1996a).

Kaplan and Norton (1996a) assume the following causal relationship between the four perspectives: *measures of organizational learning and growth → measures of internal business processes → measures of the customer perspective → financial measures.* The measures of organizational learning and growth are drivers of the measures of the internal business processes. In turn, these measures become the drivers of the measures of the customer perspective, which are drivers of the financial measures. The BSC is designed as a feed-forward model aiming to overcome some of the shortcomings of nonfinancial systems.

The Eclectic View of Multinational Corporate Sustainability

As described above, the four perspectives of the BSC approach have structural and conceptual links to widely used management models such as TQM, BPR, OL and ABM. However, the BSC's four perspectives are often criticized for not emphasizing human resource development, international scope, technological development, strategic alliance partnerships, and merger and acquisition activity (Maisel, 1992). To overcome these shortcomings, this study takes into consideration additional perspectives related to various multinational corporate constituencies and stakeholders. By broadening the model to include the aforementioned human resource development, international scope, and technology dimensions, as well as strategic alliance partners, the applicability and utility of the BSC model is enhanced to embrace a more holistic and eclectic stakeholder orientation and perspective.

This view offers a more functional perspective emphasizing multinational corporate viability and is similar to the approach used by the Financial Times' list of the "World's Most Respected Companies" (PriceWaterhouseCoopers, 2000). The list identifies 50 multinational corporations that were chosen by CEOs, top managers, business leaders and analysts as companies exemplifying the qualities most admired and desired in the global enterprise. The companies exhibited all or some of the following dimensions:

1. Relating to consumers and external stakeholders;
2. Sustaining "good" financial performance;
3. Upholding CEO's leadership capabilities and people orientation;
4. Maintaining and nurturing an innovative corporate culture;
5. Continuing to reinvent and transform processes and structure;
6. Meeting the challenges of global competitors and responsiveness to global market trends.

The eclectic view provides a platform for stakeholder engagement and gives a corporation not only a legal right but a social license to operate. The "most respected" companies are engaging in this type of market-driven reporting and nonfinancial transparency. The global investment community is realizing the benefits of disclosing "hard" bottom-line figures in conjunction with "soft" nonfinancial data. The eclectic approach allows stakeholders the ability to base their valuations on a total grasp of a company's true worth and not just its financial potential.

METHODOLOGY

Content Analysis

Content analysis of corporate annual reports and the use of taxonomies to organize data are manifestations of information categorization. Content analysis is a technique for compressing word and text volumes into fewer content categories (Berelson, 1952; U.S. General Accounting Office, 1996; Krippendorff, 1980; Weber, 1990). It is a research tool that allows words, phrases and pronouncements to be examined. Presenting financial and nonfinancial information enables external and internal stakeholders an intimate glimpse into the strategic preferences and priorities of multinational corporate decision makers. Moreover, content analysis helps managers make inferences by objectively and systematically identifying specified characteristics of corporate messages (Holsti, 1969).

Content analysis examines words and phrases within a wide range of texts, including corporate data and pronouncements. By examining the presence or repetition of certain words and phrases in these texts, a researcher is able to make inferences about the intent, assumptions and strategic options of corporate CEOs and decision makers. Researchers quantify and analyze the presence of such words and concepts, then make inferences about the messages within the text(s) and other temporal manifestations. To conduct a content analysis on any such text, the text is coded, or broken down, into manageable categories on a variety of levels — word, word sense, phrase, sentence or theme — and then examined using one of content analysis' basic methods: conceptual analysis or relational analysis (Palmquist, 1990). Traditionally, content analysis has most often been thought of in terms of conceptual analysis. In conceptual analysis, a concept is chosen for examination, and the analysis involves quantifying and tallying its presence. While explicit terms obviously are easy to identify, coding for implicit terms and deciding their level of implication is complicated by the need to base judgments on a somewhat subjective basis. Think of conceptual analysis as establishing the existence and frequency of concepts in a text. Most often, these concepts are represented by words or phrases. Relational analysis builds on conceptual analysis by examining the relationships among concepts in a text.

Content analysis is useful for examining trends and patterns in corporate mission statements and annual reports in order to make inferences about what corporations hold and value as their primary reason for existence and to help develop action plans and strategies (Stemler, 2001; Bowman, 1978; Ajami & Khambata, 1990). Moreover, content analysis provides an empirical basis for monitoring shifts in corporate priorities. The most common notion in qualitative research is that content analysis simply means doing a word-frequency count. It is assumed here that the words mentioned most frequently are the ones that reflect the greatest level of corporate concern.

Table 1. The World's 24 Largest Companies Measured by Marked Capitalization

Company (1)	Country	FY (2)	Major Industry	Listing
General Electrics	US	99/Dec.	Diversified	NYSE, BSE, CIN, MSE, PBW, PCS
Cisco Systems	US	00/Jul.	Electronics	NAS
Intel	US	99/Dec.	Electronics	NAS
Microsoft	US	00/Jun.	Electronics	MSE, NAS
NTT Mobile Communications Network	Japan	00/Mar.	Utilities	OSA, TYO
Vodafone Airtouch	UK	00/Mar.	Utilities	LON
Exxon Mobil	US	99/Dec.	Oil, Gas, Coal & Related services	NYSE, BSE, CIN, MSE, PBW, PCS
Wal-Mart Stores	US	00/Jan.	Retailers	NYSE, BSE, MSE, PCS
Nokia	Finland	99/Dec.	Electronics	FRA, HEL, LON, STO
Citigroup	US	99/Dec.	Financial	NYSE, BSE, CIN, MSE, PBW, PCS
NTT Group	Japan	00/Mar		NYSE, TYO
Oracle	US	00/May	Electronics	MSE, NAS
Deutsche Telekom	Germany	99/Dec.	Utilities	FRA
Toyota Motor Corporation	Japan	00/Mar.	Automobile	NAS, OSA, TYO
Royal Dutch/Shell	Netherlands	99/Dec.	Oil, Gas, Coal & Related services	NYSE, AMS, PAR
Lucent Technologies	US	99/Jun.	Electronics	NYSE
BP Amoco	UK	99/Dec.	Oil, Gas, Coal & Related services	NYSE, AMS, DUS, FRA, GUA, LON, PAR, TYO, OTH, ZHR
International Business Machines	US	99/Dec.	Electronics	NYSE, BSE, CIN, MSE, PBW, PCS, MON
American International Group	US	00/Dec.	Financial	NYSE, BSE, MSE, PCS
Pfizer	US	99/Dec.	Drugs, Cosmetics & Health Care	NYSE, BSE, CIN, MSE, PBW, PCS
Merck	US	99/Dec.	Drugs, Cosmetics & Health Care	NYSE, BSE, CIN, MSE, PBW, PCS
Ericsson	Sweden	99/Dec.	Electronics	DUS, FRA, GUA, LON, Osl, PAR, STO, OTH
France Telecom	France	99/Dec.	Utilities	NYSE, PAR
AT&T	US	99/Dec.	Utilities	NYSE, BSE, CIN, MSE, PBW, PCS

(1) The date for choosing the 24 largest companies measured by market capitalization is April 2000
(2) Not all companies have the same fiscal year. The most recent date for each company is being used.
Source: Financial Times, April 2000

Sample Selection

This study draws from two data sources: the Financial Times' survey (2001) entitled "'FT500" and the Financial Times' list of the "World's Most Respected Companies" (PriceWaterhouseCoopers, 2000). The FT500 identifies 500 of the world's largest companies ranked by market capitalization, while the second list incorporates a social legitimacy, respectability and sustainability orientation. Market capitalization incorporates a stock market-investor perspective. In order to measure the issues of both corporate financial success and enhanced sustainability for the legitimacy of a multinational corporation, the data mining technique of content analysis was utilized on the annual reports of the 24 largest companies on the FT500 list. The sample comprised 24 companies including the 14 largest U.S. companies, the seven largest European companies and the three largest Japanese companies. Table 1 shows the companies used in our analysis.

Tentative Propositions

The objective of employing the ODM technique of content analysis of corporations' annual reports is to quantify the frequency/presence of certain words and phrases concerned with corporate sustainability for each of the 24 firms. A further aim is to

Table 2. Sustainability Perspectives and Concepts Used in the Content Analysis

SUSTAINABILITY PERSPECTIVE	CONCEPTS USED IN THE CONTENT ANALYSIS
Shareholders	Shareholder, investor, risk
Customers	Customer, consumer, client, services, quality, delivery
Internal Processes	Flexibility, cost, time, improvement, performance
Human Capital	Human capital, employees, workforce, empowerment, personnel, education, people and knowledge
Technology and Growth	Innovation, technology, growth and learning, information, Internet
International Scope	Global, multinational, international, transnational and national culture
Others	Environment, competitors, alliance, outsourcing, merger and acquisition

quantify the importance of corporate social responsibility as viewed by top management. Specifically, the number of words in the company's annual report devoted to each stakeholder issue is examined. In order to develop a sustainability index (SI) for each firm, the words that are counted and categorized relate to shareholders, customers, internal processes, human capital, technology and growth, and international scope. Table 2 shows the sustainability perspectives and concepts employed in the study.

Adding the total number of words devoted to each stakeholder issue and comparing that figure to the total number of words provided a ratio representing the actual percentage of lines in the annual report devoted to specific stakeholder issues. The companies were then ranked from (1), the company with the highest SI, to (24), the company with the lowest SI.

Next, the SI for each firm was tabulated and correlated with the firm's return on equity (ROE). It is hypothesized that a positive relationship exists between a company's SI and ROE. The correlation analysis provides insight into the relationship between socially responsible business practices and positive financial performance. A collateral notion is that this link is positive, meaning that socially responsible management practices lead to superior financial performance in terms of ROE.

RESULTS

Table 3 presents the results of the content analysis word percentages as they relate to the various perspectives and categories. Table 4 contrasts the rate of return with total sustainability and the various dimensions of sustainability from shareholders, customers, internal processes, human capital, technology and growth, international scope and others. The firms are ranked from 1 to 24. The highest sustainability percentage is equal to 1, and the lowest score is equal to 24. Table 5 shows the results of the correlation analysis at $\alpha = 0.10$.

Table 5 shows that there is an overall positive correlation for U.S. companies and a negative correlation for non-U.S. firms. Moreover, a positive correlation exists for technology and growth as well as for human capital. There is no correlation for internal processes. Furthermore, the results of the analysis from Table 5 show that there is a positive correlation between the U.S. sample and ROE, while there is no correlation for the non-U.S. sample. The non-U.S. sample shows a positive correlation for technology and growth and human capital, while it shows a negative correlation for shareholders, customers and international dimensions.

Table 3. Rate of Return and Sustainability Score For Each Perspective Plus Overall Total

Company	ROE (5)	Shareholder Perspective	Customer Perspective	Internal process Perspective	Human Capital Perspective	Tech. & Growth Perspective	International Perspective	Other Perspective	Total Perspective
Oracle	*170.40%	0.0540%	1.0362%	0.4525%	0.6692%	1.9860%	0.7016%	0.2159%	5.11%
Vodafone Airtouch	69.66%	0.2098%	0.6386%	0.4967%	0.2098%	0.7528%	0.1203%	0.5522%	2.98%
Merck	45%	0.1552%	0.3630%	0.5257%	0.3605%	0.5958%	0.1477%	0.3905%	2.54%
Nokia	41.30%	0.4523%	0.3982%	0.4205%	0.3823%	1.0831%	0.2198%	0.2771%	3.23%
International Business Machines	39%	0.1974%	0.9775%	0.5890%	0.4394%	1.1398%	0.4935%	0.2993%	4.14%
Lucent Technologies	36%	0.0417%	2.1957%	0.2421%	0.3840%	1.5111%	0.4341%	0.5677%	5.38%
Pfizer	35.90%	0.0987%	0.2554%	0.3831%	0.1277%	0.3366%	0.1915%	0.4237%	1.82%
Microsoft	26.99%	0.2621%	0.8050%	0.4056%	0.3183%	1.5289%	0.1248%	0.1810%	3.63%
General Electrics	26.80%	0.1045%	1.3403%	0.6035%	0.2169%	1.1731%	0.3057%	0.2952%	4.04%
Intel	26.20%	0.1463%	0.5168%	0.6338%	0.2535%	1.5602%	0.0293%	0.3901%	3.53%
Wal-Mart Stores	22.90%	0.2245%	0.5948%	0.3591%	0.2132%	0.5836%	0.5051%	0.3591%	2.84%
Citigroup	22.49%	0.2056%	1.9474%	0.2834%	0.4699%	1.3998%	1.1551%	0.4013%	5.86%
NTT Mobile Comm. Network	21.30%	0.1884%	1.7762%	0.3448%	0.2085%	1.4675%	0.1884%	0.2245%	4.40%
Ericsson	18.30%	0.1383%	0.6867%	0.3261%	0.2939%	1.0696%	0.0445%	0.3705%	2.93%
American International Group	15.60%	0.4246%	1.2813%	0.3874%	0.0894%	1.3260%	0.4470%	0.5885%	4.54%
France Telecom	15%	0.2591%	2.1365%	0.4818%	0.3091%	1.6455%	0.6818%	0.3682%	5.88%
AT&T	15.20%	0.2233%	1.1670%	0.7889%	0.2203%	0.7919%	0.2501%	0.4704%	3.91%
Cisco Systems	13.93%	0.2423%	0.4984%	0.4572%	0.3475%	1.1888%	0.0686%	0.4115%	3.21%
Exxon Mobil	12.60%	0.2110%	0.1092%	0.6213%	0.1195%	0.1520%	0.0443%	0.1904%	1.45%
BP Amoco	12.40%	0.4230%	0.2204%	0.8341%	0.4766%	0.5898%	0.1311%	0.6494%	3.32%
Royal Dutch/Shell	7%	0.3276%	0.2993%	0.7025%	0.1575%	0.5198%	0.1103%	0.1796%	2.30%
Toyota Motor Corporation	*6.6%	0.2853%	0.7303%	0.7417%	0.0685%	0.7075%	0.1655%	0.2510%	2.95%
Deutsche Telekom	*5.20%	0.6479%	0.7242%	0.4574%	0.4129%	1.2260%	0.5781%	0.4447%	4.49%
NTT Group	5.01%	0.1539%	1.7902%	0.4496%	0.1904%	1.0126%	0.1296%	0.2268%	3.95%

The ROE ratio in the annual report as a measure of corporate profitability was used. However, in some instances the ROE calculated by Wright investor's service was used and are marked with *.

Table 4. Rate of Return and Sustainability Rank For Each Perspective Plus Overall Total

Company	ROE	Shareholder Perspective	Customer Perspective	Internal Process Perspective	Human and People Perspective	Tech. & Growth	International Perspective	Other	Total Sustainability
Oracle	1	23	9	14	1	1	2	21	4
Vodafone Airtouch	2	13	15	10	17	17	19	4	17
Merck	3	17	20	9	8	19	15	10	21
Nokia	4	2	19	16	7	13	11	17	15
International Business Machines	5	15	10	8	4	12	6	15	8
Lucent Technologies	6	24	1	24	6	5	8	3	3
Pfizer	7	22	22	19	21	23	12	7	23
Microsoft	8	7	11	17	10	4	18	23	12
General Electrics	9	21	6	7	15	11	9	16	9
Intel	10	19	17	5	13	3	24	11	13
Wal-Mart Stores	11	10	16	20	16	21	5	14	20
Citigroup	12	14	3	23	3	7	1	9	2
NTT Mobile Comm. Network	13	16	5	21	18	6	13	20	7
Ericsson	14	20	14	22	12	14	22	12	19
American International Group	15	3	7	18	23	8	7	2	5
France Telecom	16	8	2	11	11	2	3	13	1
AT&T	17	11	8	2	14	16	10	5	11
Cisco Systems	18	9	18	13	9	10	21	8	16
Exxon Mobil	19	12	24	6	22	24	23	22	24
BP Amoco	20	4	23	1	2	20	16	1	14
Royal Dutch/Shell	21	5	21	4	20	22	20	24	22
Toyota Motor Corporation	24	6	12	3	24	18	14	18	18
Deutsche Telekom	22	1	13	12	5	9	4	6	6
NTT Group	23	18	4	15	19	15	17	19	10

The firms are ranked by the highest sustainability percentage, where highest = 1 and lowest = 24.

U.S. firms' ROE and SI go hand in hand; whereas, a negative correlation exists for the European companies in this sample. The negative correlation between ROE and the SI for European companies may be explained by the fact that U.S. companies are more sensitive to public relations and are more pragmatic and result oriented than their European counterparts.

Furthermore, European managers may be relying more upon an objective rationalistic approach; whereas, U.S. managers are more adept at external public affairs functions as well as garnering the approval of external constituencies. Different types of organizational cultures and governance structures in various countries may put various degrees of short-term pressure on management. Therefore, performance pressures from the capital market and the need for showing responsible behavior may be higher in an Anglo-Saxon corporate governance structure than in a European or Japanese corporate governance structure (Demirag, 1998). However, as globalization accelerates in the marketplace, these differences are likely to become less pronounced.

Table 6 shows that the "World's Most Respected Companies" include 58 percent of the companies in the sample. However, those that are most respectable appear not to be the ones with the highest ROE or sustainability ranking.

Table 5. Correlation Results and Sustainability, $\alpha = 0.10$

	Total	Shareholders	Customers	Internal Processes	Technology & Growth	Human Capital	International Scope	Others
U.S.	0.2308	NC	0.1121	NC	0.2835	0.5516	0.3011	NC
Non-U.S.	-0.182	-0.1515	-0.2485	NC	0.3091	0.3333	-0.0424	0.2606

Table 6. ROE and Sustainability for the World's Most Respectable Companies

Company	Ranking ROE	Ranking Sustainability	Ranking World's Most Respectable*
Oracle	1	4	
Vodafone Airtouch	2	17	
Merck	3	21	35
Nokia	4	15	7
International Business Machines	5	8	
Lucent Technologies	6	3	
Pfizer	7	23	
Microsoft	8	12	2
General Electrics	9	9	1
Intel	10	13	9
Wal-Mart Stores	11	20	8
Citigroup	12	2	10
NTT Mobile Communications Network	13	7	48
Ericsson	14	19	
American International Group	15	5	12
France Telecom	16	1	
AT&T	17	11	
Cisco Systems	18	16	27
Exxon Mobil	19	24	26
BP Amoco	20	14	21
Royal Dutch/Shell	21	22	30
Toyota Motor Corporation	24	18	6
Deutsche Telekom	22	6	
NTT Group	23	10	

Source: Financial Times ranking of The World's Most Respectable Companies, 2000

Table 7. ROE and Sustainability Ranking for the Most Respectable U.S. Firms

Company	Ranking ROE	Ranking Sustainability	Ranking World's Most Respectable*
Oracle	1	3	
Merck	3	12	10
International Business Machines	5	5	3
Lucent Technologies	6	2	
Pfizer	7	13	
Microsoft	8	8	2
General Electrics	9	6	1
Intel	10	9	5
Wal-Mart Stores	11	11	4
Citigroup	12	1	6
American International Group	15	4	7
AT&T	17	7	
Cisco Systems	18	10	9
Exxon Mobil	19	14	8

* Re-ranking of the Worlds Most Respectable U.S. firms (PriceWaterhouseCoopers, 2000)

Table 7 shows that the world's most respected U.S. companies include 65 percent of the companies in the sample. Again, those that are the most respectable appear not to be those that have the highest ROE or sustainability ranking.

DISCUSSIONS AND CONCLUSION

ODM, particularly content analysis of corporations' annual reports, is a useful managerial instrument for analyzing, quantifying and qualifying both financial and nonfinancial multinational corporate activities and priorities. Traditional financial measures tend to reveal a great deal about a company's past actions, but not as much about its future orientation and strategic direction (Merchant, 1985; Schoenfeld, 1986; Dearden, 1987; American Institute of Certified Public Accountants (AICPA), 1994; Kaplan & Norton, 1996a). Relying on primarily financial data is problematic when the situation of the corporation is such that it feels forced to pursue short-term financial results rather than long-term organizational sustainability and viability (Dearden, 1987; Merchant, 1985; Demirag, 1998). Furthermore, Dearden (1987) suggests that managers can be reluctant to make new investments even when these actions are in the company's best economic interest, since new investments have a detrimental effect on the short-term return on investment due to asset valuations and depreciation policies. Similarly, managers often reject other investments with growth and innovation potential in order to display acceptable short-term results. While possibly improving short-term profitability, these actions may lead to low efficiency and loss of customer loyalty and satisfaction, which leaves the corporation vulnerable and exposed to competitors' attacks. The aforementioned corporate tendencies imply that the accounting system alone is an insufficient assessment tool. Corporate annual reports should also incorporate a strategic-futuristic orientation, thereby revealing a company's long-term plans and earning prospects. Content analysis, therefore, is a tool for feed-forward judgement on corporate response to emerging and anticipated social responsibility.

Lastly, it should be noted that some management models have a "legitimating" effect rather than an "efficiency"-enhancing effect. The legitimating or respectability effect is supported by Staw and Epstein (2000). They show that companies associated with some of the popular management techniques are more admired, perceived to be more innovative and rated higher in management quality, even when not matched by higher economic performance. Moreover, Polany (1944) argued that free markets are sustainable only in so far as they are embedded in a matrix of social institutions with legitimate market outcomes. Without this social acceptance, corporate legitimacy and free markets are endangered. Content analysis is, therefore, a useful assessment tool. It can sensitize corporate managers to the need for allocating the necessary space in their annual reports to adequately address nonfinancial concerns, such as corporate respectability and social responsibility. Incorporating corporate financial considerations as well as social responsibility indicators into corporate annual reports makes the narratives of these reports truly reflective of corporate performance, accomplishments and bottom-line results. Content analysis will allow all stakeholders to better assess corporate directions and priorities, and match corporate pronouncements with resource allocations.

REFERENCES

Agle, B. R., Mitchell, R. K., & Sonnenfeld, J. (1999, October). Who matters to CEOs? An investigation of stakeholder attributes and salience, corporate performance and CEO values. *Academy of Management Journal 42*(5), 507.

Ajami, R. A., & Khambata, D. (1990). Multinational corporate governance: The stakeholders paradigm. *International Journal of Management, 7*(2), 184.

American Institute of Certified Public Accountants (AICPA) Special Committee on Financial Reporting. (1994). *Improving business reporting - A customer focus: Meeting the information needs of investors and creditors* (p. 9). New York: American Institute of Certified Public Accountants.

Argyris, C. (1977). Organizational learning and management information systems. *Accounting, Organizations and Society, 2*(2), 113-123.

Argyris, C., & Kaplan, R. S. (1994). Implementing new knowledge: The case of activity-based costing. *Accounting Horizons 8*(3), 83-105.

Barney, J.B., & Hansen, M.H. (1994). Trustworthiness as a source of competitive advantage. *Strategic Management Journal, 15,* 175-190.

Berelson, B. (1952). *Content analysis in communication research.* Glencoe, IL: Free Press.

Berman, S.L., Wicks, A.C., Koth, S., & Jones, T.M. (1999, October). Does stakeholder orientation matter? The relationship between stakeholder management models and firm financial performance. *Academy of Management Journal, 42*(5), 488.

Bowman, E.H. (1978). Strategy annual reports and alchemy. *California Management Review, 20,* 32-37.

Buzell, R.D., & Gale, B.T. (1987). *The PIMS principles: linking strategy to performance.* New York: New York Press.

Cohen, M. (1999, May 28). Data mining is like looking for gold in your computer. *Boston Business Journal,* 19(19), 4-7.

Collis, D.J., & Montgomery, C.A. (1995, July-August). Competing on resources: Strategy in the 1990s. *Harvard Business Review, 73*(4), 118-128.

Dearden, J. (1987, September-October). Measuring profit center managers. *Harvard Business Review,* 65(5), 84-88.

Deming, W. E. (1986). *Out of the crisis.* Cambridge, MA: Press Syndicate.

Demirag, I. S. (1998). Short-term performance pressures, corporate governance, and accountability: An overview. In I. S. Demirag (Ed.), *Corporate governance, accountability, and pressures to perform an international study* (pp. 7-24). Hartford, CT: JAI Press Inc.

Freemann, R. E., & Gilbert Jr., D. R. (1988). *Corporate strategy and the research for ethics.* Englewood Cliffs, NJ: Prentice Hall.

Fryxell, G. E., & Wang, J. (1994). The fortune reputation index: Reputation for what? *Journal of Management, 20,* 1-14.

Griffin, J. J., & Mahon, J.F. (1997). The corporate social performance and corporate financial performance debate: Twenty-five years of incomparable research. *Business & Society, 36,* 5-31.

Hammer, M. (2001). *The agenda: What every business must do to dominate the decade.* New York: Crown Business Books.

Hammer, M., & Champy, J. (1993). *Reengineering the corporation: A manifesto for business revolution.* New York: Harper Business Press.

Harrison, J. H., & Freeman, R. E. (1999, October). Stakeholders, social responsibility and performance: Empirical evidence and theoretical perspectives. *Academy of Management Journal, 42*(5), 479.

Holsti, O. R. (1969). *Content analysis for the social sciences and humanities.* Reading, MA: Addison-Wesley.

Jones, T. M. (1995). Instrumental stakeholder theory: A synthesis of ethics and economics. *Academy of Management Review, 20,* 404-437.

Kaplan, R. S., & Norton, D. P. (1996a). *The balanced scorecard – Translating strategy into action.* Boston, MA: Harvard Business School Press.

Kaplan, R. S., & Norton, D. P. (1996b). Linking the balanced scorecard to strategy. *California Management Review, 39*(1), 53-79.

Kostova, T., & Zaheer, S. (1999). Organizational legitimacy under conditions of complexity: The case of the multinational enterprise. *Academy of Management Review, 24*(1), 64-81.

Krippendorff, K. (1980). *Content analysis: An introduction to its methodology.* Newbury Park, CA: Sage Publications.

Maisel, L. S. (1992). Performance measurement: The balanced scorecard approach. *Journal of Cost Management, 6*(2), 47-52.

Merchant, K. (1985). *Control in business organizations.* Boston, MA: Harvard Graduate School of Business.

Mouritsen, J. (2000). Valuing expressive organizations: Intellectual capital and the visualization of value creation. In M. Schultz, M.J. Larsen & M.H. Larsen (Eds.), *The expressive organization.* Oxford, UK: Oxford University Press.

Organization for Economic Cooperation and Development (OECD). (1999). *Corporate governance in OECD member countries: Recent developments and trends.* Paris: OECD.

Palmquist, M. E. (1990). *The lexicon of the classroom: Language and learning in writing classrooms.* Unpublished doctoral dissertation, Carnegie Mellon University, Pittsburgh, PA.

Polany, K. (1944). *The great transformation.* Boston, MA: Beacon Press.

Porter, M. E. (1980). *Competitive strategy: Techniques for analyzing industries and competitors.* New York: Free Press.

Porter, M. E. (1985). *Competitive advantage: Creating and sustaining superior performance.* New York: Free Press.

Prahalad, C. K., & Hamel, G. (1990, May-June). The core competence of the corporation. *Harvard Business Review, 68*(3), 79-91.

PriceWaterhouseCoopers. (2000). The world's most respected companies. *Financial Times* (December 17).

Schoenfeld, H. M. (1986). The present state of performance evaluation in multinationals. In H. P. Holzer & H. M. Schoenfeld (Eds.), *Managerial accounting and analysis in multinational enterprises* (pp. 217-252). Berlin, Germany: Walter de Gruyter.

Staw, B. M., & Epstein, L. D. (2000). What bandwagons bring: Effects of popular management techniques on corporate performance, reputation, and CEO pay. *Administrative Science Quarterly, 45*(3), 523-556.

Stemler, S. (2001). An overview of content analysis. (electronic version). *Practical Assessment, Research and Evaluation, 7*(17).

Turney, P. (1992). *Activity-based management: Making the investment in quality count.* Paper presented at a research conference in Modern Cost Management. Sponsored by American Accounting Association, Albuquerque, NM (February).

U.S. General Accounting Office. (1996). *Content analysis: A methodology for structuring and analyzing written material* (GAO Publication No. GAO/PEMD-10.3.1). Washington, D.C.: U.S. General Accounting Office.

Weber, R. P. (1990). *Basic content analysis* (2nd ed.). Newbury Park, CA: Sage Publications.

Weir, J. (1998). Data mining: Exploring the corporate asset. *Information Systems Management, 15,* 68-73.

Yoon, Y. (1999). Discovering knowledge in corporate data bases. *Information Systems Management, 16*(2), 64-74.

Chapter III

A Porter Framework for Understanding the Strategic Potential of Data Mining for the Australian Banking Industry

Kate A. Smith
Monash University, Australia

Mark S. Dale
Monash University, Australia

ABSTRACT

This chapter employs Michael Porter's Five Forces model to understand the potential strategic value of data mining within the Australian banking industry. The motivation for examining the strategic potential of data mining is to counter balance the preponderance of process level arguments for adopting this technology (e.g., risk and fraud mitigation, market campaigns, etc.) with an industry level perspective of what the technology potentially means for competition between rival firms (i.e., industry behavior). In essence, this chapter explores how data mining can affect industry structure and attractiveness by assisting businesses such as banks defend themselves against forces such as those asserted by buyers, substitute products, new entrants, and suppliers. This chapter also explores the future implications of data mining for the banking industry, the operating models of those institutions and the underlying economics of the industry. The emergence of data mining presents banks with the opportunity to either continue to develop their core competencies around the design, manufacture, distribution and support of products and/or to develop critical competencies around customer relationship management. A possible "contract banking" model supported through the application of data mining is discussed.

INTRODUCTION

Identifying the strategic potential of data mining represents a difficult and complex heuristic search. The territory occupied by the strategic application of data mining is by its very nature ill defined. Time limits are imprecise and the capacity to forecast long-term competitive benefits is contingent on the degree of volatility within the particular industry over time, as well as the management, planning and control structures that are critical to the deployment of new technology within a business environment. At an epistemological level, the concept of strategy, as it is represented in data mining literature, is also another factor causing confusion. The generally agreed understanding of strategy evident in management, business and strategy literature is that it is the point of mediation and interpretation between the organization and the external environment. Within data mining literature, however, notions of strategy are firmly fixed at the subunit or process level. Potential macroeconomic impacts of data mining technology (and data warehousing architecture) and its potential to change the underlying economics of information intensive industries are generally overlooked in deference to case studies of marketing, risk and fraud applications, where benefits are easily quantified and represent an attractive solution to managers under pressure to control costs and improve performance.

This analysis of the strategic value of data mining is based on the Five Forces model developed by Michael Porter (1980, p.4) and will focus on the Australian banking industry. The Australian banking industry is typical of information intensive industries where data mining is used at the process level. Much of the commercially available literature argues that data mining gives businesses "competitive advantage," but does not explain what the phrase "competitive advantage" actually means. Generally, notions of competitive advantage, as implied by the available literature, are focused at the process level. This corruption of the original "strategic" or enterprise level meaning of the term mirrors an incremental concept of strategy within data mining literature and research that ignores the potential industry level or intra-enterprise level impact of the technology.

Porter's model has been widely used by business, strategy and information technology researchers and practitioners as a framework of industry analysis (Christopher, Payne & Ballantyne, 1993), as a methodology for combining business and information technology strategy (Applegate, McFarlan & McKenney, 1996), and as a framework for understanding how technology can change industry structure (Porter & Millar, 1985). Evidence from the available literature, however, indicates that, in general, technology strategy research and literature has largely applied Porter's model as post facto instrument of impact evaluation or planning methodology and have not addressed the potential of the model to clarify, at a conceptual level, the enterprise or strategic value of technology investment. In *Competitive Strategy: Techniques for Analysing Industries and Competitors* (Porter, 1980), Porter outlined various macroeconomic and technical industry characteristics (e.g., entry barriers, economies of scale and scope, capital advantages, etc.) that were critical to the strength of each of the Five Forces

(Schein, 1980; Davis, 1989; Chin & Marcolin, 2001; Chan, 2000). It is not impossible to conceive that these same characteristics that Porter described as indicators of competitive intensity could also be seen as conceptual benchmarks against which the long-term impact of data mining could also be understood. For example, the strategic value of data mining could be demonstrated by its deterrence of new entrants through its intensification of scale economies, product differentiation, switching costs, capital requirements and cost advantages independent of size.

Aim of this Chapter

The aim of this chapter is to develop a generic conceptual framework through which the strategic value of data mining can be understood and clearly demonstrated. Evidence of current data mining research indicates benefits at the process level, however, enterprise-level benefits are relatively unexplored. This is in part due to the nascency of the data mining-to-business relationship and, secondly, the enthusiasm of scholars and practitioners to promote data mining as a business tool with a rapid and high return on investment.

Porter's Five Forces industry and competition framework will be used to demonstrate a macroeconomic measurement of data mining investment value. The contribution of this model will be to demonstrate how data mining, as well as other high volume analytical technologies such as online analytical processing (OLAP) can effect long-term competitive advantage by improving the profitability of the banking industry and the relative economic position of businesses within that industry. Findings within this paper can also be extrapolated across other information intensive industries where the strategic value of technology investment is less well understood.

The following sections, in outline, include: (1) a review of current data mining and information technology investment research and literature; (2) an examination of the Five Forces industry and competition model of Porter; (3) analyze the potential of data mining to influence two predominate forces within the retail banking sector (new entrants and consumers); and (4) an analysis of the potential affect of data mining and other high volume analytical technologies on the underlying economics and structure of the retail banking industry within Australia.

BACKGROUND

Literature Review: Measuring the Strategic Value of Data Mining

Literature on the value of data mining as a long-term strategic investment is limited. A persistent focus on process improvement evident in data mining literature and research reflects a bias toward more easily quantified measurements of value. Data mining investment value is usually expressed as improved efficiency through reduced expended time and effort and reduced recurrent costs. Consequently, return on investment is much clearer at the process level where data mining productivity, as a function of inputs and outputs, is clearly defined. A problem with this apparent emphasis on the "hard" financial measurement of data mining value is that research has become focused almost exclusively on cost reduction and process re-engineering to the exclusion of other levels of business-to-technology interdependency (individual, team, group, enterprise and industry), where investment value is more difficult to determine.

This bias of data mining research toward process improvement obscures strategic enterprise-level perceptions of value. Cabena, Hadjinian et al., for example, have written extensively of the many business applications of data mining in the areas of telesales, customer loyalty, forecasting financial futures and fraud detection. Business benefits derived from the application of data mining technology, whilst extensive, are limited exclusively to the process level. Though the authors aggregate their many examples upwards into categories of higher-level summaries of management functions, such as market management, risk management and fraud management, they do not specify how data mining improves the relative economic performance of the host business in comparison to other competitors. In effect, although the authors demonstrate a broad range of applications, the benefits enumerated reflect a limited strategic potential because of their one-off short-term economic effect.

Measuring technology value at the enterprise level is problematic. Numerous definitions of technology value exist ranging from "hard" quantitative financial measurements, such as efficiency ratios (cost to income, cost to asset, technology spend to labor spend, etc.), to qualitative measurements, such as those found in branches of social, organizational and cognitive psychology[1] (Prasad & Harker, 1997, p. 11). The contribution of technology to productivity in the banking industry (which is the focus of our case study) is relatively under-researched in comparison to other industries, such as manufacturing and retail. Gupta and Collins (1997) observe that there is little research assessing the contribution of information technology to the growth, profitability and efficiency of banks. Clemons and Row (1991) and Prasad and Harker (1997) argue that there is little quantitative evidence to demonstrate that information technology creates competitive advantage. This lack of a confirmed positive correlation between investment and improved productivity has given rise to research into the phenomenon of the "productivity paradox" (Sircar, Turnbow & Bordoli, 2000). However, despite the lack of empirical evidence, studies nonetheless show a continued high investment in information technology. Data from the Australian Bureau of Statistics indicates that in 2000, information technology expenditure in Australia approximated AU$62 billion and that Australia was placed in the top few nations in the world in terms of the share of Gross Domestic Product (GDP) that this scale represents (Australian Bureau of Statistics, 2001). Within Australia, information technology and telecommunications expenditure is higher in the finance and insurance industries than in any other industry. In 1997-98, total information technology expenditures within the Australian financial services industry reached AU$4.7 billion, or 20 percent of total Australian information technology expenditure (Australian Bureau of Statistics, 2001).

The confusion over the enterprise-level value of technology within the banking industry is further compounded by multiple definitions of productivity at that level. Prasad and Harker (1997) define three categories of output: assets (i.e., ratio of credit to deposits and other liabilities), user-cost (net contribution of each financial product to revenue) and the value-added approach (value added to operating costs).

A "hard" quantitative approach to the strategic value of data mining investment is impractical given the absence of any longitudinal data and the limited timeframe of this study. Alternative notions of technology value offer equally valid models for understanding the impact of data mining on performance at an enterprise level. Whereas profit and loss ratios provide one particular measure, frameworks that focus on the likely effect of core information processing competencies on industry structure offer another set of metrics based on logical cause and effect, rather than financial ratios.

Australian Banking Industry Defined

The definition of the Australian banking industry, as it applies to this study, will refer to the retail consumer activities of the four major Australian trading banks: the Australian and New Zealand Bank (ANZ), Westpac Banking Corporation (WBC), Commonwealth Bank of Australia (CBA) and the National Australian Bank (NAB), as well as smaller institutions such as Macquarie Bank that have fewer product offerings and total assets under management, but nonetheless have a sizeable market share in specialized niche markets, such as mortgage origination. Wholesale commercial operations are excluded since they are national and international in nature and are subject to much more complex forces (i.e., globalization) than those internal industry forces depicted here.

The retail market is largely regional in nature; and lending and depository practices reflect a parochial orientation as well as a consumer customer base. Typical market segments include mortgage lending, transaction and investment accounts, personal loans, bill payments, credit cards, debit cards, overdrafts, commercial bills, term loans and leasing.

In the following section, we present a framework for understanding the potential of data mining to provide information intensive business, such as banks, competitive and economic advantage over an extended time period.

FRAMEWORK FOR UNDERSTANDING THE STRATEGIC IMPACT OF DATA MINING

This section provides a functional overview of Porter's framework of industry and competition analysis, commonly referred to as the Five Forces model. Discussion is limited to the individual forces as determinants of industry competition; those factors that influence the intensity of each force; technical industry constraints that emphasize and de-emphasize particular individual forces and limitations of the model itself.

Porter's Five Forces Model

Porter's Five Forces model is a generic framework that deconstructs industry structure into five underlying competitive forces or variables. According to Porter, the economic and competitive position of a business is the result of the interplay between five generic forces. They are: (1) the bargaining power of suppliers; (2) bargaining power of buyers; (3) the threat of new entrants; (4) threat of substitute products; and (5) the rivalry of existing competitors (a function of the preceding four forces) (Porter, 1979). These five forces constitute the determinants of industry structure and attractiveness (the ability of businesses to earn, on average, rates of return on investment that exceed the cost of capital (Porter, 1980)) The interplay between these structural forces determines the intensity of competition, depending on the nature of the industry (e.g., petroleum, mineral and information technology industries) and is also a function of various underlying economic and technical factors. Figure 1 diagrams the five generic forces, detailing their respective underlying economic and technical factors.

The extent to which a company is able to defend itself against or influence the behavior of any of the individual five competitive forces is the basis of competitive advantage within a particular industry. Competitive advantage is defined by Porter as the capacity of a company to:

> "... edge out rivals when vying for the favour of customers. A competitive advantage is said to be sustainable if it cannot be copied or eroded by the actions of rivals, and is not made redundant by environment developments" (Porter, 1980, p. 339).

The ability of an institution to achieve a sustainable competitive advantage is based on its capacity to build a unique and unreplicable capability or competency that can, in turn, be transposed into desirable product and service offerings.

In any industry, however, not all forces are equal and some forces carry greater weight than others. Thus, the technical nature of the industry (manufacturing, professional services, retail, etc.) is an important consideration in determining the relative influence of each force. For example, suppliers dominate some industries, such as the petrochemical industry or manufacturing. On the other hand, in information intensive industries, such as banking, the bargaining power of consumers, the threat of new entrants and the threat of substitute products is critical, whilst the bargaining power of suppliers is less so.

Figure 1. Determinants of Industry Structure (Porter, 1985)

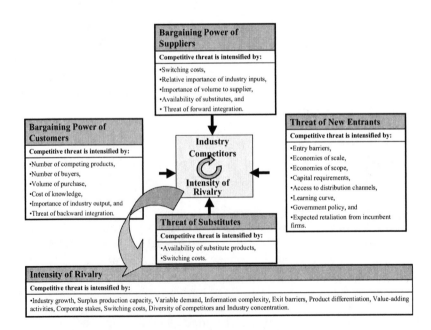

Limitations of the Five Forces Model

A fundamental limitation of Porter's Five Forces model is its failure to include those broader macroenvironmental forces (political, economic, social and technological) that also impact competition. Nellis (n.d.), Rajan (n.d.) and Llewellyn (1996) argue that the banking industry is subject to both internal and external forces. Botten and McManus (1999) argue that consideration of the wider "societal environment" is a mandatory component of any business strategy.

In terms of the Australian banking industry, four macroenvironmental forces, in particular, have profoundly affected competition in the Australian banking industry: deregulation, the economic environment, demographic trends and technological innovation. The number of Australian banks has risen prolifically as a result of deregulation, the conversion of building societies and mutual funds, as well as the introduction of foreign banks. In July 1990, the Reserve Bank bulletins noted there were 33 banks and that 10 of these banks held a further 14 subsidiary banks (Lloyd-Walker, 1999, p. 18). In 1998, the number of banks had increased to 44 with seven banks holding one subsidiary each (Lloyd-Walker, 1999). The economic environment through changes in interest rates and the failure of credit unions and state banks has adversely affected public confidence in the financial system (Lloyd-Walker, 1999). Demographic, employment and education trends have been a powerful force of change within the financial-services industry, impacting on the range of products and services offered as well as delivery channels. Life expectancy trends have encouraged governments to support superannuation initiatives that reduce dependency on the aged pension (Commonwealth of Australia, 1997). Trends toward earlier and extended retirement and longer periods in education have increased the need for services that facilitate the smoothing of cash flow over an individual's life cycle (Commonwealth of Australia, 1997).

Figure 2. Conceptual Synthesis of Porter's Five Forces and Data Mining

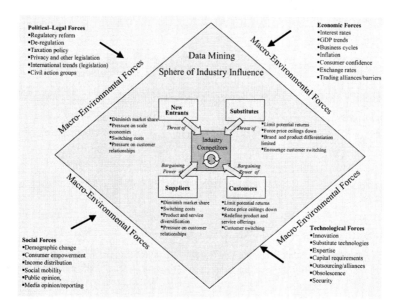

Conceptual Synthesis of Porter's Five Forces Model and Data Mining

Figure 2 defines the parameters of data mining's influence on industry competition. As is demonstrated, the influence of data mining is restricted to the mitigation of those competitive factors internal to an industry and which are initiated by new entrants, substitute products, customer and supplier power. Macroenvironmental forces that can also affect industry competition, but are extraneous to the influence of data mining, are also indicated. Antecedents of these forces are not found in interorganizational behavior, but in political, social, technological and economic change. Consequently, they are outside the scope of this study. The purpose here is to provide a conceptual industry perspective of data mining's strategic influence as a change agent and also illustrate where data mining fits in the context of Porter's Five Forces model.

THE STRATEGIC APPLICATION OF DATA MINING IN THE AUSTRALIAN RETAIL BANKING INDUSTRY

The limited scope of this chapter precludes a detailed analysis of the potential of data mining to assist banks mitigate or defend themselves against all of the four principal forces: customers, suppliers, new entrants and substitute products. The following analysis will instead focus on two predominant forces affecting competition within the Australian banking industry: the threat of new entrants and the bargaining power of customers.

The objective of the following analysis is to examine the extent to which data mining is able to mitigate the threat of new entrants and the bargaining power of customers within the Australian retail banking industry. The degree to which data mining is able to assist institutions influence those factors underpinning these two competitive forces by extension demonstrates the competitive advantage benefit of the technology.

The Potential Impact of Data Mining on the Threat of New Entrants

In mitigating the threat of entry from specialist providers as well as traditional nonbanking institutions (retail, insurance), banks must create effective barriers to entry. Porter describes six common barriers to entry. These include: economies of scale, product differentiation, capital requirements, cost disadvantages independent of size, access to distribution channels and government policy (Porter, 1980). The nonexistent deterrent effect of data mining on government policy is obvious and is, therefore, excluded from this analysis.

Economies of Scale Advantages

Expense ratios indicate that Australian banks are achieving moderate economies of scale. Figure 3 demonstrates that operating expense to income ratios have fallen incrementally from 1996, suggesting marginal improvements in scale over that time.

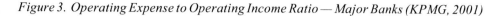

Figure 3. Operating Expense to Operating Income Ratio — Major Banks (KPMG, 2001)

Operating Expense/Operating Income

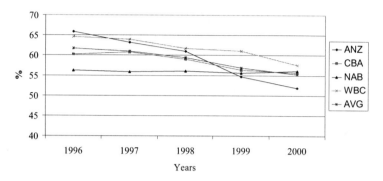

Years

Contributing factors include a continued reliance on manually intensive processes as indicated by continued high employment figures within the Australian banking industry.

Data mining can create scale advantages in activities where data analysis services are critical to performance. The magnitude of the scale advantage is proportional to the scale of operation. Large trading banks with greater than say, 5 million customers would generate lower per unit processing costs in the area of marketing campaigns or customer risk analysis, because the ratio of processing volume to operational cost is less than that of a smaller scale institution. Improvements in scale economies are also apparent at a macro end-to-end process level. Manually intensive activities can be automated, thus increasing the volume of the process output and inversely reducing the cost associated with that output. Credit scoring operations, for example, are labor intensive and based on the balanced score cards that are manually populated from preinput system data. Uploading this information directly into a specific classification or a neural network application would automatically generate the required information about the particular customer's risk rating, depending on their socioeconomic, demographic, employment, etc., details and depending on the criteria on which the institution determined credit worthiness. This process could be applied to various levels of secured and unsecured lending limits and, thus, has a generic application in the area of personal financial services, where customer fulfillment and internal probity checking processes would also be improved.

There are implicit process and human resource assumptions within data mining economies. These include the capacity of "downstream" processes to fully transform the analytic information into new or improved products. For example, the deployment of data mining technology could penalize an institution if it were unable to transpose customer behavior analysis into new products rapidly.

Learning Curve Advantages

Improvement in economies of scale automatically implies changes to existing business processes and, concomitantly, the acquisition of new expertise. Learning curve advantage refers to the development of scarce technology and process expertise that other institutions are either not able to support or would incur a premium to acquire. The organizational implications of a data-driven cognitive process presupposes structural, cultural and strategic changes necessary to leverage that analytic potential of data mining. Davenport, Harris, De Long and Jacobson (2001) identify three broad critical success factors of a broad organizational capability for transforming data into knowledge and ultimately into action. They include (1) contextual elements, such as strategy, skills and experience (including technology, analytical modeling, data and business knowledge, communication and partnering) organization and culture (including structuring analytic resources, data-oriented or fact-based culture, understanding of technology and data requirements), and technology and data; (2) transformational elements, such as analytical processes and decision-making processes; and (3) change management capability, such as behavioral, process and program change, and change in financial conditions (including revenue increase, cost decrease, improved profitability, increase market share).

The data mining learning curve is an intangible barrier and, therefore, does not automatically prohibit entry. Also, the strength of entry barriers based on internal experience and expertise implies that the expertise is proprietary and not available to competitors or potential entrants through either (1) copying, (2) the recruitment of experienced employees or (3) cannot be purchased through consultants. The difficulty of maintaining proprietary ownership over experience reduces potential advantages derived from the accumulation of expertise. Furthermore, any "pioneer" advantage can be offset by the rapidity through which second- or third-mover rivals can progress through the learning curve, since they are able to observe and learn from aspects of the pioneer's operations. Thus, competitive advantage based on the accumulation of experience is dependent on the degree to which expertise can be quarantined within the institution.

Capital Requirements Advantages

Discussion on the level of investment required to purchase a data mining application and the additional human resource costs required to support the implementation of that application is not within the scope of this study, since they are essentially commercial decisions. Discussion here will be limited to general observations regarding the technology and banking industry factors that mitigate any capital advantages derived from data mining investment.

Falling infrastructure costs negate capital advantages associated with data mining. Studies by Deloitte Touche Tohmatsu International (1995) indicate a significant and progressive reduction during the years 1979-1994 in the cost of CPU power, distributed processing, and data storage and transmission power by a factor of 100, 20 fold and a factor of 100, respectively. Banks comparatively inexpensive access to capital funding (i.e., difference between borrowing and lending rates) further lowers the deterrent effect of capital requirements.

Transposing Moore's Law (constant performance to cost improvement), there is an observable inverse relationship between technology maturity and technology costs. This phenomenon suggests that as data mining technology matures it will also decrease in cost further reducing the deterrent effect of the investment (Hosking, Kambil & Lister, 2000; Melnick et al., 2000; Wilson, n.d.).

Increased opportunities for partnering promoted by an oversupply of technology capacity within the banking industry (as evidenced, for example, by the duplication of distribution infrastructure, core banking systems, transaction systems, credit card systems, etc.) potentially lowers the deterrent effect of capital entry barriers. Data mining services could be outsourced from third parties, if it is in compliance with privacy laws. The rationalization of data mining resources and expertise, however, could further reduce capital advantages as external service providers build economies of scale in particular data mining applications, such as risk management, fraud management or product development. Axiomatically, there are also control issues associated with an operational dependency on external service providers.

Cost Disadvantages Independent of Size

This refers to the operational scale requirements of entry. In other words, investment associated with infrastructure replication. The potential of data mining to escalate operational scale requirements is considerable given the technical infrastructure requirements. The maximum economic optimization of data mining requires not only a large cross-functional data set, but also an established and mature data capture, transmission and storage infrastructure. This would suggest that the minimum level of operational scale would require substantial capital investment, since, regardless of the existing operational scale, there are fundamental prerequisite technical infrastructure components necessary to support the three- or four-tier data mining architecture, as well as secondary costs associated with the implementation of the technology, process re-engineering and change management.

Access to Distribution Channels

Data mining can significantly enhance the competitive advantage of distribution channel access by adding value to the rich stream of data captured. Distribution channel usage patterns, including preferences, frequency, intensity of usage (multiple transactions versus one transaction), etc., can be used to further enrich transaction-based data. Data mining reinforces distribution channel advantages because of the knowledge that can be inferred· from customer touch-point information (e.g., distribution channel preferences, technology preferences, merchant preferences, preferred form of payment, frequency of purchasing, intensity of contact, etc.). This information can then be used to profile the purchasing behavior of the customer and can guide decisions as to what distribution channel products to that particular customer are supported by.

The Potential Impact of Data Mining on the Bargaining Power of Customers

The influence that data mining techniques are able to bring to bear on the bargaining power of customers highlights the potential Customer Relationship Management (CRM) application of the technology. The ability of CRM to provide and extract better value from customer relationships is based on four principles: (1) customers should be managed as important assets; (2) customer profitability varies and not all customers are equally desirable; (3) customers vary in their requirements, preferences, buying behavior and price sensitivity; and (4) by understanding what motivates customer behavior and profitability, institutions can tailor their offerings to maximize customer retention and profitability (Kutner & Cripps, 2001; Ryals & Payne, 2001). Porter identifies several factors contributing to the bargaining power of customers: product differentiation and switching costs, customer concentration, relative volume of consumer purchases to vendor sales, consumer profitability, backward integration, relative quality effect and customer information. The limited scope of this study precludes a detailed analysis of the potential of data mining to influence all of those attributes of customer power identified by Porter. Instead, two attributes, consumer volume and product differentiation, will be examined.

Relative Consumer Volume to Sales

According to Porter (1980, p. 24), the bargaining power of customers is reduced if the relative volume of their purchasing to vendor sales is high. However, the previous competitive profile of the Australian banking industry indicates an oversupply of services as evidenced by reduced interest margins, falling interest revenue as well as moderate economies of scale amongst the four major banks. The existing oversupply of products would suggest that an increased production of financial products and services would increase distribution network economies of scale, but would not decrease customer bargaining power because the demand to supply ratio would be lowered further. Switching costs for customers would also be reduced, thus further diminishing advantages based on increased supply.

The potential of data mining to improve the relative volume of buyer demand to vendor supply can be realized through improved segmentation of the customer population. CRM literature advocates the incremental segmentation of the customer population using a range of socioeconomic, psychographic and demographic factors in order to better profile customer buying behavior and, in turn, improve the customer uptake of products and services. Studies of the retail financial industry indicate that the retail banking industry comprises a diverse customer population with wide ranging needs and buying behavior (Meadows & Dibb, 1998). Customer base segmentation is the established method for understanding customer requirements and needs as it better enables an institution to reflect the homogeneous subgroups within its customer community (Dibb, 1998).

Data mining techniques are ideally suited to segmentation, since relationships and deviations can be identified at various levels of abstraction (granularity), ultimately to segments of one. Neural methods, for example, are well suited to segmentation applications, such as target marketing, cross selling and customer retention, since they operate without a priori knowledge of potential common attributes. Other applicable segmentation techniques include supervised learning types such as tree induction and neural induction. Predictive methods are also well suited, since they infer possible trends within the data set and can be used to potentially predict customer needs and allow the institution to then develop new products or product features, such as contribution smoothing during periods of retraining or unemployment.

Product Differentiation Advantages

The oversupply of financial products has precipitated the imposition of ceiling and floor limits on interest rates, returns and ultimately the profits associated with various product groups. Differentiation, according to Porter (1979), either through improvement in product quality or other means is the most effective defense against over capacity. Differentiation strategies based on product-centric marketing alone, however, represent an inferior barrier in comparison to customer-centric campaigns, since they (product-based campaigns) focus on the "expression" of the relationship rather than the counterparty or variable of the relationship. Implicitly, product-based campaigns smack of "batch and blast" mass marketing approaches.

Understanding customer requirements and needs is the most effective means of product innovation. The underlying objective of supplying value and extracting value is strongly linked to CRM strategies. Data mining can provide greater understanding of customer's product requirements. The timeliness of the particular bank's capacity to assimilate learned information and transform that into a particular product or product feature, however, does assume close task interdependency between the data analysts, product design, manufacture and marketing business units. Schein (1980) argues that task interdependence within organizations inextricably links the collaborative function of technology to the on-going performance of the firm.

Predictive modeling operations are ideally suited to modeling customer requirements. Classificatory and value prediction techniques share the same objective of forecasting a particular variable of interest, but are differentiated by the nature of the variable of interest — binary ("yes" or "no") or ordinal. Classificatory techniques seek to ascribe a record to a particular class such as "most likely to require upgrading of credit limit" or "most likely to require investment advice" (i.e., after end-of-year bonuses, etc.). Value prediction techniques can be used to infer likely product requirements based on certain criteria. For example, predictive operations performed upon a data set of long standing customers, including an agreed-upon measure of financial value to date, could produce a model of likely lifetime value of new customers. For customers belonging to the so-called highly profitable group, the banking institution could review the product basket mix of that customer to supply higher value products to (1) further consolidate the relationship and (2) extract greater value from the customer.

The potential of data mining to assist banks mitigate the threat of new entrants as well as the bargaining power of consumers demonstrates a practical strategic benefit of the technology. Economies of scale in analytical management and operational areas; the optimization of capital investment advantages and expertise; the capacity to influence consumer demand and vendor supply ratios through the incrementalisation of the retail market, and also improved product differentiation through customer behavior profiling imply returns that are evident at the enterprise level rather than at the process level.

DATA MINING: FUTURE IMPLICATIONS FOR RETAIL BANKING

Disaggregation of Banking Activities

The strategic direction of banking is a complex and multidimensional problem. At an international level, there is potential for globalization of institutions through the acquisition by or merger with foreign entities. At a domestic industry level, there is potential for greater rationalization of institutions, entry of niche providers and further unbundling of banking products and services. This section will examine one possible business model for Australian banks based on the potential of data mining and high-volume analytical tools, in general, to create a closer alignment between the internal resources of an institution and the external market. Data-driven knowledge acquisition offers many possible business models, one of which is a financial products and services brokering model, based on the development of core competencies, including market analysis, fulfillment of customer needs and requirements and the management of contracts with external suppliers in order to meet customer needs. The allusion to CRM is straightforward, but the strategic implications for the business of banking go far beyond simple relationship management and, in effect, redefine the underlying economics of the retail banking industry. The emergence of data mining presents banks with the opportunity to either continue to develop their core competencies around the design, manufacture, distribution and support of products and/or to develop critical competencies around customer relationship management. Increasingly limited resources could prevent banks from developing core competencies around both specialized areas. Furthermore, niche providers have demonstrated their capacity to exploit cross-subsidies within existing banking cost structures. The significance of data mining is that it compels businesses within information intensive industries to reassess their existing business model. One possible alternative to the existing product and service-oriented model is presented below.

Traditional Product-Focused Data Processing Model

The conventional view of a bank is a vertically as well as horizontally integrated institution based on product lines and target markets (e.g., personal, small business and corporate financial services). The institution comprises business units that individually provide subcomponents of particular complete product offerings. As banks provide a range of products and services across many markets, individual business units are also horizontally linked through process interdependencies. For example, the constituent processes that combine to design, manufacture, market, sell and support a transaction account, include: marketing analysis, product development, call center operations (customer inquiries), branches (transaction initiation and fulfillment), a legal department (contract terms and conditions), risk department, a personal financial services business unit (owners and managers of the purchased product) and treasury functions (funds investment) to reinvest depository assets.

Internal processes that support products and services exist on multiple functional levels ranging from (1) strategic management processes; (2) core business processes (research and development of new products and services; and (3) resource management processes. An overview of the complex of processes that support products and services within a bank is represented in Figure 4.

Data Mining and the Underlying Economics of Retail Banking

With reference to those resource management processes depicted above, the role of information technology operations has predominantly been to support back-office functions, especially transaction and account processing functions. Consequently, the dominant data management model that banks have based their information systems planning on is characterized by a "pull" paradigm where transaction data flows into the

Figure 4. Entity-Level Model of a Bank's Operations

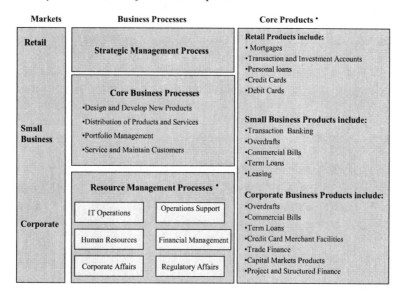

●   *Products include, but are not limited to*

transaction and account processing systems, but is essentially inert. The degree to which data processing aligned the core products and services of the bank to the external markets was low, since transaction data is ultimately managed in order to satisfy customer, management and regulatory requirements for accurate, current and retrospective reporting.

The emergence of data mining and other analytical technologies redefines the traditional "pull" model of data management. In terms of CRM applications, data mining represents a "push" paradigm, where data flowing into the organization re-enters the external environment expressed as new products or product features tailored to the consumers' requirements. This model of data management has profound implications for the perception and measurement of the strategic value of information technology, since an unbroken audit trail can be drawn from the information system, the data set and eventually to the strategic decision itself. Technology productivity and profitability can subsequently be attributed to a data source, rather tenuously linked to assets under management and other productivity and efficiency ratios.

The potential of data mining to "push" data back into the market as desirable products and services potentially redefines the economics of the retail banking industry. Through improved customer profiling and market analysis, banks could potentially reorientate their revenue streams from the origination, sales and support of financial products and instead specialize in customer relationship management services. The business model envisaged here is analogous to the vertically disaggregated model evident in some industries, such as manufacturing. In car manufacturing, for instance, some producers have sought to exploit the different scale economies and expertise in the manufacture of component parts. The finished good carries the vendor's name, but is in reality a product of the repackaging of products manufactured by other companies, based on the vendors specifications, design requirements and standards. The economic benefit to the vendor is that the cost of managing the contracts for external supply is less than the economies of scale that could be derived from the business producing all the component parts itself. In the same way, banks could, present as an apparent vertically integrated provider of a full range of products (or components) and services, whilst sourcing those products or their subcomponents from external suppliers. Furthermore, through data mining, banks would also be able to infuse the manufacturing model with a superior market analysis competency through advanced customer management techniques. Rather than responding to a specific customer request, banks could also proactively anticipate their customer's requirements and factor them in to their product and service offerings.

Data Mining and the Contract Banking Model

This vertically disaggregated model evident in other industries is contrary to the orthodox vertically integrated structure of Australian banks. Taken to its logical conclusion, the disaggregated model represents virtual banking. However, on a more practical level, the disaggregated model may be applied to individual specific markets, such as credit cards or transaction accounts, rather than globally across all retail operations. Though banks outsource some of their ancillary back-office activities, such as purchasing or technology support services, core competencies, such as loan administration, risk assessment and origination, are sourced internally.

Llewellyn (1996) refers to the transposition of the disaggregated manufacturing model into financial services as "contract banking," where a bank subcontracts out components of particular products to external suppliers on a contractual basis. That is to say, products and services purchased from a particular financial institution may not necessarily be manufactured by that financial institution. A bank may disintegrate its vertical organizational structure according to those areas in which it seeks to specialize and outsource those processes, products and services that are more efficiently done by external suppliers. For example, once creditworthiness has been assessed and a loan initiated, a bank may source the administration of that product to an external party who has a superior scale of economy in that particular activity.

The contract model is fundamentally different to the common outsourcing, shared services, strategic alliance models, since those latter models have generally related to so called noncore activities, such as procurement or the provision of technology infrastructure, applications and support services, etc. The contract model, on the other hand, is based on core activities such as those in which the institution is continually engaged (Kakabadse & Kakabadse, 2000; Quinn & Hilmer, 1994). The following discussion is based on the logical extreme of the disaggregated model — the virtual bank.

Core Competencies Based on Intelligent Data Processing — The Critical Role of Data Mining

A central issue on the supply side of the disaggregated model is the management of customer requirements. The business of banking under the model of the virtual bank is essentially the management of customer relationships, since products and subcomponents are no longer internally sourced. This means maintaining the customer interface, the design of products and services according to consumer needs, the specification of standards and the monitoring of supplier contracts. Critical to the success of this brokering process is the development of core analytical competencies in the interpretation and anticipation of uncertainty within the market environment according to the particular line of business. The optimization of this model implies an architecture that is conducive to the just-in-time analysis of customer data across multiple business units or markets.

The data management norm evidenced in some Australian banks, however, is a focus on the management of transaction data according to the line of business. For example, a standard information technology architecture would comprise the following core front-office and back-office systems. Transaction data enters via various customer interface points within the distribution network. Internet-enabled, telephone and branch transactions are processed through separate mediating systems that interface HTML and front-office platforms into the core banking system (such as Hogan), which updates account records, and via a middleware application(s) passes that data through to various line of business specific systems. The primary objective of this system configuration is the collection, updating and storage of application specific, atomic, nonredundant and current transaction data. The data flow process is described in Figure 5.

Architectural Overview of a Contract Management and Business Analysis Platforms

Unlike the singular "pull" mechanism of the orthodox data management model evident in Australian banks, the data management model of a data mining environment implies two discreet, but complementary system domains: a contract banking domain and a business analysis domain. These two domains reflect the core competencies of the business model — managing multiple product and service contracts as well as maintaining the customer interface. This involves both a "pull" and "push" data management model. A fundamental assumption that underpins the transparent interface between the two domains is a straight-through processing (one-time input of transaction data) capability. Based on the existence of legacy systems, manual interfacing, evidence of high employee numbers and moderate economies of scale, the architecture represented here is an idealized construct.

Figure 5. Typical Operational Architecture of a Bank

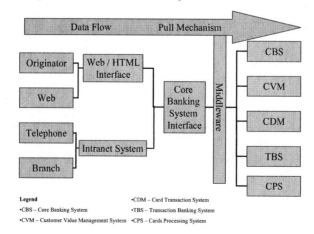

Figure 6. Contract Management and Business Analysis Architecture

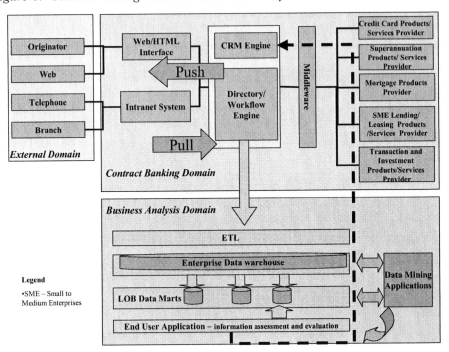

In Figure 6, the data flow arrow leading from the "End User Application" of the business analysis domain to the "CRM" module describes the flow of business information that will inform decisions regarding a particular CRM initiative. This data is ad hoc, subject specific (i.e., customer retention, profitability, products, customers, etc.), summarized, static (until refreshed), informs business decisions, and ultimately finds expression in product innovation, customer profitability initiatives, etc.

The assumption implicit here is that superior performance is determined by how efficiently the institution can establish and exploit economies of scale in aligning its product and service offerings with the requirements of consumers. This would suggest that high volume analytical technologies, such as data mining, are conducive to this model, since they would create superior market profiling capability and efficiencies in the management of customer relationships. Based on segmentation techniques, banks could anticipate client requirements (complete product or a particular feature) and negotiate product innovations, such as features that smooth contribution requirements for certain loan and superannuation products.

The disaggregated model of banking represents the transposition of a manufacturing outsourcing model into an information-intensive industry and is by its nonspecific nature generic. The generalized principle of shifting core competencies from products and services to the management of customer relationships is applicable to other information-intensive industries such as insurance and retail. The development of core competencies around the leverage of customer data could potentially change the economic basis of those industries, since business in those industries could potentially outsource core processes, products and services, and operate as customer management specialists. Distinct capabilities could be built around management of customer information (storage, security, etc.), customer requirements (product and service tailoring/innovation), contract management (compliance to terms and conditions), risk analysis and vendor management (contracts, supply, etc.), and would leverage the existing distribution infrastructure, as well as existing technology infrastructure and internal expertise.

CONCLUSION

The preceding structural analysis of the Australian retail banking industry demonstrates that data mining banks can potentially influence those competitive forces that impact on its relative economic position and market share. The intensification of entry barriers through the optimization of capital investment and product differentiation not only represents a significant reduction in the threat of new entrants and mitigation of consumer power, but is also tangible evidence of how businesses within information-intensive industries, such as banking, can achieve competitive advantage through the application of data mining and other high volume analytical technologies.

Competitive advantage, as illustrated in this chapter, is predicated on structural changes (entry barriers, switching costs, etc.) within an industry, which, in turn, affect the economic performance of enterprises within that industry. Economic benefits are realized over time as the relative position of the bank changes, rather than immediately, as is the case of process improvement initiatives. Enterprises that achieve competitive advantage, as is illustrated in the above case study, are able to alter entry barriers to their benefit, extend existing technology infrastructure investment, understand the requirements and needs of their customers and successfully differentiate their products and services within an industry.

Through the emergence of data mining, competencies based on information processing are potential drivers of profitability rather than simply cost reduction mechanisms. The degree to which data mining and the economic optimization of customer data can fundamentally alter the revenue streams of banks and other information-intensive businesses gives concrete meaning to the much used phrase, the "information economy." The productivity paradox highlights the difficulty in discerning the economic benefit of technology, since the economic benefit of capturing, storing and updating data is well nigh impossible to measure. Much of the money that has been spent on technology within the Australian banking industry has essentially been spent on an inert, previously under utilized asset. Continued investment in the dominant "pull" model of data management has increased the capital cost of the technology infrastructure, but has not contributed to competitive advantage, since all of the "runners" have been pursuing the same course. In this light, the economic, productivity and competitive value of the "pull" model of data management was extremely difficult to understand.

Data mining enables banks to finally offset data processing and storage technology investment. Through data mining, investments in technology can be assessed on the basis of returns from strategic decisions. As well, the capability to build competencies around corporate knowledge domains presents information-intensive businesses, such as banks, not only with tangible operational level benefits, but, more importantly, opportunities to reassess their existing business models and explore different strategic alternatives.

REFERENCES

Applegate, L. M., McFarlan, W. F. & McKenney, J. L. (1996). *Corporate Information Systems Management: The Issues Facing Senior Executives* (p. 49). Boston, MA: Irwin McGraw-Hill.

Australian Bureau of Statistics. (2001). *Finance 2000.* Canberra, Australia: Australian Bureau of Statistics.

Botten, N., & McManus, J. (1999). *Competitive Strategies for Service Organisations.* London: MacMillan Press.

Cabena, P., Hadjinian, P., Stadler, R., Verhees, J. & Zanasi, A. (1998). *Discovering Data Mining: From Concept to Implementation.* New Jersey: Prentice-Hall.

Chan, Y. E. (2000). IT value: The great divide between qualitative and quantitative and individual and organizational measures. *Journal of Management Information Systems, 16*(4), 225-261.

Chin, W. W., & Marcolin, B. L. (2001). The future of diffusion research. *The Database for Advances in Information Systems, 32*(3), 8-12.

Christopher, M., Payne, A. & Ballantyne, D. (1993). *Relationship Marketing* (pp. 42-43). Oxford, UK: Butterworth Heinemann.

Clemons, E. K., & Row, M. C. (1991, September). Sustaining IT advantage: The role of structural differences. *MIS Quarterly, 15*(3), 275-292.

Commonwealth of Australia. (1997, March). *Financial system inquiry final report* (pp. 81, 90). Canberra, Australia: Australian Government Publishing Service, ISBN 0642261024.

Davenport, T. H., Harris, J. G., De Long, D. W., & Jacobson, A. L. (2001). Data to knowledge to results. *California Management Review, 43*(2), 117-138.

Davis, F. D. (1989). Perceived usefulness, perceived ease of use and user acceptance of information technology. *MIS Quarterly, 13,* 319-340.

De Wit, B., & Meyer, R. (1998). *Strategy process, content, context: An international perspective.* London: International Thomson Business Press.

Deloitte Touche Tohmatsu International. (1995). *The future of retail banking: A global perspective.* London: Deloitte Touche Tohmatsu Studio.

Dibb, S. (1998). Market segmentation: strategies for success. *Marketing Intelligence and Planning, 16,* 394.

Gupta, U. G., & Collins, W. (1997). The impact of information systems on the efficiency of banks: An empirical investigation. *Industrial Management and Data systems, 1,* 10-16.

Hosking, A., Kambil, A., & Lister, A. (2000). Electronic commerce and financial services: Going for broke. In Melnick, E. L., Nayyar, P. R., Pinedo, M. L. & Seshadri, S. (Ed.), *Creating Value in Financial Services: Strategies, Operations and Technologies.* Boston, MA: Kluwer Academic, p. 181.

Jayawardhena, C., & Foley, P. (2000). Changes in the banking sector – The case of the Internet banking in the UK. *Electronic Networking Applications and Policy, 10*(1), 19-30.

Kakabadse, N., & Kakabadse, A. (2000). Critical review – Outsourcing: A paradigm shift. *The Journal of Management Development, 19*(8), 674.

KPMG. (2001, May). *Financial institutions performance survey 2001.* Retrieved on August 1, 2001 from http://www.kpmg.com.au/content/Industries/Financial_Services/Financial_Institutions_Performance_Survey_2001/docs/290309_fips_ overview_graphmarketshare.pdf.

Kutner, S., & Cripps, J. (2001). Managing the customer portfolio of healthcare enterprises. *The Healthcare Forum Journal, 4*(5), 52-4.

Llewellyn, D. T. (1996, July). *Banking in the 21st century: The transformation of an industry*. Paper presented at Reserve Bank of Australia Conference on the Future of the Financial System, Canberra, Australia.

Lloyd-Walker, B. (1999). *IT and Organisational Performance in the Australian Banking Industry*. Unpublished doctoral dissertation, Monash University, Melbourne, Australia.

Lucas, H. C. (1999). *Information technology and the productivity paradox: Assessing the value of investing in IT*. New York: Oxford University Press.

Meadows, M., & Dibb, S. (1998). Assessing the implementation of market segmentation in retail financial services. *International Journal of Service Industry Management, 9*(3), 266.

Porter, M. (1979, March/April). How competitive forces shape strategy. *Harvard Business Review: Reprint Collection*, (79208). Originally published in *Harvard Business Review, 57*(2), 137.

Porter, M. (1980). *Competitive Strategy: Techniques for Analysing Industries and Competitors*. New York: Free Press.

Porter, M., & Millar, V. E. (1985, July-August). How information gives you competitive advantage. *Harvard Business Review, 85*(4), 149-160.

Porter, M. E. (1985). *Competitive Advantage: Creating and Sustaining Superior Performance*. New York: Free Press.

Prasad, B., & Harker, P. T. (1997). *Examining the contribution of information technology toward the productivity and profitability in U.S. retail banking*. Unpublished working paper, Wharton Financial Institutions Centre, University of Pennsylvania, Philadelphia, PA.

Quinn, J. B., & Hilmer, F. G. (1994). Strategic outsourcing. *Sloan Management Review, 35*(4), 43-45.

Rajan, R. G. (n.d.). The past and future of commercial banking – Viewed through an incomplete contact lens. *Journal of Money, Credit and Banking, 30*(3), 524-550.

Ryals, L., & Payne, A. (2001, March). Customer relationship management in financial services: Towards information enabled relationship marketing. *Journal of Strategic Marketing, 9*(1), 6.

Schein, E. H. (1980). *Organizational psychology* (p. 172). Englewood Cliffs, NJ: Prentice-Hall.

Sircar, S., Turnbow, B., & Bordoli, B. (2000). A framework for assessing the relationship between information technology investments and firm performance. *Journal of Management Information Systems, 16*(4), 69-70.

Suwardy, T. (2000). *Competition: Its effect on information technology usage in Australian listed firms and industries*. Unpublished doctoral dissertation, Monash University, Melbourne, Australia.

Wilson, T. C. Pricing trends for personal computers: Moore's law, Wilson's corollary, and reality. *Library Hi Tech News, 18*(5). Retrieved on July 21, 2002 from http://zaccaria.emeraldinsight.com/vl=22743176/cl=27/nw=1/fm=html/rpsv/cw/mcb/13565362/v17n1/s2/p13.

Chapter IV

The Role of Data Mining in Organizational Cognition

Chandra S. Amaravadi
Western Illinois University, USA

Farhad Daneshgar
University of New South Wales, Australia

ABSTRACT

Data mining has quickly emerged as a tool that can allow organizations to exploit their information assets. In this chapter, we suggest how this tool can be used to support strategic decision-making. Starting with an interpretive perspective of strategy formulation, we discuss the role of beliefs in the decision-making process. Referred to as Micro-Theories (MTs), these beliefs generally concern some assumption regarding the organization's task environment, such as sales increasing in a certain segment or customers preferring a certain product. The strategic role for data mining, referred to as Organizational Data Mining (ODM) is then to provide validation for these beliefs. We suggest a four-step process for identifying and verifying MTs and illustrate this with a hypothetical example of a bank. Implications and future trends in ODM are discussed. Ultimately results of data mining should be integrated with strategic support systems and knowledge management systems.

INTRODUCTION

Data mining, the identification of useful patterns from historical data, is a step in the larger process of knowledge discovery in databases (KDD), which includes data preparation, selection, cleansing and interpretation of results as additional steps. The data to be mined is usually obtained from the company's transaction records or purchased externally from third parties. A mixture of techniques from artificial intelligence and statistics are used, including summarization, time series, regression, decision trees, rule induction and cluster analysis to name a few (Fayyad, Piatetsky-Shapiro, & Smyth, 1996). According to Nemati and Barko (2001), the majority of data mining applications (72 percent) are centered around predicting customer behavior. Business applications of mining have been in customer retention (Smith, Willis & Brooks 2000; Ng & Liu, 2000), predicting ingredient usage in fast food restaurants (Liu, Bhattacharyya, Sclove, Chen & Lattyak, 2001), effectiveness of marketing campaigns in fast food restaurants (Anonymous, 2001), and assessing the quality of health care (Hogl, Muller, Stoyan & Stuhlinger, 2001). These are operational and managerial applications in the sense that the results of such applications can be used to take specific actions, including offering discounts and incentives, modifying store layouts and reducing prices. In this chapter, we take the perspective that the role of data mining can be extended (viz. organizational data mining (ODM)) beyond managerial usage to supplementing strategic decision making in organizations. This would require viewing organizational data within the larger context of organization-environmental interactions. It is the objective of this chapter to introduce and elaborate on this strategic role and, additionally, to explore the linkages between the interpretation stage of KDD and knowledge management.

BACKGROUND

The strategic use of information technology is a mature concept in the information systems discipline. Sabherwal and King (1991) define a strategic application as one that has a profound influence on a firm's success, by either influencing or shaping the organization's strategy or by playing a direct role in the implementation or support of it. It is the former definition of a strategic application that we favor — the idea that data mining can contribute to the formation of the firm's strategy. Before examining this role, we will first review basic concepts of strategy and discuss the process by which it is formed.

Strategy is commonly defined as achieving a fit with the environment and matching capabilities with resources and environmental conditions (Kast & Rosenzweig, 1979). Organizations are subject to pressures from the environment, which originate from beyond the firm's boundaries. These pressures can arise from various sources, which can be classified into the task, institutional and general environments. The task environment is concerned with inputs and outputs relevant to the decision-making and transformation processes of the organization and can include suppliers, competitors, technologies and employees (Kast, 1980). It typically has influence on the performance of organizations. The supply of semiconductor memory, for instance, affects profitability of PC manufacturers.

The institutional environment is that part of the environment that defines the rules of operation. Banks, policy-making institutions, governments, industry standards, labor unions and special interest groups are part of this environment (Carrol & Chung, 1986). It has the effect of imposing constraints on organizations and restricting their ability to adapt to changes. Thus, union contracts govern the number of hours that union members can work. The Securities and Exchange Commission regulates the timing and quantity of stock that a company can issue. The institutional environment has been found to influence the births and deaths of organizations (Carrol & Chung, 1986).

The general environment is that part of the environment that has a broad influence on the organization and can include social mores, fashion trends, economic and political conditions, natural resources, etc. The general environment has an indirect influence on all organizations, ultimately influencing entities in the task and institutional environments. Recent accounting scandals in large companies, for instance, have affected the ability of companies to raise capital in the equity markets.

Progressive organizations attempt to adapt to environmental pressures by attempting to modify their structures, processes and other variables that affect their positioning. The process of handling environmental changes is illustrated in Figure 1 (Daft & Weick, 1984). The first stage, also referred to as environmental scanning, involves collecting various types of environmental information. "Soft," or subjective, information is collected by managers or by corporate staff and area specialists (Elofson & Konsynski, 1991). This type of information is sometimes classified as "external" information. "Hard," or quantitative, information is usually collected from the company's information archives. Banks and insurance companies, for instance, typically have data going back for dozens of years. This type of information is often referred to as "internal" information. With the prevalence of Web-based systems, both external and internal data collection is greatly accelerated, to the point where information collection is no longer a formal stage (see Figure 1).

The information gathering behavior of organizations is a function of the stability of the environment, which in turn is a function of the rate at which change occurs. If changes occur gradually, the environment will be regarded as stable and vice versa. In stable industries, such as grocery, retail, mining, metals, restaurant and consumer

Figure 1. An Interpretive Perspective of Organizational Cognition (Adapted from Daft & Weick, 1984)

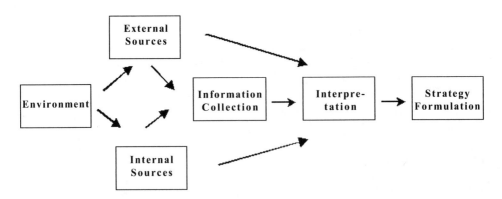

products, organizations will rely on their internal sources, while in the more unstable hi-tech industries, the reliance on external sources will be greater (Daft & Weick, 1984). Due to the slow rate of change in stable industries, organizations can rely on internal sources, especially on their archived data for environmental information.

The objective of environmental scanning is to arrive at a coherent picture of the environment. This is the interpretation phase of the strategic decision-making process illustrated in Figure 1. Decision makers attempt to address questions such as: Will a key supplier defect to a competitor?; Will a competitor raise his prices?; Will profitability increase by expanding the product line?; and Will a new product introduction cannibalize existing products? Interpretation, thus, involves acquiring and modifying belief systems. Belief systems are summaries of perceptions, observations and experiences concerning the organization's resources, markets and customers (Lorsch, 1989). They are found to have a significant impact on strategy formulation (SF) phase of the strategic decision-making process. This phase is concerned with decisions about markets, products, production levels and similar variables. It is extremely complex owing to the large number of variables that are involved and the open-ended nature of the domain.

The process is idealistic as a number of problems can arise at each of the stages. There are limitations in the amount and type of information that can be collected. Competitor's behavior is characteristically unknown. Similarly, information on tax structures in a foreign country may be unknown or unavailable. These problems will typically spill over into the other stages of the strategy-making process, resulting in interpretation and response errors (Milliken, 1990). For instance, if an organization has inadequate data on a competitor, it could misinterpret pricing moves as attempts to grab market share, when, in reality, these could be attempts to get rid of excess inventory. Misperceptions can lead to inappropriate strategies. A firm might expect an economic downturn and reduce its inventory, when, in fact, there is continued economic activity. It is here that data mining can play its biggest role by providing evidence, validated by historical data, which can be used to prove or disprove the theories that the organization holds regarding its environment. When interpretation errors are, thus, reduced, executives can make decisions with greater confidence. We will refer to this role as the ODM approach.

MAIN THRUST OF THE CHAPTER

The KDD process encompasses two modes of utilizing data mining technologies: to verify hypotheses or to discover new patterns in the data (Brachman, Khabaza, Kloesgen, Piatetsky-Shapiro & Simoudis, 1996). These have also been characterized as question-driven (confirmative) or data-driven (explorative) approaches (Hogl et al., 2001). As an example of the former, a health care institution might be interested in finding out whether or not complicated diagnoses are associated with long-term hospital stay. An example of the latter might be identifying characteristics of patients associated with long-term vs. short-term hospital stays. The techniques used in these approaches will differ. In the former case, a simple correlation test will suffice, while, in the latter case, a classification analysis will be necessary. Data-driven approaches will have an un-bounded search space, since the analyst attempts to identify all possible trends.

Obviously, hypothesis-driven approaches are likely to be more relevant to decision makers and also more computationally tractable.

The hypotheses to be tested will be derived from the belief systems of decision makers. There is empirical evidence that cognitive models play a significant role in strategy formulation. Lorsch (1989) found in a study of 12 organizations that major strategic decisions were influenced by a core set of beliefs, which included financial goals, acceptable types of risks and management's vision of distinctive competence, among other things. To some degree, the complexity of belief systems also influences success in decision-making (Nair, 2001). Clearly, beliefs need to be validated before they can be utilized. Unlike other research approaches (Lee & Courtney 1989; Nair, 2001; Ramprasad & Poon, 1983), we are not concerned so much about the inter-relationships among the beliefs (i.e., cognitive maps) as about the beliefs themselves. We will operationalize them with MTs, a term introduced by Hewitt (1986) to refer to the pre-conceptions that organizations hold about the environment.

MTs encapsulate beliefs about the environment, such as competitors announcing price cuts on certain product lines or customers preferring "grey" over "blue" color for outdoor jackets. They will be dependent on contextual factors, such as time, economic climate and state of the organization at the time. As with other organizational character-istics (structure, strategy, etc.), MTs will be similar across organizations but unique to each. Further, the number of MTs will probably be very large and will number in the hundreds. Table 1 lists a few examples of MTs for a consumer-products organization grouped by aspects of the task environment. These MTs revolve around key task entities, such as competitors, customers, suppliers and employees. While similar sets of MTs could be developed for the institutional and general environments, it is unlikely that large enough data sets would be conveniently available on the organization's interac-tions with these environments. For most purposes, MTs will be based on task entities.

Traditional application of data mining has been in the discovery mode, identifying product associations, sequential buying patterns and predicting churn and can be viewed as a managerial usage of the technology. Our view is that effective strategic decision making requires using the technology proactively, in a strategic hypothesis verification mode, to confirm/disconfirm MTs. Identifying and validating these is an extended process that consists of four primary stages (adapted from Hogl et al., 2001) as discussed below:

Initiating the Project

An ODM project will not be markedly different from other information systems projects. Resources and commitments will have to be obtained from top management (Nemati & Barko, 2001). The resources will include the infrastructure associated with the warehouse, skilled analysts as well as the time of top management. Since MTs will be interwoven with business variables, ODM analysts will require considerable domain knowledge. Resource commitments will not be possible without the support of top management. Their co-operation will have to be obtained via pilot demonstrations, using sample data and existing databases. The analysts will need to become familiar with the company's products, markets and strategies by interviewing senior executives and scrutinizing internal reports on the topic. Additionally, the analyst will need familiarity with the company's databases and capabilities of the mining software.

Identification of MTs

Once a project is initiated, the next stage is the identification of MTs. A number of manual and automated techniques for identifying strategic beliefs and assumptions have been suggested in the literature (King, 1982; Lee & Courtney, 1989; Ramprasad & Poon, 1983). In our view, automated methods are not sufficiently mature to support the assumption analysis process. King (1982) has proposed a Strategic Issue Analysis (SIA) process in which the analyst, in co-operation with top management, develops formal statements of issues, followed by a preliminary issue model and subsequently followed by revision and usage. We favor a similar, manual, co-operative process that involves the analyst developing a set of MTs and reviewing them with top management iteratively. The analyst needs to start the process by first listing the different components of the task environment. The entities that are relevant will differ from company to company and industry to industry. For a bank, the components will include customers, employees, other financial institutions and technologies. Next the relevant attributes of each of these components will need to be identified. Attributes should be selected such that they serve to predict or elaborate on the behavior of the task entity that is desired by the organization, for example, suppliers having a broad product range, customers liking/disliking the products offered and employees being competent. Examples of MTs for a consumer products organization are illustrated in Table 1. For the bank's customer component, the attributes can include service, convenience and perceived value. On the basis of discussions with company officials, key MTs, which need to be tested, are identified.

Table 1. Examples of MTs for a Consumer Products Organization

Task Dimension	Task Environment Variable	Example Microtheories
Competitor	Products	The competitor's product matches those offered by the company in price/ function.
	Markets	Competitors are strong in the New England Area. Competitors are weak in Midwest.
	Distribution	Competitor's products are readily available. Competitor has a strong distribution network.
	Management	Competitors have changed their management/strategy.
Customer	Products	Customer considers product to be superior to that of competition.
	Image	Customer has a favorable image of the company.
	Service	Customer is pleased/satisfied/very happy about service levels.
	Distribution and Availability	Customer has easy access to the product; product is available when the customer needs it.
Supplier	Reliability	Supplier has always delivered.
	Timeliness	The deliveries are on time.
	Quality of Materials	Material delivered passes inspection test barely/with flying colors.
	Cost of Doing Business	The total costs of doing business are low in comparison with other suppliers.
Employee	Work Environment	Employees have a positive work environment.
	Satisfaction	Employees are satisfied with their pay levels.
	Training	Employees are appropriately trained for their jobs.
	Contribution	Employees have produced innovative suggestions.

Selection of Technique

Depending on the type of MT to be tested, there are a variety of techniques for the analyst to choose from (see Table 2). These can be broadly grouped into predictive and descriptive techniques (not shown). Examples of the former include association and regression, while examples of the latter include classification, characterization, clustering and time-series analysis. As mentioned earlier, both techniques will be used in the hypothesis verification mode. Table 2 also illustrates the type of MTs (for a bank) for which these techniques are well suited. Predictive techniques can be used to verify hypotheses concerning the customer's behavior, such as when they would apply for a loan and what type of loan they would apply for. The descriptive techniques can be used to verify hypotheses concerning the demographic characteristics of customers. These can include income, profession, location, marital status, balance history, etc. Additionally, product characteristics, such as the most popular type of loan and the average loan amount, can also be verified.

Algorithm Selection and Model Formulation

Once a technique is identified, the analyst needs to select a suitable model with which to formulate the mining problem. This is perhaps the most challenging and confounding aspect of the ODM process, due to the large selection of models available, applicability of data at hand and their inherent complexity. Table 3 identifies some of the popular models and representative modeling issues.

For instance, in classification, CART, $C_{4.5}$, K-NN, Neural Nets and Bayesian approaches are popular algorithms. Here, the classification function needs to be defined in terms of either the values of attributes belonging to a particular class or the probability of a record belonging to a particular class. Tree-based approaches, such as CART, ID 3, $C_{4.5}$, are unsuitable for large data sets and other methods have to be used (Kumar, 2002). In clustering, the techniques can be grouped into partitioning and hierarchical approaches. Examples of partitioning-based methods include K-Means and K-Mediods. In

Table 2.   Selection of Mining Technique (Adapted from Han, 1997)

Technique	Type of problem for which the technique is suitable	Example MTs for a bank
Association	Products purchased together	Whether home loans and auto loans are obtained by same customers.
Classification	Classifying data into categories	To see if there is any demographic basis for classifying customers into credit card and non-credit card customers.
Characterization	To obtain descriptive characteristics of the data	To identify whether or not the bank has high-income customers.
Clustering	To identify naturally occurring groups in the data	To identify if the branches are serving customers in their area or not.
Prediction	To predict purchases	To predict when a customer will apply for a loan or a credit card.
Time series analysis	To obtain information on trends	To see if the loan business is increasing or decreasing in the long run.

Table 3. Popular Data Mining Models and Representative Modeling Issues

Technique	Popular algorithms	Typical model issues
Association	Apriori, Hash tree, Partitioning and Sampling (Han 1997)	Specify support levels and confidence levels.
Classification	CART, ID 3, $C_{4.5}$, K-NN, Neural nets, Discrimination analysis and Bayesian classification (Chen et al., 1996; Kumar, 2002)	Define the classification function in terms of probabilities or class attributes and values.
Clustering	K-means, K-mediod, hierarchical methods (Kumar, 2002)	Provide an initial set of clusters or distances between pair of points.
Prediction	Regression, Bayesian analysis	Identifying and specifying dependent and independent variables; prior probabilities.
Time series analysis	Simple trend analysis, Exponential, Box-Jenkins Seasonal ARIMA models and SCAN (Liu et al., 2001)	Specifying and evaluating periodicity at the correct level of aggregation. Identifying and filtering outliers.

the K-Means approach, an initial set of k centers are chosen and the "goodness of fit" is evaluated according to a prespecified criteria (distance). These are changed incrementally and the goodness of fit is again evaluated until there is no "better fit" (Han, Kamber & Tung, 2001). The challenge here is to identify and specify the initial set of clusters, since the results obtained will depend on this selection. The distances between the data points will also need to be provided. These methods are unsuitable for large data sets as well as for clusters that are irregularly shaped (Kumar, 2002). Prediction could be carried out by probabilistic or regression methods. In the former case, the prior probabilities will need to be evaluated first, while in the latter the dependent and independent variables will have to be specified. In Time-series analysis, a number of models are available for analyzing seasonal and nonseasonal data, including simple Trend analysis, Moving averages, Exponential, ARIMA, Neural Nets and SCA (see Table 3). The ARIMA model has components to capture seasonal ($\varphi(B)$ and $\theta(B)$) and nonseasonal trends ($\Phi(B^s)$, and $\Theta(B^s)$), where "B" captures the relationship between one value in the time series and the previous value, and "s" is the periodicity of the series. These parameters are estimated manually in some cases or, if the software permits, automatically. Since outliers can skew the parameters, they need to be detected and removed (Liu et al., 2001). Thus model selection and formulation is a far from straightforward process that involves expert judgment and significant effort in preprocessing, model development and data-set selection.

Testing and Evaluation of Results

Testing follows model identification and formulation. This is usually where the conventional KDD process begins. The analyst needs to select relevant data and carry out the preprocessing. Given the abundance of historical information, data selection is a nontrivial process. Obviously analysts need to guard against clerical errors such as importing the wrong columns or inadvertently missing a year. Data preprocessing can involve integration from various sources, format conversion, proper sorting and sequencing of data, especially if it involves periodicity and calculation of additional variables, such as margins and ratios. For large data sets, testing should be carried out with an experimental subset. Because of the strategic significance and computational intensity of the task, test results need to be saved. After all the tests are carried out, the analyst needs to prepare a formal report and present the results in a meeting involving the senior management of the organization. To be included in the discussions are the MTs that have been tested, the data sets utilized, the techniques used, the outputs and results of the tests and his/her perceptions of their applicability. It is expected that a majority of the MTs will be confirmed. However, for those that are not fully supported, additional testing may be required to ascertain the causes.

A Hypothetical Example

Union bank is a large Fortune 500 bank in the Midwest with branches in Des Moines, Indianapolis, Chicago, Minneapolis and Milwaukee. The bank provides full-service facilities including branch banking, ATMs, credit cards, and residential, automotive and personal loans. Recently, bank management has been concerned with decline in operating margins and hired a data mining analyst to assist them with their strategic planning efforts to remedy the situation. The consultant identified the bank's task entities as competitors, technology, customers, products and branches. On the basis of further discussions, the consultant identified key MTs as follows: (1) margin declines were associated with high charge offs in the credit card business; (2) the margin contribution from home loans and personal loans is higher than in the company's other businesses; but (3) administrative expenses, as a proportion of revenues, are relatively higher in the home mortgage business; (4) the personal loan business is on the increase; and (5) customers with high incomes contribute more to profit from personal loans.

In addition to database information on customers, the consultant also found quarterly financial data in the bank, going back 20 years, but, due to drastic differences in the general environment between the 1980s and 1990s, he decided to focus on data in the last 11 years. A sampling of the data for the credit card segment is illustrated in Table 4. [This data has been constructed based on Bank of America annual reports (www.bankofamerica.com/investor/index.cfm?section=700).]

Model Formulation

The analyst decided initially to verify the first four MTs. Due to the fairly straightforward nature of the data and hypotheses, the analyst decided to use conven-

Table 4. Sample Financial Data for the Credit Card Segment

YEAR	QTR	REVENUE	OH COSTS	COFFS
2002	2	700	303	144
2002	1	550	312	154
2001	4	600	307	164
2001	3	615	311	162
2001	2	590	287	160
2001	1	608	291	170
2000	4	560	280	126
2000	3	580	277	135
2000	2	600	276	145

Note: Qtr – quarter; OH – overheads; COFFS – charge offs. (Revenue, overhead costs and charge offs are in millions of dollars.)

tional statistical techniques. For the first MT, the analyst decided to use simple linear regression analysis with margin as the dependent variable and charge off as the independent variable and a threshold r^2 of 0.70 (assumed) for the first MT. For the second MT, the analyst decided to rely on simple hypothesis testing of the averages of the margins for home loans (computed as Revenues — Expenses — Charge offs), compared with margins from other businesses (with confidence specified at 95 percent). For the third MT, the analyst decided to perform a comparison of the average ratios of home loan administrative costs to revenues (we will refer to this as the efficiency ratio) with those in other segments (personal loans, credit cards, accounts). For the fourth MT, the analyst decided on a time-series analysis of the personal loan business. A preliminary investigation of the data revealed the most suitable model as ARIMA with autocorrelation (i.e., ARIMA(1,0,0) without integration and moving averages).

Testing and Evaluation

For testing purposes, the analyst selected quarterly data on revenues, overhead expenses and charge offs from the company's archives. He/she sorted them in chronological order and decided to ignore the two most recent quarters. He/she integrated the data from the different segments into a single file containing 44 records (four each for each of the 11 years between 1991-2001). Due to the simple nature of the MTs, the consultant utilized Minitab™ and Forecast Pro™ for testing, even though a more sophisticated mining tool (Polyanalyst™) was readily available. The results of testing were as follows:

(1)   Regression analysis for margins and charge offs resulted in an r^2 of 0.69 with a p value of 0 (i.e., the relation was nonrandom), proving for the first MT that the margins were negatively correlated with charge offs.

(2)   Hypothesis testing of the means of the margin averages proved that margins from Home loans were greater than margins from credit cards (T statistic was 5.83 and p value 0), and margins from personal loans were higher than those from credit cards (T = 18.38, p = 0) and accounts (T = 24.64, p = 0). However, the hypothesis that margins from home loans were greater than those from accounts was disproved (T = 0.78, p = 0.22). A simple comparison of (margin) means bears out this hypothesis ($\mu_{personal\ loans} = 332.66 > \mu_{home\ loans} = 109.66 > \mu_{accounts} = 106.93 > \mu_{credit\ cards} = 25.9$). Clearly margins from credit cards are problematic and this is further borne out by the high standard deviation (92.7).

(3)   Similarly, the efficiency ratio for home loans was higher than in credit cards (T = 4.55, p = 0), accounts (T = 6.67, p = 0) and personal loans (T = 11.98, p = 0), proving the hypothesis that administrative costs, as a proportion of revenues, was in general higher for the home loan segment.

(4)   For the fourth MT, ARIMA analysis indicated a trend with $r^2 = 0.67$ (the value for the constant was "574" and a trend component of "4.13" with a forecasting error of "40"). Even though the trend is not very strong, there seems to be a long-term improvement in the personal loan business.

The analyst saved these results along with the charts, prepared a report and presented it to management, who armed with this analysis, proceeded to confidently re-evaluate their strategies with respect to the credit card segment.

Technical Challenges

Despite the progress of technology, data mining presents some formidable challenges. Some of these can be attributed to the size of the data sets. The ubiquity of transaction processing systems means that warehouses of 2GB or more are very common (Fayyad, Piatetsky-Shapiro, Smyth & Uthurusamy, 1996). Statistical methods are often not preferred for such sets. For instance, a regression analysis considering 1,000 different models will find 50 of them significant at the 95 percent confidence level, due to random chance alone (King, 1997). The large number of dimensions also compounds the problem. A classification problem involving 15 variables, each with three or more possible categories, will require comparisons in the order of 500,000 for a data set containing only 1,000 records (King, 1997). Associative rule induction involves an order of complexity of $O(n.m.2^m)$, where "n" is the number of records, "m" is the number of items and 2^m is the number of times the list has to be searched to construct the candidate lists (Kumar, 2002). Thus, if there are five possible items, such as milk, eggs, etc., (m = 5) occurring in 20 grocery transactions (n = 20), the number of possible association rules are a function of "m" (i.e., the number of possible item combinations are $^5C_1 + {}^5C_2 \ldots {}^5C_{m-1}$). The number of times the item list has to be scanned to generate candidate associations is 2^5 (assuming binary search) and the total number of all operations is given by $20*5*2^5$. The algorithm is exponential in terms of the number of items. It is for this reason that a hypothesis-driven approach has been suggested. If the association rules are specified a priori, this complexity is greatly reduced. But this, in turn, raises the issue of whether or not the software provides the analyst with flexibility in adapting the discovery process to verify predetermined hypotheses.

Implications of the ODM Approach

Data mining supplements the traditional strategy formulation process rather than automating it. It is infeasible to test the full set of possible MTs, since the relevant data may not exist. Executives will still have to rely on their experience and intuition to fill in perceptual gaps. During testing, some MTs will be confirmed, while others will be disconfirmed or will lack support. For those that are not supported, further analysis may be warranted to ascertain causes. This may require referring to a different set of data than what was considered during the mining process. If basic assumptions are refuted, such as a company not offering a broad enough product line, the source data and analyses will require re-examination to ensure that there are no selection biases or clerical errors. Since critical parameters of the models utilized are estimated, it is important that special consideration be given to cases where the results are unexpected. Companies should also seek additional proof of disconfirmations. Even though a majority of MTs are expected to be confirmed, research has shown that managerial perceptions will typically exhibit divergence from information obtained through archival data (Boyd, Dess & Rasheed, 1993). This has been attributed to undue optimism or pessimism on the part of individual managers. The MT identification process should account for divergent opinions. However, if these persist, discussion and sharing of results can reduce perceptual gaps and facilitate the development of consensus.

Confirmation of an MT is not a guarantee of its validity. By definition, an MT is valid for a certain set of conditions. If these conditions change, the MT may lose its applicability. Even if environmental conditions do not change (i.e., the environment is stable), organizations should seek "soft" information concerning the MTs. The scope of interpretation errors will be further minimized.

CONCLUSION

Data mining has quickly emerged as a tool that can allow organizations to exploit their information assets. To harness its strategic potential requires considering its outputs in the context of the mosaic of belief systems that constitutes the organization's knowledge about its environment. In this chapter, we have taken an interpretivist perspective of the process by which organizations make sense of their environments. Organizations collect various types of information about the entities with which they deal. This information could arise from internal or external sources and includes information about customers, employees, suppliers, etc. The resulting data is interpreted in the context of the belief systems regarding the environment. We have introduced the term MT to refer to the individual beliefs that organizations hold regarding their customers, competitors, etc. MTs have a significant impact on strategy formulation and need to be verified. We have proposed a four-stage process of identifying, formalizing, testing and evaluating MTs, using popular data mining techniques and illustrated it with a hypothetical case study. We have discussed the approach and pointed out its technical challenges and implications. Many of the challenges stem from the large sizes of databases and the large number of attributes. These challenges are being addressed gradually as the techniques undergo refinement. During testing of MTs, it is expected that many beliefs will test positively. For those that lack support, it is necessary to examine the model and data to ensure that no biases are present. It is important also to recognize that MTs will be valid only if the environmental conditions are stable. In unstable environments, the ODM approach will not be effective. However, it is the companies that are in stable environments that will have the greatest need for data mining technologies, since these are the companies that have a history of interactions with the environment. Utilizing the technologies in a strategic mode, although suggested in the literature, has not been operationalized in the fashion indicated here. As the business environment becomes more competitive, this role will be more vital for organizations.

FUTURE TRENDS

From the user's point of view, the most important stage of the KDD process is the sharing of results. This can range from simply presenting the results in a meeting, as pointed out earlier, to incorporating it within a knowledge management (KM) system. KM systems run the gamut from simple Web-based systems to more sophisticated systems capable of intelligence (Amaravadi, Samaddar & Dutta, 1995; Amaravadi, 2001). The latter type of systems are challenging, due to the complex nature of the domain and the primitive nature of current technologies. As noted earlier, strategic planning includes large numbers of organizational variables and their inter-relationships. Strategy formulation support tools may be needed to augment this process. If data mining is to be fully integrated with strategic processes, results from mining, such as confirmations, support levels and associated data sets, will need to be tied into SF support tools. In effect the system would serve as a KM system in the area of organizational strategy. With present technologies, and sizes of data sets, it seems more prudent to keep these systems disparate. As technologies improve and mature, and managers become more sophisticated, it is expected that integration with other information systems will be required and will present fewer problems. Ultimately, ODM capabilities will need to be integrated with environmental monitoring systems, executive support systems and KM systems. This will require an advanced degree of visualization and interactivity. Decision makers will need to be able to specify models, graph the results and manipulate the representation to do "what-if" type analyses (Thearling, Becker, DeCoste, Mawby, Pilote & Sommerfield, 2001). Integrating these capabilities within existing data mining software using graphical interfaces will present substantial challenges.

ACKNOWLEDGMENTS

The authors gratefully acknowledge the critical comments of our anonymous reviewer, which led to this improved version. We also gratefully acknowledge the generous assistance in data analysis from Mr. Choonsan Kim, instructor at Department of Information Management and Decision Sciences, Western Illinois University.

REFERENCES

Amaravadi, C. S. (2001). Engineering administrative knowledge for extended office systems. *Proceedings of 2nd European Conference on Knowledge Management, Bled, Slovenia* (pp. 7-18).

Amaravadi, C. S., Samaddar, S., & Dutta, S. (1995, May). IMkIS: Computerized intelligence for marketing decision making. *Marketing Intelligence and Planning, 13*(2), 4-13.

Anonymous (2000, May). Mining the data on dining. *Nations Restaurant News, 34*(21), S22-S24.

Boyd, B. K., Dess, G. G., & Rasheed, A. M. (1993). Divergence between archival and perceptual measures of the environment: Causes and consequences. *Academy of Management Review, 18*(2), 204-226.

Brachman, R. J., Khabaza, T., Kloesgen, W., Piatetsky-Shapiro, G., & Simoudis, E. (1996, November). Mining business databases. *Communications of the ACM, 39*(11), 42-48.

Carroll, G. R., & Yang Chung P. H. (1986, January). Organizational task and institutional environments in ecological perspective: Findings from the local newspaper industry. *American Journal of Sociology, 91*(4), 838-873.

Chen, M. S., Han, J., & Yu, P.S. (1996). Data mining: An overview from the database perspective. *IEEE Transactions on Knowledge and Data Engineering, 8*(6), 866-883.

Daft, R. L., & Weick, K. E. (1984). Towards a model of organizations as interpretation systems. *Academy of Management Review, 9*(2), 284-295.

Elofson, G. S., & Konsynski, B. R. (1991). Delegation technologies: Environmental scanning with intelligent agents. *Journal of Management Information Systems, 8*(1), 37-62.

Fayyad, U., Piatetsky-Shapiro, G., & Smyth, P. (1996, November). The KDD process for extracting useful knowledge from volumes of data. *Communications of the ACM, 39*(11), 27-34.

Fayyad, U., Piatetsky-Shapiro, G., Smyth, P. & Uthurusamy R. (1996). *Advances in knowledge discovery and data mining.* Menlo Park, CA: AAAI Press/MIT Press.

Han, J. (1997). Integration of data mining and data warehousing technologies. *Proceedings of the International Conference on Data Engineering (ICDE'97), Birmingham, UK.* Available at: http://db.cs.sfu.ca/sections/publication/kdd.kdd.html.

Han, J., Kamber, M., & Tung, A. K. H. (2001). Spatial clustering methods in data mining: A survey. In H. Miller & J. Han (Eds.), *Geographic data mining and knowledge discovery.* New York: Taylor and Francis. Hewitt, C. (1986, July). Offices are open systems. *ACM Transactions on Office Information Systems, 4*(3), 271-287.

Hogl, O. J., Muller, M., Stoyan, H., & Stuhlinger, W. (2001). Using questions and interests to guide data mining for medical quality management. *Topics in Health Information Management, 22*(1), 36-50.

Kast, F. (1980). Scanning the future environment: Social indicators. *California Management Review, XXIII*(1), 22-32.

Kast, F. E., & Rosenzweig, J. E. (1979). *Organizations and management: A systems and contingency approach.* New York: McGraw Hill.

King, D. (1997). *An overview of data mining.* Retrieved August 2002 from http://www.cc.gatech.edu/~kingd/datamine/datamine.html#hard.

King, W. R. (1982). Using strategic issue analysis. *Long Range Planning, 15(4),* 45-49.

Kumar, V. (2002, January 14). *Data mining algorithms.* Tutorial presented at IPAM 2002 Workshop on Mathematical Challenges in Scientific Data Mining. University of California, Los Angeles.

Lee, S., & Courtney, J. F. (1989). Organizational learning systems. *Proceedings of the Hawaii International Conference on System Sciences, III,* 492-503.

Liu, L. M, Bhattacharyya, S., Sclove, S. L., Chen, R., & Lattyak, W. J. (2001). Data mining on time series: An illustration using fast-food restaurant franchise data. *Computational Statistics and Data Analysis, 37,* 455-476.

Lorsch, J. W. (1989). Managing culture: The invisible barrier to strategic change. In A. A. Thompson & A. J. Strickland (Eds.), *Strategy formulation and implementation* (pp. 322-331). Homewood, IL.: BPI/IRWIN.

Milliken, F. J. (1990). Perceiving and interpreting environmental change: An examination of college administrators' interpretation of changing demographics. *Academy of Management Journal, 33*(1), 42-63.

Nair, U. K. (2001). Cognitive maps of managers and complex problem solving. In T. K. Lant & Z. Shapira (Eds.), *Organizational cognition* (pp. 211-239). Mahwah, NJ: Lawrence Erlbaum and Associates.

Nemati, H., & Barko, C. D. (2001). Issues in organizational data mining: A survey of current practices. *Journal of Data Warehousing, 6*(1), 25-36.

Ng, K., & Liu, H. (2000, December). Customer retention via data mining. *Artificial Intelligence Review, 14*(6), 569-590.

Ramprasad, A., & Poon, E. (1983). A computerized interactive technique for mapping influence diagrams (MIND). *Strategic Management Journal, 6,* 377-392.

Sabherwal, R., & King, W. R. (1991). Towards a theory of strategic use of information resources. *Information and Management, 20*(3), 191-212.

Smith, K. A., Willis R. J., & Brooks, M. (2000, May). An analysis of customer retention and insurance claim patterns using data mining: A case study. *Journal of the Operational Research Society, 51*(5), 532-541.

Thearling, K., Becker, B., DeCoste, D., Mawby, B., Pilote, M., & Sommerfield, D. (2001). Visualizing data mining Models. In U. Fayyad, G. Grinstein & A. Wierse (Eds.), *Information visualization in data mining and knowledge discovery* (pp. 312-329). San Mateo: Morgan Kaufman.

Chapter V

Privacy Implications of Organizational Data Mining

Hamid R. Nemati
University of North Carolina at Greensboro, USA

Charmion Brathwaite
University of North Carolina at Greensboro, USA

Kara Harrington
University of North Carolina at Greensboro, USA

ABSTRACT

Technological advances and decreased costs of implementing and using technology have allowed for vast amounts of data to be collected, used and manipulated for organizations to mine. If correctly deployed, Organizational Data Mining (ODM) offers companies an indispensable decision-enhancing process that optimizes resource allocation and exploits new opportunities by transforming data into valuable knowledge (Nemati & Barko, 2001). These tools have the potential to significantly reduce a company's costs by helping to identify areas of potential business, areas that the company needs to focus its attention on or areas that should be discontinued because of poor sales or returns over a period of time. However, this information, if used in the wrong context, can be very harmful to an individual. As a result, ODM may "pose a threat to privacy" in the sense that discovered patterns can reveal confidential personal attributes about individuals. This paper examines a number of issues related to the privacy concerns that are inherent with the use of ODM.

PURPOSE OF ODM

Companies' interactions with their customers have changed dramatically over the years. There is no longer the guarantee of a customer's loyalty. Factors such as niche marketing, the decreased attention spans of customers, the availability of alternative products as well as others complicate the situation even more. "Your customers are not your customers. You are merely their caretaker until one of your competitors can provide and communicate a better offer" (Berson et al., 1997). As a result, many companies have realized that in order to remain competitive, they need to understand their customers better and to quickly respond to their customers' wants and needs. To succeed, these companies must anticipate customer desires, satisfy these desires and, at the same time, encourage continued business.

Gone are the days where the shopkeeper would simply keep track of all of his customers in his head, and would know what to do when a customer walked into the store. Today shopkeepers are faced with a much more complex situation: more customers, more products, more competitors and less time to react. Thus, understanding customers is now much harder to do. Also, in this new technology age, with businesses moving at "Internet speed," uncertainty over a business' sustainability has increased significantly: Competition is global, and businesses are trying to minimize costs while customers and prospective customers want to negotiate their own terms. To remain competitive in this environment involves using the best tools available that will allow the company to take care of customers better than its competition. As a result, both the customer and the company will benefit from the successful analysis and determination of customer needs. The customer will be satisfied that he/she is being served in a timely manner, and the company will reduce costs associated with providing products or services that are of little interest to the customer. Improved customer service and reducing costs, exemplify the importance of collecting data for analysis.

TECHNOLOGY IMPROVING DATA MINING

Technological advances and decreased costs of implementing and using technology have allowed for vast amounts of data to be collected, used and manipulated for data mining. Traditionally, data collection was done manually through market surveys conducted by companies. This data was then summarized and categorized for use by the company to assess their clientele's needs. The questions usually focused on the usage of particular products and comparisons to competitors' products. Because these surveys tended to be anonymous (at least initially), consumers had few, if any, reservations about providing data. By analyzing sales records (provided either through the stores or directly from salespeople) companies knew which areas had greater sales and which needed additional marketing or support to increase market share. This type of analysis, however, tended to be long and laborious producing large volumes of paperwork because almost everything was done manually.

With automation, work became more efficient and less labor intensive. Vast amounts of data could be processed in shorter time spans so analyses became more accurate and up-to-date. As transaction processing became more automated, it became easier for companies to collect and store vast amounts of transactional data on their customers. The cost of data storage also decreased further fueling the data collection frenzy. The data was stored for future analysis in repositories or databases called data warehouses.

With increasing use of the Internet, especially for online purchasing, companies are able to collect this data instantaneously and track users' movements with or without their knowledge.

> "*The advent of the Internet and the associated explosive growth in databases has thrust business intelligence into the forefront of many corporate technology initiatives — from internal business reporting to direct marketing to Web traffic analysis. For the modern organization, business intelligence, often defined as the process of turning raw data into insightful, consumable pieces of information, has never been more prevalent throughout organizations than it is today*" (MicroStrategy, www.microstrategy.com, 2001).

Data that the user previously had the option of providing could now be collected without the user's permission. This new data, called clickstream data, adds a new dimension to the individual profile. Companies can now track user interests and can target their marketing campaigns directly at the user before purchases are even made. Clickstream data is obtained from Web sites as the user/consumer browses. It is an important source of data collection for the data warehouse because of its detailed nature. It allows companies to better complete the customer profile because companies can integrate Web-based data with traditional data. Due to its large volume, this data can be very difficult to sort through in order to determine valuable information. There are many tools available that make sorting through this clickstream data easier. These tools provide extraction, transformation and load facilities to combine the desired data from the clickstream with the traditional data. The clickstream data dimensions are combined with traditional data dimensions for analysis in data marts/warehouses. The most important sources of the clickstream data are query strings and cookie fields, which are used to gather customer data. Clickstream data, however, can be collected from many other Internet sources through background processes built into the technology. Technology also automates the mining process, presenting it in a relevant way for business users. The data warehouse is the foundation of and the means for data integration that leads to a strategic data usage (Berson et al., 1997). Data mining techniques are applied to the cleaned and rationalized data stored in a data warehouse, which can lead to effective customer relationship management.

There are a number of different ODM techniques (Nemati & Barko, 2001). The first method utilizes statistics. Statistical techniques are driven by the data and are used to discover patterns and build predictive models. Through regression analysis a model is created that maps values from predictors, so that the fewest errors occur when making a prediction.

Two of the oldest techniques, clustering and the nearest neighbor prediction, are often used in data mining. Clustering is described as the grouping or clustering of like records together. Clustering is usually done to give the end user a high-level view of what is going on in the database. It can also mean segmentation, which is useful to marketing people for coming up with a birds-eye view of the business. Sometimes, however, clustering is performed not so much to keep records together, but to make it easier to see when one record sticks out from the rest. These "outsiders" could spark new areas of business or can help identify failing areas of the business. When clustering is used in business, the clusters are often dynamic, changing weekly to monthly, and decisions concerning which cluster a record should be placed in can be difficult. The nearest neighbor technique is quite similar to clustering. In order to predict what a prediction value is in one record, the nearest neighbor method looks for records with similar predictor values in the historical database and uses the prediction value from the record that is "most similar" to the unclassified record. The nearest neighbor prediction algorithm works in very much the same way except that nearness in a database may consist of a variety of factors, such as where a person lives or their gross income. Nearest neighbor techniques are among the easiest to use and understand, because they work in a way similar to the way that people think by detecting closely matching examples. They also perform quite well in terms of automation, because many of the algorithms are robust with respect to dirty data and missing data. Finally, they are particularly adept at performing complex return on investment (ROI) calculations because the predictions are made at a local level, where business simulations could be performed in order to optimize ROI. Because they enjoy similar levels of accuracy compared to other techniques, the measures of accuracy, such as lift, are as good as from any other technique (Berson et al., 1997).

As its name implies, a decision tree is a predictive model that can be viewed as a tree. Each branch of the tree is a classification question, and the leaves of the tree are partitions of the data set with their classification. Because of their tree structure and capability to easily generate rules, decision trees are the favored technique for building understandable models. Because of this clarity, they also allow for more complex profit and ROI models to be added easily in on top of the predictive model (Berson et al., 1997).

Neural networks have probably been of greatest interest through the formative stages of data mining technology. True neural networks are biological systems (that is, they function like human brain) that detect patterns, make predictions and learn. The artificial neural networks are computer programs that implement sophisticated pattern detection and machine-learning algorithms on a computer to build predictive models from large historical databases. Artificial neural networks derive their name from their historical development, which started off with the premise that machines could be made to "think," if scientists found ways to mimic the structure and functioning of the human brain on the computer. Neural networks are very powerful predictive modeling techniques that can be applied to a variety of different types of problems, but some of the power comes at the expense of ease-of-use and ease-of-deployment, since it requires all of the predictor values to be in numeric form. The output of the neural network is also numeric and needs to be translated if the actual prediction value is categorical. Neural networks, however, are used in a wide variety of applications. They have been used in all facets of business, from detecting the fraudulent use of credit cards and credit risk prediction to increasing the hit rate of targeted mailings. They also have a long history of application in other areas: the military (for the automated driving of an unmanned vehicle at 30 miles per hour on paved roads) and biological simulations (learning the correct pronunciation of English words from written text).

Rule induction is one of the major forms of data mining and is a common form of knowledge discovery in unsupervised learning systems. It represents the idea of "mining" for gold through a vast database. The gold, in this case, would be a rule that is interesting — a rule that tells you something about your database that you did not already know and probably were not able to explicitly articulate. Rule induction on a database can be a huge undertaking, where all possible patterns are systematically pulled out of the data, and then accuracy and significance are added to them to tell the user how strong the pattern is and how likely it is to occur again. In general, however, the rules that are "mined" are relatively simple.

ODM is defined as leveraging data mining tools and technologies in an organizational context to acquire and maintain a competitive advantage (Nemati & Barko, 2001). ODM techniques have had widespread appeal and are implemented in most industries around the world. If correctly deployed, ODM offers companies an indispensable decision-enhancing process that optimizes resource allocation and exploits new opportunities by transforming data into valuable knowledge (Nemati & Barko, 2001). These tools have the potential of significantly reducing a company's costs by helping to identify areas of potential business, areas that the company needs to focus its attention on or areas that should be discontinued because of poor sales or returns over a period of time. ODM, therefore, helps the decision makers make informed, and hopefully timely, decisions on where the business should be. It provides facts or information that can help the company focus or direct the company along the most profitable path, and, at the same time, provide better management and service to customers.

FOOD FOR THOUGHT

Whereas the idea behind using this information to target advertising specifically to suit the needs of the consumer is advantageous, this information, if used in the wrong context, can be very harmful to an individual. Focused marketing saves a company money they would have otherwise spent on general, blanket advertising, and the return on investment would be minimal. The information obtained from tracking user preferences allows the company to utilize targeted advertising. The company knows beforehand that the consumer is interested in a particular product, so they target the customer with a product that they are more likely to purchase, increasing the opportunity for a sale. For example, Amazon.com uses this technique for recommending books to readers based on their previous purchases; Blockbuster Entertainment uses it to recommend video rentals to individual customers based on their rental history and American Express uses it to suggest products to its cardholders based on an analysis of their monthly spending patterns (Information and Privacy Commissioner, 1998).

This technique is not only beneficial to retailers' suppliers can also use the data to their advantage. For example, Wal Mart captures point-of-sale transactions from over 2,900 stores in six countries and continuously transmits this data to its massive 7.5 terabyte data warehouse. Wal Mart allows more than 3,500 suppliers to access data on their products and perform data analyses. These suppliers use this data to identify customer buying patterns at the store-display level. They use this information to manage local store inventory and identify new merchandising opportunities (Information and Privacy Commissioner, 1998).

However, because companies collect data from so many different sources, not all of the data may be correct and/or available, and, as companies substitute default values for data not available, the individual profile may become skewed and produce undesired results. For example, a company may purchase a list of consumers that are likely to buy a particular product. If that data is inaccurate, the company could end up wasting resources targeting unlikely consumers. There are all kinds of stories of pets, children, etc., receiving marketing information that they cannot possibly act upon. Differences in culture and legal requirements can also influence results. What may be acceptable in one culture may have the completely opposite effect in another. In light of the recent terrorist attacks, an inaccurate profile could have legal ramifications, as well as influence public perception, and have an adverse affect on opportunities available to that person. What financial, emotional and social affects would occur if someone was inaccurately profiled as a terrorist? Data mining "poses a threat to privacy, in the sense that discovered patterns classify individuals into categories, revealing in that way confidential personal information with certain probability. Moreover, such patterns may lead to generation of stereotypes, raising very sensitive and controversial issues, especially if they involve attributes such as race, gender or religion. An example is the debate about studies of intelligence across different races" (Estivill-Castro, Brankovic & Dowe, 1999).

In this new economy, it is not uncommon for a company's data to be a major asset. The existing market of personal data postulates that the gathering institution owns the data. Thus, many companies, such as the Gartner Group, base their business on the sale of data and related information. The sale of data, in this case, can be a good revenue earner; however, there can also be some negative outfall from its sale. In 1989, the Californian Department of Motor Vehicles earned over $16 million by selling the driver-license data of 19.5 million Californian residents. A deranged man used this data to obtain the home address of actress Rebecca Schaeffer and killed her in her apartment. The sale of driver-license data ended after this tragedy. In 1990, Lotus Development Corp. announced a release of a CD-ROM with the data on 100 million U.S. households. The data was so detailed that it generated strong public opposition, and Lotus abandoned the project. However, this mostly affected small business, as large companies already had access and continued to use Lotus data sets. At least 400 million credit records, 700 million annual drug records, 100 million medical records and 600 million personal records are sold yearly in the U.S. by 200 superbureaus. Among the records sold are bank balances, rental histories, retail purchases, criminal records, unlisted phone numbers and recent phone calls. When combined, this information provides data images of individuals that are sold to direct marketers, private individuals, investigators and government agencies (Estivill-Castro et al., 1999). A company may choose not to sell the data and only use it internally. They may have a privacy policy that protects a consumer's personal data; however, if the company files bankruptcy, then the asset (data) can be sold to satisfy debt obligations. The consumer whose data has been collected has no control over the use of the data once it is sold. Concerns about informational privacy generally relate to the manner in which personal data is collected, used and disclosed. When a business collects, discloses or uses data without the knowledge or consent of the individual to whom the data relates, the individual's privacy may be violated (Information and Privacy Commissioner, 1998).

Regulations

Consumers are concerned about the collection and use of their personal data (FTC survey, 1998). They are concerned that the data will be manipulated (data mined), and the resulting information will be used in ways that may be detrimental to them. For example, medical information located in databases has been accessed by persons who were able to mine the data and combine it to identify individuals' private medical data and contact information. A Florida abortion clinic sued Compuserv for providing access to a database that allowed users to mine information. The users were able to compile personal data to create a list of clinic patients along with their contact information, such as addresses and telephone numbers (obtained from driver's license data). A pro-life supporter used the information to contact many of the clinic's patients. This egregious violation of individual privacy resulted in a lawsuit and the database base being shut down (CNET News Staff, 1999). Legislators are aware of the need to update current laws and create new ones to accommodate changing technology and to protect personal privacy.

LAWS AND ENFORCEMENT

Data mining and accompanying technologies have advanced at a rapid rate and have outpaced legislation designed to protect consumers. The Federal Trade Commission (FTC) is the primary federal agency responsible for the enforcement of various laws governing the privacy of an individual's information on the Internet. The FTC Act (FTCA), 15 U.S.C. § 45(a), gives the FTC investigative and enforcement authority over businesses and organizations engaged in interstate commerce. While waiting on the enactment of new legislation, the FTC utilizes existing laws to protect consumers from unfair and deceptive trade practices. The FTC has allowed most businesses to self-regulate. However, the government has regulated some industries, such as healthcare and financial services. They also require Web sites to follow specific rules when obtaining information from children.

Health information is subject to Health Insurance Portability and Accountability (HIPPA) Act of 1996. The original legislation went into effect in 2001, and the final modifications take effect in April 2003. The act applies to health information created or maintained by health care providers who engage in certain electronic transactions, health plans and health care clearinghouses. The Office for Civil Rights (OCR) is responsible for implementing and enforcing the HIPPA privacy regulation (OCR Web site, 2002). The act sets standards to protect privacy in regards to individuals' medical information. The act provides individuals access to their medical records, giving them more control over how their protected health information is used and disclosed and providing a clear avenue of recourse if their medical privacy is compromised (HHS, 2002). Data miners must take care not to violate this regulation, or they will face stiff penalties, which may include fines and/or imprisonment.

Financial information is routinely minded to improve customer service and marketing and to increase an organization's bottom line. It is essential that this data be adequately protected from fraudulent use. The illegal and fraudulent use of financial information is widespread, causing harm to individuals and opening the organization and individual(s) responsible for the lapse in security to liability for the damage and hardship caused for not adequately protecting personal financial data. Financial information is subject to the Gramm-Leach-Bliley Act (15 U.S.C. §§ 6801 et seq.). The act requires financial institutions to protect data collected from routine transactions (i.e., names, addresses and phone numbers; bank and credit card account numbers; income and credit histories; and social security numbers). Financial institutions must develop a written information security plan that describes their program to protect customer information. All programs must be appropriate to the financial institution's size and complexity, the nature and scope of its activities and the sensitivity of the customer information at issue (FTC, 2002). Experts suggest that three areas of operation present special challenges and risks to information security: employee training and management: information systems, including network and software design; information processing, storage, transmission and retrieval and security management, including the prevention, detection and response to attacks, intrusions or other system failures. The rule requires financial institutions pay special attention to these areas (FTC, 2002).

Special care must be taken when dealing with information obtained from children. The Children's Online Privacy Act of 1998 (COPPA) (15 U.S.C. §§ 6501 et. seq.) governs the online collection of personal information from children under the age of 13. The regulation requires that Web sites get parental consent before collecting personal data from children. Web sites are also required to post a privacy statement detailing what information will be collected, how it will use that information, if it will make the information available to third parties and a contact at the site. When utilizing data mining, one should be aware of how the data to be used for mining was obtained. The user can be held responsible for utilizing data that was illegally obtained. This is not limited to solely to children and pertains to all data.

The FTC would like to see self-regulation of industries. However, if businesses don't effectively comply with the FTC, the agency is prepared to step in and apply existing laws to protect consumers. FTC Chairman Robert Pitofsky, on July 21, 1998, stated that, "new laws may be needed to eliminate concerns raised by the online collection of personal information. ... While some industry players may form and join self-regulatory programs, many may not. ... This would result in a lack of uniform privacy protections that the Commission believes are necessary for electronic commerce to flourish. The Commission believes that unless industry can demonstrate that it has developed and implemented broad-based and effective self-regulatory programs by the end of 1998, additional governmental authority in this area would be appropriate and necessary" (Consumer Privacy on the World Wide Web, 1998). The FTC proposed the following four fair information practices that Web sites collecting information on consumers should comply with:

Notice and Awareness: notify consumers of their data collection practices and how they use the information.

Choice and Consent: online users must be given the choice and give permission regarding how their data is used.

Access and Participation: consumers must have "reasonable" access to their data to be able to correct inaccuracies.

Security and Integrity: sites must take "reasonable steps" to ensure the security and integrity of the data they collect.

These regulations were prescribed to protect the privacy of personal information collected from and about individuals on the Internet, to provide greater individual control over the collection and use of that information and other purposes. However, how well these self-regulatory programs work is very questionable. In the space of six months, TRUSTe, a nonprofit privacy initiative, had three of its licensees — RealNetworks, Microsoft and Deja News — investigated for privacy violations. In 1998, just the year before, yet another TRUSTe licensee, Geocities (now owned by Yahoo Inc.), settled with the FTC after being cited for improperly collecting data from children under 13 (Lemos, 1999a). Organizations, such as TRUSTe, provide Web site owners with seals once they meet certain criteria relating to consumer privacy. Sites qualify for the seals by agreeing to post their privacy policies online, and allowing the seal providers to audit their operations to ensure they're adhering to the policy. When violations are discovered, TRUSTe and other privacy services "come in after the fact and say what the company did was bad, but they don't do anything to solve the problems," said Richard Smith, an independent Internet consultant, who has uncovered several of the worst incidences of online privacy infringement (Lemos, 1999b). Can the consumer really trust that his or her privacy is being protected? Is the government really doing enough? Can they do more? The government is enacting regulations and is trying to monitor the situation, but it is unclear when, if ever, the legislation will be able to keep pace with the technology.

New Legislation: The Patriot Act

The events of September 11, 2001, have led to new legislation designed to help the authorities combat terrorism. The Patriot Act (Uniting and Strengthening America by Providing Appropriate Tools Required to Intercept and Obstruct Terrorism Act, H. R. 3162, Oct. 24, 2001) covers a broad range of topics including: wiretapping and intelligence surveillance, criminal justice, student privacy, financial privacy and immigration. The legislation increased law enforcement's powers, lowered the burden of proof needed for searches and surveillance and decreased checks and balances that protect individual rights and privacy.

"Both the surveillance provision in the 'Patriot' Act and Attorney General Ashcroft's new domestic spying guidelines opens up the very real prospect that the FBI will return to the pre-Watergate days, when political dissenters ranging from Dr. Martin Luther King to average largely unknown Americans, were routinely spied on or had their lives disrupted" (Steinhardt, 2002).

Due to the Patriot Act, the government has been given easier access to individuals' records. These records could be personal, such as medical, educational, mental health, as well as financial. All the FBI needs to do to gain access is to certify that the records may be relevant to an investigation. The FBI will undoubtedly be collecting more data than it has in the past, and the government will be more active in applying data mining technology in the hunt for suspected terrorists. The government is actively investing in data mining, providing research grants and leading the effort to increase the ability of technological tools to be used for law enforcement and surveillance:

"...the tool that probably has the most potential to thwart terrorism is data mining. Think of it as a form of surveillance that casts its eye on computer networks" (Businessweek, 2001).

Governmental Use of Data Mining and Surveillance Tools

Technologists will need to assist investigators with the current technology and develop new or improve current data mining tools. The U.S. government utilizes some very powerful surveillance tools. There are legitimate concerns regarding accuracy of data and privacy of the material these tools produce. This material is often the subject of analysis using data mining or other techniques. It is imperative that those who utilize data mining and other technologies be aware of the potential abuses and limitations of the technology. The concern is that if the tools are blindly relied upon, then costly mistakes could occur, such as missing something vital to national security and perhaps allowing another attack or the guilty to go free, or, on the other hand, wrongly accusing an innocent person.

The chasm between pre- and post-September 11, 2001 views on privacy and what is acceptable government intrusion into our lives is significant. What was once unacceptable is now, not only being considered, but also being implemented. Judicial requirements for searches and wiretapping are being lessened and in some instances virtually removed. The idea of "Big Brother watching us" has become more real as technological advances provide the tools to conduct surveillance (Carnivore, Echelon, facial recognition software, etc.). There were considerable concerns regarding the use of surveillance tools by privacy advocates prior to the terrorist attacks. The government, judiciary and law enforcement struggled to keep up with the technological changes, and the debate raged on about how and what could be monitored. This changed substantially after September 11, 2001. There are still many concerns with privacy and civil liberties; however, a shift towards security and increasing law enforcement power has occurred. The government is allocating resources to improve its technology and change legal procedures to allow them to conduct investigations appropriate for the technology. Data mining is a key technology that will undoubtedly be utilized for national security purposes. The government has several tools in its arsenal to obtain personal data for mining. It is important for those using data mining techniques to understand how the data is obtained. They should ask questions such as: Was the data legally obtained? Was it taken in violation of an individual's privacy? What context? The results of the data mining could have a profound effect on an individual, or society as a whole, if the predictions, relationships or correlations are not accurate. In our current environment of heightened tensions, the data miner should be aware of the possibility of abusing the additional powers granted to law enforcement and violating individuals' right to privacy.

Government Tools

The government has a number of tools for electronic eavesdropping. They are reluctant, of course, to share how these tools work beyond basic concepts. The most prominent of these tools are Carnivore (DCS 1000), Data Interception by Remote Transmission (DIRT), Echelon and Transient Electromagnetic Monitoring Pulse Standard (Tempest). There are serious concerns for proper oversight to be maintained when utilizing these technologies so that abuses do not occur. There must be a balance between the individual's rights and national security. It is essential for those who will be conducting analysis to understand the issues surrounding the collection of data. The analysts and technologists will be part of this process and must be aware of the legal, privacy, security and ethical concerns, and also the ramifications their results may have on individual lives.

Carnivore

The FBI developed Carnivore to monitor the Internet for illegal activity. The FBI describes Carnivore as a software-based tool that examines all Internet IP packets on an Ethernet and records only the packets with very specific parameters. These parameters refer to the data, which is subject to lawful order, and disregards communications that are not allowed to be intercepted. The FBI refers to this as Carnivore's "surgical ability" to intercept and collect data. Prior to September 11, the FBI stated that law enforcement needed to get high-level authorization from the Department of Justice (DOJ) to apply for judicial approval for the use of Carnivore. They also point out that there are significant penalties for those who misuse the system. However, there are concerns about the FBI's description and implementation of Carnivore. Since it is a secretive tool, the FBI will not disclose the source code or how the system actually works. How do we know that its "surgical ability" works? Can it really discern and separate communications approved by the court from those that are not allowed? Who will oversee law enforcement to make certain there is no misuse? Is the intercepted data secure? Are businesses willing to allow the FBI to install unknown software on their systems?

The DOJ requested an independent technical review of Carnivore, which was conducted by the Illinois Institute of Technology Research Institute (IITRI). The DOJ's own review (only the draft was available) stated that Carnivore does not adequately protect the data it is intercepting. Academics and technical personnel from AT&T Laboratories, University of Pennsylvania, SRI International and Purdue University reviewed the IITRI's report. Their paper entitled, "Comments on the Carnivore System Technical Review" identified several concerns with the DOJ report and its results. The review summed up its results in the following statement: "Unfortunately, serious technical questions remain about the ability of Carnivore to satisfy its requirements for security, safety and soundness" (Illinois Institute of Technology, 2000).

Aside from technical concerns, there were other issues addressed by the reviewers. They were troubled by the fact that a single agent determines what data is collected and deleted. (This seems to contradict the FBI's "surgical ability" to separate communications.) Also, the FBI states that Carnivore is not intended to collect all data, but the researchers disagreed with that characterization. They also questioned the FBI's reliance on the "pen register statute" — the law that allows agents to obtain the phone numbers a suspect has called — as the basis of using Carnivore to capture e-mail headers. "The statute falls short of such use because headers could reveal the correspondence of two parties not included in a search warrant, if they carbon copy a third, suspected, person" (Lemos, 2000).

DIRT

DIRT has the ability to monitor and intercept data from any Windows PC in the world. This tool is only available to law enforcement and military. The DIRT Bug operates as a Trojan horse and sneaks inside a Windows PC by an attachment, macro or program. Once inside the system, it allows law enforcement complete control of the system without the user's knowledge. It has the ability to track each keystroke and transmit logs to law enforcement monitoring the PC. When the PC is online, it will invisibly behave like an anonymous File Transfer Protocol (FTP) server, giving the monitor 100 percent access to all resources on the targeted computer (Schwartau, 1998). Encrypted files can be opened because DIRT is able to capture passwords and decrypt the files. The manufacturer, CODEX Data Systems, claims that if you have a PC at home there is very little you can do to keep DIRT out (Schwartau, 1998).

Echelon

Echelon is a satellite surveillance system developed during the Cold War, primarily by the U.S. and Great Britain. The UKUSA Alliance also includes Canada, New Zealand

and Australia. Individual states in the UKUSA Alliance are assigned responsibilities for monitoring different parts of the globe, providing surveillance coverage of the entire earth. They achieve this coverage by using satellites, ships, planes, radar and communication-interception sites located around the world. It is believed that Echelon has the capability to intercept every international telephone call, fax, e-mail and radio transmission. The fact that Echelon can intercept any phone conversation, e-mail, etc., is impressive, but what is more remarkable, is that they can make sense out of it all. Imagine all the telephone conversations that occur everyday and in every language. How does any agency sift through that amount of data and produce worthwhile results and useful data?

"The UKUSA states have positioned electronic-intercept stations and deep-space satellites to capture all satellite, microwave, cellular and fiber-optic communications traffic. The captured signals are then processed through a series of supercomputers, known as dictionaries that are programmed to search each communication for targeted addresses, words, phrases or even individual voices" (Goodspeed, 2000). It is mind boggling to conceptualize the amount of data these computers must sift through to identify keywords and identify pertinent data. Echelon must utilize incredibly powerful data and knowledge mining tools to accomplish this task. The data compiled naturally contains data outside of the scope (searching for terrorists) of the original search. This data may contain confidential economic or private matters, and the temptation will exist to inappropriately use this data.

Echelon is very powerful and has the capability of being incredibly intrusive. This has prompted cautious comments regarding proper oversight from members of the government. A primary concern is how can there be proper oversight on a secretive system. Sen. Frank Church was quoted as saying:

"...the capability at any time could be turned around on the American people and no American would have any privacy left, such is the capability to monitor everything: telephone conversations, telegrams, it doesn't matter. There would be no place to hide. If this government ever became a tyranny, if a dictator ever took charge in this country, the technological capacity the intelligence community has given the government could enable it to impose total tyranny, and there would be no way to fight back ... I don't want to see this country ever go across that bridge ... we must see to it that this agency and all agencies that possess this technology operate within the law and under proper supervision, so that we never cross over that abyss. That is the abyss from which there is no return" (Poole, 1999/ 2000).

Concerns are justified due to prior abuses of the system. The following are examples of past inappropriate usage of Echelon:

Mike Frost, a former Communications Security Establishment employee and author of Spyworld, which is about his career in Canada's secret service, claims that as far back as 1981 Canada was using its U.S.-produced spy technology to eavesdrop on the American ambassador to Ottawa. In one instance, Canadian spies managed to overhear the ambassador discussing a pending trade deal with China on a mobile telephone and used that data

> *to undercut the Americans in landing a $2.5-billion Chinese grain sale (Goodspeed, 2000).*

> *On another occasion, in 1983, Mr. Frost says British intelligence officials invited their Canadian counterparts to come to London to eavesdrop on two British cabinet ministers whose political loyalty was doubted by Margaret Thatcher, then the British prime minister. Since it would have been illegal for British officials to do the surveillance themselves, they had the Canadians do the job using eavesdropping equipment in the Canadian embassy. After three weeks of snooping, the Canadians quietly turned over all their findings to the British, Mr. Frost says (Goodspeed, 2000).*

After the end of the cold war, the concerns of other nations, especially in the European Union (EU) focused on whether Echelon was being used for economic espionage or to violate individual rights. The EU commissioned reports regarding Echelon in 1997 and, again, in 2001 to first prove Echelon's existence and then to consider the economic ramifications of the system on their industries. Although its existence has been known for years, it has not been officially sanctioned. This system was established to spy on other countries, particularly the former Soviet Union. The EU report found evidence of Echelon and routine U.S. spying and interception of communication between firms. The U.S. justifies this eavesdropping by stating that they are trying to combat bribery.

The U.S. operation is believed to be run by the National Security Agency (NSA). The NSA does admit it collects intelligence but says it does not violate individual citizen's rights in the U.S. or abroad. The privacy issue is tricky because laws generally only protect individuals of a particular state. Therefore, the EU would like to see rules established to protect against industrial and economic espionage and assure individuals right to privacy. The NSA's position regarding surveillance is that they provide the U.S. government with valuable intelligence data on terrorism and narcotics and weapons trafficking, stating that, because of the intrusive nature of their job, they are subject to strict regulations and oversight from different governmental bodies. In light of recent events and expanded governmental powers, the question that arises is of the degree of oversight and what is the proper balance between individual rights and national security.

Tempest

Tempest is a classified government program, based on the knowledge that all electronic devices emit low-level electromagnetic radiation that can be remotely captured and later displayed. Compromising emanations radiate from many sources including computer monitors, tape drives, scanners, printers and power cables, which can be captured. There is no way to detect Tempest surveillance, and it is unclear whether a court order would be needed to collect Tempest data.

The NSA has some limited data regarding the tool on their Web site, which confirms the existence of the tool. The NSA did not disclose if, how or which agencies use this tool.

OTHER AREAS OF CONCERN
Wiretapping and Intelligence Surveillance

The role of a judge in wiretapping is to ensure that surveillance is conducted legally and with proper justification. This role is now minimized. Under the new legislation, Foreign Intelligence Surveillance Act (FISA) surveillance can be used in a criminal investigation. FISA authority had been reserved for matters of national security. Internet tools, such as Carnivore, can be utilized with a lower burden of proof to obtain a court order. Searches can be conducted without probable cause. A pen register or trap and trace order can be obtained by law enforcement by simply certifying that it is relevant to an ongoing investigation.

Criminal Justice/Legal Concerns

The government can request to keep searches secret. In the past, they were required to notify those subjects of the search.

The government can now share data between agencies without guards for future use or dissemination of that information. The data included can be obtained from wiretaps and other searches. Once that data is spread out among agencies, it is difficult to recall. Who else will have access to it? How long will it be available? Who is responsible for certifying accuracy of the data or error correction and updating data among agencies? As it stands now, there are no measures in place to address these concerns. This data would be a prime candidate for data mining by combining data from these different sources and evaluating it. For these results to be credible, it is essential to use accurate and up-to-date data.

Proposal of a National Identification Card

A national identification card was proposed, but quickly rebuffed by many diverse factions because it raised concerns about the potential of the card to collect vast amounts of personal data. Although it does not have enough support currently, it is still on the table as an option.

Why not have an ID card? Many other countries have national ID cards. In our political culture, the thought of being tracked by an ID number or card and listed in an official registry (database) is not appealing. This may appear to be a contradiction because we have Social Security numbers and are often tracked by them. However, having an official registry and a database that can track our actions is a frightening thought to many. Some questions that should be considered when discussing the viability of adopting a card are: What data would be required?; Who would have access?; and Would the card include a computer chip capable of tracking use.

In Malaysia the government is issuing a "multipurpose card" for their citizens. The card will include a computer chip (smart chip). The chip will allow the card to be used as a driver's license, cash card, National Health Service card and a passport (*Businessweek*, 2001).

This will allow the Malaysian government to track an incredible amount of data on each citizen. In the U.S., if a card was enabled with a smart chip and the data stored in a database, how long would it take before other government agencies or companies would want to tie into the database? The Social Security number is a prime example. It was originally intended for tax purposes, but over time, other government agencies, health care providers and companies began using it as an identifier. The number's usage is so widespread that even simple transactions require a person to give his Social Security number. For example, it is common when applying for video store membership that a person will be asked to supply her Social Security number. The video store has no legal right to require it, but it is so commonplace that most people supply it without even thinking it inappropriate.

There are additional concerns that would also need to be addressed such as: cost, fraud (counterfeiting and identity theft), the potential threat of tracking and monitoring people's actions and movements (internal passports), the establishment of a data base of all Americans, increased harassment and discrimination (non-native looking people would be asked at greater rates to provide their card) and, most importantly, would it solve the problem it was developed for: the prevention of terrorism.

CONCLUSION

The gathering of data for data mining purposes was initially an attempt by companies to learn as much as possible about their customers so that they could provide customized or personable service and increase sales. The development and use of computer/data technology helped speed this process, as it made the gathering and analyzing process easier. However, recent developments have caused individuals to lose control over that data about them. As technology advanced, the tools became more invasive and thorough and accuracy increased. It is possible that this data, available to anyone (individuals, businesses, governments), can be manipulated in such a way as to produce an in-depth profile of an individual or group.

Concerns have arisen regarding the use of data mining, because an individual has to interpret the results and data and knowledge gained can be taken out of context. For example, if Echelon picked up a phone conversation where a person stated they are picking up a kilo of Columbian, someone would have to determine what that would mean. Are they trafficking drugs or picking up coffee? Individuals have their own preconceptions and bias, which must be acknowledged and taken into consideration when interpreting and analyzing data. Profiles may be misleading, for example, in many countries military service is obligatory for certain individuals. These countries may also have a state religion. An innocent person could easily be considered suspect, because they fit some predetermined profile of a terrorist by having military experience and religious ties.

The U.S. government utilizes some very powerful surveillance tools to gather data. There are legitimate concerns regarding accuracy of data and privacy of the material these tools produce. The data mining technology is limited and can produce inaccurate results. What is the cost of a mistake? Is it a type-one or type-two error? What if you wrongly accuse an innocent person or allow a guilty person to go free? What percentage of accurate results is acceptable? Is an 85 percent accuracy rate good? If you are sending out a flyer or picking a stock, then yes it is. If you are deciding if a person should be questioned and possibly detained by the police, is that percentage still acceptable? What if you are one of the 15 percent wrongly accused? What are the implications? (Under the Patriot Act, if the accused is an immigrant, they may be detained indefinitely.) These are questions that must be seriously considered. The end users of the technology must understand these concerns and the limitation of the technology they employ.

There are serious concerns that current technology and technology being developed will allow governments extraordinary abilities to monitor their citizens. There is a legitimate concern that "Big Brother" has arrived. Proper oversight and usage is essential to limit abuses:

> *"All of these technologies are built on ones and zeros so it is possible to blend them together — just as TV's computers, video games, and CD players are converging — into one monster snooping technology. In fact, linking them together makes each one exponentially more effective. Unifying the various surveillance systems makes sense from a technological standpoint, and there is likely to be strong pressure, once the tools are in place to try to make them work better. It is useful to keep this scenario in mind, if only as a warning beacon of some of the hazards ahead. Left unchecked, technologists could create a nearly transparent society," says David J. Farber, a pioneering computer scientist who helped develop the Net. "All the technology is there," he says. "There is absolutely nothing to stop that scenario — except law." Surveillance can be checked by laws that require regular audits, that call for citizens to be notified when they are investigated and that give people the right to correct data collected about them. That's the best way of guaranteeing in our efforts to catch the next terrorist, we don't wind up with Big Brother instead (BusinessWeek, 2001).*

Concerns about surveillance tools were abundant prior to September 11, since then they have lessened with the understanding that the technology will be used for national security. However, the new legislation increasing law enforcement and governmental powers are not limited solely to terrorism. In our rush to protect ourselves, we must be certain not to trample on individual rights in such a way that we regret it in the future. The balance between individual rights vs. national security should be carefully weighed. Those mining data obtained by business or governmental surveillance tools need to consider how the data is obtained, its accuracy and the limitations of the tools. They must be especially aware of the potential use of their analysis. Reliance on inaccurate results could have profound effects on individuals or our society as a whole.

REFERENCES

Berson, A. & Smith, J. (1997). *Data warehousing, data mining, and OLAP*. McGraw-Hill.

Computer Professionals for Social Responsibility. (2001, May). *Privacy and civil liberties*. Retrieved December 2002 from http://www.cpsr.org/cpsr/privacy.

Estivill-Castro, V., Brankovic, L., & Dowe, D. L. (1999, August). *Privacy in data mining*. Retrieved October 15, 2002 from Australian Computer Society – NSW Branch at: http://proxy-mail.mailcity.lycos.com/bin/redirector.cgi?c lass=1&url =http%3a%2f%2fwww%2eacs%2eorg%2eau% 2fnsw%2farticles%2f1999 082%2ehtm&uuid=13622&partner_key=mailcity"\t"newwin"—http:// www.acs.org.au/nsw/articles/1999082.htm.

Federal Trade Commission (FTC). (2000, May). *Privacy online: Fair information practices in the electronic marketplace*. Retrieved Fall 2001 from the FTC website: http://ftc.gov/bcp/conline/pubs/alerts/safealrt.htm.

France, M., Green, H., Kerstetter, J., Black, J., Salkever, A. & Carney, D. (2001, November 5). Privacy in an age of terror. McGraw-Hill. *BusinessWeek,* 83-91.

Goodspeed, P. (2000, February 19). The new space invaders spies in the sky. *National Post Online.* Retrieved Fall 2001 from http://www.fas.org/irp/program/process/docs/000219-echelon.htm.

Illinois Institute of Technology (2000, December 3). *Comments on the carnivore system technical review.* Retrieved November 27, 2001 from http://www.crypto.com/papers/carnivore_report_comments.html. Section 2.

Information and Privacy Commissioner/Ontario. (1998, January). *Data mining: Staking a claim on your privacy.* Retrieved October 18, 2002 from http://www.ipc.on.ca/english/pubpres/papers/datamine.htm#examples.

Lemos, R. (1999a, November 2) *Can you trust TRUSTe?* Retrieved October 14, 2002, from ZDNet News at http://zdnet.com.com/2100-11-516377.html?legacy=zdnn.

Lemos, R. (1999b, October 31). *RealNetworks rewrites privacy policy.* Retrieved October 14 from ZDNet News at http://zdnet.com.com/2100-11-516330.html?legacy=zdnn.

Lemos, R. (2000, December 4). *Experts: Carnivore review limited.* Retrieved Fall 1999 from www.zdnet.com.

Macavinta, C. (1999, January 6), CNet News Staff. (1999, January 8). *Florida clinic sues Compuserv.* Retrieved October 15, 2002 from http://news.com.com/2100-1023-219927.html?tag=bplst.

Magouirk, J. (2001, September 18). *Partners in privacy.* Intelligent Enterprise MicroStrategy. *Investor information.* Retrieved from http://www.microstrategy.com.

Microstrategy (2001, Fall). http://www.corporate-ir.net/ireye/ir_site.zhtml?ticker=mstr@script=100.

National Broadcasting Company. (1975, August 17). *Meet the press.* Washington DC: Merkle Press. Quoted in *Puzzle Palace,* 477.

Nemati, H. R., & Barko, C. D. (2001, Winter). Issues in organizational data mining: A survey of current practices. *Journal of Data Warehousing, 6*(1), 25-36.

Online Discussion. (2002, June 19). Steinhardt, *Homeland Security and Digital Privacy.* Retrieved from www.washingtonpost.com/wp-srv/technology/transcripts/archive_steinhardt_061902.htm.

Prepared Statement of the Federal Trade Commission (1998, July). *Consumer privacy on the World Wide Web.* Retrieved September 16, 2002 from the FTC website. http://www.ftc.gov/os/1998/9807/privac98.htm.

Safeguarding customers' personal information: a requirement for financial institutions. Retrieved from the FTC at http://www.ftc.gov/bcp/conline/pubs/alerts/safealrt.htm.

Schwartau, W. (1998, July 6). It's getting easier to dig up DIRT on criminals. *Network World.* Retrieved Fall 2001 http://www.nwfusion.com/forum/0706schwartau.html.

U.S. Deparment of Health and Human Services. (2002, August). *Issues first major protections for patient privacy.* Retrieved from the U.S. Dept. of Health and Human Services website from http://www.hhs.gov/news/press/2002pres/20020809a.html.

ZDNet News. (2000, December 4). Lemos Report. *Experts: Carnivore review limited.* Retrieved from http://zdnet.com.com/2100-11-526074.html.

Section II

Business Process Innovations Through ODM

Chapter VI

Knowledge Exchange in Organizations is a Potential, Not a Given: Methodologies for Assessment and Management of a Knowledge-Sharing Culture

Richard E. Potter
University of Illinois at Chicago, USA

Pierre A. Balthazard
Arizona State University West, USA

ABSTRACT

Team collaborations generate rich collections of information that are valuable inputs to the knowledge management (KM) process. But such effectiveness is not guaranteed. Team members may possesses considerable knowledge, but their tendency and ability to contribute that knowledge — and transform it from a personal tacit resource that has value only to them to an explicit resource that can have value to the team or organization — is only a potential. This chapter provides readers with an understanding of the human dynamics of expert knowledge exchange in the realm of virtual teams who interact via computer-controlled communication (CMC). We present the research, theory and the methodologies now in professional use to assess information exchange potential for KM-related activities at the team level as well as from the perspective of organizational culture.

INTRODUCTION

Data mining is an important part of KM for competitive advantage, and perhaps currently the most powerful technology available for extracting useful information and ultimately competitive knowledge from organizational data. But the power of data mining to achieve this end is naturally constrained by the availability and suitability of the data resources to which it is applied. A number of authors (e.g., Nonaka, 1994; Teece, 1998; Spender, 1996) have stressed that competitive advantage through KM is realized by identifying the valuable tacit knowledge possessed by organizational members and making that knowledge explicit. Once made explicit, the knowledge can be mined, organized, stored and, perhaps most importantly, shared throughout the organization to spur innovation.

Data mining is typically done once the tacit knowledge has been made explicit in some form, for example as text files generated by a team of people collaborating on a project (Leonard & Sensiper, 1998). Here, the root source of the data to be mined is in the minds of the people who are interacting. Given the tremendous popularity of team-based work in organizations as well as the rise of virtual teams, these teams are an increasingly common organizational unit and can be viewed as a source of competitive advantage through their ability to quickly form with often a diverse group of experts all collaborating and sharing knowledge to solve organizational problems. When effective, their collaborations represent rich collections of information that through exchange have achieved a level of unique synergy and problem-solving effectiveness (Cooke & Szumal, 1994; Potter, Balthazard & Cooke, 2000). Accordingly, such interactions are valuable inputs to the KM process.

But effectiveness is not guaranteed. Although the amount (and value) of knowledge that any of the team member possesses may be considerable, their tendency and ability to contribute that knowledge — and transform it from a personal tacit resource that has value only to them to an explicit resource that can have value to the team and the organization — is best understood as a potential. When viewed in this way, the success of data mining and other aspects of KM is, by extension, also only a potential, and not a given.

This chapter provides readers with an understanding of the human dynamics of expert knowledge exchange. First we describe how groups and teams exhibit interaction styles — patterns of communication behavior that have profound effects on knowledge exchange, group problem-solving and decision-making performance, and process outcomes, such as solution acceptance and team cohesiveness. Second, we present an overview of research that extends this area into the realm of virtual teams who interact via CMC. We provide an introduction to our methodologies and tools, as well as results that detail (a) how interaction styles affect knowledge exchange and performance in both media; (b) how expert knowledge is linked to performance via the interaction style; (c) how individual team members' personalities can drive the formation of constructive or nonconstructive interaction styles; and (d) the much greater effect that interaction styles have on team performance compared to the media used. Third, we inform readers about the utility of our methodologies and tools for use with real KM and organizational development (OD) in real organizations. Though our Web-based virtual team versions have been recently developed and validated and are now just becoming commercially available, the traditional paper-based versions have been in use around the world by KM and OD professionals — some for over 25 years. Fourth, we introduce our tools and methodologies for related KM activities that go beyond small group or team knowledge exchange to address the phenomenon from the perspective of organizational culture.

INTERACTION STYLES, KNOWLEDGE EXCHANGE AND TEAM PERFORMANCE

Members of problem-solving teams face two types of pressures in achieving quality solutions and high solution acceptance (Maier, 1963, 1967). On the one hand, there is pressure on each member to contribute unique, and possibly controversial, information to maximize the team's resources. On the other hand, members of teams tend to believe that closure to team problem solving and strong solution acceptance are best achieved through conformity of opinions (e.g., Festinger, 1950; Hoffman, 1979; McGrath, 1984). The way in which a team deals with the conflicting "task" and "maintenance" pressures is reflected in the team's interaction style (Hirokawa, 1985; Hirokawa & Gouran, 1989; Watson & Michaelsen 1988; Cooke & Szumal, 1993). Building on the Watson and Michaelsen (1988) typology and others (e.g., Maier, 1967; Hoffman, 1979), Cooke and Szumal (1994) showed that group interaction, aggregated from stable personality factors of the individual group members, can be categorized as constructive, passive and aggressive styles. The constructive style is characterized by a balanced concern for personal and group outcomes, cooperation, creativity, free exchange of information and respect for others' perspectives. The constructive style enables group members to fulfill both needs for personal achievement as well as needs for affiliation. The passive style places greater emphasis on fulfillment of affiliation goals only, maintaining harmony in the group and limiting information sharing, questioning and impartiality. The aggressive style places greater emphasis on personal achievement needs, with personal ambitions placed above concern for group outcome. Aggressive groups are characterized by competition, criticism, interruptions and overt impatience.

Groups whose interactions are characterized by a dominant style achieve different levels and patterns of effectiveness. Specifically, predominantly constructive groups produce solutions that are superior in quality to those produced by passive groups and superior in acceptance to those produced by either passive or aggressive groups. Predominantly passive teams produce solutions that are inferior in quality to those of constructive (and sometimes aggressive) groups and inferior in acceptance to those of constructive groups. Similarly, groups with predominantly aggressive styles produce solutions that are not as consistently high quality as those generated by constructive groups, but not as consistently low quality as those produced by passive groups. The solutions produced by aggressive groups generate less overall acceptance than those developed by constructive groups and about the same level of acceptance as those generated by passive groups (Cooke & Szumal, 1994).

Group interaction style is theorized to affect performance outcomes, such as decision quality, because it can impede or enhance team members' ability to bring their unique knowledge and skills to bear on the task, and the extent to which they develop and consider alternative strategies for approaching the task (Hackman & Morris, 1975). This is particularly critical for groups with heterogeneous levels of expertise. Communication by most expert group members is positively correlated with group performance, though it will be so only if the team exhibits an interaction style that permits the expert knowledge to be heard, considered and, when possible, improved upon.

As noted above, interaction styles affect process-related outcomes such as solution acceptance. Similarly, information exchange is often positively related to higher levels of cohesion, collaboration and satisfaction with decision quality in virtual teams. Solution acceptance and satisfaction with the decision process are functions of the perceptions of process quality and fairness, and are characteristic of teams with a constructive interaction style. To summarize, the research above has established that for traditional face-to-face (FTF) groups and teams, the stable personality characteristics of members manifest themselves in communication behaviors that can be construed as styles and these individual styles can be aggregated to manifest a group or team interaction style. These interaction styles affect group performance by facilitating or depressing the exchange of knowledge. They also have strong effects on contextual outcomes.

INTERACTION STYLES, KNOWLEDGE EXCHANGE AND PERFORMANCE IN VIRTUAL TEAMS

Virtual team members are geographically and often temporally distributed, possibly anywhere within (and beyond) their parent organization. The team members possess relevant knowledge and need to collaborate to accomplish tasks. Typically, the members have different areas of expertise and often work in different functional areas (Lipnack & Stamps, 1997; Townsend et al., 1998; Duarte & Snyder, 1999). Although definitions vary, most researchers would agree that to qualify as a virtual team, the members would have a minimum of FTF interaction and rely heavily on CMC. As we noted in the introduction, the text-based CMC of virtual teams often represents a valuable explicit form of expert knowledge — a very appropriate target for KM.

Building on research that examined information exchange in FTF teams (e.g., Stasser & Titus, 1985), Hightower and Sayeed (1996) found information exchange to be positively linked to virtual team performance on an intellective decision task. Tan, Wei, Huang and Ng (2000) found information exchange positively related to virtual team performance on a preference task. Warkentin, Sayeed and Hightower (1997) found that perceptions of shared norms and expectations of task process were types of relational links positively related to a higher level of team cohesion and information exchange in virtual teams. Mennecke and Valacich (1998) also found information sharing to be positively related to decision quality for group support system- (GSS) supported groups whose members had unique information. This research stream provides an important link between knowledge exchange via CMC or GSS and performance on group intellective tasks.

However, it stops short of asking if a propensity to share knowledge might be more directly related to individual personality or the interaction of the personalities, rather than to characteristics of communication mode.

TOWARD A MORE INTEGRATED AND ACCURATE PICTURE

Our research agenda over the past four years concerns (1) whether or not virtual teams also exhibit interaction styles; (2) whether those interaction styles have effects on performance and process outcomes similar to those seen in FTF teams; (3) the relative magnitude of those effects in the two media; (4) how the prevalence of certain personality factors in team members manifests itself in the team's interaction style; and (5) whether team composition, via targeted personality factors and interaction styles, can be managed to produce high performing teams.

Our first study (Potter & Balthazard, in press) was conducted to answer the first two of these questions and its primary focus was to validate a digital version of a methodology used by Cooke and Szumal (1993, 1994) originally developed to assess interaction styles in FTF groups.

STUDY 1: VALIDATING THE INSTRUMENTS
Methodology and Technology

Group style, task and contextual performance data were collected from 186 members of 42 virtual teams who completed the Internet version of the "Desert Survival Situation" (Lafferty, 1974; Human Synergistics, 1987; Balthazard, 1999a), a structured problem-solving exercise used for management development and team building in classroom and corporate settings. Subjects were either mid-level managers participating in an organizational development program or students in executive MBA and MBA and senior undergraduate courses in management information systems. During an initial meeting, participants were introduced to a Web-based system designed to support geographically and/or temporally dispersed teams as they discuss issues and solve problems. Participants were randomly assigned to a virtual team and asked to provide a team name. As individual participants (with no interaction yet permitted), they were provided with the URL for the simulation and supporting instruments.

After providing biographical information, participants were directed to peruse the Web page that described the decision task. The desert survival simulation places teams in a desolate region of the Sonora Desert in the middle of summer (where their chartered plane has crashed) and challenges them to correctly rank 15 items they have salvaged in order of their importance for the teams' survival. To further understanding, participants also viewed a five-minute digitized video stream of the situation. Before entering into a group discussion, each participant ranked the 15 items on an individual basis and submitted their personal solution for processing by the Web system. Each team was then provided its own URL of a password-protected threaded discussion Web and given seven consecutive days to interact (exclusively using the system) to produce a group solution on a consensus basis. Team members could access the discussion Web from any location (with a computer, browser and Internet connection) and at any time. Upon achieving a consensus solution, each member independently submitted the consensus ranking and completed group process (assessing effectiveness and solution acceptance) and group interaction style questionnaires. The questionnaires were both answered after ranking the items as a group, but before receiving feedback on the "experts' ranks" or the quality of their team's and individual solution.

Task Performance

In our studies, task performance was assessed by comparing individual members' rankings and their team's ranking against that suggested by the situation expert (Cooke, 1994; McGrath, 1984). A high performing team will perform well beyond the capabilities of its "average" member prior to the team interaction. Alternatively, lower task performance scores reflect poor team processes and low solution quality.

Four measures of contextual or process outcomes were captured for each team: "solution acceptance," "cohesion," "group commitment" and "effectiveness."

Group Interaction Styles

To assess a group's interaction style, participants answered 33 questions that captured their perceptions of their group interaction. The items were an adaptation and subset of the Group Styles Inventory™ (GSI) described in Cooke and Szumal (1994). The items (statements) assess 12 behaviors that aggregate into three distinct, yet interrelated, group style clusters: constructive, passive and aggressive. Each member's scores along each of the three interaction styles are calculated by averaging his or her responses to the items composing each of the respective scales. These items describe specific collective behaviors that might characterize a group to a very great extent (response option 5) or, at the other extreme, not at all (response option 1). For the Study 1 data set, the Cronbach alpha coefficients for the three style measures are 0.90 for constructive, 0.83 for passive and 0.89 for aggressive, indicating that the items composing each scale were answered in a fairly consistent manner by respondents.

Analysis and Results

We first sought to determine if virtual team interaction styles were essentially the same as those found in conventional groups. We, thus, followed the strategy employed with the validation of the original GSI instrument, as detailed in Cooke and Szumal (1994). The interaction styles, although distinct, are expected to be interrelated. For our Study 1 sample, analysis of the individual-level data showed that the constructive scale correlates negatively and significantly ($p < 0.01$) with the passive ($r = -0.45$) and aggressive ($r = -0.22$) scales. Further, the aggressive scale correlates positively and significantly ($p < 0.01$) with the passive scale ($r = 0.70$). Constructive interaction styles appear to suppress the passive and aggressive styles, and the latter styles appear to reinforce one another. That is, the aggressive behaviors of some beget passive behaviors from others.

The predicted pattern of relationships between interaction styles and performance, as suggested by the literature on conventional teams, were supported by the pattern of correlations of our examination of virtual teams. That is, a constructive interaction style improves both team performance and contextual outcome measures. Passive and aggressive styles reduce task performance and contextual measures of performance.

Beyond the validation of the digital methodology, the results support the assertion that individual team members' behavioral and psychological communication characteristics do not fundamentally change in geographically and/or temporally dispersed virtual teams, and the resulting interaction styles affect performance and process outcomes similarly in both FTF and virtual teams. A second study provided a direct comparison of the dynamics of interaction styles and performance of FTF and virtual teams.

STUDY 2: AN FTF VERSUS VIRTUAL TEAM COMPARISON

Methodology and Technology

Group interaction style, task and contextual measures of performance were collected from 556 members of 147 groups who had completed the "Ethical Decision Challenge," a content-full structured problem-solving exercise used for management development and team building in classroom and corporate settings (Balthazard, 2000; Cooke, 1994). The 284 members of 78 teams completed the exercise in a traditional FTF setting and another 272 members completed the exercise as members of 69 virtual teams.

Our research methodology for our virtual teams mirrored that reported in Study 1 above, except that we restricted the time for our virtual team trials to 55 minutes, and we substituted a different task prior to the post-task self-assessments. The "Ethical Decision Challenge" requires participants to rank 10 biomedical and behavioral research practices — all of which involve human subjects — in terms of their relative permissibility and acceptability (Balthazard, 2000; Cooke, 1994). The experts' solution is based on the decisions of over 800 Institutional Review Board (IRB) members who are responsible for reviewing proposals for research involving human subjects. Our technologies for our virtual teams were identical to those used in Study 1, whereas FTF teams used the paper-based tools and an identical protocol.

Results and Directions

Study 2 provides a number of important insights. First, virtual teams are less successful than FTF teams on performance measures, especially those that deal with contextual outcomes (see Table 1). Second, the development of a group interaction style (reported as an aggregated factor score in Table 1) appears to be dependent, at least in part, on media type. Virtual teams, in comparison to FTF teams, have fewer tendencies to develop constructive or aggressive styles and more tendencies to develop a passive interaction style.

Third, our results are consistent with previous studies on conventional teams (e.g., Cooke & Szumal, 1993, 1994) and Study 1 above: Group interaction styles predict performance in both media. Finally, Study 2 showed us that adhering to the FTF protocol of having our virtual participants complete the interactive portion of the exercise within 55 minutes did not affect our results, nor did using a different simulation. This gave us

Table 1. T-Test for Equality of Means Between FTF and Virtual Teams

Measures	Face-to-Face		Virtual		
	Mean	S.D.	Mean	S.D.	t
Constructive Style	.27	.54	-.25	.66	5.23**
Passive Style	-.18	.68	.19	.63	-3.40**
Aggressive Style	.14	.77	-.15	.66	2.39*
Team Error	19.88	5.24	20.48	5.25	-0.68
Team Synergy	-2.30	3.98	-4.42	4.78	2.91**
Solution Acceptance	3.65	.55	3.43	.62	2.27*
Cohesion Group	4.40	.38	4.01	.53	4.39**
Commitment	4.16	.68	3.78	.76	3.14**
Effectiveness	4.08	.59	3.73	.58	3.53**

further evidence that the results of Study 1 were not an artifact of those participants having a longer trial time.

STUDY 3: PERSONALITY, INTERACTION STYLES AND PERFORMANCE IN VIRTUAL TEAMS

As we stated earlier, individual communication and interaction behaviors are rooted in stable personality characteristics. Five personality factors have been identified that constitute the fundamental dimensions of personality (Fiske, 1949; Hogan, 1991; McCrae & John, 1992): extraversion, agreeableness, conscientiousness, openness and neuroticism. Extraversion refers to the degree to which individuals are gregarious, friendly, compliant, cooperative, nurturing, caring and sympathetic versus introversion, which is characterized by those who are shy, unassertive and withdrawn. Extraversion affects interpersonal relations through the quality of social interactions (Barry & Stewart, 1997; McCrae & John, 1992). Extraverts are usually active participants in group interactions and often have high intragroup popularity (Barry & Stewart, 1997). Barrick and Mount (1991) found that extraversion and conscientiousness were the two personality factors that consistently related to success in the work place. They concluded that extraversion correlates positively with individual performance in tasks involving social interaction. The proportion of group members that are high in extraversion may affect or shape the groups' interaction style, which in turn, affects both the objective group performance (i.e., task solution quality) and subjective process outcomes, such as acceptance of the group solution. Barry and Stewart (1997) found that the proportion of high-extraversion group members was related curvilinearly to task focus and group performance. Too few extraverts can result in low performance, whereas too many extraverts can lead to a decrease in group performance due to the group's lessened ability to remain focused on task completion (McCrae & Costa, 1989). Study 3 (Balthazard, Potter & Warren, 2002) examined the effects of extroversion on interaction styles and performance in virtual teams.

Methodology and Technology

Extraversion, group interaction style, task and contextual performance data were collected from 248 members of 63 groups who had completed the Internet version of the "Ethical Decision Challenge" (Balthazard, 2000; Cooke, 1994). Our methodology and technology mirrored that used for our virtual teams in Study 2 but also included an instrument to assess individual personality type, administered several weeks prior to the group exercise. Our independent variables included level of extraversion within a team (i.e., an average of individual levels), differences in individual levels of extroversion within a team, as well as similar measures of expertise (derived from the individual error scores explained in Study 1).

Results

Based on a three-step multiple regression analysis, we found that expertise is the most powerful predictor of performance (β = -0.54, p < 0.01). We also found that the importance of extraversion is limited, though the difference in extraversion had a role in explaining contextual performance. The second step indicated that a difference in extraversion explains a marginally significant portion of added variance (β = -0.23, p < 0.10) in solution acceptance and (β = -0.23, ns) effectiveness. In the third step, when all variables are entered, interaction styles explained the largest portion of unique variance in solution acceptance and effectiveness. In effect, when interaction styles are included in the model, effects from all other variables are greatly reduced or disappear, except with team errors, which are best predicted by expertise in the group. Extraversion leads to both constructive and/or aggressive styles and differences in extraversion within a team lead to passive styles. Variances in extraversion within virtual teams (which connotes the presence of both extraverts and nonextraverts) appear to trigger largely negative interaction characteristics. Variances in extraversion generally have negative impacts on process outcomes, except for solution acceptance. We found that in this particular virtual setting, extraversion is an important personality trait to promote that interaction and that teams with lower variances in extraversion do best, especially in teams with good knowledge to start off with. Perhaps most importantly, we found that it is mostly group styles, and not individual personality or the expertise of one individual, that have predictive power on outcomes in virtual teams.

DISCUSSION: WHAT WE KNOW AND WHAT IT MEANS FOR KM

Although space considerations do not permit us to share all the methodological and analytical details of the three studies here (or the more subtle myriad findings), readers should be able to discern some basic points about this research stream. First, virtual team members do not leave their personalities at the virtual door. People's personalities drive how they interact with one another in both the FTF world and the virtual world. Second, just as in the FTF setting, members can accurately assess each other's individual interaction style and these assessments can be accurately aggregated as a group interaction style. Third, the three interaction styles have very similar effects on virtual groups' performance and process outcomes as they do on FTF groups. However, the styles differ in strength of effect on performance across the two media. A constructive style that has a very positive effect on an FTF group loses some of its strength in the CMC world. Alternatively, the passive style is somewhat more pernicious in the virtual realm. It is simply easier for those with passive tendencies to contribute minimally in CMC, particularly until the group or team develops norms about communication length, frequency, relevance and so forth. In addition, related to issues with constructive behaviors, nontextual cues and mechanisms are not available online to draw passive members into the dialogue. Fourth, the interaction styles have a much greater effect on performance and process outcomes than does the medium.

What do these findings mean for KM? First, the results support the theoretical links between human interaction, knowledge exchange and group/team performance and process outcomes. Those involved with KM may not be particularly concerned with a team's performance or process outcomes, but they probably should be. A positive virtual team collaboration (whether one considers either or both performance or process outcomes) will naturally lead members to expect that future experiences of this nature would also be positive. The more collaborative work that is done online means more knowledge that goes from being tacit to being explicit and more input for KM and data mining. Some interventions may help virtual teams adopt constructive interaction styles either before or while they tackle a task. They also suggest a clear formula to improve the effectiveness of computer-mediated work. Interfaces and communication techniques or protocols should be designed to promote participation in the process and a constructive interaction. At a minimum, members of current virtual teams should be made aware of the characteristics and manifestations of constructive, passive and aggressive styles in the virtual setting.

The bottom-line implications of these studies for KM are that virtual teams are a great potential source of knowledge, but that knowledge may or may not be fully made explicit and exchanged (and subsequently captured and exploited for KM purposes), depending on how the team interacts. Regardless of the strategy chosen, KM professionals should realize that some proactive awareness and management of CMC-based collaboration challenges will go a long way in creating constructive interaction and free exchange of knowledge online.

A Bigger Picture

From a theoretic as well as an empirical standpoint, it is clear to see how some factors of individual personality drive the communication behavior that aggregates into a group interaction style. But certainly other factors combine with personality to shape how one interacts. Political and social realities shape all forms of human conduct, and there is no a priori reason to believe that these factors disappear when one goes online to work with others. Regardless of professionalism and joint buy in of a professed common goal, organizational collaborators may be reluctant to contribute or exchange knowledge unless they discern some reward for doing so. Measurement of contribution to a project, incentives and rewards are among the organizational structures whose harmony or dissonance with the prevailing culture have strong impacts on behavior, including group work. Within any organization there may be a variety of cultures, shaped by characteristic differences in professional orientation, status, history, power, visibility or other factors. Understanding these cultures in terms of expected behaviors can explain why some organizational units (or the entire organization) exhibit behaviors that are counter to the organization's expressed values or mission. On a more practical level, behavior expectations can also drive the level of cooperation in a group or team, which like personalities, aggregate into an interaction style. Thus, culture creates expectations of behaviors, some of which can result in nonconstructive interaction styles that hamper knowledge exchange.

As with our research on interaction styles and knowledge exchange in virtual teams, we are taking a quantitative and empirical approach to the assessment of culture in organizational units. As we have done with the conversion of Human Synergistic's instruments, such as the GSI, we are developing a virtual compliment to their Organizational Culture Inventory (OCI) (Human Synergistics, 1989; Cooke & Lafferty, 1989), used to assess the culture of traditional organizations and subunits. The virtual version will also be able to assess the culture of virtual organizations or organizational subunits via measurement of behavioral expectations (Cooke & Szumal, 1993). Equipped with either the traditional methodology or the virtual version, the KM professional will have greater insight into how an organization's culture drives behaviors that nurture or inhibit knowledge exchange. This insight, properly managed, will be key to harvesting knowledge for organizational data mining.

In conclusion, we have tried to show in this chapter how KM professionals can benefit from understanding the very human dynamics involved in knowledge exchange in conventional and virtual teams and groups. Knowledge exchange makes the tacit explicit, and it is explicit knowledge that can be most advantageously exploited. As the raw and potentially abundant raw material for organizational data mining, explicit knowledge is thus a potential that can only be fully realized if the participants — for personal or cultural reasons — have constructive interaction.

REFERENCES

Balthazard, P. A. (1999a). *Virtual version of the Desert Survival Situation* by J. C. Lafferty and A. W. Pond. Arlington Heights, IL: Human Synergistics/Center for Applied Research.

Balthazard, P. A. (1999b). *Virtual version of the Group Styles Inventory* by R. A. Cooke and J. C. Lafferty. Arlington Heights, IL: Human Synergistics/Center for Applied Research.

Balthazard, P. A. (2000). *Virtual version Ethical Decision Challenge* by R. A. Cooke. Arlington Heights, IL: Human Synergistics/Center for Applied Research.

Balthazard, P. A., Potter, R. E., & Warren, J. (2002). The effects of expertise and extraversion on virtual team interaction and performance. *Proceedings of the 53rd Annual Hawaii International Conference on System Sciences, Honolulu, Hawaii.* (January 7-10) (CD/ROM), Computer Society Press.

Barrick, M. R., & Mount, M. K. (1991). The big five personality dimensions and job performance: A meta-analysis. *Personnel Psychology, 44,* 1-26.

Barry, B., & Stewart, G. L. (1997). Composition, process and performance in self-managed groups: The role of personality. *Journal of Applied Psychology, 82*(1), 62-78.

Cooke, R. A. (1994). *The Ethical Decision Challenge.* Arlington Heights, IL: Human Synergistics/Center for Applied Research.

Cooke, R. A., & Lafferty, J. C. (1989). *Organizational culture inventory.* Plymouth, MI: Human Synergistics.

Cooke, R. A., & Szumal, J. L. (1993). Measuring normative beliefs and shared behavioral expectations in organizations: The reliability and validity of the organizational culture inventory. *Psychological Reports, 72,* 1299-1330.

Cooke, R. A., & Szumal, J. L. (1994). The impact of group interaction styles on problem-solving effectiveness. *Journal of Applied Behavioral Science, 30*(4), 415-437.

Duarte, D.L & Snyder, N.T. (1999). *Mastering Virtual Teams.* San Francisco, CA: Jossey-Bass.

Festinger, L. (1950). *Theory and experiment in social communication.* Ann Arbor, MI: Research Center for Dynamics, Institute for Social Research, University of Michigan.

Fiske, D. W. (1949). Consistency of the factorial structures of personality ratings from different sources. *Journal of Abnormal and Social Psychology, 44,* 329-344.

Hackman, J. R., & Morris, C. G. (1975). Group tasks, group interaction process, and group performance effectiveness: A review and proposed integration. *Advances in Experimental Social Psychology, 8,* 45-99.

Hightower, R. T., & Sayeed, L. (1996). Effects of communication mode and prediscussion information distribution characteristics on information exchange in groups. *Information systems Research, 7*(4), 451-465.

Hirokawa, R. (1985). Discussion procedures and decision-making performance: A test of a functional perspective. *Human Communication Research, 12*(2), 203-224.

Hirokawa, R., & Gouran, D. S. (1989). Facilitation of group communication: a critique of prior research and an agenda for future research. *Management Communication Quarterly, 3*(1), 71-92.

Hoffman, L. R. (1979). Applying experimental research on group problem solving to organizations. *Journal of Applied Behavioral Science, 15,* 375-391.

Hogan, R. T. (1991). Personality and personality measurement. In M. Hough, *Handbook of industrial and organizational psychology* (pp. 873-919). Palo Alto, CA: Consulting Psychologists Press.

Human Synergistics. (1987). *Desert survival situation.* Plymouth, MI: Human Synergistics.

Human Synergisitics. (1989). *Organizational culture inventory.* Plymouth, MI: Human Synergistics.

Lafferty, J. C. (1974). *The desert survival situation.* Plymouth, MI: Human Synergistics

Leonard, D., & Sensiper, S. (1998). The role of tacit knowledge in group innovation. *California Management Review, 40*(3), 112-132.

Lipnick, J. & Stamps, J. (1997). *Virtual Teams: Reaching Across Space, Time and Organizations with Technology.* New York: John Wiley & Sons.

Maier, N. R. F. (1963). *Problem-solving discussions and conferences: Leadership methods and skills.* New York: McGraw-Hill.

Maier, N. R. F. (1967). Assets and liabilities in group problem-solving: the need for an integrative function. *Psychological Review, 74,* 239-249.

McCrae, R. R., & Costa, P. T. J. (1989). The structure of interpersonal traits: Wiggin's circumplex and the five-factor model. *Journal of Personality and Social Psychology 56*, 586-595.

McCrae, R. R., & John, O. P. (1992). An introduction to the five-factor model and its applications. *Journal of Personality 60*, 175-215.

McGrath, J. E. (1984). *Groups: Interaction and performance.* Englewood Cliffs, NJ: Prentice-Hall.

Mennecke, B. E., & Valacich, J. S. (1998). Information is what you make it: the influence of group history and computer support on information sharing, decision quality, and member perceptions. *Journal of Management Information Systems, 15*(2), 173-197.

Nonaka, I. (1994). A dynamic theory of organizational knowledge creation. *Organization Science, 5*(1), 14-37.

Potter, R., Balthazard, P. A., & Cooke, R. A. (2000). Virtual team interaction: Assessment, consequences, and management. *Team Performance Management, 6*(7-8), 131-137.

Potter, R. E., & Balthazard, P. A. (in press). Virtual team interaction styles: Assessment and effects. *International Journal of Human-Computer Studies.*

Spender, J. C. (1996). Making knowledge the basis of a dynamic theory of the firm. *Strategic Management Journal,* Winter Special Issue(17), 45-62.

Stasser, G., & Titus, W. (1985). Pooling of unshared information in group decision making: Biased information sampling during groups discussion. *Journal of Personality and Social Psychology, 48,* 1467-1478.

Tan, B. C. Y., Wei, K.-K., Huang, W. W., & Ng, G.-N. (2000). A dialog technique to enhance electronic communication in virtual teams. *IEEE Transactions on Professional Communication, 43*(2), 153-165.

Teece, D. (1998). Capturing value from knowledge assets: The new economy, markets for know-how, and intangible assets. *California Management Review,* Spring, *40*(3), 55-79.

Townsend, A., DeMarie, S. & Hendrickson, A. (1998). Virtual teams: Technology and the workplace of the future. *Academy of Management Executive, 12*(3), 17-29.

Warkentin, M. E., Sayeed, L., & Hightower, R. (1997). Virtual teams versus face-to-face teams: An exploratory study of a web-based conference system. *Decision Sciences, 28*(4), 975-996.

Watson, W. E., & Michaelsen, L. K. (1988). Group interaction behaviors that affect group performance on an intellective task. *Group & Organization Studies, 13*(4), 495-516.

Chapter VII

Organic Knowledge Management for Web-Based Customer Service

Stephen D. Durbin
RightNow Technologies, USA

Doug Warner
RightNow Technologies, USA

J. Neal Richter
RightNow Technologies, USA

Zuzana Gedeon
RightNow Technologies, USA

ABSTRACT

This chapter introduces practical issues of information navigation and organizational knowledge management involved in delivering customer service via the Internet. An adaptive, organic approach is presented that addresses these issues. This approach relies on both a system architecture that embodies effective knowledge processes, and a knowledge base that is supplemented with meta-information acquired automatically through various data mining and artificial intelligence techniques. An application implementing this approach, RightNow eService Center, and the algorithms supporting it are described. Case studies of the use of eService Center by commercial, governmental and other types of organizations are presented and discussed. It is suggested that the organic approach is effective in a variety of information-providing settings beyond conventional customer service.

INTRODUCTION

The phrase "organizational data mining" in the title of this book suggests the importance of tapping all sources of information within an organization. The bare term "data mining" is most often applied to the extraction of patterns and relationships from databases or other structured data stores, enabling the productive use of information otherwise buried in overwhelming quantities of raw data. More recently, methods have been developed to extract information from relatively unstructured text documents, or, at least, to render that information more available via techniques of information retrieval, categorization and extraction. But in spite of such progress, one major source of organizational knowledge often remains inadequately managed.

It is widely recognized that much of the knowledge of any organization resides in its people. A major difficulty in tapping this key resource is that much of this knowledge is not "explicit" but rather "tacit." For our present purposes, we call explicit the sort of knowledge that could be captured relatively easily in a document, such as a memorandum, a manual or a white paper. In contrast, tacit knowledge is generally not committed to any permanent, structured form, because it tends to be strongly dependent on context or other variables that cannot be described easily. Because of its difficult nature, as well as its importance, the concept of tacit knowledge has received much attention in the recent literature (e.g., Nonaka & Takeuchi, 1995; Stenmark, 2000; Richards & Busch, 2000), though its roots go back at least to Polanyi (1966). It has become clear that the obstacles to capturing such knowledge are not merely technical, but psychological, sociological and even philosophical. No simple solution can be anticipated to this inherently difficult problem. Nevertheless, one can hope to identify certain features of the problem that are likely to be important in designing systems to deal with it.

In the following, we shall present our view of some key aspects of human-centered knowledge acquisition and dissemination. We do this within the context of a specific software application, RightNow eService Center (RNeSC), which was originally developed and is primarily used for Web-based customer service. This is not the limited domain it might at first appear, for the basic paradigm of knowledge exchange between producers (e.g., customer service representatives, university staff or government agencies) and consumers (e.g., customers, students or citizens) can be applied very generally. To cover this broad spectrum using a common terminology, we shall refer to the producers as "experts" and the consumers as "novices" or "end-users," while the general term "users" will encompass both groups.

Focusing on the knowledge management aspects of our application, the fundamental goal is to facilitate information finding by end-users and information providing by experts. We recognize that the information transfer, though asymmetric, occurs in both directions. Indeed, one of our main points is that for end-users to learn effectively, the experts must also learn about the end-users and their information needs. Furthermore, we note that the same basic paradigm can also apply to the situation where experts and end-users are the same population. (Our software is actually used in that way within a number of organizations, including our own.)

Data mining is key to the function of RNeSC in more than the metaphorical sense of eliciting knowledge from experts or the conventional sense of extracting information to generate various reports on the system status, history and use. Beyond these, the continuous analysis of text exchanges and the mining of user interaction logs represent embedded data mining functions that are crucial to the performance of RNeSC. Their main purpose is to extract what could be considered tacit knowledge of both experts and end-users about the relationships among knowledge items in the knowledge base. This metaknowledge would be both tedious and overly demanding for users to provide directly, but greatly improves the operation of the system in terms of user experience, as we shall describe.

Our aim in this chapter is to present our approaches to knowledge acquisition and access, and show how they are implemented in the RNeSC application. We outline various statistical and artificial intelligence techniques that are used in the process. Based on extensive usage information provided by companies and educational and governmental institutions that have used RNeSC, we describe some practical aspects of deploying and using the application. Finally, we discuss future trends and draw several conclusions.

KNOWLEDGE MANAGEMENT FOR CUSTOMER SERVICE

Knowledge Management Issues

We begin with a few general observations relating to the tasks of collecting or acquiring knowledge from people and providing it to others. We make no attempt to survey the vast literature on knowledge management, but simply note that a great deal of effort has gone into analyzing the nature of knowledge in its various forms and, in particular, the feasibility of capturing it for re-use or training. As mentioned, much discussion has centered around the distinction between explicit and tacit knowledge (Nonaka & Takeuchi, 1995; Stenmark, 2000; Sternberg, 1999). Though not clearly separable, these two types of knowledge are equally significant. Because tacit knowledge is often unique to an organization, it is considered a major source of competitive advantage, distinguishing that organization from others. Furthermore, tacit knowledge presents special management problems as personnel changes. For some authors (Polanyi, 1966; Cook & Brown, 1999), tacit knowledge is by definition that which cannot be expressed, while others (Nonaka & Takeuchi, 1995; Stenmark, 2000; Richards & Busch, 2000) consider "externalization" of tacit knowledge to be possible in appropriate settings. We believe the latter view is more appropriate to the domain of generalized customer service.

The process of conveying knowledge — both explicit and tacit — from expert to novice can be divided into stages, each associated with certain artifacts. This division is not unique. One traditional approach, exemplified by the creation of product documentation, models the process in two stages: (1) the expert writes the documentation, and

(2) the novice reads it. While straightforward and familiar, this approach places a heavy burden on the expert to anticipate all the knowledge that could be required and present it in a way that can serve all those who might need it. An equally heavy burden is placed on the novice who must extract from the resulting large body of knowledge just that part corresponding to his or her need. Naturally, it often happens that what the novice needs is not fully provided, or the context is different enough that the novice fails to find the separate "nuggets" that, combined, would meet the need.

For example, it is difficult, if not impossible, to write a service manual for some piece of equipment that covers all repair situations. Yet an experienced repairperson can usually figure out what is needed on a particular job. If that specific repair procedure is described, elements of tacit knowledge are implicitly captured. In most organizations, as described in Brown and Duguid (1991), such stories are circulated informally within a community of practice. If they can be recorded and made more widely available, as was done with the well-known Eureka system at Xerox, the resulting knowledge base can be of extraordinary value to the organization (Powers, 1999; Fischer & Ostwald, 2001).

A second traditional approach is simple dialogue between expert and novice, in which the expert can both assist in the expression of the novice's needs and convey the knowledge in the most effective way for the particular novice. Such a model is the ideal of the conventional help desk. It typically results in the greatest benefit to the novice, but, depending on the setting, it may be highly burdensome and expensive to have an expert always available for each novice.

The model of the knowledge transfer process embodied in the architecture of RNeSC comprises elements of both the traditional approaches described above. Our interactive approach starts with the novice's specific information need. This is not necessarily clearly formulated, so we provide various means for the novice to satisfy the need via a self-service knowledge base. If that effort is unsuccessful, the novice must express the need in the form of a text message, which is sent to an expert. The expert then responds, drawing on accumulated experience, including appropriate elements of tacit knowledge. The response is, thus, much more limited in scope and tailored to the immediate need. In this setting, tacit knowledge, which might not have found its way into a manual, is activated; the expert realizes intuitively what will work best in the case at hand. This leads to what we consider an important aspect of any approach that aims to capture such knowledge: it is easiest to do so at the point of application, that is, in the consideration of a particular situation that calls for such knowledge. In a final stage of the process, the expert can choose to add the newly articulated knowledge to the knowledge base, thus enhancing self-service capability on the part of other novices.

Knowledge management in our model contrasts with that in the traditional model in several key regards. First, knowledge creation by the expert occurs not in a relative vacuum but in a specific, situated context. This facilitates application and capture of tacit knowledge, which is stored in the knowledge base along with the context. The knowledge transfer is not limited to transmission via a static artifact, such as a manual, but either by direct, personal response of expert to novice or via the novice's ability to locate the knowledge on his own. Since the latter is preferred, it is important to provide tools that assist the novice in navigating the knowledge base. Finally, utilization of the knowledge tends to be more effective under our model because of increased relevance to the particular situation of the novice.

Note that we have so far taken the expert to be omniscient. In most real cases, the expert also might need to refer to the knowledge base in the course of responding to a novice, especially if the expert is really an expert-in-training.

The Customer Service Domain

Customer service represents a quintessential knowledge management problem. Answers, i.e., information or knowledge, must be identified, transcribed or acquired by or from experts (e.g., customer service representatives) and then provided to novices (end-users) in response to their questions. Because of the economic importance of customer satisfaction, significant resources may be devoted to this function. In recent years, many companies and other entities have found it necessary to maintain a presence on the World Wide Web, and customer service is naturally one of the functions that can be provided by this means. However, the journey has not always been easy or successful.

Historically, the first step toward Web-based service was that of simply listing contact phone numbers and e-mail addresses on a Web page; end-user inquiries were then handled through these more traditional channels. This approach has the advantage of using existing infrastructure, but is typically very expensive per transaction, especially as there is now a general expectation of rapid response, even 24 hours a day. The majority of organizations are still at this level.

A second generation of Web-based service provides a set of answers to frequently asked questions (FAQs) on a support Web page. The composition of such a FAQ list is based on the accumulated experience of customer service representatives (CSRs). If well written and organized, this can significantly reduce the number of repeated inquiries received by CSRs, reducing their overload and increasing their productivity. However, unless the common inquiries are quite stable over time, this method requires a significant maintenance effort to keep the FAQ list organized and up to date. In many cases, depending on the organization, change can be relatively great on a weekly or monthly time scale. This change can also be unpredictable. Although it may be easy to see that introduction of a new product will lead to inquiries related to that product, it is not so easy to foretell what external events, such as a new law or regulation, or new products offered by competing companies, will cause a shift in end-user information needs. A further problem with this type of service is that as the number of FAQs grows larger, it becomes increasingly difficult for users to find answers to their questions.

A third level of Web-based service involves the provision of search capability over a set of indexed documents that constitute the online knowledge base. With such a system, answer-containing documents can be added independently of each other, and the structure is essentially the invisible one provided by the search facility. Related documents are, by definition, those returned together in response to a specific search query. Depending on the design of the search engine, it may or may not provide additional features, such as natural language input or matching to related words such as word-form variants (drive, driver, driving, etc.) or synonyms (car, automobile, etc.). These well-known search engine problems have led some companies to deploy conversational question-answering systems, or "chatbots." Unfortunately, at their current stage of development, such systems require extensive knowledge engineering in the form of identifying input question patterns that should be recognized and the links to the corresponding answers. Beyond pre-scripted patterns, the performance degrades rapidly. Furthermore, this type of system either does not support overviews and browsing of the knowledge base, or again requires knowledge engineering to create and maintain a taxonomy and relate it to the collection of knowledge base documents.

At present, there is a wide range of levels of customer service available on the Internet. Some organizations have managed a good fit between what they need and what they provide. But many are still struggling with expensive, cumbersome systems that do not serve them well. In some cases, organizations simply don't have a good understanding of what state-of-the-art customer service can or should be. But probably most often it is a lack of resources — both human and financial — that limits the quality of service. For this reason, a constant aim in the development of RNeSC was to minimize the effort necessary to establish and maintain the system. This entailed an architectural design in accordance with the above and other considerations, as well as integration of data mining and artificial intelligence techniques to reduce the burden on users.

AN ORGANIC KNOWLEDGE BASE
The Organic Approach

To find a way to meet the sometimes conflicting needs of experts and end-users, we believe that attention must first be focused on the core of the system where knowledge is stored, namely the knowledge base. In the type of system we envision, this is a publicly available (via the World Wide Web), dynamic collection of documents that we shall refer to as Answers. We assume here that it is created and maintained by the experts (e.g., CSRs). In actuality, there may be distinct managers who perform various important functions, but whose role is outside the scope of this paper.

The knowledge base must first of all contain the knowledge sought by end-users. How does one know what this is? Within our organic approach, the reply is simple: Let the end-users identify what is needed by the questions they ask. This implies that the knowledge base does not exist in isolation; it must be closely coupled to channels through which end-users ask questions.

As a concrete example, take the case of a computer services help desk that receives several complaints about problems with a new software version. Though one might expect certain problems to arise with such upgrades, it would be extremely difficult to attempt to forestall complaints by preparing a comprehensive troubleshooting guide. In contrast, it is relatively easy for a technician to answer a specific question in a given context and easier for the end-user to understand that answer than the full troubleshooting procedure. If the Answer is published in the knowledge base, incoming questions on the topic may be reduced either because only that single case led to problems, or because other users could resolve their problems also by following the approximate answer. If not, new support requests will come in, and then either the first answer could be modified or expanded, or a new answer added. This adaptive "just-in-time" approach is very efficient in terms of experts' effort.

Thus, along with the knowledge base itself, end-users must have direct access to experts when they don't find the information they need in the knowledge base. It is their needs that drive knowledge creation, while the experts' effort is conserved. A similar concept of experts backing up a knowledge base in a system for organizational memory, an application close in spirit to customer service, has been described and studied by Ackerman (1998).

According to the organic growth scenario, the knowledge base is initially seeded with a fairly small set of Answers to known or anticipated FAQs. After that, Answers are added as needed to respond to new incoming questions frequent enough to merit creation of a public Answer. (Of course, Answers to predictable concerns can also be added even before questions arise.) Depending on the organization, the threshold could range from one to perhaps hundreds.

This approach has a number of advantages for experts:

- Tacit as well as explicit knowledge can be brought to bear on the specific questions.
- Answers can be based on existing private responses (made before reaching the threshold).
- No time and effort are spent creating unneeded Answers.

Furthermore, experts have a natural motivation to upgrade private responses to publicly available Answers: A single Answer can eliminate the need for many private responses. As in any knowledge management endeavor, it is also important for the organization to create a culture in which such contributions are recognized or rewarded in one way or another.

End-users also benefit. Unlike a traditional call center or contact center, this approach develops an authoritative, self-service knowledge base, accessible 24 hours a day, in which an end-user can generally locate information faster than she can compose, say, an e-mail describing her question or problem. This is especially true if the initial problem description is unclear and a series of back-and-forth communications would be necessary for clarification. End-users with novel or inherently personal questions can still receive service through the traditional channels, now improved because of the reduced load on the experts.

Critical to success of this approach is the ease with which end-users can actually navigate the knowledge base to find information. Frustration leads not only to negative attitudes towards the organization but, if anything, increases the burden on experts. In contrast, a positive experience for the end-user enhances trust and loyalty, key assets for noncommercial as well as business entities. Ensuring such a positive interaction requires attention to the psychology as well as the statistics of searching. To support each end-user's quest, the interface to the knowledge base must be as intelligent as possible and be adaptable to the range of search skills that different users may have. This entails use of natural language and artificial intelligence (AI) methods. Appropriately integrated, these techniques can also be applied to improving performance of the system from the experts' point of view.

Feedback from end-users to experts, in addition to that implicit in the asking of questions, should be such as to facilitate various forms of optimization, as well as provide understanding of end-user behavior that may be significant to the organization. This can be accomplished by mining records of user interactions with the knowledge base.

In the following, we detail how this organic approach is embodied in RNeSC. After briefly introducing the overall system, we focus on those aspects related to the knowledge base, since this is where most of the AI and data mining techniques come into play. We describe the use of the system in practice, as well as the algorithmic techniques employed and their multiple roles.

System Architecture

RNeSC is an integrated application that combines e-mail management, Web self-service, live collaborative chat, and knowledge management. The core of the application, from our present perspective, is the publicly accessible Answer knowledge base and the tools by which it is created, maintained and accessed. In addition, there is a database of customer-service Incidents, i.e., messages from end-users, which are fully tracked from initial creation—via e-mail, Web form or live chat—through resolution and archiving. Figure 1 illustrates these key components and how they are involved in end-user and CSR (or other expert) knowledge-related transactions.

As indicated in the previous section and in Figure 1, the architecture of RNeSC provides a strong interaction between question and answer channels. As CSRs respond to the questions submitted by end-users, they naturally become aware of trends and commonalities among them. At any time, a private CSR reply can be proposed as a potential public knowledge base item, or a new Answer can be composed on the basis of previous replies or predicted information needs. Depending on organizational practices, the item might be reviewed or edited by collaborators or managers before being made a publicly available Answer.

In typical operation, the main knowledge flow (in terms of volume) is from the knowledge base to end-users who are successful in their searching. But even if they are unsuccessful, or if they make no attempt at self-service, the contents of their question may suggest that one or more relevant Answers actually exist. In that case, Answers can be suggested automatically, based on search technology described later. These Sug-

Figure 1. Principal Knowledge-Related Transactions in RNeSC (End-users search the Answer knowledge base for information; if they cannot find what they need, they submit a question, which is stored and tracked in an Incidents database, and replied to by a CSR. CSRs also use the knowledge base, and add to it by creating new Answers, typically suggested by frequently asked questions. Answers to questions can be suggested from the knowledge base either to assist CSRs in forming replies or as auto-replies to end-users. See text for a fuller description.)

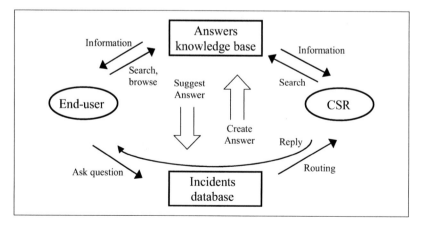

gested Answers can either be routed directly to the end-user as an auto-reply or to the CSR engaged in formulating a personal reply. Naturally, CSRs also make direct use of the knowledge base for their own information, especially novice CSRs.

In this paper we leave aside the multiple administrative functions of RNeSC, though these are vital to its overall ease of use (especially from a CSR's point of view). Some of these use AI techniques also employed in the central knowledge management functions. For example, one of the criteria that can be used in routing incoming questions to individual CSRs is an emotive index that estimates the degree to which the tone of a message is angry, neutral or happy. This determination uses the same natural language processing algorithms described later, in combination with wordlists and grammar rules. As RNeSC is available in about 15 languages and dialects, implementing this feature takes a significant effort. Also not indicated in Figure 1 is a module that generates a wide variety of reports to aid in evaluating transaction statistics, CSR performance and Web-site usage. These are developed through both batch and incremental analysis of system interaction records. Finally, except to mention a notification function that allows a user to be informed of any changes in a selected Answer, we won't detail here the many customization options that users can set.

Using the Knowledge Base

It is widely appreciated that knowledge comprises not only facts, but relationships among these, as well as perspective on their importance, relevance, etc. A knowledge base organized to incorporate or reflect such metaknowledge provides a much better match to user habits and expectations and is consequently easier to use. In RNeSC this metaknowledge is acquired through several techniques. In addition to intelligent searching, these include adaptive clustering and classification of text documents (the knowledge base Answers), and collaborative filtering techniques that mine usage patterns to extract implicit user feedback on importance, timeliness and relatedness of knowledge base items. We will describe these techniques as they might come into play while a user navigates a knowledge base.

An illustration of a simple end-user view of a knowledge base is shown in Figure 2. This page is reached after first selecting the "Answers" link on the support home page, before any search has been made. The Answers shown are listed in order of historical usefulness — called solved count — which measures how helpful an answer is likely to be based on the experience of previous users. If the knowledge base is not too large and the end-user is looking for information that is commonly sought, there is a fair probability that the appropriate Answer will be listed in the first set. If the solved count of answers happens to follow a Zipf distribution, then even with 500 items in the knowledge base, there is nearly a 50 percent chance that the appropriate Answer will be within the top 10.

The solved count is obtained from a combination of explicit and implicit user feedback. If enabled, each Answer page carries evaluation buttons (e.g., labeled 0 percent, 25 percent, 50 percent, 75 percent and 100 percent) that the user can select to indicate the degree to which his or her question was answered; these contribute proportionately to the solved count. Since relatively few users make the effort to provide explicit feedback, we also derive an implicit evaluation from the user's actions. Simply choosing to view a particular Answer is taken as a partial vote for its usefulness. If the Answer is the last one viewed, it is assumed that it provided the information sought, and the vote is given a higher weight (though still less than an explicitly approved Answer).

Figure 2. Portion of the Web Browser Display from the Support Page of the University of South Florida Information Technology Division [The page is configured to list by default the historically most useful Answers (i.e., highest solved count). Users may search in various modes by entering search text, and they may contact a CSR via the "Ask a Question" tab.]

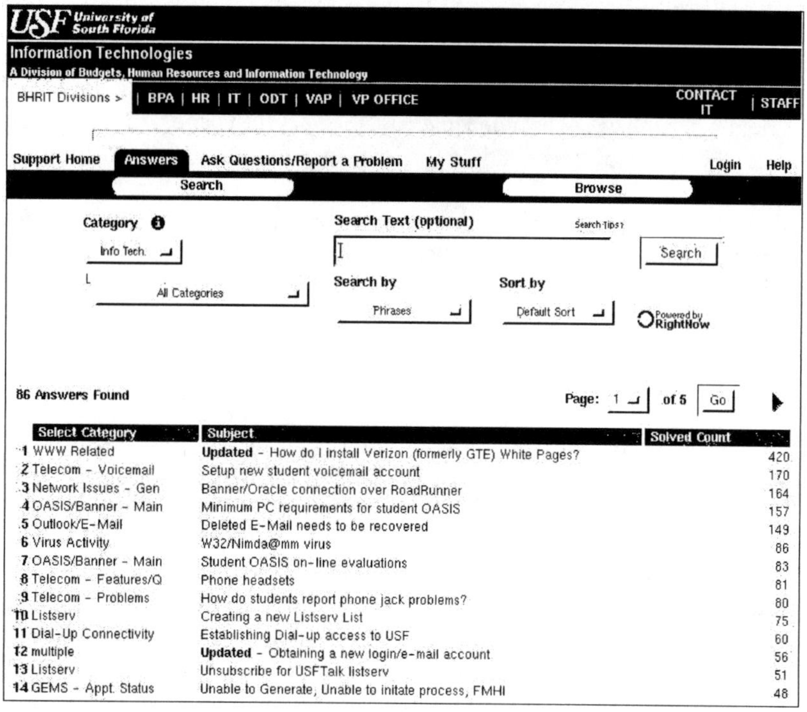

An Answer that appeared promising from its title might prove insufficient. If so, to the extent the title represented the content, an Answer with similar or related content might help the user. Each Answer page can be provided with links to a variable number of the most closely related Answers. The relatedness ranking, like the solved count, has explicit and implicit components. The explicit relatedness is derived from text similarity, currently based on the vector model common in information retrieval (see, e.g., Manning & Schutze, 1999, p. 296), with stopword removal and conflation of words having the same stem. To obtain an implicit relatedness score, the application maintains a link matrix, the corresponding element of which is incremented each time an end-user navigates from one Answer to another, presumably related one. The increment is larger if the second Answer is the final one viewed or is given a high explicit rating.

The methods just mentioned for capturing user perceptions of usefulness and relatedness are inspired by both collaborative filtering (Levy & Weld, 2000) and swarm intelligence (Dorigo, Di Caro & Gambardella, 1999) approaches. In our application, rather than software agents traversing a network as in the usual form of swarm intelligence, it is human users whose paths leave a trace as a pheromone-like record. The resulting link matrix certainly contains noise in the sense that not every item-to-item transition is made by users only on the basis of perceived relatedness. Nonetheless, averaged over many users who each tend to be searching for information related to a specific need, we have found that the strong links indicate useful relationships. By means of the accumulated links, the application learns which other items in the knowledge base are most closely related to a given one.

The algorithm as described so far would be appropriate for a static knowledge base but not for a changing one. Just as an insect pheromone trail evaporates with time, so we perform an aging process by which both solved count and link values are periodically reduced in strength when not reinforced. This aging keeps the knowledge base responsive by enforcing the primacy of recent usage patterns. By this means the most useful Answers float to the top of the list and appear on the very first page. For a more complete discussion of these collaborative and swarm intelligence methods, see Warner, Richter, Durbin and Banerjee (2001).

Both the solved count and the link matrix represent a form of knowledge acquired from users about items in the knowledge base. From a knowledge management point of view, the role of this metaknowledge is to aid in the principal knowledge transfer by making it easier for end-users to find the Answers they need.

To find Answers to less frequently asked questions, end-users may need to perform a search of the knowledge base. Intelligent search is a prerequisite for easy access to information. In RNeSC, queries entered into the search box (Figure 2) can be processed according to a variety of search modes, including natural language input and similar phrase searching (which carries out spelling correction and synonym expansion). Searches can also be restricted to predefined products and categories, if such taxonomies have been established. The results of a search can be displayed in order of relevance or solved count.

End-users may or may not come to a support Web site with specific questions, but, in either case, they may find it convenient to browse the knowledge base from a more distant perspective, gaining an overview of the available information. Our system offers a browse mode of access in which categories of documents are displayed as folders, labeled with the key terms most descriptive of their contents (Figure 3). Clicking on a folder opens it to display documents and subfolders corresponding to more specific categories. The automatically determined labels on the folders give a summary of the contents. Because the user can navigate by selecting subfolders and individual documents without needing to type search terms, the browse mode is especially helpful when the user is unfamiliar with the terminology used in the Answers, and, hence, might have difficulty formulating a productive search query. If desired, it is also possible to search within a browse category. In a sense, the ease of browsing is related to the tacit knowledge of a user about the subject area. Most people are able to recognize what they're looking for much more easily than they can articulate it.

The browse function is made possible by a hierarchical categorization of the text items in the knowledge base. For this we employ a modification of the fast, hierarchical clustering algorithm BIRCH (Zhang, Ramakrishnan, & Livny, 1996), the result of which is used to learn RIPPER-style classification rules (Cohen, 1995). The final topic hierarchy is determined by classifying all knowledge base items according to the learned rules. Because of the inherent multiplicity and subjectivity of similarity relationships, we allow single items to be classified in multiple places where they fit well. This makes using the browse interface much more convenient, as the user can locate an item along various paths and does not have to guess what rigid classification might control the listing. New

Figure 3. Web Browser Display from the Support Page of the University of South Florida Information Technology Division [This page displays a hierarchical set of folders and subfolders, where a given folder (like a typical computer file system) may contain both subfolders and Answer documents.]

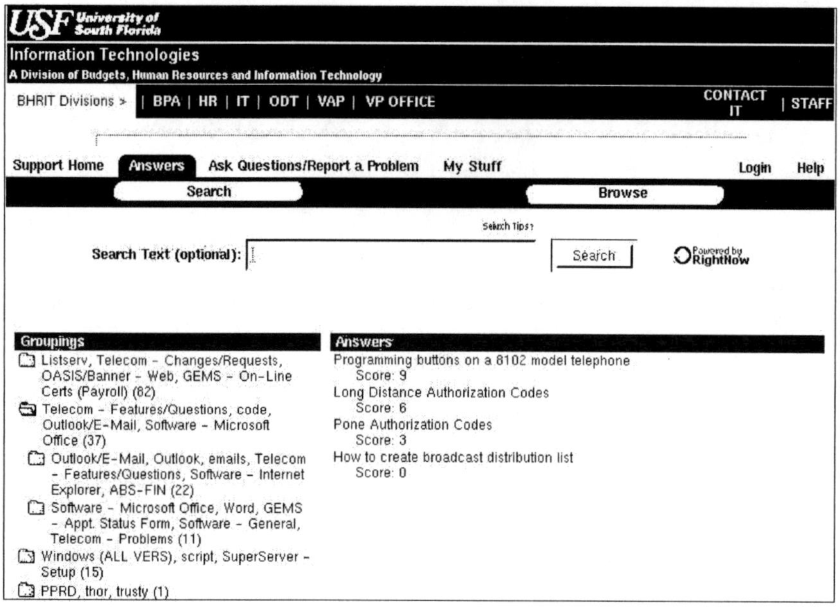

Answers are, on creation, simply inserted into the hierarchy according to the classification rules. After a predetermined amount of change in the knowledge base, due to modification or addition, a reclustering is performed so that the browse hierarchy reflects the current state of the contents, rather than a fixed hierarchy.

The features on the basis of which the clustering is performed are obtained from the document texts by shallow parsing. The natural language processing starts with part of speech tagging via a transformation-based tagger (Brill, 1994). Rules are the used to identify noun phrases, which receive the highest weight as features, though other selected words are also used. In addition, customer-supplied keywords and product or category names provide highly weighted features. The weights of feature words are additionally adjusted on the basis of the frequency with which users have searched for them, as reflected in a table maintained with the knowledge base. The clustering procedure is actually carried out several times with different sets of parameters, and the best clustering, according to a composite figure of merit, is chosen.

To assist CSRs in composing responses, as well as to optionally supply automated responses to end-users submitting questions, RNeSC can be configured to automatically suggest Answers. This is done by first processing the text of the question as if it were a search query. Simply taking the top-ranked Answers returned can result in spurious matches. Hence, they are filtered by checking whether they would appear in the same cluster as would the question text, now treated as an Answer for categorization. If this feature is used by a CSR, the suggested Answers are directly pasted into a reply form, where they can be edited by the human expert.

As with the solved count and the link matrix, the clustering represents automatically generated metaknowledge that serves to aid knowledge acquisition by end-users. To evaluate scientifically the utility of such aid would require extensive human testing, which we have not carried out. However, both our own observations and, more importantly, the experience of RNeSC users, as described in the next section, indicate that the benefits can be significant.

USER EXPERIENCE WITH RNESC

The system we describe has been used, through several versions, by a wide variety of commercial, educational, and governmental organizations. Drawing from their accumulated experience, we present both aggregate statistics and case studies illustrating the dramatic reduction of time and effort for knowledge-base creation and maintenance, and the increase in satisfaction of knowledge base users. This holds across the spectrum of organizations and applications, including those outside the area of conventional customer service.

Different organizations use the system in a variety of ways. The Rotherham England Metropolitan Borough Council uses it as a community clearinghouse where answers are provided to all kinds of questions about which one might contact a city office. As of this writing, it contains 476 answers to questions ranging from regularly recurring ones, such as "Can I report a pothole in the road?," to more timely ones, such as "Do you have any information regarding the Queen's Golden Jubilee?" Statements by the council make it clear that they view this information service for citizens, part of an e-government initiative, as very analogous to a business' support for customers. Although the majority of the 16,000 daily hits on the site are from the UK, there are also high numbers from the U.S., Taiwan, Germany, France, Sweden and Denmark, some of which, it is hoped, may represent people looking to invest in the UK and attracted by Rotherham's assets.

Within our own company (RightNow Technologies), independent instances of RNeSC are used for external customer support and for internal company information. More interesting is its use as a resource for developers, who answer each other's questions — a case of experts and end-users being the same population. It also provides a defect posting and tracking system shared by the development and quality assurance departments. The resulting history of bug fixes, with each incident often carrying contributions from several developers and testers, is a heavily used company resource. In terms of knowledge management theory (see, e.g., Brown & Duguid, 2000), each bug history document constitutes a "boundary object," collaboratively produced by two groups within the organization, serving to facilitate communication between them.

Due to the high degree of automation of RNeSC, the ease of installation is such that it has been accomplished in as little as a few days, or even one day. Once set up, the knowledge base can grow rapidly. For example, the United States Social Security Administration started with 284 items in their initial knowledge base, and over 200 new items based on user-submitted questions were added within two weeks. After two years, the number has stabilized at about 600, though the composition continues to change. Due to the public availability of the knowledge base, the number of telephone calls has dropped by 50 percent, from 50,000 to 25,000 daily. Similar experiences are common.[1]

Table 1. Self-Service Index for Various Types of Organizations Using RNeSC [The self-service index is the fraction of end-users that find needed information in the Answer knowledge base, rather than initiating contact (escalating) with a support person via e-mail or online chat.]

Industry	Visits	Escalations	Self-Service Index
General Equipment	342,728	4,144	98.79%
Manufacturing	22,784	489	97.85%
Education	8,400	317	96.23%
Entertainment/Media	113,047	4,622	95.91%
Financial Services	40,574	1,972	95.14%
Contract Manufacturers	77,838	4,203	94.60%
Utility/Energy	19,035	1,122	94.11%
ISP/Hosting	147,671	8,771	94.06%
IT Solution Providers	53,804	3,277	93.91%
Computer Software	449,402	27,412	93.90%
Dot Coms	267,346	20,309	92.40%
Medical Products/Resources	17,892	1,451	91.89%
Professional Services	24,862	2,142	91.38%
Insurance	40,921	3,537	91.36%
Automotive	3,801	373	90.19%
Retail/Catalog	44,145	6,150	86.07%
Consumer Products	1,044,199	162,219	84.46%
Computer Hardware	101,209	15,759	84.43%
Government	108,955	17,347	84.08%
Travel/Hospitality	27,099	4,610	82.99%
Association/Nonprofit	14,620	2,772	81.04%
Telecommunications	809,320	202,158	75.02%
Overall Total	**3,779,652**	**495,156**	**86.90%**

The ability of a Web self-service system to handle dynamic fluctuations in usage can be very important. As one example, an announcement of a rate hike by the U.S. Postal Service led to a short-term increase in visitors to the support site of Pitney-Bowes, which provides mailing services, of nearly 1,000 percent over that for the previous rate hike. Attempting to handle such volume via telephone or e-mail would have resulted in huge backlogs.

One quantitative measure of end-user success in finding information is the self-service index, is defined as the percentage of end-users who are able to find Answers online, rather than sending a message to a CSR. Table 1 is excerpted from a Doculabs study (Watson, Donnelly & Shehab, 2001) in which it was found that the self-service index for organizations using RNeSC ranged from 75 to almost 99 percent, averaging 85 to 90 percent. The lower values for some categories of organization, such as telecommunications or travel services companies, may be due to a greater number of end-user-specific questions in these areas. Nonetheless, given typical costs of $30 per telephone transaction, $10 per e-mail exchange and $1 per Web interaction, such high self-service rates can lead to dramatic savings. According to anecdotal reports from users, the benefits described are largely attributable to the features of RNeSC described in this paper.

DISCUSSION AND FUTURE TRENDS

We believe that the performance of the RNeSC application in a range of settings is evidence that the underlying principles have a sound practical basis. Nevertheless, there is certainly room to do better. Some improvements are incremental, such as making the clustering algorithm more adaptive to knowledge bases that may differ significantly in the nature and length of the documents they contain, and in the granularity of the product and category divisions they use, if any. More difficult is the issue of descriptive labels for the clusters; the area of multidocument summarization is one of active current research (see, e.g., Mani & Maybury, 1999).

More qualitative enhancements can be obtained from applying AI techniques to a greater number of functions. Advanced machine learning techniques can potentially be employed wherever rules are used, including incident routing, text categorization and natural language processing. In the latter area, sophisticated question-answering systems will probably soon reach the point of being commercially viable, at least within restricted subjects. A fluent conversational interface to a knowledge base would fulfill many developers' dreams. Until that is available, the art is to provide some approximation with capabilities that outweigh the disappointments.

Another trend is toward greater personalization of user interfaces. Care must be exercised to ensure such customization facilitates rather than constrains. The extent to which significant personalization is feasible for frequent and for one-time users remains to be investigated.

Along other lines, the pursuit of applications in different sectors of knowledge management could suggest a new mix of features. RNeSC is already quite flexible and user-configurable and could evolve in many different directions. We believe that many of its advantages as a customer-service application could be realized in related areas as well.

CONCLUSION

We have presented an organic approach to knowledge creation and delivery that emphasizes rapid response for dynamic information environments. The user-driven architecture helps mobilize tacit knowledge and dramatically reduces the time and expense of creating a knowledge base. Facilitated and cooperative creation of knowledge base documents takes place as an extension of the normal activities of experts. Continuous mining of implicit end-user recognition of the importance and relationships of information items enables the system to adapt quickly, while remaining easy to use through automated re-organization. As embodied in the Web-based customer service application Right Now Service Center, the system uses a number of AI techniques to facilitate construction, maintenance and navigation of a knowledge base of answers to frequently asked questions. These techniques include collaborative filtering, swarm intelligence, natural language processing, text clustering and classification rule learning. Many of these individual techniques have been similarly employed in other commercial applications, but we know of no other system that combines all of them. Customers using RNeSC report dramatic decreases in support costs and increases in customer satisfaction due to the ease of use provided by the "self-learning" features of the knowledge base.

We have argued that the principles and methods of our approach are also applicable in other settings, for example, government agencies reaching out to concerned citizens. In fact, organizations and associated constituencies with information needs are ubiquitous in modern society. Ubiquitous also is the need for software tools to assist them. "Since it is the value added by people — context, experience and interpretation — that transforms data and information into knowledge, it is the ability to capture and manage those human additions that make information technologies particularly suited to dealing with knowledge" (Davenport & Prusak, p. 129).

ENDNOTES

[1] See more case studies at http://www.rightnow.com/resource/casestudies.php.

REFERENCES

Ackerman, M. S. (1998). Augmenting organizational memory: A field study of Answer Garden. *ACM Transactions on Information Systems, 16*(3), 203-224.

Brill, E. (1994). Some advances in transformation-based part of speech tagging. *Proceedings of the Twelfth National Conference on Artificial Intelligence.* Menlo Park, CA: AAAI Press, pp. 722-727.

Brown, J. S., & Duguid, P. (1991). Organizational learning and communities-of-practice: Toward a unified view of working, learning, and innovation. *Organization Science, 2,* 40-57.

Brown, J. S., & Duguid, P. (2000). *The social life of information.* Boston, MA: Harvard Business School Press.

Cohen, W. H. (1995). Fast effective rule induction. *Machine Learning: Proceedings of the Twelfth International Conference.* Lake Tahoe, CA: Morgan Kaufmann, pp. 115-123.

Cook, D., & Brown, J. S. (1999). Bridging epistemologies: The generative dance between organizational knowledge and organizational knowing. *Organization Science, 10,* 381-400.

Davenport, T. H., & Prusak, L. (1998). *Working knowledge.* Boston, MA: Harvard Business School Press.

Dorigo, M., Di Caro, G., & Gambardella, L. M. (1999). Ant algorithms for discrete optimization. *Artificial Life, 5*(2), 137-172.

Fischer, G., & Ostwald, J. (2001). Knowledge management: Problems, promises, realities, and challenges. *IEEE Intelligent Systems, 16,* 60-72.

Levy, A. Y., & Weld, D. S. (2000). Intelligent Internet systems. *Artificial Intelligence, 118,* 1-14.

Mani, I., & Maybury, M. T. (Eds.). (1999). *Advances in automatic text summarization.* Cambridge, MA: MIT Press.

Manning, C. D., & Schutze, H. (1999). *Foundations of natural language processing.* Cambridge, MA: MIT Press.

Nonaka, I., & Takeuchi, H. (1995). *The Knowledge creating company: How Japanese companies create the dynamics of innovation.* New York: Oxford University Press.

Polanyi, M. (1966). *The tacit dimension*. London: Routeledge & Kegan Paul.

Powers, V. J. (1999). Xerox creates a knowledge-sharing culture through grassroots efforts. *Knowledge Management in Practice* (18), 1-4. American Productivity & Quality Center.

Richards, D., & Busch, P. (2000). Measuring, formalising, and modeling tacit knowledge. *Proceedings of the ICSC Symposium on Intelligent Systems and Applications*. Millet, Alberta, Canada: NAISO Academic Press.

Stenmark, D. (2000). Leveraging tacit organizational knowledge. *Journal of Management Information Systems, 17*, 9-24.

Sternberg, R. J. (1999). What do we know about tacit knowledge? Making the tacit become explicit. In R. J. Sternberg & J. A. Horvath (Eds.), *Tacit knowledge in professional practice* (pp. 231-236). Mahwah, NJ: Lawrence Erlbaum Associates.

Warner, D., Richter J. N., Durbin, S. D., & Banerjee, B. (2001). Mining user session data to facilitate user interaction with a customer service knowledge base in RightNow Web. *Proceedings of the Seventh ACM SIGKDD International Conference on Knowledge Discovery and Data Mining* (pp. 467-72). New York: Association for Computing Machinery.

Watson, J., Donnelly, G., & Shehab, J. (2001). The self-service index report: Why Web-based self-service is the ROI sweet-spot of CRM. Retrieved on March 25, 2003 from http://www.doculabs.com.

Zhang, T., Ramakrishnan, R., & Livny, M. (1996). BIRCH: An efficient data clustering method for very large databases. *Proceedings of the 1996 ACM SIGMOD International Conference on Management of Data* (pp. 103-114). New York: Association for Computing Machinery.

Chapter VIII

A Data Mining Approach to Formulating a Successful Purchasing Negotiation Strategy

Hokey Min
University of Louisville-Shelby, USA

Ahmed Emam
Western Kentucky University, USA

ABSTRACT

A successful path to purchasing negotiation often hinges on the buyer's ability to gain relative bargaining strength. The buyer's bargaining strength, in turn, depends upon the extent of the buyer's preparation and preplanning for the negotiation. We postulate that the buyer's level of expertise and/or simulated negotiation experiences through the experiential learning process help him/her better prepare for the negotiation and, thereby, increase his/her bargaining strength. Under such a premise, this study empirically investigates the impact of expertise and experiential learning on the bargaining position of purchasing professionals and their subsequent negotiation outcomes. The main objective of this chapter is to use both statistical data analysis and data mining techniques and demonstrate their usefulness in the optimal performance of business-to-business negotiations.

BACKGROUND

Purchasing negotiation is the effective means of resolving interorganizational conflicts with suppliers over the essentials of a purchasing contract, such as price, quality assurance, specifications, payment terms and delivery schedules. Since the success of purchasing negotiation depends largely on the buyer's ability to establish bargaining strength, much of the negotiation literature (e.g., Dwyer & Walker Jr., 1981; Day, Michaels & Perdue, 1984; Dwyer, 1984; Greenhalgh, Neslin & Gilkey, 1985; Schurr & Ozanne, 1985; Perdue, 1989; Dabholkar, Johnston & Cathey, 1994; King Jr. & Hinson, 1994; Min, LaTour & Jones, 1995) to date have focused on the identification of salient variables that affect the buyer's (negotiator's) bargaining strength. Examples of these variables include negotiator personality, team size, time pressure, rewards, situational power, relationship preferences, bargaining stance toughness, sex and equity sensitivity, and so forth. Most of these variables, however, are often situational and dynamic (time-sensitive); therefore, the extent of their impact on the bargaining strength and negotiation outcome may vary over time. The rationale is that, as negotiators have gained similar negotiation experiences over time, their negotiation skill may improve and, consequently, their control over these variables may also improve. Herein, negotiation experiences refer to self-learning processes through hands-on industry experiences and simulated negotiation exercises (role-playing games). As such, today's savvy purchasing managers often train their apprentice negotiators using simulated negotiation exercises (Long, 1993). Earlier Burt (1982) also recognized the importance of simulated negotiation experiences to the successful purchasing negotiation, because they would help negotiators become aware of many potential issues and controversies surrounding actual negotiations apriori. Given the importance of such experiences to the dynamics of purchasing negotiation, it is clear that understanding of the link between negotiators' experiences and bargaining power is essential for formulating successful purchasing negotiation strategies. Nevertheless, little attention has been given to this line of research. To initiate this line of research, this chapter attempts to examine the effects of self-learning through experiential games on the negotiation outcome.

PRIOR LITERATURE ON DATA MINING

With rapid technological advances in retrieving, storing and integrating data, a growing number of organizations have to deal with large volumes of data sets. Such data expansion calls for data mining techniques that can help decision makers systematically uncover hidden patterns and trends in the large data sets. In contrast with traditional statistics, that intend to answer specific questions through hypotheses testing, data mining often deals with data that has already been collected for other purposes, such as record keeping (Hand, Mannila & Smyth, 2001). Although the field of data mining is still young and evolving, it has been widely applied to various practical domains. These include: discovery of genetic causes and DNA sequences (Baxevanis & Ouellette, 1998), loan payment performance (Higgins, 1997), target marketing (Westphal & Blaxton, 1998), customer profiling (Min, Min & Emam, 2002), customer relationship management (Berson, Smith & Thearing, 1999), telecommunication traffic patterns (Chen, Hsu & Dayal, 2000), time series forecasting (Hill, O'Connor & Remus, 1996) and satellite imaging (Gibson, Kreinovivh, Longpre, Penn & Starks, 2001).

With respect to its intended applications, data mining techniques can be classified into four categories: classification, clustering, association rule mining and sequence pattern mining. Classification is the process of finding the set of models (or functions) that describe and distinguish data classes to predict unknown or future values of variables of interest (Han & Kamber, 2001). The models can take a variety of forms, such as IF-THEN rules, decision trees, neural networks, case-based reasoning, rough sets and genetic algorithms. Clustering is the process of partitioning a data set into a set of distinctive classes (or groups) to maximize intraclass similarity, while minimizing interclass similarity. The examples of clustering data mining techniques include partitioning, hierarchical, density-based and model-based algorithms. Association rule mining is the process of finding interesting correlations among large sets of data. These correlations can explain how different data items (e.g., products and services) relate to each other, or how they tend to occur together in a transaction. A typical example of association rule mining is a market basket analysis that aims to infer customers' preferences and habits from their purchase patterns in shopping baskets. Sequential pattern mining is the process of finding frequently occurring patterns over time or in sequence and an example of which includes the Apriori property techniques developed by Agrawal and Srikant (1995). Despite proven success, when applied to practical problems, data mining has not been utilized to develop negotiation rules. Recognizing this gap, this chapter first attempts to use data mining techniques to formulate effective negotiation strategies in the industrial purchasing environment.

RESEARCH ISSUES

Subject

The participants in this study were 197 students who produced 192 valid data sets. Specifically, the student data for this study was collected from role-playing negotiation games conducted with both undergraduate and graduate (MBA) students, taking purchasing management and marketing courses at a major southeastern public university in the United States. Since a majority of the student subjects participating in the experiments did not have extensive prior experience with real-world purchasing negotiations, it is noted that these student subjects may have lacked negotiations skills that professional buyers and suppliers possess. However, they were taught to utilize what personal traits and expertise might lead to negotiation success and the formulation of effective negotiation strategy.

Research Instrument

Despite realistic scenarios, simulated negotiation experiments may not fully reflect the complexity of real-world negotiations. Nonetheless, the use of simulated negotiation experiments for determining the effects of various negotiating environments and the negotiator's personal traits on negotiation outcomes is not uncommon and serves as a valuable learning tool (Pruitt & Kimmel, 1977). In fact, much of the negotiation literature (e.g., Burt, 1982; McFillen, Reck & Benton, 1983; Clopton, 1984; Dwyer, 1984; Greenhalgh et al., 1985; Graham, 1986; Kersten, 1988; Alexander, Schul & Babakus, 1991; Eyuboglu & Buja, 1993; Min et al., 1995) used simulated experiments, such as role-playing games, to investigate the dynamics of negotiation. Likewise, three separate role playing games were used in this study to examine how significantly the negotiators simulated negotiation experiences, through a series of role playing games, influence negotiation outcomes.

The first exercise involves purchasing and selling a used personal computer (PC). Once the subjects completed the first exercise and evaluated their performances, they were instructed to participate in the second experiment. Prior to the second experiment, all the participants were given extensive lectures about the Stagner and Rosen's (1965) model of negotiation, psychology of negotiation (Rubin & Brown, 1975), negotiation styles (Perdue, Day & Michaels, 1986) and various negotiation strategies formulated by the Purchasing Staff Report (1962), Karass (1974) and Nierenberg (1983). The second experiment is based on the role-playing game that involves purchasing and selling either a minivan or a house. Both of these exercises were designed to give no distinctive advantage (negotiation leverage) to either the buyer or the seller. Neither the buyer nor the seller had access to complete information, although the seller was contingently rewarded with a commission when he/she settled for a price above a certain amount. Also, prior to negotiation, each participant was instructed to review his/her assigned negotiation task, detailed bargaining scenario, major negotiating issues related to price haggling (e.g., obsolescence, product life cycle, rarity, pending offer, product quality), potential payoff/loss (e.g., commission, sales below current market price) and negotiation deadline (e.g., two weeks to sell or buy). Furthermore, each participant was given a worksheet on which the record of his/her offers and his/her opposing party's counteroffers was summarized as the negotiation progressed. Under the above game scenario, the total of 192 dyads were created for each game by randomly pairing one buyer to one seller, with some pairings being between opposite sexes. Tryads were eliminated from the experiment because they may not fully reflect the individual learning effects. For these games, each subject was allowed a maximum of 25 minutes to read the given scenario, plan his/her bargaining strategies and settle with the opposing party. All of the student subjects were able to reach an agreement within 25 minutes for both exercises.

At the end of each exercise, each participant was asked to fill out an exit questionnaire to not only evaluate the negotiator's performance, but also assess the negotiator's understanding of the scenario (see Appendix for an exit questionnaire). Based on the exit questionnaire survey, we discovered that five pairs did not seem to clearly understand the scenario because the buyer's final price was greater than the highest offer of the seller. Therefore, these responses were not included in the final data. To extract valuable statistical information from these experiments, the results obtained from the first experiment were compared to those of the second experiment to assess the extent of learning effects using paired t-tests. Further analyses of the experimental data were conducted using both the correlation analysis and the stepwise linear regression analysis of the Statistical Packages for Social Sciences (SPSS) for Windows (Statistical Packages for Social Sciences (SPSS) Inc., 2000).

Research Hypotheses

Evans and Steele (1982) stated that preparation is one of the most important stages of negotiation. Complementary to this statement, Bloom (1984) and Heinritz, Farrell, Giunipero and Kolchin (1991) note that the buyer's bargaining strength is considerably affected by the extent of his/her preparation for the upcoming negotiation. Both Burt

(1982) and Long (1993) indicated that a number of industrial marketing representatives and purchasing managers often used simulated negotiation exercises in an effort to enhance their negotiators' preparedness. To verify the usefulness of such exercises, we examined how crucial experiential learning is to successful negotiation planning/preparation and which variables constitute experiential learning. In this examination, the following hypotheses were advanced:

H_1:   The more interaction a negotiator has with his/her opponent, the larger the degree of concession from the opponent. That is to say, the negotiator's learning experience during negotiation and the subsequent bargaining strength is positively affected by the frequency of communications between two negotiating parties.

Negotiation is a back-and-forth communication process that involves continuous offers and counter-offers. During the continuous offers and counteroffers, traditional wisdom has suggested that both the buyer and the seller would reveal some confidential information about their actual needs and preferences and subsequently such information exchanges between the two negotiating parties might help them narrow the differences. That is to say, the frequent interaction with the opposing negotiating party may facilitate the negotiator's self-learning experience and, thereby, lead to more favorable negotiation outcomes. As a matter of fact, Hogarth (1981) argued that negotiation experience through increased interaction would generally provide negotiators with feedback that they could use to correct negotiation errors. Also, Graham (1986) found that cooperative buyer-supplier information exchange tended to result in negotiation outcomes beneficial to the negotiators. As such, Pruitt and Lewis (1975) used a number of different proposals as a surrogate measure of the extent to which the negotiator was exploring a variety of alternative solutions. Clopton (1984) also added that the negotiator's coordinative behavior exhibited by frequent proposals and counterproposals usually led to a more favorable negotiation outcome. In light of the above, we posit that the number of proposals and counterproposals is a good indicator of the extent of clear information about the opposing negotiating party's needs and preferences which, in turn, may provide a better insight into the potential sources of conflicts and payoffs.

H_2:   The more negotiation experiences negotiators have, the more likely the imbalance between two negotiating parties will be reduced. In other words, a negotiator's negotiation skill is positively affected by the learning effect.

According to the classical French Jr. and Raven paradigm (1959), one of the important sources of social power is expertise. By analogy, a negotiator with the expertise may possess a stronger bargaining power. This notion was congruent with the study conducted by Kersten and Szapiro (1986) in that they viewed negotiation as a "knowledge-based" communication process. Since a negotiator may increase his/her expertise from one negotiation session to another, we can extend such a notion by hypothesizing that the negotiator with experiential learning will gain relative bargaining strength. Furthermore, Dwyer and Walker Jr. (1981) found that more powerful negotiators tended to make their initial offers closer to the ultimate agreement. Thus, we also postulate that negotiators with experiential learning tend to make their initial offers closer to the final agreed price and, consequently, reduce their bargaining range. However, despite the popularity of simulated experimental games in the negotiation literature (e.g., Pruitt & Kimmel, 1977), no prior study has paid attention to the negotiator's self-learning adaptation in the repeated experimental games.

H_3: Due to reciprocity, the lower initial offer of a buyer is likely encountered by the higher initial counteroffer of a supplier. In other words, highly incompatible initial offers will lead to more contentious or protracted bargaining.

In theory, a tough negotiator may gain favorable outcomes when the opposing negotiating party's aspirations or expectations are lowered (Schurr & Ozanne, 1985). The rationale may be that tougher negotiators tend to demand more from their opposing parties and, consequently, are likely to concede less than their opposing parties. Although bargaining toughness can lead to more favorable agreements for a negotiator, it may create more conflict due to the opposing negotiating party's reciprocal behavior. Putman and Jones (1982) suggested that negotiators would tend to match one another's bargaining stance and could create reciprocal responses. Thus we posit that the buyer's tough bargaining stance would be responded to by the supplier's reciprocal responses and, consequently, would prolong the negotiation process.

H_4: The high degree of contentiousness between negotiating parties will likely increase a frequency of communications. That is to say, a large difference between the supplier's initial offer and the buyer's initial offer tends to require more frequent communications between two negotiating parties.

Since contentious negotiation involves an effort to force one's will on another negotiating party, it is likely to favor one's own interest at the expense of another. In this situation, when both parties maintain a tough stance and become rigid in their demands, the negotiation process is likely to be much delayed (Pruitt, 1983). Bartos (1974) also indicated that tougher offers decreased the chances of agreement and could lead to a deadlock. Since a deadlock results in status-quo (i.e., zero) payoffs for both negotiating parties, efforts of getting out of a deadlock may require more interactions and, subsequently, take more time.

RESULTS AND DISCUSSIONS

To test hypothesis H_1, we designated the degree of a buyer's concession (i.e., a buyer's final agreed price — a buyer's initial offer) as a dependent variable, while using the number (frequency) of a supplier's proposals (or counterproposals) as an independent variable. As a preliminary testing procedure, Pearson correlation analysis was performed to detect any statistically significant relationships between the variables. Pearson correlation coefficient ($r = 0.252$) reveals that the degree of a buyer's concession is significantly correlated to the number of proposals made by his/her opponent (i.e., a supplier) at $\alpha = 0.001$. Since significant correlation was identified between the variables, we conducted additional statistical test by using a simple regression analysis. The result of a simple regression analysis verified that the degree of a buyer's concession is significantly related to the number of a supplier's proposals ($t = 3.586, p < 0.001$). By the same token, we designated the degree of a supplier's concession (i.e., a supplier's initial offer — a supplier's final agreed price) as a dependent variable, while using the number of a buyer's proposals as an independent variable. Both Pearson correlation coefficient ($r = 0.327, p < 0.001$) and simple regression ($t = 4.764, p < 0.001$) reveal that the extent of a supplier's concession is significantly correlated with the number (frequency) of a buyer's proposals. Therefore, hypothesis H_1 is fully supported by the test results.

To validate hypothesis H_2, we measured the difference between the supplier's degree of concession (a supplier's initial offer — a supplier's final agreed price) and the buyer's degree of concession (a buyer's final agreed price — a buyer's initial offer), and then compared the difference to determine who made more price concessions than his/her opponent. On the average, in the case of the first negotiation experiment involving the purchase of PCs, the buyers made approximately 54 percent more price concessions than did the suppliers. Another first negotiation experiment involving the purchase of a minivan showed that the buyers made an average of 67 percent more price concessions than did the suppliers. On the other hand, in case of the second negotiation experiment involving the purchase of a house, the same group of buyers made only 5 percent more price concessions than did the supplier. This result suggests that, as the negotiator gains more experience with additional negotiation exercise, he/she tends to settle at the price that is less skewed to either party. In other words, the more negotiation exercise a negotiator gets involved in, the more balance between two negotiating parties will be created. Therefore, H_2 is supported.

To test hypothesis H_3, Pearson correlation analyses were conducted for three separate negotiation experiments. Test results indicate that there is a negative correlation between the buyer's initial offer and the supplier's initial offer at $\alpha = 0.05$ ($p = 0.03$) for the negotiation experiment involving the purchase of a minivan, whereas we found no significant correlation between the buyer's initial offer for the other negotiation experiments involving the purchases of a PCs and a house. That is to say, we found the evidence of reciprocity only in the negotiation experiment involving the purchase of a minivan. Thus, H_3 is not fully supported by the test results.

Hypothesis H_4 was tested by measuring the extent of contentiousness (i.e., a supplier's initial offer — a buyer's initial offer) between two negotiating parties and its impact on the frequency of communication between the two parties (i.e., the number of proposals or counterproposals made by both the buyer and the supplier). Pearson correlation coefficient ($r = 0.370$) shows positive correlation between the degree of contentiousness and the number of a buyer's proposals at $\alpha = 0.01$ ($p < 0.001$). A simple regression analysis result confirms that the degree of contentiousness significantly affects the number of buyer proposals ($t = 5.468, p < 0.001$). Similarly, Pearson correlation coefficient ($r = 0.379$) and simple regression ($t = 5.645, p < 0.001$) reveal that the degree of contentiousness significantly affects the number of supplier proposals. These results indicate that the high degree of contentiousness between two negotiating parties leads to more frequent proposals and counterproposals between the buyer and the supplier. Thus, we fully support H_4.

NEGOTIATION RULE DISCOVERY THROUGH DATA MINING

In the prior section, we conducted a series of hypotheses testing to examine whether the negotiation outcome is significantly affected by the negotiator's learning experience and perceived expertise. However, as Glamour, Madigan, Pregibon and Smyth (1996) contended, hypothesis testing could be inconsistent unless the level of statistical significance was decreased as the sample size increased. Hypothesis testing is also limited to either substantiating or disproving a preconceived notion. In other words, although hypothesis testing may allow us to validate some of intuitive premises, causal inferences made by hypothesis testing may not be sufficient for us to accurately predict behavioral patterns of a negotiator in different negotiation settings. To overcome such a potential shortcoming, we employed data mining techniques. We also chose data mining techniques over traditional statistical techniques, due to their ability to integrate multiple data sources, remove inconsistent data, identify the truly interesting patterns and visualize the patterns in different forms. In general, data mining is a process of searching for previously unknown but meaningful information, such as decision-making patterns and trends, by sifting through large data sets and utilizing a combination of pattern-recognition, model-building and validation techniques. In particular, we used decision trees among various data mining methods due to its visual appeal and simplicity in setting useful rules. Decision trees aim to classify data into a finite number of classes by generating a hierarchy of IF-THEN statements (Menon & Sharda, 1999). To construct decision trees, we followed four major steps as shown in Figure 1 and described below.

Data collection: The raw data were collected using a structured questionnaire. The questionnaire contained 10 different questions related to the negotiator's initial offer, final agreed price, preparedness, perceived power, negotiation styles and the frequency of offers/counteroffers. One of the key pieces of information (i.e., descriptive statistics) that we obtained through this questionnaire was the final agreed price, which represents the negotiation outcome and, thus, indicates which negotiation party arrived at a favorable agreement.

Data formatting: The quality of a decision tree depends on the classification accuracy (Chen, Han & Yu, 1996). To improve the classification accuracy, we formatted data sets in such a way that they could be easily queried, and then their patterns could be specified with distinctive categories. Thus, all data sets were recorded and displayed in a spreadsheet format.

Data normalization: Our database contains three different sets of data summarizing the results of three negotiation experiments, involving the purchases of a PC, a house and a minivan. The scales on which these data are measured may differ from one experiment to another. For instance, the price range of a PC is quite different from that of a house. To extract more meaningful information from these data sets of different scales, we rescaled the given data sets through normalization.

Rule induction: Decision trees are intended to generate sets of rules that can be easily understood by a negotiator and can be replicated in other negotiation settings. These rules may give important clues as to how the supplier will respond to the buyer's offers/counteroffers and, consequently, help the buyer to formulate a winning negotiation strategy. Among a variety of algorithms, such as Classification and Regression

Figure 1. Steps of Data Mining

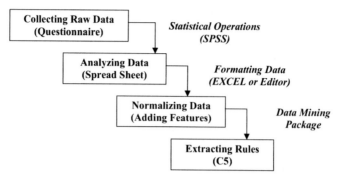

Trees (CART), C5 and Chi-squared Automatic Interaction Detection (CHAID), for building decision trees, we selected C5.0 due to its speed, small memory requirement and boosting and cross-validation features, which greatly improve predictive accuracy. Since C5.0 can generate rules that have a straightforward interpretation, it is also quite robust in the presence of problems, such as missing data and large numbers of fields (Statistical Packages for Social Sciences (SPSS) Inc., 2001). Basically, C5.0 is a decision-tree algorithm that was introduced by J. Ross Quinlan to produce trees with varying numbers of branches per node. By running C5.0 under the UNIX platform operating system, we developed the decision trees shown in Figures 2, 3 and 4.

Figure 2 graphically displays a collection of "IF-THEN" rules that classify the negotiation outcome as either "win" (favorable) or "loss" (unfavorable) to a particular negotiator (i.e., a buyer or a supplier), depending on where the final agreed price is set. In the case where both parties reach an agreement within the range of a middle ground

Figure 2. A Decision Tree Describing a Negotiation Rule Involving the Purchase of PC

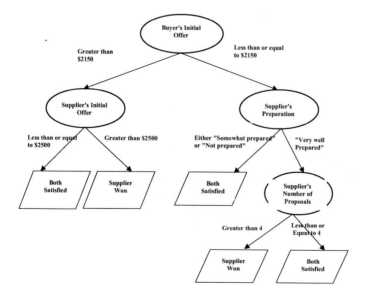

Figure 3. A Decision Tree Describing a Negotiation Rule Involving the Purchase of a House

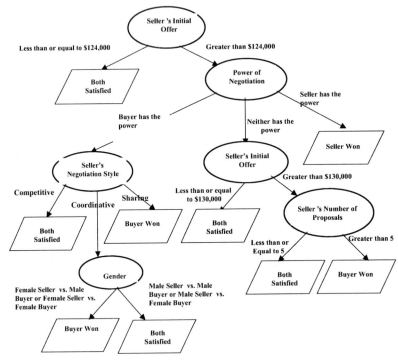

between the extreme initial offers of both parties, both parties are considered "winners" (satisfied with the settlement). A decision tree that developed a negotiation rule for the purchase of a PC was drawn with the root node at the top, child nodes at the middle and leaf nodes at the bottom (see Figure 2). Notice that this decision tree drawn by C5.0 includes only the rules that are really useful in formulating a negotiation strategy.

Figure 2 shows that a root node (i.e., the buyer's initial offer) has one child node in a left path (the supplier's initial offer) and two children in a right path (i.e., the supplier's preparedness, the number of proposals). Figure 2 illustrates that if the buyer's initial offer is greater than $2,150 (slightly above the average initial offer of the buyer) and is countered by the supplier's initial offer less than or equal to $2,500, then both the buyer and the supplier would be satisfied. On the other hand, if the same initial offer of the buyer is countered with the supplier's initial offer greater than $2,500 (slightly above the average final agreed price of $2,473), the supplier tends to have more favorable outcome than the buyer. This rule makes intuitive sense, because the supplier's tough initial stance usually helps increase his bargaining strength (Min et al., 1995). On the other hand, even though the buyer's initial offer is low (less than or equal to $2,150), if the supplier is very well prepared and interacts with the buyer frequently (greater than four times), the supplier still tends to obtain a favorable negotiation outcome.

A decision tree shown in Figure 3 has three children nodes with a mixture of binary and ternary paths. It illustrates negotiation rules dictating the purchase of a house. Highlighting some of the rules described in Figure 3, there are at least three ways that

Figure 4. A Decision Tree Describing a Negotiation Rule Involving the Purchase of a Minivan

a buyer can perform better than his counterpart. First, if the seller's initial offer is greater than $124,000 (approximately $10,000 or 8 percent above the average final agreed price), but such a seller is encountered with the buyer who has the power (negotiation leverage) and he/she exhibits a less aggressive (i.e., sharing) negotiation style, the buyer tends to obtain the more favorable outcome than the seller. Interested readers should refer to Perdue, Day and Michaels (1986) for an excellent classification of negotiation styles. Second, in a similar situation where the female seller makes an initial offer greater than $124,000 and maintains a collaborative negotiation style against a buyer who has the power (e.g., a seller is more anxious to reach an agreement than the buyer), then the buyer is likely to obtain the more favorable outcome than the seller.

Third, if the seller, who feels neither he/she nor the buyer has the distinctive negotiation advantage over his/her counterpart, makes an initial offer greater than $130,000, and interacts with the buyer frequently (more than five times), the buyer is likely to obtain the more favorable outcome than the seller. Other IF-THEN rules can be created by following the paths from the root to each leaf depicted in Figure 3. Figure 4 illustrates a simple decision tree representing two possible outcomes: (1) If the supplier's initial offer is approximately 3.3 percent above the average final agreed price of $130,570, then the supplier emerges with the more favorable outcome than the buyer. (2) Otherwise, both parties will be satisfied with the negotiation outcome.

FUTURE TRENDS

In this chapter we used data mining techniques to extract valid, potentially useful and meaningful patterns from the negotiation data. Although some of the patterns simply confirmed the conclusions drawn from the traditional statistical data analysis, others produced an interesting and novel insight into the process of developing winning negotiation strategy. Despite the proven merits of the proposed data mining techniques, there are avenues for future research that extend the current study. These avenues include:

1.   The current database can be expanded to include larger numbers of negotiation experiments through which we can develop "scalable" data mining algorithms. In particular, the inclusion of dynamic (nonstationary) data may capture changes in negotiation behavior over time.

2. The future study may integrate all the steps of knowledge discovery process by linking a database, machine learning, statistics and information retrieval. Such integration can be a stepping stone for developing an expert system from the negotiation rules that we have already discovered.

3. Further research is needed to refine the proposed data mining algorithm in such a way that we can improve the interpretability of sets of negotiation rules. Rather than IF-THEN rules that we developed in this study, future research may use different forms of representing patterns. These forms include neural networks and mathematical equations.

CONCLUSION

As a growing number of purchasing professionals cope with countless contract negotiations with suppliers, their professional success has often paralleled their purchasing negotiation success. Recognizing such a trend, this study examined the impact of the buyer's experiential learning, initial offer, preparedness, perceïved power, the number of proposals/counterproposals, gender and negotiating styles on the negotiation outcome. From a practical point of view, several findings are noteworthy.

First, the most important finding is that, the negotiator's bargaining strength seems to increase with greater negotiation experiences as evidenced by the fact that the final settlement is less skewed to either the buyer or the supplier with increased participation in negotiation exercises. That is to say, there is a learning effect. This finding reassures our intuitive prediction that the negotiator would perform better as he/she gains more experience.

Second, an increase in the number of proposals/counterproposals made by a negotiator will likely enhance his/her bargaining strength. The possible explanation for this finding is that as the negotiator interacts with his/her opposing party more frequently, he/she would learn more about his/her opposing party's accommodation limits, desired goals, bargaining position and sense of urgency for a deal (e.g., how badly the buyer or the supplier wants the deal). In particular, the high degree of contentiousness (a large differential between the initial offer of a supplier and that of a buyer) is likely to require more frequent communications between both negotiation parties because frequent communications may help them search for alternative solutions together and then arrive at a settlement that is mutually satisfactory.

Although one who starts with a more demanding initial offer is likely to obtain more favorable negotiation terms at the end of negotiation, a tougher initial stance alone will not necessarily dictate the final negotiation outcome. Indeed, a tougher initial stance may simply increase the chance of unwanted deadlocks and affect the negotiation outcome negatively. As our data mining results indicated, some combination of an initial offer, negotiation styles, perceived power, communication frequency and sex-role composition exerted more influence on the negotiation outcome than toughness of an initial offer. Therefore, in formulating a successful purchasing negotiation strategy, one should consider a multitude of variables comprised of personality characteristics, market conditions, power balance, mutual dependence and experiences.

ACKNOWLEDGMENT

The authors would like to express sincere gratitude to Dr. David Page of the University of Wisconsin-Madison (USA) for providing valuable suggestions on the earlier draft of this paper.

REFERENCES

Agrawal, R., & Srikant, R. (1995). Mining sequential patterns. *Proceedings of International Conferences in Data Engineering* (pp. 3-4), Taipei, Taiwan.

Alexander, J. F., Schul, P. L., & Babakus, E. (1991). Analyzing interpersonal communications in industrial marketing negotiations. *Journal of the Academy of Marketing Science, 19*(2), 129-139.

Bartos, O. J. (1974). *Process and outcome of negotiation.* New York: Columbia University Press.

Baxevanis, A., & Ouellette, B. F. (1998). *Bioinformatics: A practical guide to the analysis of genes and proteins.* New York: John Wiley & Sons.

Berson, A., Smith, S., & Thearing, K. (1999). *Building data mining applications for CRM.* New York: McGraw-Hill.

Bloom, H. (1984). Principles and techniques of negotiation. *Guide to Purchasing.* Tempe, AZ: National Association of Purchasing Management.

Burt, D. N. (1982). Simulated negotiations: An experiment. *Journal of Purchasing and Materials Management, 18*(1), 6-8.

Chen, M., Han, J., & Yu, P. S. (1996). Data mining: An overview from database perspectives. *IEEE Transactions on Knowledge and Data Engineering, 8*(6), 866-883.

Chen, Q., Hsu, M., & Dayal, U. (2000). A data-warehouse/OLAP framework for scalable telecommunication tandem traffic analysis. *Proceedings of International Conference in Data Engineering* (pp. 201-210). San Diego, CA.

Clopton, S. W. (1984). Seller and buying firm factors affecting industrial buyers' negotiation behavior and outcomes. *Journal of Marketing Research, 11,* 39-53.

Dabholkar, P. A., Johnston, W. J., & Cathey, A. S. (1994). The dynamics of long-term business-to-business exchange relationships. *Journal of the Academy of Marketing Science, 22,* 130-145.

Day, R. L., Michaels, R. E., & Perdue, B. C. (1988). How buyers handle conflicts. *Industrial Marketing Management, 17,* 153-160.

Dwyer, F. R. (1984). Are two better than one? Bargaining behavior and outcomes in an asymmetrical power relationship. *Journal of Consumer Research, 11,* 680-693.

Dwyer, F. R., & Walker Jr., O. C. (1981). Bargaining in an asymmetrical power structure. *Journal of Marketing, 45,* 104-115.

Evans, E. F., & Steele, P. T. (1982, December). Preparing yourself for the negotiation. *Procurement Weekly, 16,* 8-9.

Eyuboglu, N., & Buja, A. (1993). Dynamics of Channel Negotiations: Contention and Reciprocity. *Psychology and Marketing,* 10(1), 47-65.

French, Jr., J. R. P., & Raven, B. (1959). The bases of social power. In D. Cartwright (Ed.), *Studies in social power* (pp. 150-167). Ann Arbor, MI: University of Michigan.

Gibson, S., Kreinovivh, V., Longpre, L., Penn, B., & Starks, S. A. (2001). Intelligent mining in image databases, with application to satellite imaging and to Web search. In A. Kandel, M. Last & H. Bunke (Eds.), *Data mining and computational intelligence* (pp. 309-336). Warsaw, Poland: Physica-Verlag.

Glamour, C., Madigan, D., Pregibon, D., & Smyth, P. (1996). Statistical inference and data mining. *Communications of the ACM, 39*(11), 35-41.

Graham, J. L. (1986). The problem-solving approach to interorganizational negotiations: A laboratory test. *Journal of Business Research, 14,* 271-286.

Greenhalgh, L., Neslin, S. A., & Gilkey, R. W. (1985). The effects of negotiator preferences, situational power, and negotiator personality on outcomes of business negotiations. *Academy of Management Journal, 28,* 9-33.

Han, J., & Kamber, M. (2001). *Data mining: Concepts and techniques.* San Francisco, CA: Morgan Kaufman.

Hand, D., Mannila, H., & Smyth, P. (2001). *Principles of data mining.* Cambridge, MA: The MIT Press.

Heinritz, S., Farrell, P. V., Giunipero, L., & Kolchin, M. (1991). *Purchasing: Principles and applications* (8th ed.). Englewood Cliffs, NJ: Prentice-Hall.

Higgins, R. C. (1997). *Analysis for financial management.* New York: Irwin/McGraw-Hill.

Hill, T., O'Connor, M., & Remus, W. (1996). Neural network models for time series forecast. *Management Science, 42*(7), 1082-1092.

Hogarth, R. (1981). Beyond discrete baises: Functional and dysfunctional aspects of judgmental heuristics. *Pyschological Bulletin, 90,* 197-217.

Karass, C. L. (1974). *Give and take: The complete guide to negotiating strategies and tactics.* New York: Thomas Y. Crowell Co.

Kersten, G. E. (1988). A procedure for negotiating efficient and non-efficient compromises. *Decision Support Systems, 4,* 167-177.

Kersten, G. E., & Szapiro, T. (1986). Generalized approach to modeling negotiations. *European Journal of Operational Research, 26,* 124-142.

King, Jr., W. C., & Hinson, T. D. (1994). The influence of sex and equity sensitivity on relationship preferences, assessment of opponent, and outcomes in a negotiation experiment. *Journal of Management, 20*(3), 605-624.

Long, B. G. (1993). Training your negotiating team for success. *NAPM Insights, 3,* 14-15.

McFillen, J. M., Reck, R. R., & Benton, W. C. (1983). An experiment in purchasing negotiations. *Journal of Purchasing and Materials Management, 19*(2), 2-8.

Menon, S., & Sharda, R. (1999). Data mining update: New models to pursue old objectives. *OR/MS Today, 26*(3), 26-29.

Min, H., LaTour, M., & Jones, M. (1995). The effects of a negotiator's initial offer, time, gender, and team size on negotiation outcomes. *International Journal of Purchasing and Materials Management, 31*(4), 19-24.

Min, H., Min, H., & Emam, A. (2002). A data mining approach to developing a profile of hotel customers. *International Journal of Contemporary Hospitality Management, 14*(6), 274-285.

Nierenberg, G. I. (1983, February). Negotiation strategies and counter strategies: How to develop win/win techniques. *Management Review,* 48-49.

Perdue, B. C. (1989). The size and composition of the buying firm's negotiating team in rebuys of component parts. *Journal of the Academy of Marketing Science, 17,* 121-128.

Perdue, B. C., Day, R. L., & Michaels, R. E. (1986). Negotiation styles of industrial buyers. *Industrial Marketing Management, 15,* 171-176.

Pruitt, D. G. (1983). Strategic choice in negotiation. *American Behavioral Scientist, 27*(2), 167-194.

Pruitt, D. G., & Kimmel, M. J. (1977). Twenty years of experimental gaming: critique, synthesis, and suggestions for the future. *Annual Reviews Psychology, 28,* 363-392.

Pruitt, D. G., & Lewis, S. A. (1975). Development of integrative solutions in bilateral negotiations. *Journal of Personality and Social Psychology, 31,* 621-633.

Purchasing Staff Report. (1962, March). How to negotiate-part III. *Purchasing, 12,* 87-89.

Putman, L. L., & Jones, T. S. (1982). Reciprocity in negotiations: An analysis of bargaining interaction. *Communication Monographs, 49,* 171-191.

Rubin, J. Z., & Brown, B. R. (1975). *The social psychology of bargaining and negotiation.* New York: Academic Press.

Schurr, P. H., & Ozanne, J. L. (1985). Influence on exchange processes: Buyer's preconceptions of a seller's trustworthiness and bargaining toughness. *Journal of Consumer Research, 11,* 939-953.

Stagner, R., & Rosen, H. (1965). *Psychology of Union-Management Relations.* Monterey, CA: Wadsworth.

Statistical Packages for Social Sciences (SPSS) Inc. (2000). *SPSS base 10.0 user's guide.* Chicago, IL: Author.

Statistical Packages for Social Sciences (SPSS) Inc. (2001). *Clementine 6.0 user's guide.* Chicago, IL: Author.

Wesphal, C., & Blaxton, T. (1998). *Data mining solutions: Methods and tools for solving real-world problems.* New York: John Wiley & Sons.

APPENDIX

Exit Questionnaire

1. Do you have an agreement?
    (1) Yes   (2) No

2. What was your initial offer (in dollar terms) for the negotiation?

3. What was your negotiated price after the final settlement?

4. In general, how prepared are you for this negotiation?
    (1) Very prepared   (2) Somewhat prepared   (3) Not prepared

5. Who do you think has the power (leverage) for this negotiation?
    (1) Seller   (2) Buyer   (3) Neither

6. Identify your negotiation style during the negotiation.
    (1) Collaborative   (2) Competitive   (3) Sharing

7. Generally, how would you rate the results of your negotiation?
    (1) Outstanding   (2) Very good   (3) Good
    (4) Fair   (5) Poor

8. Do you think you improved your negotiation skills compared with your previous
    role-playing game? If so, how much?
    (1) Substantial improvement   (2) Minor improvement
    (3) Same as before   (4) Worse than before

9. Negotiation Worksheet

Number of proposals	Price of your offer	Price of seller's counteroffer

Chapter IX

Mining Meaning: Extracting Value from Virtual Discussions

William L. Tullar
University of North Carolina at Greensboro, USA

ABSTRACT

This chapter focuses on the pattern detection and extraction step in text data commonly called text data mining. I examine some of the literature on natural language processing and propose a method of recovering value from the text of virtual group discussions based on methods derived from the communication field. Then, I apply the method in a case using data from 216 different groups from a virtual group experiment. The results from the case show that higher performing groups are characterized by higher frequencies of acts of dominance and higher frequencies of terms concerning cognition, communication and praise. Higher performing groups were also characterized by lower frequencies of acts of equivalence and lower frequencies of leveling terms and numerical terms. Ways to use this knowledge to improve the groups' performance are discussed.

INTRODUCTION

Text mining may be considered a subspecialty of the broader domain of Knowledge Discovery from Data. This in turn can be defined as the computational process of extracting useful information from huge amounts of data by mapping low-level data into richer, more abstract forms and by detecting meaningful patterns implicitly present in the data. Knowledge Discovery from Data is typically conducted on structured, relational databases, and data mining is one of its subtasks. When the data are ill-structured text data, the data mining process becomes somewhat more difficult. Moreover, data mining itself is only one of the steps within the Knowledge Discovery from Data process. The full process usually includes data storage and access, data cleansing, pattern detection and extraction and data interpretation. Data mining refers more narrowly to the particular step of applying specific algorithms for detecting and extracting patterns (Liddy, 2000).

This chapter focuses only on the pattern detection and extraction step in text data. It proposes one method of recovering value from the text of virtual group or team discussions and deliberations. Thus, mining meaning in the text of group discussions requires an approach that is iterative between human and machine. It is my purpose here to outline a strategy for recovering valuable meaning from this data.

MINING TEXT DATA

Large text databases potentially contain a great wealth of knowledge. However, text represents factual information (and information about the author's communicative intentions) in a complex but opaque manner. Unlike numerical and fixed field data, it cannot be analyzed by standard statistical data mining methods. Relying on human analysis results in either huge workloads or the analysis of only a tiny fraction of the database (Nasukowa & Nagano, 2001). Mining text data is the science and art of extracting meaningful factual information from masses of text, usually by means other than the statistical approaches that have produced value in numerical and fixed-field data.

Many of the most successful text mining systems are focused on document retrieval. But in order to begin extracting the full value out of text, a truly useful system must go beyond simple retrieval. It must provide a broad range of information access and analytic capabilities. The way that text mining can accomplish this goal is through reliance on Natural Language Processing (NLP). NLP consists of a range of computational techniques for analyzing and representing naturally occurring texts at all levels of linguistic analysis to achieve human-like language processing that can support this kind of analysis. A fully featured text miner should be one that combines both information retrieval and text mining capabilities (Liddy, 2000). Such a technology would:

- detect the specific sources that contain information worth mining;
- recognize and extract meaningful entities that convey valuable knowledge;
- produce a semantic interpretation of the information;
- store the semantically interpreted information in an efficient data structure; and
- provide means for easy access and utilization of this knowledge base for new insights or for utilization in decision-making tasks.

Several firms (e.g., IBM and SAS) are hard at work at producing text miners that can do all these things. SAS has recently acquired the rights to use Inxight's LinguistX Platform, a natural-language text solution for analyzing words, phrases and sentences, and Inxight's Thing Finder, which identifies and extracts from documents key content, such as company names, products, people, addresses and dates. SAS offers a product called Text Miner that takes advantage of Inxight's technology for analyzing documents that contain text in a variety of languages. Text Miner can access and run analysis against as many as 15 types of data files, including unstructured data sets, such as e-mail, Microsoft Office applications and PDF and HTML files (Sullivan, 2002).

GROUP DISCUSSION TEXT MINING

Text mining in group discussions offers a number of organizationally valuable outcomes. First, it would allow managers to monitor the performance of groups, especially groups that have a long-term life. Second, it would allow the assessment of group process so that managers could see the points at which virtual groups become bogged down or lose track of their objective. Third, it would help to prevent free riding and social loafing. If group members knew that the discussions are monitored by an efficient text miner, they would be more likely to participate actively in group work. Fourth, text mining could also help managers to alter group process for the better. They could remove unproductive or disruptive group members; they could form better groups by choosing the right mix of skills and abilities; they could provide better training for group members and they could provide facilitation for those groups that need it.

Group process — the text of the discussion — is all that groups have to accomplish their goals. Every working day teams of workers separated by geography and sometimes by time communicate using the Internet and various types of software. However, such virtual groups face many of the problems common to traditional face-to-face groups, plus some additional ones (Maznevski & Chudoba, 2000). Some studies have shown that virtual groups may suffer from free riding (Tullar, Kaiser & Beach, 2000), social loafing (Suleiman, 1998) and inferior group product (Shaila & Bostrum, 1999). In addition, there are a number of well-explored problems such as groupshift and groupthink that have yet to be studied in geographically distributed virtual groups. Text mining could potentially help interventions in all these group problems.

Communication among virtual group members occurs at two levels: the relational level and the content level. It is likely that differences between satisfying and dissatisfying, successful and unsuccessful groups lie in the interaction that takes place (Glauser & Tullar, 1985). Having the text of the group's discussions available for examination provides the data miner with the opportunity to see the extent to which satisfying and dissatisfying or successful and unsuccessful groups differ from each other in terms of relational control and content. Moreover, it allows the possibility of classifying ALL the groups in the text data base in terms of their interaction. As we shall see, this permits forming teams instead of groups and better facilitation of group interaction once the team is formed.

RELATIONAL CONTROL

A substantial number of researchers and therapists have argued for the application of a systems theory approach to the study of human interaction (e.g., Friedlander & Heatherington, 1989, 1990). Much of the foundational work for this was done in the '70s and '80s (e.g., Fisher, 1975, 1983; Fisher, Glover, & Ellis, 1977; Fisher & Hawes, 1971;

Hawes, 1973; Watson, 1982a, b). Called the pragmatic perspective, this approach produces a set of basic propositions which were explicated in other publications (Fisher, 1978, 1983). For our purposes in this chapter, the following principles will suffice: (a) communication occurs in a social system, in this case a virtual group or team; (b) communicative acts constrain future communication behavior so that unique patterns in communication develop and recur in communication among group members; (c) the structure of the system is defined by the redundancy or predictability of its recurring communication patterns; and (d) the function of a system is determined by the nature and complexity of its communication patterns.

The pragmatic perspective holds that a clear understanding of the functioning of any group requires the empirical elaboration of the communication patterns relevant to that group. The important observable components of a communication system are codable units of verbal or, in this case, written conversational behavior. The smallest codable unit is an act — one single statement written by a group member. A larger unit of communication is called an interact. This unit of analysis is a contiguous pair of messages — the antecedent and subsequent acts together comprising a single interact (Glauser & Tullar, 1985). From the standpoint of mining virtual group data, interacts are problematic. Such discussions are usually done in threads and branches. Since there is a variable amount of time between the addition of each thread and each branch, it is often quite difficult to say to which previous thread a new thread relates. The character of discussion boxes is that often a remark is made in a branch that refers to a remark that someone else made in the previous branch. Thus, it is not possible to pair acts into interacts. However, it is possible to classify the basic acts.

While it is true that much of the developmental work in this area was done on interacts, the acts themselves to a large extent determine the affective responses and outcomes experienced by group members. It is reciprocal behavior — what is written in response to something someone else has written — that characterizes the relationships that develop in groups. This methodology has been used to investigate interaction patterns in decision-making groups for more than 25 years (e.g., Ellis, 1979; Ellis & Fisher, 1975; Glauser, 1984; Hirokawa, 1980; Mabry, 1975).

Relational control itself is measured with category systems based on Bateson's (1958) three functions of relational communication: attempts to dominate (one-up), attempts to be equivalent (one-across) and attempts to be submissive (one-down). Ellis (1976) refined and extended these categories. He broke dominance down into dominance and structuring, left equivalence the same and broke submission down into deference and submission. Dominance is usually said to restrict the behavioral options of the other party. Dominance in this system is giving responses of nonsupport, demanding an answer to a question, not answering others' questions and changing the subject. Structuring is an attempt to restrict the behavioral options of the other person, while leaving a variety of options open. Examples of structuring would be expanding on a previous statement in the conversation or extending the discussion to a new topic. Equivalence is usually an attempt at mutual identification. It would include statements like "that's interesting" or "tell me more about that." Deference is an attempt to relinquish behavioral options to another, while retaining some choice of options. Examples of deference would be statements like "don't you think so?" or "isn't it true that ... ?" Deference questions are not seeking information so much as seeking support from other group members. Last, there is submissiveness. This is an attempt to relinquish almost all behavioral options and retain little or no choice at all. A submissive statement might be a question such as "how should we solve this?" or "what do you think we should do?"

Glauser and Tullar (1985) in a study of police/citizen interaction found that dissatisfying interactions were characterized by a higher frequency of dominance acts and a lower frequency of structuring acts by police officers. They reasoned that this result was due to the fact that both the officer and the citizen were trying to control the conversation, and both were frustrated in their attempts to do so by the other. Greater amounts of structuring in the conversations meant that the police officers were providing more information and guidance, and this was found in more satisfying conversations.

More recently, Courtright, Fairhurst, and Rogers (1989) examined relational control in different types of organizations. They compared a plant with an organic, self-managing team philosophy to a plant managed by a mechanistic, authority-based philosophy. They found that interchanges in the authority-based plant were characterized by competitive interchanges, interruptions and statements of nonsupport and typified interaction at the authority-based plant. They interpreted these findings as empirical support for theories suggesting that communicative forms are consultative in organic systems and command-like in mechanistic systems.

Heatherington and Friedlander (1990) in their studies of relational control in family therapy concluded that better therapy results were associated with families that evidenced complementary (one up/one down) rather than symmetrical interactions (one up/one up). Buchanan (1997), in a dissertation using Heatherington and Friedlander's (1987) methodology, found that the more interaction was characterized by openness in the interaction, then the groups' perception of their openness differentiated the quality of their decision-making processes and effectiveness. That is, groups that dominated less and showed more structuring and equivalence produced better outcomes.

These results indicate that poorer group process is characterized by a preponderance of dominating, whereas better group interaction is characterized by more structuring. Though this is not always the case, for purposes of data mining this is a reasonable place to begin searching for reasons for group ineffectiveness.

CONTENT

Content has been a major focus of text mining. Since Bales (1950) introduced his content coding scheme more than five decades ago, researchers have been examining the content of group discussions. The content level refers to "what is said" in interaction. Therefore, content is focused on informational and topical issues. For purposes of mining text, it is important that the content categories engage the topics and information. In order insure this, it is necessary to use a grounded-theory approach to make certain that the category system actually engages the discussion. Failure to identify key content categories or failure to develop a full understanding of the categories in their context could lead to trivial or embarrassing findings (Neuendorf, 2002).

Some readers, who are accustomed to the idea that hypotheses should always occur before proceeding to empirical work, may find this approach troubling. However, experience (mine and hundreds of others who have tried them) with a priori category systems have found categories that don't contain a single hit in all the data. Moreover, it is often true that when extreme cases are considered (e.g., highly satisfying versus highly unsatisfying groups), there is no difference at all between them on the content categories that have been used.

The approach I am taking here proceeds in part from Glaser and Strauss' (1967) original formulation of grounded theory. Grounded theory is based on the premise that we don't understand what part of group process actually causes performance problems. As group structures are produced and reproduced, the unfolding of each group is different depending on the contingencies that govern behavior in the group (Giddens, 1979, 1984). Since virtual groups' discussions are written, it is a simple matter to examine the transcript of the group discussion after the discussion has concluded. A careful examination of these discussions will often reveal the process and content factors in the group that lead to success or failure.

The traditional grounded-theory approach requires that we develop a well integrated set of concepts that provide a thorough theoretical explanation of the social phenomenon under study. Data collection and analysis are linked in grounded theory. This linkage enables the researcher to capture all potentially relevant aspects of the topic as soon as they are perceived (Strauss & Corbin, 1998). The investigator must carefully read through the transcript of several groups located at the extremes of some criterion of group effectiveness to build an explanation of group performance. Choosing whether to base the theory on group performance or group satisfaction will make a considerable difference in the content categories arrived at. It is not advisable to assume that because a category scheme discriminates well between high satisfaction and low satisfaction groups that it also discriminates well between high performing and low performing groups.

The approach of finding two sets of groups at the extreme ends of some criterion variable is often called the extreme case study method. Stake (2000) notes that "... a researcher may jointly study a number of cases in order to investigate a phenomenon, population or general condition" (p. 437). While Stake cautions his readers about potential false inferences that may result from focusing on separation of groups by one variable, it is precisely this risk that must be taken in order devise a useful category scheme.

As noted above, it is critical to choose the proper criterion by which to measure group behavior and, thus, classify the groups into the best and worst cases. In most instances, virtual groups produce some product: a decision, a recommendation or a report. The outcomes can be scored by two or more judges. While it is often quite difficult to differentiate among the performances close to the average, it is usually possible to isolate a few truly outstanding groups and a few truly abysmal ones. By this means the investigation of the discussions of hundreds or thousands of groups can be reduced to the five to 10 best and the five to 10 worst. This renders the task of carefully reading the full text of the group interaction manageable.

Armed with the content categories and a dictionary of words and phrases that emerge from this reading, the data miner can do category counts for individuals, for groups and for the whole sample. Moreover, in this phase, it is imperative to prepare the dictionary of phrases that classify one act into a given content category. This is an iterative process. That is, one uses the content system to classify each act and then examines the classification of acts to check for correctness of classification of actual text.

It is usually necessary to refine the dictionary a number of times before classification accuracy is satisfactory.

The process I have outlined above is not currently in use in any organization. In order to explicate this process, I have included the following case. The case shows how data on virtual groups could be mined to produce valuable data on group process that could improve the efficiency and effectiveness of virtual groups in any organization.

CASE

Participants: Participants were 1,164 volunteer college students from three different universities working in 216 virtual groups. All participants had sufficient typing and computer skills to use the Internet and participate in a threaded discussion. All of them had been previously trained to use the computers in laboratories where the experiments were held. Thus, they were familiar with the lab and the computers there, so no instruction time on computers was necessary. Groups were made up of five or six students each.

Procedure: Participants were given materials on a fictitious position at a fictitious university, Pine Ridge State. Via a Web page, they were given the candidates' résumés and a position description as well as a description of the university. Participants were distributed at various computer labs in two different universities. The experiment was conducted in such a way that participants could log on and participate in the experiment when they chose to.

Each subject was randomly assigned to a group. Each group met online through a threaded discussion format. An example of the discussion boxes used is shown in Figure 1. The participants discussed (threads) are listed down the left hand side of the page, and comments on the participants (branches) are listed on the right hand side of the page. Participants were asked to rate three candidates for an international programs director's position. After they read all the materials, they were asked to rate the three candidates

Figure 1. Discussion Box Format Used to Gather Participants' Discussions

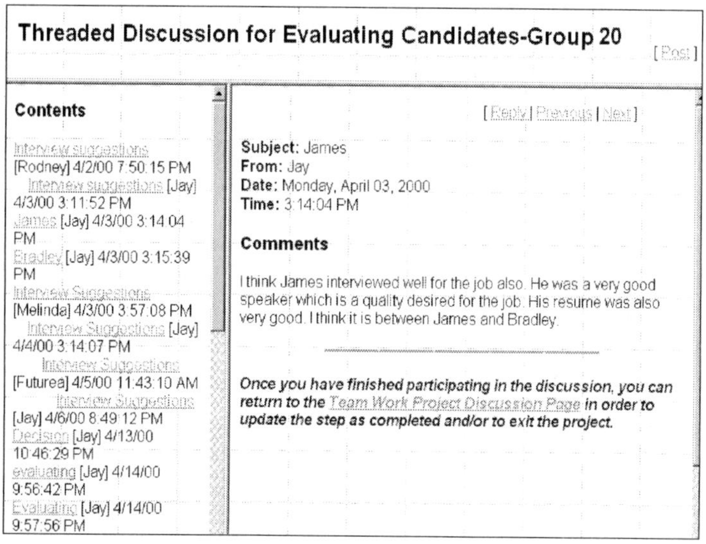

on their overall suitability for the job based on their paper credentials. Then they saw 20-minute digitized videos of each of the three candidates being interviewed by a professional interviewer. They then participated in a lengthy threaded group discussion (three weeks) as to which of the candidates was best for the job. At the conclusion of the discussion, they rated the three candidates again and then tried to come to a group consensus in order to write a memo of recommendation for one candidate. All the stimulus materials were displayed, all discussions were carried on and all ratings were performed via the Web page. The entire experiment was completed in less than four weeks.

Criterion Measure: The measure used was the distance of the group's consensus solution from the ideal. Human resource experts ($N = 15$) rated each of the candidates on a scale of 1 to 100. The average of their ratings was said to be the ideal. The absolute value of the difference between each group's ratings and the expert ratings summed across all three candidates was the distance score.

High Criterion and Low Criterion Groups

Using the measure described above, the 10 best and 10 worst groups of the 216 were identified. Five of the 10 best were chosen randomly to be in the validation group and the rest were place in the cross-validation group. The same was done with the low criterion groups.

For the relational control portion of the study, a special dictionary of words and phrases found in a manual coding of the validation sample was constructed. The manual coding was done by the author and a graduate student, coding independently of one another using Atlas ti. The high criterion and low criterion groups were mixed so that neither coder knew whether she/he was coding a high or low criterion group. Five high criterion and five low criterion groups were included in the reliability test of the manual coding. Two hundred and five total acts were included in the reliability check. The reliability estimate of this coding using Guetzkow's coefficient (Guetzkow, 1950) was 0.85. This compares favorably with similar estimates of reliability for this type of coding (e.g., Tullar, 1989).

Based on the phrases that the two coders agreed on, using Diction, special dictionaries were made of phrases that commonly indicated each of the relational categories. The statistics displayed in Table 1 are based on counts from those dictionaries.

For the content portion of this study, the author and a graduate student went through the list of content categories commonly counted by Diction 5.0. They carefully read a sample of text from three high and three low criterion groups. Based on this reading, they independently chose eight of the 31 constructs that Diction scores as being likely to differentiate between high criterion and low criterion groups. Since both knew the words that the dictionaries actually count, they were simply estimating the different use of words in the two groups.

Cross Validation

Both the high criterion and the low criterion groups were divided into a validation sample of five groups and a cross-validation sample of five groups. This is to ensure that the results are not simply taking maximum advantage of chance. In the case of relational control, it was not possible to do a statistical test of cross validation, but only to see that the results were similar in the two samples. In the case of content, 0.8 of a standard score was chosen as an arbitrary standard. Since the content analysis involves word counts, ordinary statistical analysis is generally meaningless, since the counts are in the thousands and any tiny difference will be statistically significant. The 0.8 rule was chosen so that a very substantial, practical difference had to occur in order to claim that the construct differentiated between the high criterion and low criterion groups in both validation and cross-validation samples.

RESULTS

Table 1 shows the results for the relational measures. As may be seen from this table, the 10 most accurate groups and the 10 least accurate groups were randomly split into a five group validation and five group cross-validation sample. In the validation sample, the five groups produced 114 total acts (threads) classified. Both the validation and the cross-validation sample produce χ^2 statistics of 3.97 and 15.11, respectively. Both of these are significant at $p < 0.05$.

The high performing group differed from the low performing group on two of the four relational measures. High performing groups were characterized by more than twice as high a frequency of one up pluses as the low performing groups. In the cross-validation sample, the difference is even stronger, where the frequency of one up plus is almost three times that of the low performing groups.

There is relatively little difference between the one ups in the high performing as opposed to the low performing groups in the validation sample or the cross-validation sample. There is, however, a considerable difference between the equivalences in both the validation and cross-validation samples. Low performing groups had percentages of 43 and 46 in the validation and cross-validation groups, whereas high performing groups had 34 and 23, respectively. Clearly, there was a relational difference between high performing and low performing groups: high performers did more dominating and less

Table 1. Relational Control in High Performing and Low Performing Groups

Validation Sample

Criterion Group		1 up +	1 up	1 across	1 down	Totals
High Performing	Count	19	40	39	16	114
n = 5	Percent	.17	.35	.34	.15	
Low Performing	Count	9	36	41	14	100
n = 5	Percent	.08	.36	.43	.14	

$\chi^2 = 3.97, p < .05$

Cross Validation Sample

Criterion Group		1 up +	1 up	1 across	1 down	Totals
High Performing	Count	30	66	35	21	152
n = 5	Percent	.20	.43	.23	.14	
Low Performing	Count	6	29	37	9	81
n = 5	Percent	.07	.36	.46	.10	

$\chi^2 = 15.11, p < .01$

Table 2.   Content Analysis of Discussions in High Performing and Low Performing Groups

Validation Sample

Standard Dictionary Totals	Low Performing Groups (n = 5) 5385 words		High Performing Groups (n = 5) 7334 words	
Variable	% words analyzed	Standard Score	% words analyzed	Standard Score
Cognition	2.67	0.81	3.53	1.69
Communication	1.66	0.27	2.62	1.27
Leveling Terms	2.16	0.50	1.13	-0.83
Numerical Terms	12.56	7.48	10.53	6.11
Praise	1.64	0.59	2.46	1.79
Rapport	2.12	4.31	1.29	2.13
Satisfaction	2.09	2.56	1.37	1.26
Temporal Terms	1.60	-1.05	2.87	-0.11

Cross Validation Sample

Standard Dictionary Totals	Low Performing Groups (n = 5) 13,324 words		High Performing Groups (n = 5) 13, 278 words	
Variable	% words analyzed	Standard Score	% words analyzed	Standard Score
Cognition *	2.47	0.61	2.76	1.82
Communication *	1.50	0.11	2.53	1.18
Leveling Terms *	2.40	0.80	1.55	-0.29
Numerical Terms *	16.14	9.91	8.90	5.00
Praise *	2.21	1.43	2.75	2.23
Rapport	0.40	1.18	1.05	1.52
Satisfaction	0.70	0.08	0.82	0.28
Temporal Terms	2.88	-0.11	1.84	-0.88

* Variable holds up on cross validation

equivalence. This is not what we would have expected. Glauser and Tullar (1985) found that higher frequencies of dominance by police officers lead to less citizen satisfaction. However, as noted above, it is difficult to say what relational control category should be associated with better performing groups. Empirically, at least for this type of group and setting, it appears that higher frequencies of dominance and lower frequencies of equivalence are associated with better decisions.

Table 2 shows the same groups' discussions content analyzed. The eight constructs chosen based on a careful reading of the text did show differences on the validation sample, but only five of them held up on cross validation: cognition, communication, leveling terms, numerical terms and praise. The other three constructs washed out in cross validation. No statistical tests of significance are included in these tables, since the sample sizes are so large. Instead, as noted above, the critical difference between the high and the low performing groups was set at 0.80 of a standard score. Only if the construct differentiated the two groups by at least that much and in the same order in both samples was the cross validation deemed accomplished.

Cognition shows a lower frequency for high performing groups in both the validation and cross-validation samples. This means that words from the cognition dictionary showed up with a lower frequency in high performing groups than in low performing groups. The cognition dictionary features words such as: analysis, belief, choose, compare, etc. The words are those that indicate that the interaction was about thought and its products. It is not surprising that the better performing groups in this analysis had more of their interaction concerned with thought and its products — the groups were chosen by the criterion of which of them made the best decision.

The next area that showed a consistent difference between the high and low performing groups across validation and cross-validation samples was communication. The communication dictionary contained words such as: acknowledge, advise, advocate, agree, speak, tell and wrote. In other words, these are terms that describe some communicative act. Here the difference is quite pronounced. The high performing groups have a higher frequency and much higher standard score than the low performing groups. Again, it is as predicted that the better performing groups are more focused on the communication, and the poorer performing groups less focused on it.

Leveling terms also were sustained by validation and cross validation. Leveling terms are words like: actually, decidedly, definitely, completely, totally, wholly, etc. They are words used to accentuate points and to convince. Apparently, in the groups that had poorer process, it was relatively more difficult to convince other group members of the correct ratings of the candidates. The better performing groups have much less leveling in their conversations, and, in fact, in both the validation and cross-validation sample, the better performing groups are below average on the frequency of leveling terms in their conversations.

A fourth area where the content analysis performed as predicted was the area of numerical terms. The dictionary for numerical terms includes such words as: all cardinal and ordinal numbers, add, count, calculate, subtract, digit, divide, number and percent. Here the poorer performing groups focused more on the numbers than the better performing groups. The relative size of the standard scores seems outlandish, but the reader should bear in mind that each of the threads and branches were marked with numbers, so that accounts for the high frequency. The point is that however high the frequency was in the high performing groups, the low performing groups were more than two standard deviations higher. Even a cursory reading of the text of the group discussions indicates that the poorer performing groups got to the business of ranking the candidates very quickly. They did not discuss the criteria to be used in employing the rankings, but usually went directly to ranking the candidates. This proved (often) to be their downfall in rating accuracy.

Lastly, Table 2 shows the difference between the two groups in praise. The praise dictionary includes such words as: admirable, brave, commendable, clear, clever, competent, kinder, loyal and supreme. In determining which content categories were likely to be useful, we saw that one factor that differentiated the two types of groups was how group members argued for their choices. In better performing groups, group members lauded the candidate they felt was best. In poorer performing groups, group members denigrated the other candidates in order to make their choice appear the best. This tendency appears to be the source of this difference.

The other three constructs, rapport, satisfaction and temporal terms, showed promise in the validation sample, but did not hold up in cross validation. The changes in the frequencies of the words between validation and cross-validation samples gives some idea of the random variability that one reasonably expects between samples.

In summary, then, the cross-validated results show higher performing groups contained a higher frequency of dominating statements and a somewhat lower frequency of equivalence statements. High performing groups were characterized by higher frequencies of cognition, communication and praise words. They were characterized by lower frequencies of leveling terms and numerical terms. Five of the eight categories chosen to engage the differences in the high performing vs. the low performing groups actually did so and held up on cross validation.

DISCUSSION

Several clear differences emerged between high performing and low performing groups. First, dominance appears to be an advantageous act in virtual groups, where it is not in studies of dyads. In fact, in dyads, dominance tends to be associated with dissatisfaction and poorer performance. This may be due to the medium. Discussion boxes lend themselves well to digressions. Groups where one or more members are forcefully pulling other group members back to the subject at hand seem to make more accurate decisions.

As for the content categories, higher frequencies of cognition, communication and praise words and lower frequencies of leveling terms and numerical terms being associated with better performance makes perfect sense for this context. But it is important to remember the context. We had students participating in a university hiring via discussion boxes. Because of the subject and the medium, the conversation was limited and stereotyped for the most part. If that had not been the case, making a phrase dictionary for relational control would have been much more difficult.

From a data mining standpoint, these results cannot be generalized to other samples. However, it is also true that most effective data mining strategies will have utility limited to the specific application for which they are produced. Groups' context, purpose and dynamics vary enormously. Data miners should approach each sample of group text as a new field. It is extremely important for data mining to have two or more people read samples of the text to get a feel for what categories will work. The grounded theory approach discussed in the literature review section is a critical starting point. The relational control and content categories that differentiated in this sample will not necessarily work in other samples — in fact, unless the groups are similar in make-up and task, it is unlikely they will work.

For the 216 groups that were examined here, the benefit of this data mining would be to identify the lowest performing third. These 72 groups could then be measured on both relational control and content of their discussions. For those groups that lacked a member who dominated and brought the group back to the matter at hand, such a person from the remaining 144 groups could be substituted for one of the group members. Similarly, the groups' profiles on cognition, communication, leveling terms, numerical terms and praise should be carefully examined. Once more, group members should be added to the low performing groups such that people whose communication embodies the better profile of the above listed categories are substituted for lower performing group members. In this way, group process could be improved in these virtual groups. Then performance of these 72 groups should be monitored further to see that their performance has improved. Group process cannot always be improved by changing one or two people in a group, so further monitoring is warranted. The point here is that data mining enables better performing groups by allowing management to substitute group members who provide missing competencies.

We need also to note that there are at least two other performance enhancers that might be gleaned from the data we have mined. First, we could include training for new groups given this decision-making task. Such training could be based on the information we have mined from our text base. The author has done such a mining operation and the resulting participant training improved both process and outcomes (Tullar & Kaiser, 2000). Second, we could use the information we have mined from the data set to train facilitators. Shaila and Bostrum (1999) showed the advantages of process facilitators in their study of decision-making groups. Data mining can provide facilitators with the specific process issues they need to be looking for. In this case, higher frequencies of cognition, communication and praise words and lower frequencies of leveling terms and numerical terms were associated with better performance. Facilitators could encourage participants to do these things more frequently. Moreover, facilitators could encourage group members to dominate more and pull the group back on task. I have data that show that facilitation in groups performing this task does, in fact, produce better process and better outcomes.

Each of these three approaches, substituting group participants, training and facilitation would produce improvements in group process. Such improvements are possible for all virtual groups if mined data are used to produce the three group manipulations.

OTHER USES

Data mining in virtual groups might well serve many other purposes. One of these might be to evaluate the performance of individual members in the groups. Such performance evaluation might be qualitative or quantitative. For instance, it would be easy to count the total words or threads contributed by a given person. Similarly, people whose performance in the groups is suspect (they might be free riders) might have their contributions read carefully for content to see if they are contributing half-heartedly. Where virtual groups are important, management must emphasize this importance by appraising employee performance in the virtual group setting.

Similarly, value might also be extracted from focus groups. Many companies have hundreds or thousands of focus groups on videotape. Using content and relational analysis, the discussions could be evaluated. Response to the product could be evaluated by examining evaluative words occurring before and after the product's name. Lag sequential analysis might be used to examine how participants pick up on facilitator suggestions in the focus group discussion.

As text becomes more widely stored in organizational data bases, strategies for mining it for value will become relatively more sophisticated. In this chapter, I have outlined two simple strategies for getting value from the discussion of virtual decision-making groups. As investigators dig into the problem of extracting value from text, the approaches used will become more automated and complex. As they do this, they will come closer and closer to extracting meaning from the text itself.

REFERENCES

Bales, R. F. (1950). *Interaction Process Analysis: A Method for the Study of Small Groups*. Cambridge, MA: Addison-Wesley.

Bateson, G. (1958). *Naven*. Stanford, CA: Stanford Press.

Buchanen, D. (1997). Unique contributions of differentiation, consistency, and identity in predicting congruence and job satisfaction. *Dissertation Abstracts International Section A: Humanities and Social Sciences, 58*(3-A): 0749.

Courtright, J. A., Fairhurst, G. T., & Rogers, L. E. (1989). Interaction patterns in organic and mechanistic systems. *Academy of Management Journal, 32*, 773-802.

Ellis, D. G. (1979). Relational control on two group systems. *Communication Monographs, 46*, 153-166.

Ellis, D. G., & Fisher, B. A. (1975). Phases of conflict in small group development: A Markov analysis. *Human Communication Research, 1*, 195-212.

Fisher, B. A. (1975). Communication study in system perspective. In B. D. Reuben & J. Y. Kim (Eds.), *General systems theory and human communication*. Rochelle Park, NJ: Hayden Book Company.

Fisher, B. A. (1983). Communication pragmatism: Another legacy of Gregory Bateson. *Journal of Applied Communication Research, 10*, 38-49.

Fisher, B. A., & Hawes, L. C. (1971). An interact system model: Generating a grounded theory of small groups. *Quarterly Journal of Speech, 57*, 444-453.

Fisher, B. A., Glover, T. W., & Ellis, D. G. (1977). The nature of complex communication systems. *Communication Monographs, 44*, 231-240.

Friedlander, M. L., & Heatherington, L. (1989). Analyzing relational control in family therapy interviews. *Journal of Counseling Psychology, 36*(2) 139-148.

Giddens, A. (1979). *Central problems in social theory*. Berkeley, CA: University of California Press.

Giddens, A. (1984). *The constitution of society: Outline of a theory of structuration*. Berkeley, CA: University of California Press.

Glaser, B. J., & Strauss, A. L. (1967). *The discovery of grounded theory: Strategies for qualitative research*. Chicago, IL: Aldine.

Glauser, M. J. (1984). Self-esteem and communication tendencies: An analysis of four self-esteem/verbal dominance personality types. *The Psychological Record, 34*, 115-131.

Glauser, M. J., & Tullar, W. L. (1985). Citizen Satisfaction with police officer/citizen interaction: Implications for the changing role of police organizations. *Journal of Applied Psychology, 70*, 514-527.

Guetzkow, H. (1950). Unitizing and categorizing problems in coding qualitative data. *Journal of Clinical Psychology, 6*, 47-48.

Hawes, L. C. (1973). Elements of a model for communication processes. *Quarterly Journal of Speech, 59*, 11-21.

Heatherington, L. & Friedlander, M. (1990). Complementarity and symmetry in family therapy communication. *Journal of Counseling Psychology, 37*(3), 261-268.

Hirokawa, R. Y. (1980). A comparative analysis of communication patterns within effective and ineffective decision-making groups. *Communication Monographs, 47,* 312-321.

Liddy, E. (2000). Text mining. *American Society for Information Science. Bulletin of the American Society for Information Science, 27*(1), 13-17.

Mabry, E. A. (1975). Exploratory analysis of a developmental model for task-oriented small groups. *Human Communication Research, 2,* 66-74.

Maznevski, M. L., & Chudoba, K. M. (2000). Bridging space over time: Global virtual team dynamics and effectiveness. *Organization Science, 11,* 473-492.

Nasukawa, T., & Nagano, T. (2001). Text and knowledge mining system. *IBM Systems Journal, 40*(4), 967-984.

Neuendorf, K. A. (2002). *The content analysis guidebook.* Thousand Oaks, CA: Sage.

Shaila, M., & Bostrum, R. P. (1999). Meeting facilitation: Process versus content interventions. *Journal of Management Information Systems, 15*(4), 89-114.

Stake, R. E. (2000). Case studies. In N. K. Denzin & Y.S. Lincoln (Eds.), *The Handbook of Qualitative Research* (2nd ed., pp. 435-454). Thousand Oaks: Sage.

Strauss, A., & Corbin, J. (1998) *Basics of qualitative research: Techniques and procedures for developing grounded theory.* Thousand Oaks, CA: Sage.

Suleiman, J. (1998). *Influencing social loafing in electronic workgroups.* Unpublished doctoral dissertation, University of Georgia, Athens, GA.

Sullivan, T. (2002). SAS uncovers text mining deal. *Infoworld, 24*(4), 28-30.

Tullar, W. L. (1989). Relational control in the employment interview. *Journal of Applied Psychology, 74*(6), 971-977.

Tullar, W. L. & Kaiser, P. R. (2000). The effect of process training on process and outcomes in virtual groups. *Journal of Business Communication, 37,* 408-427.

Tullar, W. L., Kaiser, P. R., & Beach, S. S. (2000, October). The virtual free rider. Presentation at the *Meeting of the International Association of Business Communication*, October 18-21, 2000, Atlanta, GA.

Watson, K. M. (1982a). An analysis of communication patterns: A method for discriminating leader and subordinate roles. *Academy of Management Journal, 25,* 107-120.

Watson, K. M. (1982b). A methodology for the study of organizational behavior at the interpersonal level of analysis. *Academy of Management Review, 7,* 392-402.

Section III

ODM Analytics
and Algorithms

Chapter X

An Intelligent Support System Integrating Data Mining and Online Analytical Processing

Rahul Singh
University of North Carolina at Greensboro, USA

Richard T. Redmond
Virginia Commonwealth University, USA

Victoria Yoon
University of Maryland Baltimore County, USA

ABSTRACT

Intelligent decision support requires flexible, knowledge-driven analysis of data to solve complex decision problems faced by contemporary decision makers. Recently, online analytical processing (OLAP) and data mining have received much attention from researchers and practitioner alike, as components of an intelligent decision support environment. Little that has been done in developing models to integrate the capabilities of data mining and online analytical processing to provide a systematic model for intelligent decision making that allows users to examine multiple views of the data that are generated using knowledge about the environment and the decision problem domain. This paper presents an integrated model in which data mining and online analytical processing complement each other to support intelligent decision making for data rich environments. The integrated approach models system behaviors that are of interest to decision makers; predicts the occurrence of such behaviors; provides support to explain the occurrence of such behaviors and supports decision making to identify a course of action to manage these behaviors.

INTRODUCTION

Increasing complexities in decision problems and an exponential growth in the volume of data available for analysis are characteristic of contemporary decision problems. Systems support for managerial decision-making in today's environments requires precision and accuracy in the problem representation, intelligence in the selection of data relevant to the specific decision problem and flexible analytical support to alleviate the cognitive burden on the decision maker. Intelligent decision support systems (IDSS) that provide accurate models to understand the decision problem and flexible mechanisms to examine the multiple dimensions of the problem can enhance the analysis and support the decision-making process. A goal of IDSS design is a decision-making environment with flexible mechanisms to analyze the relevant data using the models of the problem domain as a reference.

This research presents a model to integrate the unique benefits of two very promising technologies — data mining and OLAP — to develop a model for an IDSS. Data mining techniques are used to provide accurate and sophisticated models of the process based on historical data from the business processes. Actively mining the data enables dynamic models that capture emerging relationships in the data. Analysis, based on such models, is accurate and current in its depiction of the problem environment. OLAP is used in decision support systems (DSS) to provide the decision maker with fast and flexible analytic capabilities for large amounts of data. As an improvement on existing approaches, the model supports explanatory and predictive capabilities that are based on mined models of the process.

The following section presents background information in the use of artificial intelligence (AI)-based techniques for decision support. After presenting the theoretical basis and some approaches to incorporate AI-based techniques in DSS, we review the concepts of data mining and OLAP and present some arguments for their integration to support decision-making. The next section presents the architecture of the IDSS, based on the integration of data mining and OLAP. Components of the model are discussed in detail and directions for implementation are offered. We conclude with a synopsis of our prototype and discuss some future directions for research to further the state of the art in intelligent decision systems.

BACKGROUND RESEARCH
Systems Support for Decision-Making

Administration of an organization involves making decisions to determine appropriate courses of action that help the organization achieve its objectives (Simon, 1976). Such decision-making is the primary function of administrators and managers in an organization. DSS have been developed to aid managers in the critical decision-making process. Keen and Scott Morton (1978) define a DSS as "a coherent system of computer based technology, including hardware, software, and supporting documentation, used by managers as an aid to their decision-making in semi-structured tasks." These systems help the decision maker examine more alternatives and evaluate the complex relationships between the alternatives and their associated outcomes, while satisfying the objectives of the decision-making process. Contemporary business decision problems are semi- or ill-structured and often require the decision maker's judgment as a vital input. DSS are developed for problems where there is a sufficient amount of structure for analytical aids to be helpful, yet the nature of the problems makes the judgment of managers critical to the decision-making process (Keen & Scott Morton, 1978). The challenge for DSS design is to frame decision problems in accurate models to facilitate the decision makers' understanding of the problem domain and providing a flexible analytical environment for exploration of the dimensions of the decision problem.

A model is a concise representation of the problem domain and presents an organized view of problem aspects. It may use simplification to facilitate understanding of the problem, without losing critical elements of the problem in the simplification. DSS are constructed with pre-existing knowledge of the decision problem. The representation models are chosen based on suitable analysis for the decision problem. For example, a multiple criteria DSS using the analytical hierarchy process (AHP) for problem representation can only analyze the problem domain in conformance with the analysis methodology of AHP. The extent to which a problem can be reduced into known models is the extent to which their solution can be simplified (Simon, 1976). Ill-structured problems present a challenge since there may be a lack of fit of problem characteristics into known solution models. Typically, decision problems are ill-structured due to lack of models and their solution often requires judgment on the part of the decision maker (Keen & Scott Morton, 1978). The design of computer-based systems to support the flexible analysis required in solving ill-structured problems is a challenging task.

Intelligent Systems

AI seeks to explain and emulate intelligent behavior in uncertain environments through computational processes by creating machines with the ability to perform appropriate actions that increase the probability of success in achieving the subgoals in support of the systems goals (Albus, 1981). AI has been used in a number of application areas, such as robotics, intelligent manufacturing, marketing, banking and finance. Feigenbaum, McCorduck and Nii (1988) list several applications of expert systems in such diverse areas as agriculture, communications, computers, construction, geology and medicine. The application of AI in decision-making focuses on the automation of human thinking activities such as decision making, problem solving and learning (Bellman, 1978).

Early applications of AI to support decision making is through the development of knowledge-based expert systems that can perform the role of a focused, problem-specific domain expert. Expert systems provide a means of formalizing a lot of mostly experiential and subjective knowledge that may have been heretofore unexpressed and unrecorded, thereby, creating a formal body of knowledge that the organization can draw upon in solving problems (Dhar, 1987). AI supports expert systems by trying to solve fundamental problems related to development of knowledge representation techniques that help decision makers efficiently use knowledge in their tasks (Goldstein & Papert, 1977). The scope of application of expert systems is limited to the specific problem domain for which they are developed. Problems usually involve ambiguous and incomplete data from which an expert must be able to judge reliability of facts to clarify the problem and evaluate competing conceptualizations of the problem (Dhar, 1987). As the problem domain changes, any attempts to add new knowledge to the system may affect the system in unforeseen ways. There is no learning involved in expert systems; if there are changes in the problem domain, a new expert system needs to be built.

Besides the complex, yet structured and algorithmic approach provided by operations research and management science models, another direction in the evolution of systems support for modeling decision problems comes from the AI community. There is debate in the AI community on whether its purpose is to create machines that act rationally, thereby, replacing human actions, or to create machines that think rationally and can support human cognitive activity. These opposing points of view are reflected in the debate on the role of AI in the DSS area. Expert systems aim to replace the human decision maker with an artificial one — the system. AI's contribution to DSS with intelligent components is to support the decision maker, as in traditional DSS. Goul, Henderson and Tonge (1992) propose that "Artificial intelligence can broaden DSS research beyond its original focus on supporting rather than replacing human decision-making by selectively incorporating machine based expertise to deliver the potential of DSS in the knowledge era." This proposition calls for synergy between research in both fields to find aspects of AI that can help decision support and conversely find areas of DSS that can benefit from machine intelligence.

DATA MINING, ONLINE ANALYTICAL PROCESSING AND THEIR INTEGRATION

Data Mining: A Process to Extract Models for Business Decision Problems

Knowledge discovery from organizational data is defined as: "the non-trivial process of identifying valid, novel, potentially useful and ultimately understandable patterns in data" (Fayyad, 1996). Fayyad et al. (1996) place the process of data mining in the context of the knowledge discovery process and define it as: "the process by which patterns are extracted and enumerated from the data." From these definitions, it is clear that data mining is central to the process of knowledge discovery in databases; these terms are often used interchangeably in the literature. Data mining uses techniques to acquire knowledge from organizational data that can eventually be used to support the decision-making activity in organizations. Data mining uses techniques and algorithms from a number of related fields of study, including statistics, machine learning and pattern recognition to achieve a better understanding of large volumes of data through developing means of classification and discovering patterns and associations in the data. Fayyad et al. (1996) define three major components of most data mining algorithms:

- **Models** that contain parameters to be determined from the data;
- **Preference criteria** that form the basis for preference of one model over another;

- **Search algorithm** to find particular models and parameters given the data, a family of models and preference criteria.

The literature classifies data mining into two major forms (Simoudis, 1996; Fayyad et al., 1996):
1. **Verification-driven data mining:** This form of data mining presumes that users already have postulated a hypothesis that they want to verify from the data. The data mining algorithms are selected to verify, or nullify, the a priori hypothesis. Statistical techniques are often used for this form of data mining.
2. **Discovery-driven data mining:** New rules and associations are extracted from the data in this form of data mining in which hypotheses are not postulated a priori. Discovery-driven data mining relies heavily on AI techniques, such as symbolic processing, association discovery and supervised induction.

Some common data mining operations are listed below:
1. **Classification:** Classification refers to the rapid discovery of categories that observational data can be divided into. Classification looks at the difference between dimensions of an observation and categorizes the observation based on that dimension. Some common techniques used for classification of data include clustering analysis, nearest neighbor analysis and factorial analysis.
2. **Link analysis:** Discovery of associations in data that may lead to the explanation of causality and reveal previously unknown associations between variables in a data set. It is common to find variables that covary, particularly in large data sets. Such associations may provide useful insight and provide a powerful tool for the reduction of the dimensionality in data.
3. **Regression techniques:** Regression attempts to establish relationships between variables in the data set so that associations between the rules can be inferred. This is a relatively simple, yet powerful, technique for the induction of rules and associations in the data set.
4. **Visualization techniques:** These techniques contend that people who are familiar with the application area can identify patterns in the data if they have powerful tools available that allow them to view the data in multiple ways. This class of techniques provides a way to form hypotheses about relationships in the data that can be further verified.

A mapping between data mining techniques and the objective of the data mining task is found in Bose and Mahapatra (2001). Additional case studies in the literature report on the success or failure of the data mining provide valuable experiential and anecdotal guidance to practitioners and researchers. The reader is referred to a variety of white papers that can be found online with various levels of regularity from sources such as Pilot Software (http://www.pilotsw.com) and KDD Nuggets (http://www.kdnuggets.com). Data mining can provide managers with effective solutions to utilize transactional and historical data stored in corporate data warehouses. Spangler, May and Vargas (1999) report on the capabilities of multiple classification approaches for multidimensional problems. Such approaches are typically applied to predict classifications of data as well as to develop explanatory models for classification. Sung, Chang and Lee (1999) developed mining models to classify and support interpretation and explanation of the causes of bankruptcy in normal and crisis conditions with very accurate results, highlighting the need for mining information with consideration of the environment where the data was collected. Feelders, Daniels and Holsheimer (2000) provide a very useful guide of the data mining process and emphasize the knowledge of tools and processes used in data mining. Development of data mining techniques and their various applications to business problems continues to be an active area of research for academics and practitioners alike.

OLAP

OLAP is a class of technologies that provides multidimensional views of data and is supported by multidimensional database technology. These multidimensional views provide the technical basis for the calculations and analysis required by intelligent applications for providing fast, responsive analysis of data (Han, 1997). OLAP provides powerful analytical processing for applications and is optimized for analysis of information. This technology is especially suitable for multidimensional data that includes a temporal component (Simoudis, 1996). OLAP provides multidimensional structures and summarization techniques that enable fast and intuitive access for complex analytical queries (Thomsen, 1997). OLAP technologies are commonly used in the increasingly popular organizational data warehouses in which many large organizations are investing (Elkins, 1998). Organizations store data about their various business processes in data warehouses. Due to the large variety of the business processes, typical organizational databases contain vast amounts of data. This data is stored for the purpose of managerial decision-making. OLAP presents a multidimensional logical view of the data to facilitate analysis. OLAP operations are provided to allow users to interact with the data for multidimensional data analysis to facilitate decision-making. OLAP alone does not generate any models about the nature of the data and these are normally developed at the time of the development of the OLAP system. Hence, these models are developed prior to the analysis for which the data is used. OLAP systems interact with statistical analysis algorithms, such as trend analysis or linear modeling, to allow for statistical analysis of the data. The models that the analysis is based on are a task for the designers of the OLAP system or for the analyst. Given models of the environment, OLAP technologies can provide an efficient method for easy and flexible access to data to facilitate analysis for decision-making purposes.

Rationale for Integration

The data stored in typical organization-wide data repositories has multiple dimensions, stemming from the numerous entities and processes with which the business is involved. Any combination of these dimensions may be important for a decision maker faced with a specific, multidimensional business problem. Therefore, analysis of decision problems requires flexible views of multiple dimensions of the data and various levels of analytical support for the decision-making activity. OLAP has demonstrated its ability for efficiently processing large amounts of data and for providing intuitive, multidimensional views of the data along the dimensions of the problem with a view to facilitate analysis. OLAP uses multidimensional database technology with its corresponding multidimensional data structures and summarization methods for fast and intuitive access for complex analytical queries. These multidimensional views provide a basis for the analysis required of intelligent applications and in turn provide fast and responsive analysis of data. Though OLAP provides the decision maker with an efficient means of analyzing data by providing flexible views and summary information on multiple dimensions of the data, it does not provide support for identification of the dimensions that may be relevant to a specific decision problem. The decision support capabilities of OLAP largely depend on the identification of dimensions that are relevant to a decision problem. As the dimensionality of the data stored in organizational data repositories and the complexity of decision problems continue to grow, the need to identifying dimensions germane to a decision problem is ever increasing.

An effective intelligent decision support approach should combine the knowledge of the problem domain with the means to analyze relevant data to provide support for decision-making. Techniques that not only develop accurate models, but also provide summary information of the data on the dimensions identified and facilitate the decision-making process are required. Analysis of the capabilities and limitations of DM and OLAP reveals their complementary roles. Integration of these approaches may significantly enhance the ability of DSS to assist a decision maker, by augmenting the analytical capability of OLAP with knowledge gained from DM to provide knowledge-driven analysis of complex, multidimensional decision problems. For example, the generation of marketing strategy is frequently a segmentation task wherein the decision maker analyzes the discrimination power of multiple dimensions of consumer behavior to develop the criteria upon which potential customers can be identified. The manager also has the task of identifying the relative range of values in each of the discriminating criterion that separate one class of customer from another. The critical task of discovery of problem dimensions, in this case the discovery of discriminating dimensions of consumer behavior using OLAP alone, is not supported by the system. Data mining can provide significant assistance in helping the decision maker identify the problem dimensions in such decision problems using a variety of algorithms, such as clustering, segmentation, k-nearest neighbor and inductive learning. However, data mining alone does not provide any analytical tools to help the decision maker analyze the volume of data that may be available to the decision maker. Here, OLAP can play a critical role in providing the decision maker with fast and flexible analytic capabilities to

Work by Han (1997) and others (Kelkar, 2001; Parsaye, 1997) investigates the integration of data mining and OLAP to support knowledge driven decision making for data-intense decision problems. The OLAP mining approach (Han, 1997) involves data cubes that are generated based on ad-hoc or decision maker specified dimensions and the mining task is verification oriented, in that it verifies the relevance of the dimensions of the cube to the specific decision problem. Such an approach requires the decision maker to identify problem-relevant dimensions in the vast volume of data, with hundreds or thousands of data fields and hundreds of thousands of records — thus resting the bulk of the problem-solving, cognitive burden on the decision maker. The approach presented in this paper takes a discovery driven data mining approach by using mining to identify problem-relevant dimensions in the data and using these dimensions to analyze problems as they occur. We believe such an approach reduces the cognitive burden on the user and allows the system to identify relevant data based on models of the problem generated by data mining techniques. The following section presents the integrated model discussed in the paper and describes individual components of the model in greater detail.

INTEGRATED MODEL

The integrated system is developed using data mining and online analytical processing components to discover useful relationships in the data and present the information for analysis. The system interacts with the user by providing the status of the system and responding to queries of the user. A model of the proposed integrated system is shown in Figure 1. This model is based on identifying error conditions in a process, analyzing the conditions that lead to the errors and suggesting possible actions that may be taken to correct the problem. A prototype of the model was implemented and tested for the manufacturing process of a large, fully-automated chemical processing plant that routinely collects and stores a large volume of process data from multiple parts of the manufacturing process. Models were developed to identify errors in complex manufacturing processes and explain their cause. The following sections describe the operation of the components of the integrated system.

Data Mining Component

Data mining is used for creating and maintaining the models of the process and for interacting with the OLAP component to provide the correct model parameters for analysis. The data mining component of the model searches for frequently occurring patterns and trends in data that precede an error condition. These may involve establishment of acceptable parameters for data elements, composite or otherwise, that lead to an error condition. Initially, the models are created from the complete data repository of the system in an off-line mode. They are tested and validated on historical data before being deployed in the system. The set of models is updated on a regular basis, especially if known changes are made to the process parameters.

A primary requirement of the integrated approach model is the ability to identify imminent failures of the system and provide early warning. The system needs to learn the historical patterns that have historically led to failure by using data mining techniques. An artificial neural network, trained using process data from the process, is used to

Figure 1. Model of Integrated System

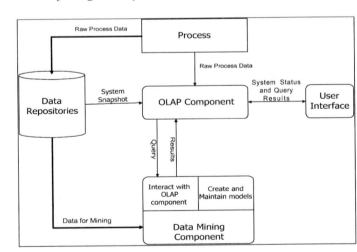

predict whether critical variables are within their established ranges. The predicted values of these critical variables obtained from the neural network are used to predict failure of the process. This is different from other methods of error detection in that the prediction is obtained from nonlinear models of the system that consider the autocorrelation between process variables.

The data mining component identifies the views that the OLAP component needs to support the efficient analysis of the data. This is done using decision trees that identify causes for errors in the process. The OLAP component provides analysis of the variables that are responsible for error conditions as they occur. For this, the data mining component will react to requests by the OLAP component and provide models required for analysis based on the current error condition being analyzed. The application of the data mining techniques gives the system a set of models to describe causes of possible error conditions in the data. A model of the system would identify a set of trends in the process that should continuously be checked. A model also defines a "time-window" that defines the number of data points required to make valid and accurate predictions of imminent failures from the incoming, real-time process data. It also defines a set of parameters that identify and describe a set of key variables that can be used as event triggers to identify possible error conditions in the process. These variables are identified by the decision trees of the data mining component. On identification of nonconformity to the process model, the OLAP component queries the data mining component for either a changed model or an error condition. This information is passed back to the OLAP component. If there is no conformance to any model present in the data mining component's model base, then an error condition is said to occur, and this information is passed to the OLAP component. Otherwise, a different set of trends and

Figure 2. Expanded Model of the Integration Between Data Mining and OLAP

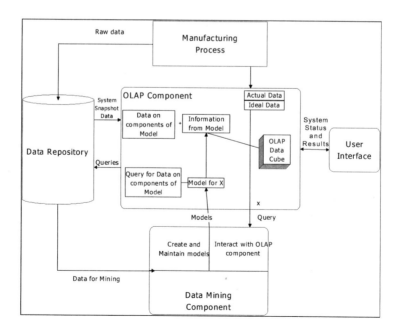

parameters are passed to the OLAP component and a process model changeover occurs. New data may be obtained from the data repository and the process starts to be monitored. Figure 2 expands the components of the integrated model we presented in Figure 1 and provides the implementation prototype model of the architecture elucidated in this chapter.

OLAP Component

The OLAP component accepts event trigger data from the multiple data collecting devices of the process and analyzes them to see if sufficient evidence can be found for the likelihood of an error condition. This process follows the simplistic view of error identification, where certain variables or clusters are checked for conformity to known models of a normal state of operations. These models are derived from data mining algorithms that consider the normal operation of the process. For this research, this would be the trained neural network that analyzes process data to see if the process is in or out control as defined by abnormal variations in these critical variables. When the critical variables are within appropriate ranges, the OLAP component does not do anything. The actual results obtained by the process would serve as a confirmation of the fact that the process is not going out of control. When an event trigger detected by the OLAP component identifies an imminent problem in the process, action is required. The first course of action is to flag the process to be leaving the normal operating range and, hence, inform the user of an imminent problem in the process. This can be done by a simple comparison of the predictions from the neural net and normal operating range means of the critical variables of the process. This is further reinforced by comparison with the observed values from the process.

When an error occurs, the analysis of the system needs to identify causes of these errors as defined by abnormal variance in the variables that occur before the critical variable that signals the occurrence of the error. The system also needs to identify the normal values of these variables to provide indication of corrective action required. The data mining component develops decision tree models for relationships between the critical variables and all variables that occur downstream. Once an unsteady variation is identified, the model(s) pertaining to the out-of-control variables is requested by the OLAP component from the data mining component. In such situations, the OLAP component requests a snapshot of the current state of the system from the production data repository. For example, the OLAP module may require all process data from the last hour of operation, or it may require data from a defined cluster of variables for a certain period of time. The content of this data cube is defined by the model of the effect of the critical variable that is out of control and the set of process characteristics that it is known to affect. The fact that these models are predictive and descriptive in nature allows for forecasting of results from the out-of-control condition. Figure 3 shows a sample screen shot of the variables. The explanations offered by the decision tree component are used by the OLAP component of the integrated system to generate analytical views of the data and present this to the decision makers for analysis.

Figure 3 shows a screenshot of the analysis interface with fictitious variable names in order to mask the process characteristics of the actual data used in the study. The variables listed in the selection box labeled "1". Variables to Plot" are variables that are offered by the decision tree as explanations for the causes of errors. Users may choose

Figure 3. Sample Screenshot Showing the Analysis Interface for the Integrated Model

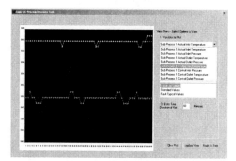

to view observed values, standard control values or values that are typical of the errors that are presented in the given situation.

If sufficient evidence of error is not discernible from the event triggers, then the system must conclude that models for the current condition do not exist. The OLAP component passes the variables under consideration to the data mining component, and new associations must to be derived for those data items as relationships between the critical variables and the process variables under consideration. Depending on the observed data and the extent of system information, the OLAP component may query the data mining component for its data for error conditions that may possibly be developing. If this query returns a positive result, then the result is passed to the user with explanations of possible errors that may be developing and possible remedies. In either case, a set of output and input variables are passed to the data mining component for it to search for associations.

DISCUSSION

The components of the integrated system interact between the AI components that comprise the data mining part of the integrated system and the data components, which make up the OLAP components. The system is implemented using object-oriented methods with objects for the data mining and OLAP components. The purpose of the system is to model the relationships that exist in the data and extract. These relationships are then used by the OLAP component of the integrated system to provide analytical support for making decision about the process. A primary requirement of the integrated system model is to detect errors by examining the process data. This is achieved by identifying critical process variables that are key indicators of process stability. The purpose of the system to provide causes for this error in addition to the ability of predicting these errors in order to provide better input to the decision-making process. Therefore, the system must be able to offer explanations of the cause of the error and support the decision maker in deciding a course of action to correct the error. For our purposes, an error is a set of observations in which at least one of the critical process variables is outside of its acceptable range of operation. OLAP alone can easily identify all the variables that are out of range at the same time as the critical process variable. Thus, the explanation from OLAP alone is a set of variables that are outside their specified range at the same time that the output is out of its specified limits. At best, this approach offers information on out-of-range covariance of the input variables with the output variables.

The integrated approach is able to detect and explain errors through the integration of data mining and OLAP components. The OLAP component detects a process error by detecting a condition where an output variable is outside of its established range. The out-of-control output variable is used to traverse a decision tree of the data mining component to determine the variables that may explain the causes for the error. These variables are then used to retrieve summary information via the OLAP component to inform the user of the causes and their behaviors leading up to the detected error in the process. Hence, the integrated system detects the errors in the process, offers causes for these errors and provides information related to these causes to allow the user to make an informed decision regarding the cause and subsequent correction of the error. This approach relies on the availability of a path on the decision tree, created by sufficient training examples, so that the tree has been trained in this type of error. For this reason, the integrated approach may not be able to explain all instances of process errors, without retraining the data mining-based components of the integrated system. Specifically, the integrated approach will not be able to offer explanations for errors that are novel, in that they were not part of the training set and, hence, new to the learning-based components of the integrated approach.

Intelligent DSS should be flexible enough to handle changes in the environment and be able to adapt to changes in the standards for any given product. Flexibility and adaptability in this context address the ease with which the underlying assumptions of the system can be modified, so the system works with a new set of descriptors of the environment. Changes in the environmental characteristics are a frequent occurrence in dynamic modern processes. By using OLAP alone, a change in the assumptions that represent the environment must be updated. This process can be as easy as loading these parameters from a file. Therefore, using OLAP alone, it is relatively easy to modify the underlying assumptions of the system. Changes in the environment imply that the inherent relationships in the environment have also changed. The data mining component of the integrated approach models these relationships in the environment. Therefore, if there are any changes in the environmental conditions, the data mining components need to be trained to incorporate the new relationships in the environment. If any of the underlying assumptions are altered, the system needs to be retrained. Changes in these assumptions may be due to a change in any external or internal conditions that affect the process. In each case, the models that are used by the data mining component of the integrated system will have to change. This requires retraining of the data mining components of the integrated system, so that these changes in the operating environment can be incorporated into the models maintained by the system. At any point in time, the system should be able to provide the user with summary information regarding the various process and product characteristics to support decision-making regarding the process. The system should be able to respond to queries for summary information, as well as provide some process critical information, on a regular basis as an indication of process stability at any given point in time. The presentation and content of this information should be done to facilitate making decisions regarding the process. Flexible and efficient access to summary information about multiple aspects of the environment is a major strength of the OLAP. However, in using OLAP alone, this information is based on dimensions that must be supplied by the user. Given the dimensions along which the data is to be analyzed, OLAP provides efficient access to historical and summary information. The integrated approach incorporates all the benefits of using OLAP through its OLAP component. The primary difference between the two approaches is that the integrated approach generates the summary information based on the dimensions that are identified by the data mining components of the integrated approach. Hence, the integrated approach can provide efficient access to summary information on the dimensions based on explanatory and predictive models of the process in addition to those identified by users' queries.

The ability of a system to accurately predict the conformance of the process to established standards by examination of the process characteristics is a desirable feature of an intelligent DSS. Using OLAP alone does not offer any predictive capabilities. There is no information with respect to what may happen to the critical process characteristics in the future based on the current characteristics of the environment. Data mining offers the ability to develop predictive models of the system that can predict the future state of the system based on current characteristics. The artificial neural network component of the integrated approach has predictive capabilities in determining future values of outputs based on the current values of the inputs. The neural network can be trained on inputs in the present to predict outputs at a later point in time. Therefore, the integrated model offers an approach that allows for the analysis of the current state of the system and its effects on the future states. This is a desirable capability of the integrated approach over the capabilities of using data mining or online analytical process alone.

CONCLUSIONS AND FUTURE RESEARCH

The proposed solution relies on the integration of data mining and OLAP to build accurate and dynamic models of the process and provide analytical views of the data that support decision-making in this environment. The integrated solution is compared against using only data mining or OLAP. The discussion illustrates that the functionality offered by the integrated model is better than using data mining or online analytical processing alone. The integrated approach is able to identify and explain errors in the process data. It also offers explanations that provide information for decision making about the environment. The integrated approach offers content rich explanations about the state of the process. The integrated approach is capable of identification of errors and provides additional information about these causes of error that is useful in making decisions about the process. This may be achieved though decision tree models that supply information about the process characteristic under question and its associations with other descriptors of the system. These explanations may take the form of an explanation of the association between variable's states, or take the form of queries used to materialize multidimensional views of the data from actual, as well as model, states of the system. This information is knowledge-based, multidimensional and concerns the state of the system under consideration and can provide valuable information to support the decision-making process. This integrated approach can be used to analyze incoming real-time data to predict, identify and explain possible error conditions in the process. As an improvement on existing approaches, this approach offers explanatory and predictive capabilities based on accurate and adaptive models of the process and offers early warning of imminent failures. The integrated system uses data mining to discover the complex relationships hidden in large volumes of process data to identify and classify error conditions. These relationships are discovered from real process data, using an artificial neural network component used for prediction of future states of the environment and a decision tree component used to offer explanations for states of the environment. The knowledge in these models is used to support intelligent decision making for the process. This data is organized and presented for decision-making using OLAP to support multidimensional views of the data. These multidimensional views are created by the results from the models discovered by mining the data from the process. We suggest an evolutionary approach in which these models can be constantly updated, whenever there are any changes in the environment, which may cause changes in the relationships modeled by the system.

The model for integration of data mining and OLAP to support intelligent decision making developed in this research can help the decision-making process by providing a set of models derived from the data, and the ability to explain the different states of the system. It provides a means for knowledge-driven analysis of large volumes of data by combining methods to develop analytical models of data and means for analysis of large volumes of multidimensional data at multiple levels of abstraction as required by the decision problem. This approach needs to be tested on other environments and problem contexts in order to address the approach's generalizations. There needs to be sufficient amounts of data for the data mining models to be developed for this approach to be applicable to a problem domain. This is necessary for the opportunity to discover complex and, heretofore, unknown relationships in the data that may be potentially useful for making decisions in the problem domain. There are many business environments, such as financial markets, credit analysis, marketing analysis, banking, among others, that share these characteristics. Research has been done on the individual applicability of data mining and OLAP in these areas with reasonable success. This research focuses on off-line data mining of the environment to develop explanatory and predictive models of the environment or provide multidimensional views of the data as seen appropriate by the decision maker. There is little that has been done in methods for integrating the two approaches to provide a systematic method for decision making that allows users to examine multiple views of the data that are generated using knowledge about the environment and the decision problem. Further research on the applicability of systems that focus on the use of such technologies to support intelligent decision-making can further the state of the art in data mining and OLAP research and improve intelligent DSS.

REFERENCES

Alavi, M., & Henderson, J. C. (1981). An evolutionary strategy for implementing a decision support system. *Management Science, 27*(11).

Albus, J. S. (1991, May/June). Outline for a theory of Intelligence. *IEEE Transactions on Systems, Man, and Cybernetics, 21*(3).

Bellman, R. E. (1978). *An introduction to artificial intelligence: Can computers think?* San Francisco, CA: Boyd & Fraser Publishing Company.

Bose, I., & Mahapatra, R. (2001). Business data mining – A machine learning perspective. *Information and Management, 39*

Dhar, V. (1987, Summer). On the plausibility and scope of expert systems in management. *Journal of Management Information Systems, 4*(1).

Elkins, S. B. (1998, April). Open – OLAP. *DBMS*.

Fayyad, U. M., Piatetsky-Shapiro, G., & Smyth, P. (1996a). From data mining to knowledge discovery: An overview. In U. M. Fayyad, G. Piatetsky-Shapiro, P. Smyth & R. Uthurusamy (Eds.), *Advances in knowledge discovery and data mining.* Menlo Park CA: AAAI Press/The MIT Press.

Fayyad, U. M., Piatetsky-Shapiro, G., & Smyth, P. (1996b). The KDD process for extracting useful knowledge from volumes of data. *Communications of the ACM, 39*(11).

Feelders, A., Daniels, H., & Holsheimer, M. (2000). Methodological and practical aspects of data mining. *Information and Management, 37*.

Feigenbaum, E., McCorduck, P., & Nii, P. (1988). *The rise of the expert company.* New York: Times Books.

Goldstein, I., & Papert, S. (1977). Artificial intelligence, language, and the study of knowledge. *Cognitive Science, 1*.

Gorry, A. G., & Scott Morton, M. S. (1971). *A framework for management information systems.* Sloan Management Review.

Goul, M., Henderson, J. C., & Tonge, F. M. (1992, November/December). The emergence of artificial intelligence as a reference discipline for decision support systems research. *Decision Sciences, 23*(6).

Han, J. (1997, October). OLAP mining: An integration of OLAP with data mining. *Proceedings of the 1997 IFIP Conference on Data Semantics (DS-7).* 1-11

Hurst Jr., E. G., et al. (1983). Growing DSS: A flexible evolutionary approach. In J. L. Bennett (Ed.), *Building decision support systems* (pp. 133-172). Reading, MA: Addison-Wesley.

Keen, P. G. W., & Scott Morton, M. S. (1978). *Decision support systems: An organizational perspective.* Reading, MA: Addison-Wesley.

Kelkar, B. (2001, December). Exploiting symbiosis between data mining and OLAP for business insights. *DM Direct*.

Liang, T., & Jones, C. V. (1987, Summer). Design of a self-evolving decision support system. *Journal of Management Information Systems, 4*(1).

Murray, T. J., & Tanniru, M. R. (1987, Summer). A framework for selecting between knowledge-based and traditional systems design. *Journal of Management Information Systems 4*(1), 42-58.

Parsaye, K. (1997, February). OLAP and data mining: Bridging the gap. *Database Programming and Design*.

Simon, H. A. (1976). *Administrative behavior: A study of decision-making processes in administrative organization.* New York: The Free Press.

Simoudis, E. (1996, October). Reality check for data mining. *IEEE Expert*.

Spangler, W. E., May, J. H., & Vargas, L. G. (1999, Summer). Choosing data-mining for multiple classification: Representational and performance measurement implications for decision support. *Journal of Management Information Systems, 16*(1).

Sung, T. K., Chang, N., & Lee, G. (1999, Summer). Dynamics of modeling in data mining: Interpretive approach to bankruptcy prediction. *Journal of Management Information Systems, 16*(1).

Thomsen, E. (1997). *OLAP solutions: Building multidimensional information systems.* John Wiley and Sons Inc.

Chapter XI

Knowledge Mining in DSS Model Analysis

David M. Steiger
University of Maine, USA

Natalie M. Steiger
University of Maine, USA

ABSTRACT

The three stages of mathematical modeling include model formulation, solution and analysis. To date, the primary focus of model-based decision support systems (DSS), in general, and Management Science/Operations Research (MS/OR), specifically, has been on model formulation and solution. In fact, with a few notable exceptions, computer-assisted model analysis has been ignored in both information systems (IS) and MS/OR literature (Swanson & Ramiller, 1993).

This lack of attention to model analysis is especially noteworthy for two reasons. First, the primary bottleneck of modeling is in the analysis and interpretation of model results (Greenberg, 1993). Second, the basic purpose of DSS and mathematical modeling is insightful understanding of the modeled environment through insightful analysis (Geoffrion, 1976; Steiger, 1998). Developing insight into the complex decision-making environment is ultimately a process of discovery, finding trends and surprising behaviors and comparing the behavior of the model to what is expected or observed in the real system (Jones, 1992). Thus, insightful understanding often entails the inductive analysis of several (if not many) model instances (i.e., what-if cases), each of which has one or more different values for input parameters in an attempt to understand the associated changes in the modeled output.

INTRODUCTION

We hypothesize that there are two reasons for this relatively scant attention to model analysis: (1) a lack of clear understanding of what the model analysis tasks are, and (2) a lack of understanding of how knowledge mining tools can be used to extract valuable organizational knowledge from a DSS model and the associated what-if cases. Therefore, the objective of this paper is twofold: (1) to identify the primary inductive model analysis tasks in a DSS and (2) to suggest specific artificial intelligence- (AI) based data mining tools and techniques to facilitate those analysis tasks, i.e., tools and techniques that can be used to mine the multiple what-if cases of a DSS, and, thus, facilitate the various analysis tasks. To our knowledge, this assignment of the appropriate data mining technologies to the various analysis tasks has not previously appeared anywhere in the DSS, MS/OR or IS literature.

The chapter is organized as follows. We present our taxonomy of inductive model analysis tasks and then briefly introduces various AI-based knowledge mining technologies that are potentially appropriate for the mining of knowledge from model analysis tasks. The chapter also specifies the various knowledge mining techniques applicable to each analysis task identified. This is followed by an illustrative example of using one knowledge mining technique for analyzing model solutions for a specific analysis task. The chapter concludes with some ideas for further research.

MODEL ANALYSIS TASKS

Once a model is built and run for an initial set of assumptions and instantiating values the decision maker's job has just begun. That is, practically no decision is based on the first model run. A manager develops his/her confidence in the model, as well as an understanding of a problem and its solution, as she/he specifies and runs several (if not many) what-if model instances, i.e., as she/he iteratively specifies and analyzes pertinent what-if cases and understands the interrelationships between changes in the model variables/parameters and corresponding changes in the model solution (Little, 1970; Jones, 1992). This analysis can be divided into seven basic analysis tasks, covering the different phases of the model's life cycle. Each analysis task addresses a specific set of questions, is based on the analysis of anywhere from two to hundreds (or even thousands) of solved model instances and demands specific AI-based technologies.

Several researchers (Brennan & Elam, 1986; Elam & Konsynski, 1987; Geoffrion, 1987; Hillier & Lieberman, 1990; Kosy & Wise, 1984, 1986; Little, 1970) have suggested several DSS analysis and interpretation tasks that could be addressed by the use of various data mining technologies. We suggest that there are seven inductive analysis tasks used to enhance the development of insights into the decision problem: validation, sensitivity/planning, comparison, causation, recommendation, implementation and post audit. While some of the tasks may contain components of deductive analysis tasks, our focus is on identifying and defining analysis tasks that are primarily inductive in nature. Thus, these represent only a subset of the total set of analysis tasks that a modeler might consider. Each analysis task is discussed individually and illustrated with general questions that are addressed by the task.

Validation

Validation consists of making comparisons between model results and actual, real world situations. How do the results of the model compare with the historical results? Does the model provide answers that are consistent with reality? Does a change in a parameter affect the solutions in the same way that you would expect? If different, are the differences reasonable, explainable and traceable? The results of validation may be one or more modifications in either the mathematical model or the decision maker's mental model, the confidence on the part of the decision maker in the validity of the mathematical model and/or the newly developed insights into the decision-making environment.

Sensitivity Analysis/Planning

Sensitivity analysis consists of "identifying the relatively sensitive parameters (i.e., those which cannot be changed without changing the solution), so that such parameters may be better estimated, and then to select a solution which remains a good one over the range of likely values of the sensitive parameters" (Hillier & Lieberman, 1990, p. 40). How does the model behave under small changes in its assumptions? Are certain model solutions and corresponding decisions particularly robust?

Planning addresses the questions concerning which what-if case should be tried next. For example, which what-if instances should be run next to test the underlying model assumptions or determine alternative solutions that might be better than those already under consideration? What paradigm-specific model settings might be changed (and in what direction) to provide a better model solution? It can be viewed as an extended sensitivity analysis.

Given a set of solved model instances, or what-if cases, the planning function can be viewed as a form of multiple, nonlinear regression analysis in which one wants to determine which parameters are most important in causing the desired change in the variable of interest. This analysis is complicated by the fact that the decision maker does not know which subset of parameters should be included in the regression, which power(s) these parameters should be raised to or what degrees of interaction between parameters is most appropriate.

The primary result of good sensitivity/planning analysis should be a better understanding on the part of the decision maker of the sensitivity of the solution to changes in model parameters or solution settings and greater insight into the critical factors of the decision making environment.

Comparison

Comparison consists of detecting, explaining and suggesting reasons for surprising or unexpected model behavior; e.g., Why did a specific decision variable increase from one model run to another or from one model year to another?; Why did modeled expenses remain flat in 2001 instead of increasing?; Why does the addition of one warehouse change the total costs so much?; or Why does increasing a customer's demand cause its source warehouse to change? These comparisons may concern different parameters or decision variables in a single model instance (e.g., costs in different years of a multi-period model) or different variables in different model instances (e.g., cost differences when demand for a given customer increased by 20 percent). Some researchers suggest that managerial decision makers analyze problems on the basis of differences between model output and similar historical experiences. Little (1970) states that a manager often compares model output with his intuition; substantial differences in the two initiate an iterative process of determining the causes of the differences, and many times lead the manager to learning something new about the interaction of a number of factors and updating his/her intuition. The results of good comparisons include better insight into the model behavior and decision-making environment.

Causation

Causation consists of identifying and quantifying causal relationships between the model solution and the model variables, intermediate variables and/or parameters. What are the key parameters that can most affect the model solution and corresponding decision? Are several decision parameters and/or intermediate variables interrelated and does some combination of changes in these parameters adversely affect my decision? How are these parameters interrelated, i.e., is there a simple, deterministic relation between them and the model solution?

Causation may take the form of generating simplified auxiliary models, or metamodels, that help develop insights into system behavior (Geoffrion, 1976; Sharda & Steiger, 1996). For example, the classic warehouse location problem, which is modeled using mixed integer linear programming, can be reduced (using simplifying assumptions suggested by experienced operations research consultants) to several simple mathematical equations that highlight the key factors and their interrelationships in determining the optimal number and locations of the warehouses. Other researchers have suggested similar metamodels, also developed by experienced human experts, for simulation-based models.

The result of good causation analysis includes (1) identifying the critical factors, (2) defining their interrelationships in simple, mathematical, deterministic terms, and (3) using these relationships to formulate and test hypotheses about the decision-making environment.

Recommendation

Recommendation consists of identifying, evaluating and choosing the most appropriate, or satisfactory, solution to a given problem based on one or more decision maker-specified objective(s). For example, what is the best solution, given a set of assumed or specified evaluation criteria? In some situations, this is a function of trying several (or perhaps many) what-if cases until one is found that satisfies all objectives. In other situations, optimization techniques may be employed to provide the best solution, given the assumed parameter values and objective function.

Implementation

Implementation consists of comparing the current modus operandi with the recommended solution to suggest a minimal, or least offensive, set of changes that would result in a substantial fraction (e.g., 80 percent) of the total improvement promised by the recommended solution. For example, which model solution and corresponding decision could be implemented with the least offensive set of changes (to the current modus operandi or operational status quo) and still realize some large percentage (say 80 percent) of the benefits of the heretofore "best" solution? Can we rank order the best 10 solutions in terms of difficulty to implement or required changes from the status quo? Which changes to the status quo should be implemented first to realize the most benefits early in the implementation process? Implementation might be viewed as a stepwise, multiple, nonlinear regression of the recommended operational changes against levels of the objective, assuming multicollinearity, since some of the changes may be interrelated, i.e., the implementation of one operation change may reduce the impact of a different recommended change.

The output of an implementation analysis consists of an ordered set of changes with the corresponding cumulative and incremental benefits generated by each. For example, if the optimal solution of a warehouse location model recommends building five new warehouses in specified locations, perhaps building three new warehouses in the most opportune locations would result in achieving 90 percent of the target profits with much less capital risk. Thus, the implementation analysis would consist of a list of warehouses and their locations, based on the best order of their construction, and the resulting cumulative and incremental projected profit for the building of each.

Post Audit

Post audit consists of comparing the presumed or forecasted impact of an implemented, model-recommended decision against what actually happens. For example, when this model was used two years ago to help make a decision, did actual results closely correlate to those predicted by the model? Did the actual benefits materialize as forecasted by the model? Has the environment changed significantly since then to require an update or rework of the model? Differences of actual versus forecasted results might be caused by several factors, including poor implementation, bad forecasts, model oversimplification, erroneous assumptions, changes in economic environment and/or erroneous model values. The challenge is to determine what happened, why it happened and how to compensate for such occurrences in the future to improve decision-making.

POTENTIAL KNOWLEDGE DISCOVERY TECHNOLOGIES

As noted previously, the need for such analysis tools is critical, especially with the recent widespread explosion of desktop computing and the associated growth in end-user computing, i.e., the decision makers building and running models and analyzing the results. Researchers have seen this growing need for analysis tools and have proposed various technologies that could be applied. These technologies include classic knowledge discovery technologies (Adriaans & Zantinge, 1998; Cabena, Hadijinian, Stadler, Merhees & Zanasi, 1998; Ebecken & Brebbia, 2002; Han & Kamber, 2001; Witten & Frank, 2000) as well as other related tools, such as the group method of data handling, case-based reasoning, etc. Each of these technologies, along with its potential application to model instance analysis, is discussed briefly below.

Data Visualization

In the classic sense, data visualization is the formation of mental visual images to enhance the process of interpreting data in visual terms. More applicable for model analysis, data visualization is a tool or method for interpreting image data fed into a computer, generating images from complex multidimensional data sets. Specifically, the multidimensional data sets may include the multiple model parameters represented in a set of related model instances, along with the associated solutions. The primary potential uses of data visualization in model analysis include the causation task, where it could be used to help the decision maker picture the effects of changes to various model parameters and their effects on the solution in the form of multidimensional hills and valleys or other pictorial representations.

Example applications of data visualization to industry problems include recognizing potential approach problems in aviation (Smith, 2001) and promoting user confidence in the telecommunication data mining processes (Sterritt, Curran, Adamson & Shapcott, 2002).

Fuzzy Logic

Fuzzy logic is a method of reasoning that allows for partial or fuzzy descriptions of rules. The power of fuzzy logic comes from the ability to describe a particular phenomena or process linguistically and then to represent that description in a small number of very flexible rules (Dhar & Stein, 1997). In model analysis, fuzzy logic is primarily applicable to the validation and post audit tasks, where it would be most advantageous in correlating the fuzzy real world concepts with the more specific mathematical model concepts. It might also be applicable to the recommendation task, when converting the model output to the fuzzy terms of some human decision makers.

Example applications of fuzzy logic in industry include early detection and assessment of assembly problems in manufacturing operations (Yang & Tsai, 2002), reduction of cutting tool times in manufacturing (Anonymous, 2002), and controlling and managing start-ups of offshore oil drilling/production facilities (Campos & Satuf, 2001).

Decision Trees

Decision trees provide a useful method for showing how a problem can be decomposed into a series of smaller subproblems as well as showing the sequential nature of the decision process. They can also be derived inductively from the analysis of case data. In model analysis, decision trees are applicable to the sensitivity analysis and planning task as well as the causation task. In these situations, decision trees can be used to display several trees that might provide insight into the key factors and their influence on the modeled solution. In addition, decision trees might be used in the recommendation and implementation tasks to depict the rationales and probabilities associated with the range of potential solutions.

Example applications of decision trees in industry include potential profit analysis of new drugs in pharmaceutical companies (Boer, 2002), medical diagnosis (Baker, 2002) and risk management analysis in petroleum pipeline construction (Dey, 2002).

Case-Based Reasoning

Case-based reasoning (CBR) is characterized by the decision maker making his inferences and decisions based directly on previous cases recalled from memory rather than general knowledge (Kolodner, 1988). That is, the decision maker tries to avoid or reduce the potential for failure by recalling previous failures, and avoiding the associated pitfalls or changing key factors in those previous failures. He also can speed the decision making process by not having to generate and evaluate all alternatives from scratch. Finally, he can generalize from the attributes of recalled cases to improve decision making in the future (Hammond, 1988).

CBR involves, in the simplest case, the following set of steps: (1) previous case recall, (2) focus on the relevant parts of the recalled case (i.e., the decision maker's current reasoning goals, if the recalled case was successful, or the recalled case's reasons for failure, if it failed) and (3) making a case-based inference or decision based on the parts of the pervious case that are appropriate for the current decision (Kolodner, 1988). The primary advantage of CBR is that it generates knowledge from stored cases (or model instances, in our terms). Assuming that the decision maker's specification of instances has some directed, though unspecified goal (e.g., to learn more about the interaction of variables and their effect on the system being modeled), the set of instances generated during what-if sessions should have some bit(s) of knowledge buried (perhaps perspicaciously) within the instances themselves. Thus, it makes perfect sense to analyze such instances and derive as much knowledge from them as possible. CBR works on this principle. The primary limitations of CBR are: (1) its initial screening of cases and corresponding loss of potential knowledge contained in them, (2) its lack of ability to generate multiple variable relationships, explicitly, to help the decision maker better understand the system, (3) its algorithm limitation associated with changing one or more of the variables in a recalled case to change its outcome and (4) its simulation of changed cases to test the efficacy of any attribute changes.

Example applications of CBR in industry include recording successful knowledge discovery in databases (KDD) experiments and findings (Rodrigues, Ramos & Henriques, 2002), aiding in the recall of applicable legal precedents (Sartor & Branting, 1998) and profiling Web site users by capturing their domain and behavioral preferences (Smyth & Cotter, 2002).

Artificial Neural Networks

Artificial neural networks are biologically inspired by the architecture of nerve cells in the human brain, i.e., they are massively parallel networks consisting of neurons (or nodes) and interconnecting synapses (or arcs) arranged in multiple layers with a large number of interconnections. Neural networks are not programmed; they learn by example. That is, they accept as input a training set consisting of a group of examples from which the network can learn. Each example, in turn, consists of values for each input variable and a correct value from the output variable. Neural networks use these training examples to adjust parameters associated with the interconnections between neurons; the rate of learning is dependent on the rate of interconnection updates.

Neural networks excel at problems involving pattern mapping, pattern completion and pattern classification. They are especially adept at completing noisy and incomplete patterns (i.e., those with segments missing), translating financial time series data into financial predictions, and analyzing and recognizing patterns in visual and acoustic data. Another area in which they excel is in "generalizing on the tasks for which they are trained, enabling the network to provide the correct answer when presented with a new input pattern that is significantly different from the inputs in the training set" (Dayoff, 1990, p. 13).

Applications of artificial neural networks (ANNs) in industry include improving direct mail responses in retail operations (Cabena et al., 1998), fraud detection in credit card accounts (Albrecht & Albrecht, 2002), retail sales analysis and prediction (Ziechick, 2001) and customer satisfaction research (Garver, 2002).

Group Method of Data Handling (GMDH)

The group method of data handling (GMDH) is an inductive, self-organizing technique that employs a multilayered, cascading network of interconnected nodes. Each node induces and represents input/output relations in the form of a quadratic and/ or incomplete cubic polynomial as opposed to the arc weights and sigmoidal transfer functions of neural networks. Like back propagation neural nets, GMDH models are trained via supervised learning on a set of input tuples, each of which contains one or more independent parameter values (objective function coefficients, right-hand side values and/or constraint coefficients) and the corresponding objective function value (dependent parameter). Also like neural nets, GMDH models can be generalized to instances that are not represented in the training data and are commonly applied to forecasting, process control, etc.

GMDH was developed in Russia in the late 1960s (Ivakhnenko, 1971) as an analysis technique for identifying nonlinear (and perhaps complex) relations between system inputs and outputs. By basing the model totally on actual observed data, GMDH eliminates the requirement that the modeler assume and specify relations about the system that are generally impossible to know a priori, e.g., the fertility levels of fish by age group, when modeling fisheries, or the lead/lag relationships between interest rates and the national economy, when modeling economic growth (Farlow, 1984). In essence, GMDH induces such relationships and determines their importance directly from the data.

Applications of GMDH in industry include fraud detection in credit card accounts (Albrecht & Albrecht, 2002), automated target recognition (Drake, Kim, Tony & Kim, 1994) and general business predictive modeling (Abtech Corporation, 1995).

Task-Appropriate Knowledge Mining Technologies: A Proposal

Based on the definitions of the analysis tasks and the promise and potential of the knowledge mining technologies, this section presents our suggestions on the appropriateness of these and other traditional technologies for the model analysis tasks identified in this paper. It is based on our understanding of what these technologies offer today, and what we need for each analysis task. Table 1 summarizes these recommendations. Validation tasks can be aided by statistical analyses of actual data with the results generated by the model, as well as fuzzy logic in using both concrete and fuzzy logic in the validation task. Considerable domain specific work (as in the case of linear programming) already is used for sensitivity analysis. However, decision trees and case-based reasoning that allow generation of rules from examples can be used for sensitivity analysis and planning next analyses. Comparison tasks can be aided by techniques, such as ANNs, GMDH and case-based reasoning.

One of the key tasks of the inductive model analysis is causation: to determine the key factors and relationships among the model parameters. This can be approached by solving the model a number of times under different scenarios and then estimating a relationship among the factors. While relationships among variables may be estimated by using standard statistical techniques, such as multiple regression, techniques such as artificial neural networks, GMDH, visualization and decision trees, might provide more appropriate answers, because these techniques are not subject to the assumptions of normal distribution of data. In generating what-if scenarios, it is difficult to ensure that the model instances will be generated based on normal distribution of underlying uncertain parameters. Recommendation and implementation tasks imply a step beyond traditional optimization. These steps might be able to benefit from decision trees and logic-based optimization, since the analysis is qualitative as well as quantitative. Finally, post audit analysis tasks can benefit from relationship building techniques, such as ANNs, GMDH, CBR and fuzzy logic.

AN EXAMPLE: KNOWLEDGE MINING IN THE CAUSATION TASK

To illustrate the application of one knowledge discovery technology to one analysis task, we formulated a facility location model for a test case. Geoffrion (1976) used a similar model to illustrate an insight-generating simplified auxiliary models developed through mathematical simplification requiring significant human knowledge and exper-

Table 1. Analysis Tasks and Related Technologies

Inductive Analysis Task	Potential AI and Other Technologies
Validation	Statistical Tools, Fuzzy Logic
Sensitivity Analysis and Planning	Knowledge-Based Systems, CBR, Decision Trees, GMDH
Comparison	GMDH, Neural Nets, CBR
Causation	Neural Networks, GMDH, CBR, Data Visualization, Decision Trees
Recommendations	Decision Trees, Data Visualization
Implementation	Decision Trees
Post Audit	GMDH, Neural Nets, CBR, Fuzzy Logic, Data Visualization

tise. The general facility location model, formulated using mixed integer linear programming, is as follows:

$$\text{Min} \quad \Sigma_i \quad \Sigma_j \quad t_{ij} * x_{ij} + \quad\quad \Sigma_j \, f_i * y_i$$

S.T. $\Sigma_i \, x_{ij} = p_j$ for every j

$\Sigma j \, x_{ij} - M * y_i \leq 0$ for every i

$y_i = 0,1$ for every i

$x_{ij} \geq 0$ for every i, for every j

where $x_{i,j} =$ product shipped from the warehouse in city i to satisfy demand in city j

$t_{i,j}$ = transportation cost ($/unit) from warehouse i to demand point j

f_i = fixed costs associated with building a warehouse in city i

p_j = product demand in city j

y_i = a binary variable: 1 if a warehouse is acquired/opened in city i, and

0 otherwise.

To this formulation, Geoffrion (1976) added seven simplifying assumptions, and then used human expertise and mathematical manipulation to generate the following insight-generating simplified auxiliary model for the optimal number of warehouses, n^*, for an area having A square miles of area: $n^* = A/3.05 * (p * t / f)^{2/3}$.

Our illustrative model incorporates approximately the same set of assumptions used by Geoffrion. However, in our model, demand is evenly distributed among the 13 potential cities, instead of being uniformly distributed throughout the plane. Thus, our model represents lumpy demand located in 13 fairly centrally located (but not exactly equidistant) cities, where distances between cities are actual highway miles. Our model depicts the cities in Central Texas, an arbitrary locale chosen simply because a map showing city-to-city driving distances was handy at the time.

The facility location model was formulated as a 13X13 city mixed integer linear programming model using the What's Best! (Savage, 1992) software package to solve specific instances. As an illustration of the causation analysis task and using the INSIGHT software developed in Sharda and Steiger (1996), we generated and solved a set of 24 model instances, each with a different value of one or more of the following variables: total demand, p; warehouse-to-customer transportation rate, t, and/or warehouse fixed costs, f.

Any instance that resulted in an optimal number of warehouses greater than one and less than 13 was accepted as one of the instances to be analyzed. In addition, we ensured that there were at least two model instances that depicted different values for each of the three model variables mentioned above. Both of these restrictions, concerning the selection of model instances to be used in the analysis, could easily be implemented in an expert system module.

GMDH algorithms cannot generate simple models for common terms such as 1/x, sqrt(x) and cos(x). For example, cos(x) would be approximated by an 18th order polynomial, patently unsuitable for our simplified auxiliary model. To address this potential problem, we included in INSIGHT a routine to automatically add 1/x and sqrt(x) for each of the independent input variables specified in Scenario Manager, since these are common terms that might be potential components of any simplified auxiliary model. (A future enhancement to INSIGHT will include the capability for the user to specify such terms at his discretion.)

Based on these 24 model instances, the INSIGHT tool generated the following simplified auxiliary model: $n^* = 700 * (p * t / f)$, using the same three key variables as used in the Geoffrion model in an even more simplified form. This single term explained 92 percent of the total variation from average of the optimal number of warehouses, i.e., $R^2 = 0.92$.

In this model, at least, the INSIGHT results degrade gracefully (with respect to R^2) down to the 10-15 instance range. This indicates that only a modest number of rationally selected instances were required to generate the insightful results shown. Actual results in other models would depend on the model, modeling paradigm, specific instances, complexity of relationship, etc.

Thus, the INSIGHT software, using inductive analysis technologies as applied to the analysis of multiple model instances, was able to duplicate the insight-generating simplified auxiliary model produced by Geoffrion, without using human expertise or mathematical manipulations based on simplifying assumptions. This provides a preliminary illustration (but not a proof) of the productive application of knowledge discovery, when applied to the analysis of multiple, related model instances.

Note that this relation between p, t, f and n^* is valid when all other model parameters are held constant. If other parameter values were varied, those additional parameters, their value and the associated model solutions could be added to the set of instances included in the INSIGHT analysis. Then, if they had a significant impact on the output parameters, they would be included as key factors and included in a (new) relation; or else, they would be ruled out as key factors and would not enter into the key relation. In some models, knowing that a parameter, varied over an appropriate range of values, would not affect the output might be very valuable information indeed.

CONCLUSIONS AND FUTURE TRENDS

This paper has presented a set of inductive model analysis tasks and developed the definitions that can be used in identifying appropriate technologies to implement those tasks. We also provided an example of how these analysis tasks and applicable knowledge discovery technologies could be applied to develop the key factors and key relationships among the model variables based on an analysis of several model instances.

Other model analysis tasks similarly need to be investigated. The operations research (OR) community has emphasized model solution the most. Recently, there have been some enhancements in the formulation stage of the modeling support. It is now time to focus on model analysis.

We also need to explore other pattern recognition technologies that would provide potential key relations. Such technologies might include self-organizing nonlinear regression techniques, based on something other than second- or third-degree polynomial representations, and/or other techniques that employ quality measures more conducive to filtering out unimportant terms and keeping only key terms.

REFERENCES

Abtech Corporation. (1995). *AIM*. Charlottesville, VA.

Adriaans, P., & Zantinge, D. (1998). *Data mining*. Reading, MA: Addison-Wesley.

Albrecht, W. S., & Albrecht, C. C. (2002). Root out financial deception. *Journal of Accountancy, 193*(4), 30-34.

Anonymous. (2002). Hydraulics are the heart of FAST machines. *Manufacturing Engineering, 128*(3), 34-44.

Baker, J. J. (2002). Medicare payment system for hospital inpatients: Diagnosis-related groups. *Journal of Health Care Finance, 28*(3), 1-13.

Boer, F. P. (2002). Financial management of R & D 2002. *Research Technology Management, 45*(4), 23-35.

Brennan, J. J. & Elam, J. J. (1986). Understanding and validating results in model-based decision support systems. *Decision Support System, 2,* 49-54.

Cabena, P., Hadijinian, P., Stadler, R., Merhees, J., & Zanasi, A. (1998). *Discovering data mining*. Upper Saddle River, NJ: Prentice Hall.

Campos, M., & Satuf, E. (2001). Intelligent fuzzy system helps offshore platform start-up. *Oil & Gas Journal, 99*(13), 45-49.

Dayoff, F. (1990). *Neural network architectures*. New York: Van Nostrand Reinhold.

Dey, P. K. (2002). Project risk management: A combined analytic hierarchy process and decision tree approach. *Cost Engineering, 44*(3), 13-26.

Dhar, V., & Stein, R. (1997). *Intelligent decision support methods*. Upper Saddle River, NJ: Prentice Hall.

Drake, K., Kim, C., Tony C., & Kim, R. (1994, February). A multi-technology approach to automated target recognition. *Proceedings of the 11th Night Operations Symposium* (pp. 213-223). Las Vegas, NV. Cambridge, MA: MIT Press.

Ebeken, N., & Brebbia, C. B. (2002). *Data mining II*. London: WIT Press.

Elam, J. J., & Konsynski, B. (1987). Using artificial intelligence techniques to enhance the capabilities of model management systems. *Decision Sciences, 18*(3), 487-501.

Farlow, S. J. (Ed.) (1984). *Self-organizing methods in modeling: GMDH type algorithms*. New York: Marcel Dekker.

Garver, M. S. (2002). Using data mining for customer satisfaction research. *Marketing Research, 14*(1), 8-17.

Geoffrion, A. M. (1976). The purpose of mathematical programming is insight, not numbers. *Interfaces, 7*(1), 81-92.

Geoffrion, A. M. (1987). An introduction to structured modeling. *Management Science, 33*(5), 547-588.

Greenberg, H. J. (1993). Enhancements of ANALYZE: A computer-assisted analysis system for linear programming. *ACM Trans. on Math'l Software, 19*(2), 223-256.

Hammond, K. F. (1988, May). Case-based planning. *Proceedings of a Workshop on Case-based Reasoning* (pp. 12-20). University of Wisconsin. Madison, WI.

Han, J., & Kamber, M. (2001). *Data mining: Concepts and techniques*. San Francisco, CA: Morgan Kaufmann.

Hillier, F. S., & Lieberman, G. J. (1990). *Introduction to operations research* (5th ed., pp. 20-23). New York: McGraw-Hill.

Ivakhnenko, A. G. (1971). Polynomial theory of complex systems. *IEEE Transactions on Systems, Man and Cybernetics 4,* 364-384.

Jones, C. V. (1992). User interfaces and operations research. In E. G. Coffman, J. K. Lenstra & A. Y. Kan (Eds.), *Handbook of operations research, vol. 3* (pp. 603-668). Amsterdam: North-Holland/Elsevier.

Kolodner, J. L. (1988, May). Extended problem solver capabilities through case-based inference. *Proceedings of a Workshop on Case-Based Reasoning* (pp. 21-30). University of Wisconsin. Madison, WI.

Kosy, D. W., & Wise, B. P. (1984, August). Self-explanatory financial planning models. *Proceedings of the National Conference of Artificial Intelligence* (pp. 176-181). Cambridge, MA: MIT Press.

Kosy, D. W., & Wise, B. P. (1986). Overview of Rome: A reason-oriented modeling environment. In L. F. Psu (Ed.), *Artificial intelligence in economics and management* (pp. 21-30). Amsterdam, North-Holland: Elsevier Science Publishers.

Little, J. D. C. (1970). Models and managers: Concept of a decision. *Management Science, 16*(8), B466-B489.

Rodrigues, R. & Henriques (2002). A case-based reasoning framework to extract knowledge from data. In Ebecken, N. & Brebbia, C. (Eds.), *Data mining II* (pp. 102-125). London: WIT Press.

Sartor, G., & Branting, K. (1998). *Judicial application of artificial intelligence.* Dordrecht: Kluwer Academic Publishers.

Savage, S. L. (1992). *What's best!* Chicago, IL: LINDO Systems Inc.

Sharda, R., & Steiger, D. M. (1996). Inductive model analysis systems: Enhancing model analysis in DSS. *Information Systems Research, 7*(3), 328-341.

Smith, B. (2001). Visualization software. *Aviation Week & Space Tech, 155*(5), 17+.

Smyth, B., & Cotter, P. (2000). A personalized television listings service. *Communications of the ACM, 43*(8), 107-111.

Steiger, D. M. (1998). Enhancing user understanding in a decision support system. *Journal of Management Information Systems, 2,* 199-200.

Sterritt, D., Curran, S., Adamson, S., & Shapcott, D. (2002). Visualization for data mining telecomm network data. In Ebecken & Breggia (Eds.), *Data Mining II* (pp. 57-69). London: WIT Press.

Swanson, E. B., & Ramiller, N. C. (1993). Information systems research thematics: Submissions to a new journal, 1987-1992. *Information Systems Research, 4*(4), 299-330.

Witten, I. H., & Frank, E. (2000). *Data mining – Practical machine learning tools and techniques.* San Francisco, CA: Morgan Kaufmann Publishers.

Yang, T., & Tsai, T. (2002). Modeling and implementation of a neurofuzzy system for surface mount assembly defect prediction. *IIE Transactions, 34*(7), 637-646.

Ziechick, A. (2001, October). How data mining makes businesses smarter. *Red Herring, 3,* 23+.

Chapter XII

Empowering Modern Managers: Towards an Agent-Based Decision Support System

Rustam Vahidov
Concordia University, Canada

ABSTRACT

This chapter discusses recent advances in the use of agent technology in Decision Support Systems (DSSs) and introduces a model for an agent-based DSS. The chapter analyzes the modern requirements for the nature of decision support and argues in favor of adopting active situated paradigm as the basis for building DSS. The benefits of agent technology are highlighted in relation to the desired features of DSS and the past research in this direction is reviewed and systematically categorized. The description of an agent-based DSS elaborating on the architecture of the system and the potential use of data mining techniques is then introduced. The approach is illustrated with an agent-based DSS for investment decisions. The chapter informs the readers about the state of art in agent-based DSS, and provides a framework that can be used as a reference model in future research in the area.

INTRODUCTION

The modern business environment is characterized by the abundance and accessibility of information available from a variety of heterogeneous sources. The success of a business largely depends on its capabilities of mining, filtering, processing, transforming and translating this information into timely and effective managerial decisions. The focus of this chapter is on the new generation of tools for facilitating modern managerial decision-making, based on recent developments in agent technologies.

The category of systems that directly targeted managerial decision making known as DSSs were conceived in the early 1970s as the tools for informing decision making processes (Alter, 1981; Sprague & Carlson, 1982). The classical vision behind DSS was in synergistically combining human judgment with the computational power of machines. DSSs were envisaged as incorporating data and modeling tools, borrowing heavily from such areas as statistics, operations research/management science and, later, artificial intelligence. Thus, the decision maker having recognized the problem situation would invoke DSS capabilities (e.g., linear programming, Monte-Carlo simulations) in order to gain insights into the situation, assess the consequences of actions and exercise judgment to make a final decision. He or she would then take the consequent implementation of the decision into the real world.

In the past 30 years, since the conception of DSSs, the business and technological environments have changed in a number of significant ways. The most profound of these changes include:

- globalization of economy and the growing complexity of economic relationships;
- increased need for fast response in the dynamic competitive environment;
- flattening of organizations and growing employee empowerment;
- explosion of information accessible through electronic networks;
- emergence and growth of electronic commerce; and
- better-informed, better-empowered customers, competitors and suppliers.

In light of the above influences, the traditional model of DSS does not adequately serve the objectives of today's decision makers. The concept of a DSS as an isolated passive toolbox can hardly fit in the modern technological picture. There is a need for new frameworks, architectures and tools that could bring the DSS research up to the demands of the day.

One promising technology that has recently gained tremendous popularity is intelligent agents. Although intelligent agents apparently defy precise definition, they are normally characterized by a number of attributes including autonomy, reactivity, proactiveness, social ability, situatedness in the environment, purposefulness, mentalistic ascription, and others (Franklin & Graesser, 1997; Shoham, 1993; Wooldridge & Jennings, 1995). One useful metaphor to employ when thinking of agents is that of a software robot that perceives the cyber-environment in a continuous autonomous fashion, reacts to certain developments, performs delegated tasks and communicates with the principle (user) or other agents.

The development of the Internet, the increased accessibility of information, dramatic decline of computer hardware costs, development of friendly user interfaces, proliferation of information technologies into numerous aspects of business processes and personal lives and other factors paved the road for the increased level of automation, and, hence, triggered huge interest in agent-based technologies. A number of agent-oriented approaches to the business domain have been proposed and demonstrated including business-process management (Jennings, Norman & Faratin, 1998), e-commerce mediation (Maes, Guttman & Moukas, 1999), customer empowerment (Conway & Koehler, 2000; Sen & Hernandez, 2000), supply chain management (Collins, Bilot & Gini, 2000; Nissen, 2000), and others.

The purpose of this chapter is to introduce a new framework for DSSs based on agent technologies. In the subsequent sections, we will analyze the changing requirements for DSS in more detail and argue in favor of employing agent technologies as a basis for the new type of DSS. We will further review the state of the art in agent-based DSS and position our approach in light of the past research. We will further develop a framework for the agent-based DSS, describe a generic architecture for an agent-based DSS and illustrate our vision using a prototypical multi-agent DSS for investment decisions.

THE CHANGING ROLE OF DECISION SUPPORT

The increased use of networked in business environments means there is access to large volumes of internal and external information, creating a possibility for quick and direct response to arising problems and opportunities. We have seen an increasing integration of information systems in business environments, including e-commerce and enterprise resource planning systems. The classical "island" model of DSS is no longer consistent with today's requirements. As it is stressed in Shaw, Gardner and Thomas (1997), the DSS researchers must incorporate the ubiquitous network model in the design of modern DSSs. The concept of "managing by wire" largely reflects the need of today's decision makers to sense and respond to changes in the business environment in real time. "Managing by wire" provisions use Information System power to combine high-level decision making with automation and support of various business operations and monitoring the performance of delegated responsibilities (Haeckel & Nolan, 1993).

The above considerations correlate with the concerns raised by the DSS researchers regarding the passive nature of traditional "toolbox" DSS (Angehrn, 1993; Manheim, 1988). Thus, the notion of active DSS has evolved into a powerful research stream in DSS community (Angehrn, 1993; Carlsson, Kokkonen & Walden, 1999; Limayem & DeSanctis, 2000; Manheim, 1988; Raghavan, 1991; Rao, Sridhar, & Narain, 1994). The basic idea behind active DSS is that the system would take initiative in performing some of the tasks and actively collaborate with the user as opposed to simply enabling the user to invoke its tools.

While activeness is argued to be a desired feature of DSS, the question of synthesizing active DSS and decision makers still remains unresolved. Silver (1991), elaborating on the concept of DSS restrictiveness, noted that the perceived restrictiveness of DSS would be high for the systems with low absolute restrictiveness. He demonstrated it in a form of a paradox, where the system with more capabilities (lower absolute restrictiveness) would be more difficult to use for users lacking appropriate knowledge and skills, and, hence, would be viewed as more restrictive (Silver, 1991). Therefore, DSS's complexity is one of the key barriers to its effective use by decision makers (Carlsson et al., 1999; Chung, Willemain & O'Keefe, 2000; Limayem & DeSanctis,

2000). This is especially true due to the advance of relatively new technologies, such as neural networks, genetic algorithms and others (Dhar & Stein, 1997; Fazlollahi & Vahidov, 2001), and the advance of the Internet and new information-service brokering architectures, like CORBA, that make it possible to "construct" a DSS from a rather large arsenal of DSS components scattered throughout electronic networks (Bhargava, Krishnan, & Muller, 1997; Lang & Whinston, 1999).

Decisional guidance has been used by DSS researchers to help users in search for appropriate decisions (see, e.g., Montazemi, Wang, Nainar & Bart, 1996). However, the danger of any advisory mechanism (suggestive guidance) is that it can potentially lead the user to some limited region in the problem space and also facilitate "user miscalibration (Kasper, 1996).

In our view, there is a need for an additional layer between DSS and the user that would fit the decision-making needs of the user, on one hand, and the technical capabilities of the toolbox. On the other hand. Such a layer would help shift the DSS view from technocratic to managerial. The idea of intermediation is not new in DSS literature. Over two decades ago, Alter (1980) pointed at the mode of DSS use through a human intermediary. We argue that this (non-human) intermediating layer should be organized around human problem-solving/decision-making processes. One popular model in this connection is Simon's three-phase model of Intelligence/Design/Choice (Simon, 1960). We will adopt this model here, since it has served as a reference model extensively in DSS literature.

To summarize, we have argued that DSS in the modern era should be (Table 1): directly connected to the problem domain/business environment, i.e., situated in that environment (Vahidov, 2002); be active participants in the decision process and provide intermediation organized around human decision processes.

EMPOWERING DSS WITH AGENT TECHNOLOGIES

A Model for "Enwrapped" DSS

Figure 1 shows our vision for a new DSS as it relates to its user and the environment. With the increased need for tighter integration of DSS with users and business environments, the additional wrapping layer is envisaged to "enwrap" the "naked" toolbox-like DSS. On the user side, the intermediating layer will conduct the dialogue with

Table 1. Summary of New DSS Requirements

Requirement	DSS Characteristic	Description
Direct sensing and response	Connectedness, situatedness	The ability to directly access important information and directly affect the state of affairs
Timely decisions, reduction of information and work overload	Active nature of support	Automation of some of the decision related tasks, active collaboration
Managerial orientation	DSS-user intermediation	Using human decision-making model to provide adequate support with technical capabilities of DSS

Figure 1. Enwrapped DSS

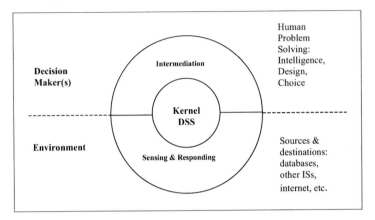

the user to support his/her decision making utilizing kernel DSS capabilities as needed. In a nutshell, this layer will help the user learn more about situation, propose diverse alternative courses of actions and provide quantitative and qualitative feedback on the alternatives to support decision maker's judgment. On the environment side, the layer will provide possibly advanced sensing and affecting capabilities to "situate" the DSS in the problem environment. Such linking can facilitate direct and timely (and possibly partially automated) response to external challenges. There is a temptation to call this model an "encapsulated" DSS by analogy with an object-oriented approach. However, while in proper object-oriented settings the "internals" of the objects should be strictly hidden from the outside, here we do not impose such requirements. For instance, it could be appropriate to allow access to the "naked" DSS tools for some proficient decision makers.

The kernel contains models and data and can be thought of as a "traditional" DSS. Nonetheless, the kernel may have an active component (other than the ones embedded in the intermediation and sensing and responding layers).

We propose the use of agent technologies as a basis for building a new type of DSS. Viewed as one of the most important computing paradigms of the near future, these software units are often characterized by autonomy, reactivity, proactiveness, social ability and situatedness in some environment (Franklin & Graesser, 1997; Jennings, 2000; Wooldridge & Jennings, 1995). The key human-agent relationship in agent-based computing is that of delegation. The idea is to transform a human worker into a manager (Yen, 2000). As Negroponte (1997, p. 58) puts it: "future human-computer interface will be rooted in delegation, not the vernacular or direct manipulation." Since organizational DSS users are mostly managers, a delegation-centered approach that agent technologies provide is a very promising direction of future human-DSS collaboration.

Table 2 links the characteristics for DSS we outlined before to the features of software agents. In order to promote "connectedness," or "situatedness," DSS agents can be utilized in the sensing and responding layer. The possibility of directly affecting the environment as a consequence of decision-making has been largely ignored in the past DSS research. Agent technology adds this radically new insight to the design of DSSs. Furthermore, the social ability and autonomy of agents enable them to act as intermediaries between the system and the user. Agents have been used as mediators

Table 2. Desired DSS Characteristics and Features of Software Agents

DSS Characteristic	Agent Features	Explanation
Connectedness, situatedness	Situatedness, sensors and effectors	Agents are situated in and have means of direct interaction with the target environment. DSS can be "situated" through agents
Active nature of support	Autonomy, reactivity, proactiveness	Agents can perform tasks on their own, react to changing conditions, and take initiative in setting and accomplishing goals. This can facilitate active support in DSS
DSS-user intermediation	Social ability, autonomy	Due to autonomy and social ability agents are good candidates for intermediaries

in other areas, including e-commerce (Chavez, Dreilinger, Guttman & Maes, 1997; Karacapilidis & Moraitis, 2001; Maes et al., 1999) and human-system interaction (Koutsabasis, Darzentas, Spyrou & Darzentas, 1999).

Agent-Empowered DSSs: State of the Art

Agent technologies have been applied to enhance decision support in the recent past. From a system point of view agents have the highest level of abstraction and modularity known in computer science, thus promising to facilitate and simplify the development of complex software systems (Jennings, 2001). Large systems comprised of multiple interacting agents are referred to as multi-agent systems (MAS). MAS are naturally characterized by the distributed nature of processing. The units of distribution include: data, control, expertise and resources (Jennings & Wooldridge, 1998). Since DSS can include/interact with multiple agents (a single-agent DSS being a trivial subset of MAS), we can adopt the nature of distributedness as a basis for categorizing past research in the area. We can distinguish the following units of distribution: decision task (entire DSS), DSS components, information sources, expertise and stakeholders (people). These units will serve as a basis for categorizing agent-based DSS applications in the past. Note that this categorization is not strict in the sense that a particular approach may suit several categories. Nonetheless, we tried to classify the existing work according to the focus as it relates to the above categories.

In the "DSS as an agent" approach, the entire DSS is viewed as an agent that automates all tasks that are amenable to automation. Such DSS are characterized with high level of activeness as opposed to the traditional systems. For example, in Hinkkanen, Kalakota, Saengcharoenrat and Whinston (1997), the idea of an agent acting as a DSS for supply-chain decisions has been proposed. The approach would enable the system to react in real time to changing conditions and relieve human decision makers from most routine activities. Such a DSS would carry out most decisions automatically and alert the user if something unexpected happened. The authors provided an example incorporating raw materials agent, production agent and finished good inventory agent. In Tseng and Gmytrasiewicz (2002), an agent DSS has been described for real-time portfolio management. The architecture of the agent included KB, Decision Models, Interface and Executors. The authors demonstrated the system using experiments with 12 stocks. The "DSS as agent" approach promotes the vision for active DSS. The main disadvantage is in the uniqueness (lack of generality) of the solutions and, hence, the difficulty of using the same agents for other problems.

In "DSS components" model, various parts and functionalities of DSS are provided by agents. Such a DSS could incorporate one or more agents that perform specific decision-related tasks. In Hess, Rees and Rakes (2000), agents were utilized to encapsulate basic DSS components. Five types of agents were utilized: data-monitoring, data-gathering, modeling, domain manager and preference learning. The early work by Angehrn (1993) is an example of an idealistic vision for high cognitive level human-DSS collaborative problem solving, using a virtual team of agents that provide continuous stimuli to human decision makers. The agents were envisaged to be providers, servants, experts or mentors, composing virtual teamwork. Use of agents in DSS during the "choice" phase of problem solving is exemplified through the automated critiquing approach. In O'Connor, Cochran and Moynihan (2000), the Prompter system is described for assisting in the planning and managing of software projects. In Vahidov and Elrod (1999) two types of critiquing agents were introduced: positive and negative critics. The critics produced the qualitative feedback on the alternative decisions during the "what-if" process, in addition to the traditional numeric feedback. "Agents as DSS components" is a promising venue for future research as it facilitates development of potentially reusable agents.

Agent technology is one of the key solutions to gathering information in distributed heterogeneous environments (March, Hevner & Ram, 2000). From a DSS perspective, information agents are helpful in delivering information that is relevant to a given decision or an on-going decision-making process. Sycara and Zheng (1996) proposed an elegant architecture for information gathering and decision support. The approach distinguished three types of agents: information agents, task agents and interface agents. Information agents handle the issues of selecting, accessing information sources, conflict resolution and other information-centric processing. Task agents perform decision support through formulating and solving decision-related problems and communicating with information agents, if necessary. Interface agents are responsible for interacting with the users and capturing user preferences. Various task agents can serve different interface agents. This framework has been illustrated using portfolio management problem (Sycara, Decker & Zeng, 1997). In Shaw, Mian and Yadav (2002), an architecture for an agent-based information retrieval system has been proposed. The architecture included five types of agents: including intelligent user information (intermediating user-system interaction), query enhancing (enhancing queries based on user profile), searching and routing (accessing distributed information sources), filtering (filtering data based on user profile) and analysis and synthesis (data mining, report generation, etc.). A prototype system AgentRAIDER illustrated some of the aspects of the architecture. Effective information gathering is an important prerequisite to sensing the environment and successful decision-making, and the work in this area is very important. This capability should be included in DSS and combined with other supporting tools used in decision-making.

Complex problems may be decomposable to subproblems that require variety of expertise. For example, to conduct a thorough diagnosis a physician can send a patient to different specialists and then incorporate their feedback in final diagnosis. Hence, in DSS for complex decision tasks, the unit of distribution could be the expertise necessary to handle various subtasks. Rao et al. (1994) proposed architecture for active agent-based DSS with multiple knowledge processors (agents) that specialize in specific areas. The agent called "facilitating element" handled the system-user interactions. The problem solving started with facilitating element extracting from the description of the user's problem. The agents were then assigned subproblems and set to work on them. The coordinating agent synthesized the individual solutions into the composite solution, using simple conflict resolution method, if it was necessary. The DSS for air fleet control was used for the illustration. Pinson, Louca and Moraitis (1997) proposed a design for a multi-agent DSS for strategic planning. In devising a global strategic plan, coordination among several actors is necessary. The approach utilized multiple cooperating agents that were competent in carrying out specific tasks and attempting to maximally automate the overall process. The process focused on specifying a number of alternatives and trying to come up with the satisfactory solution. The difficulties with this approach lie in the necessity of providing mechanisms for problem decomposition and allocation, solution integration and conflict resolution.

Another possibility for the use of agents as a part of a multi-agent DSS is to associate them with different stakeholders in the decision. Shaw and Fox (1993) discussed the application of distributed artificial intelligence (multi-agent) system to group DSS. A Networked Expert System Testbed (NEST) prototype had been implemented to illustrate the approach. NEST had a blackboard architecture through which several expert agents cooperated. The Group Decision Support System (GDSS) for concurrent design, including marketing, manufacturing, distribution and other expert agents, was discussed. The agents acted as advisers and coordinated solutions. Ito and Shintani (1997) described an approach to GDSS where agents used persuasion to achieve consensus. Individual agents associated with group participants maintained the user preferences in form of an Analytic Hierarchy Process (AHP) model. The agents communicated with each other trying to persuade others to adopt their proposals. During the process, the agents interacted with the user to revise their AHPs. After successful persuasion, the agents formed groups. The session ended when overall consensus was reached. Another use of agents in group work coordination was reported in Bordetsky and Mark (2000). Here the agents were not associated with individual parties, but rather acted as facilitators in active retrieval and storage of relevant cases in the group collaboration process. The approach was tested in a German government ministry.

GDSS-type uses for agent technologies is appropriate for situations where tightly coordinated or common decisions need to be made by several parties.

Table 3 summarizes the above overview. Since our primary interest here is the design of DSS, we chose to adopt the components category of agent-based DSS. In this view, the DSS is composed of agent components that work together with the user to support managerial decision-making.

ARCHITECTURE FOR AN AGENT-BASED DSS

Situated DSS: Sensing and Responding

Table 4 exposes the relationships between artificial intelligence (AI), agents and DSSs. The field of AI had produced expert systems as a means of mimicking expert

Table 3. Summary of Agent-Based DSS Categories

Unit of Distribution	Description	Advantages	Disadvantages
Decision task	"DSS as agent." The entire DSS acts as a semi-autonomous agent automating most of the routine tasks.	High level of activeness.	Lack of generality. Idiosyncratic design.
DSS components	Some components of DSS or aspects of problem solving are organized as agents.	Provides activeness, has more generality.	Provision of coordination procedures between component agents may be necessary.
Information sources	Facilitates extraction and pre-processing of information from heterogeneous sources.	Delivers timely information from a variety of sources.	Information delivery only partially supports decision-making process.
Expertise	Large problems are decomposed and sent to different agents that have diverse expertise.	Brings together all necessary competence to approach a global problem.	Is applicable to rather complex large problems. Problem decomposition and solution synthesis issues need to be handled.
Stakeholders	When a group of people have to make a common decision or work together on a problem.	Helps to automate some of the intra-group interactions.	Is not applicable to single-user decisions.

decision-making. Situating these systems in the problem environments led to the development of intelligent agents. We strongly believe that situating DSSs within problem environments, linking them to the means of directly sensing the relevant data and issuing control signals to change the environment can bring about the type of decision support that today's organizations need. Having such a system at their disposal, the decision makers could "buckle up" and use it to sense what's going on in their respective problem domains, utilize traditional DSS facilities to inform their decisions, make the choices and change the state of affairs through the digital tentacles of the situated system. Moreover, the situatedness of the system will allow delegation of some of the tasks to the system.

Situating the DSS should involve adding two major capabilities: the capability to assess the state of affairs (sensory capability) and the capability to change the state of affairs (effectory capability). These capabilities provide the sensing and responding layer in Figure 1. The generic architecture for our vision for a situated DSS comprises four main parts: kernel, sensors, effectors and intermediaries (Figure 2).

The kernel is composed of the DSS facilities in a traditional sense. Sensors are agents that capture, filter and transform the data from the variety of sources. Effectors are the agents that a situated DSS uses to send a signal to the problem environment with the purpose of directly altering the current state of affairs. The effectors are not necessarily simple vehicles of decision execution or communication, but may engage in different activities required to implement a decision (e.g., converting the decision into

Table 4. Comparison of DSS, Expert Systems and Intelligent Agents

	Decision Support	Artificial Intelligence
Traditional	DSS	Expert Systems
Situated	Situated DSS	Intelligent Agents

Figure 2. A Generic Architecture for a Situated DSS

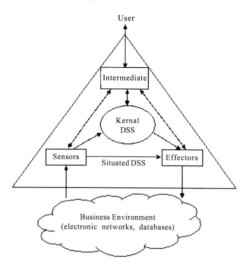

more detailed plans, optimizing the well-structured aspects of a decision, conducting negotiations, etc.).

Note that the separation of sensors and effectors here is prompted by the distinct roles they play in carrying out the interactions with the problem domain. Implementation-wise these parts can be integrated into a single module. Intermediaries are agents that use system resources to support managerial decision-making. These will be discussed later in the chapter.

In the trivial case, the sensors would just import relevant information into the DSS from the environment. More advanced sensors, though, would have the capabilities to locate, filter, transform relevant information and also generate alerts, if necessary. For example, in Nunes-Suarez, O'Sullivan, Brouchoud, Cros, Moore and Byrne (2000), agents access information from airline databases as necessary to support travel planning. In Das and Grecu (2000), a "cognitive" agent is described that is designed to amplify human perception and cognition in critical environments. In the realm of e-commerce, classical examples of agents for information gathering include: BargainFinder, Jango, Firefly and Tete-a-tete (Maes et al., 1999). In general, we identified the following set of sensor functions: accessing, filtering, conversion, monitoring information and generating alerts, if a critical situation arises. We also envisage such advanced features as identifying new sources of information (e.g., through interacting with search engines or crawling the Web), and even tuning some of the sensing functions (e.g., adjusting thresholds that trigger alert generation).

The focus on the intelligence/design/choice trinity in DSS research largely led to the oversight of the implementation phase. This probably has not been a significant impediment in the past, since the means of linking DSS outputs to the problem environ-ment were rare. In a modern world, there is less need to "switch media" while moving from decision making to decision implementation (McDonald & Tobin, 1998). The common means of manipulating virtual objects on the Internet include such tools as ftp, telnet, mail and others (Etzioni & Weld, 1997). Moreover, the effectors can potentially reach beyond the virtual world and into the physical one. In fact, 98 percent of the computing power is embedded in different types of devices facilitating proactive computing with humans placed "out and above the loop" (Tennenhouse, 2000). Implementation, in general, involves carrying out the decisions, and also may entail corresponding planning and optimization activities, monitoring of execution, reviewing and even negotiating, if necessary. For example, production decision may require purchase of certain items from suppliers, and effectors could award bids to the winning suppliers (Nissen, 2000). The functions that effectors need to be able to perform include affecting the state of environment, converting the decisional outputs into actions, monitoring the execution of actions, alerting if a problem is encountered, negotiating the details of decisions or transactions and planning execution of actions.

DSS-User Intermediation

As we have mentioned earlier, it is important to organize the DSS around human decision-making processes. The basic idea, elaborated in greater detail elsewhere (Vahidov, 2000), is that the agents will be using the DSS tools to support different phases of decision0-making. Not all of the tools may be used by all agents in every type of problem, and the agents will also have interactions among them as well as directly with sensing and responding layers, as required. In accordance with Simon's model, we included three types of agent intermediaries: agents of intelligence, design and choice groups. It is important to note that these do not form a mere trivial "interface" to the DSS capabilities but are active collaborators in the decision-making process. They make use of the DSS toolbox (kernel) to serve the purpose of human decision maker in the intermediation mode.

The intelligence agents are primarily concerned with the delivery and interpretation of relevant information to the user. They interact primarily with sensors and local databases (in DSS kernel) to receive information, assess situations, request further information from the sensors, if necessary, and provide the user with the informative description of the problem. These agents may also employ data mining methods to obtain a better insight into the problem domain. The results of data mining can be used to warn of developing problems/opportunities.

The design phase is primarily concerned with alternative generation. We emphasize the role of pluralistic models in generating diverse alternatives. The use of pluralistic models has been advocated before. Jones and Jacobs (2000) considered the inclusion of multiple perspectives (points of view) as one of the "tenets" of effective human-machine cooperation. Malhotra, Sharma and Nair (1999) proposed the use of multiple diverse classification models within a DSS, where consensus is sought among the models to produce the final outcome.

We have sought to incorporate the pluralistic philosophy in our alternative generating agents. The design group agents generate their alternative decisions based on their "views" and "values." The "views" reflect different opinions on the relationships between key variables in the domain or on the ways to achieve a given set of objectives. For example, in security analysis, fundamental and technical analysis are two different schools of thought representing different "views." The "values" refer to different sets of objectives that define the set of "good" alternatives. For example, trying to capture market share (maximize sales) and maximizing profit could be considered as "good" alternatives and could be sought by different agents with corresponding "values." Here also, data mining techniques could be used to build different models, reflecting different views and values. In short, the design agents use the data, models and knowledge to generate diverse alternatives according to their "views" and "values."

The choice phase is where the decision maker systematically analyzes the alternatives and makes a final decision. We have chosen a critiquing system approach as a kernel for our choice agents. Critiquing systems take a proposed decision as an input, in addition to the description of situation at hand, and provide a critique of the decision as an output, if necessary (Fischer & Mastaglio, 1991; Silverman, 1992). We mentioned earlier one example of critiquing systems in DSS (O'Connor et al., 2000). Our approach to modeling choice agents is based on the insight that human beings tend to evaluate alternative courses of actions in terms of pros and cons. We, therefore, adopted the approach reported in Vahidov and Elrod (1999), where distinction between the positive and negative critique had been made. Data mining techniques can be used in this respect to assess the possible consequences of decisions.

DSS Architecture

The summary of agents used to facilitate active interaction of DSS with its environment and the user is given in Table 5. Figure 3 provides an expanded generic architecture for the agent-based situated DSS. The intermediaries' box has been enriched by the three types of agents discussed above. The agents communicate via blackboard during environment monitoring and decision-making.

The DSS architectures represented in Figures 2 and 3 are qualitatively different from the traditional models. We propose a label "Decision Station" for such a "situated" DSS. Ideally the user of a Decision Station would be able to directly access timely and relevant information, interact with the system to arrive at a decision and execute the decision directly through the system.

DSS FOR INVESTMENT DECISIONS

In order to illustrate our approach, we have developed a prototype DSS for supporting investment decisions. The problem of investments requires selection of a

Table 5. Summary of Agents in DSS

DSS Agents	Layer	Functions
Sensors	Sensing and responding	Accessing, filtering, pre-processing, monitoring information, alerting
Effectors	Sensing and responding	Affecting , converting decisions to actions, monitoring execution, negotiating the details of transactions
Intelligence	Intermediary	Information delivery and interpretation, situation assessment & presentation to the user
Design	Intermediary	Generating diverse alternatives by views and values
Choice	Intermediary	Critiquing alternatives, identifying pros and cons

Figure 3. Expanded Architecture of an Agent-Based DSS

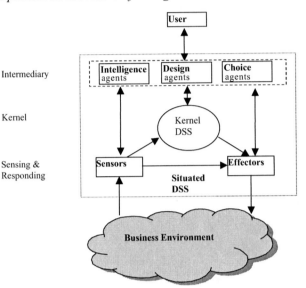

weighted portfolio of securities that suits the investor's objectives (Elton & Gruber, 1995). The purpose of the prototype DSS is to assist the user (decision maker) in his/her investment decisions by determining a portfolio of securities. The prototype specifically targets equity instruments (stocks) selected from the software industry. At the time of writing, the prototype includes the sensors and intermediary agents of the Design and Choice groups.

The design group consists of four intermediaries. These agents differ on value dimension by their attitude towards risk (risk taking vs. risk aversion), and on the view dimension by their views (fundamental vs. technical schools). Therefore, the four intermediaries are: risk-taking technically-minded; risk-averse technically-minded; risk-taking fundamentally-minded and risk-averse fundamentally-minded.

The intermediaries use the knowledge and models for fundamental and technical analysis incorporated in DSS. The fundamental analysis has been essentially restricted to a simplified ratio analysis. The major categories of ratios include profitability ratios, solvency ratios and value ratios. The technical analysis tools include trend determining models and knowledge for identifying the securities that are likely to grow in value. Technical indicators include moving averages (MAs) of price and their crossovers, momentum, relative strengths and others (Pring, 1991). The intermediaries determine the portfolios of the fixed size (10 securities). The risk-taking agents look for maximizing the expected return and accepting somewhat high risk, while risk-averse agents try to keep risk under control and earn moderate return.

The Choice Team consists of two critiquing agents (negative: "devil" and positive: "angel") that analyze and critique the proposed portfolios. There are a number of important factors taken into consideration while making investment decisions, including expected return and risk, user preferences and the source of alternative portfolios. Generally, one seeks to maximize return while controlling risk. This knowledge is used for providing objective-related critique. If the user chooses a portfolio with the expected return being high, the "angel" detects this and tells user "the expected return of this portfolio is high." The "devil," on the other hand, may detect high risk associated with the proposed allocation and prompt the user. The preference-related critique examines the solution from the point of view of the user's preferences. If the user is a risk taker, high risk would trigger the positive critique. On the other hand, if the user is risk averse, the negative critique would identify the inappropriate risk level.

Figure 4 shows the user interface of the prototype. The available stocks (actual symbols are coded by Xs) are listed in a list box on the left. The return and risk estimates of the portfolio are displayed in the upper right corner. Every time these are recalculated, critiquing agents start analyzing the newly defined portfolio. The central part of the screen contains portfolios generated by the design agents.

The prototype could be enhanced by effectors as well as intelligence agents. The effectors could link to various online brokerage firms as alternative outlets for the ordering. They could support different types of order and can monitor execution of the orders.

Intelligence agents could continuously assess market and portfolio performance information provided by sensors to decide if intervention is necessary. They could also customize presentation of this information to the needs and style of the decision maker. Such a system would be active, collaborative and highly responsive to the changes in the market. A more detailed discussion of the prototype is given elsewhere (Vahidov, 2000).

CONCLUSION

Organizations can fully realize the vast potential of the information age if they learn to utilize the abundance of accessible information for timely and effective managerial decision-making. DSSs have been used for the past three decades or so for informing managerial decision-making. In this chapter, we have postulated that in the modern business environment the DSS should be active, situated in the environment and

Figure 4. Investment DSS Prototype

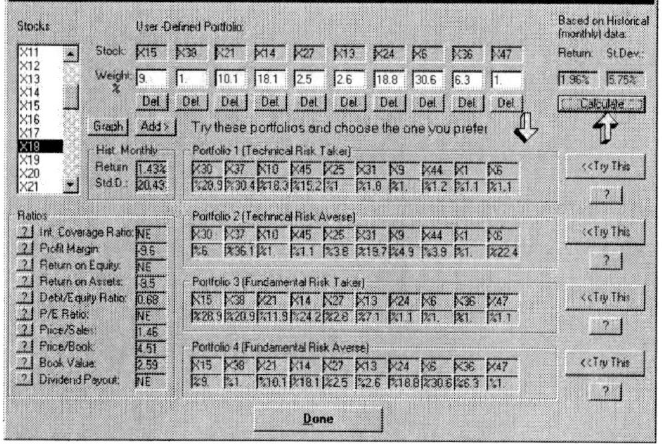

organized around managerial decision processes. We have argued that use of agent technologies could empower the traditional DSS with such capabilities. After systematically reviewing the existing applications of software agents to DSS, we have proposed an architecture comprised of the kernel DSS enwrapped into the sensing and responding and intermediary layers. We labeled such a system a "Decision Station." We have elaborated on the composition of these layers and discussed possible use of data mining techniques by the agents. We have illustrated our vision using a prototype system for investment decision support.

One limitation of our conceptual model for DSS is the fact that it does not explicitly address group and cooperative decision-making. While we can envisage these types of interactions and communications conducted through sensors and effectors, a more thorough future examination of this issue is needed. Another apparent problem is the complexity of the proposed architecture. However, not all types of agents may be needed for particular applications. Moreover, with the development of component technologies, the DSS could possibly be assembled from distributed prebuilt components, instead of having to develop the system from the scratch.

Future research should be directed towards developing and assessing a prototype with full functionality and exploring other problem areas. Furthermore, more theoretical work needs to be done regarding elaboration of the implementation phase of decisions. We believe that the new generation of DSS will benefit from the employment of software agent technology in a fashion described in this chapter.

REFERENCES

Alter, S. (1980). *Decision support systems: current practice and continuing challenges.* Reading, MA: Addison-Wesley.

Alter, S. (1981). *Transforming DSS jargon into principles for DSS success.* Paper presented at the Transactions of the International Decision Support Conference. Execucom Systems Corporation, Atlanta, GA (June 18-10).

Angehrn, A. A. (1993). Computers that criticize you: Stimulus-based decision support systems. *Interfaces, 23*(3), 3-16.

Bhargava, H. K., Krishnan, R., & Muller, R. (1997). Decision support on demand: Emerging electronic markets for decision technologies. *Decision Support Systems, 19,* 193-214.

Bordetsky, A., & Mark, G. (2000). Memory-based feedback controls to support groupware coordination. *Information Systems Research, 11*(4), 366-385.

Carlsson, C., Kokkonen, O., & Walden, P. (1999). *On the improvement of strategic investment decisions and active decision support systems.* Paper presented at the 32nd Hawaii International Conference on System Sciences. Maui, Hawaii.

Chavez, A., Dreilinger, D., Guttman, R., & Maes, P. (1997). A real-life experiment in creating an agent marketplace. In H. S. Nwana & N. Azarmi (Eds.), *Software agents and soft computing* (pp. 160-179). Berlin, Germany: Springer-Verlag.

Chung, Q. B., Willemain, T. R., & O'Keefe, R. M. (2000). Influence of model management systems on decision making: Empirical evidence and implications. *Journal of the Operational Research Society, 51,* 936-948.

Collins, J., Bilot, C., & Gini, M. (2000, June). *Mixed-initiative decision support in agent-based automated contracting.* Paper presented at the Fourth International Conference on Autonomous Agents, Barcelona, Spain.

Conway, D. G., & Koehler, G. J. (2000). Interface agents: Caveat mercator in electronic commerce. *Decision Support Systems (Decision Support System), 27*(4), 355-366.

Das, S., & Grecu, D. (2000, June). *COGENT: Cognitive agent to amplify human perception and cognition.* Paper presented at the Fourth International Conference on Autonomous Agents, Barcelona, Spain.

Dhar, V., & Stein, R. (1997). *Intelligent decision support methods: The science of knowledge work.* Upper Saddle River, NJ: Prentice-Hall.

Elton, E. J., & Gruber, M. J. (1995). *Modern portfolio theory and investment analysis* (5th ed.). New York: John Wiley & Sons.

Etzioni, O., & Weld, D. (1997). A softbot-based interface to the Internet. In M. N. Huhns & M. P. Singh (Eds.), *Readings in agents* (pp. 77-81) San Francisco, CA: Morgan Kaufmann.

Fazlollahi, B., & Vahidov, R. (2001). A method for generation of alternatives by decision support systems. *Journal of Management Information Systems, 18*(2), 229-250.

Fischer, G., & Mastaglio, T. (1991). A conceptual framework for knowledge-based critic systems. *Decision Support Systems, 7*, 355-378.

Franklin, S., & Graesser, A. (1997). Is it an agent, or just a program? A taxonomy for autonomous agents. In J. P. Muller, M. J. Wooldridge & N. R. Jennings (Eds.), *Intelligent agents III: Agent theories, architectures, and languages* (pp. 21-36). Berlin: Springer Verlag.

Haeckel, S., & Nolan, R. (1993, September-October). Managing by wire. *Harvard Business Review, 71*(5), 122-132.

Hess, T. J., Rees, L. P., & Rakes, T. R. (2000). Using autonomous software agents to create next generation of decision support systems. *Decision Sciences, 31*(1), 1-31.

Hinkkanen, A., Kalakota, R., Saengcharoenrat, P., & Whinston, A. B. (1997). Distributed decision support systems for real-time supply chain management using agent technologies. In R. Kalakota & A. Whinston (Eds.), *Readings in electronic commerce* (pp. 275-292). Reading, MA: Addison Wesley Longman.

Ito, T., & Shintani, T. (1997, August). *Persuasion among agents: An approach to implementing a group decision support system based on multi-agent negotiation.* Paper presented at the 15th International Joint Conference on Artificial Intelligence (IJCAI-97), Nagoya, Japan.

Jennings, N., & Wooldridge, M. (1998). Applications of intelligent agents. In N. Jennings & M. Wooldridge (Eds.), *Agent technology: Foundations, applications and markets.* Berlin, Germany: Springer-Verlag.

Jennings, N. R. (2000). On agent-based software engineering. *Artificial Intelligence, 117*(2), 277-296.

Jennings, N. R. (2001). An agent-based approach for building complex software systems. *Communications of the ACM, 44*(4), 35-41.

Jennings, N. R., Norman, T. J., & Faratin, P. (1998). ADEPT: An agent-based approach to business process management. *ACM SIGMOD Record, 27*(4), 32-39.

Jones, P. M., & Jacobs, J. L. (2000). Cooperative problem solving in human-machine systems: Theory, models, and intelligent associate systems. *IEEE Transactions on*

Systems, Man, and Cybernetics - Part C: Applications and Reviews, 30(4), 397-407.

Karacapilidis, N., & Moraitis, P. (2001). Building an agent-mediated electronic commerce system with decision analysis features. *Decision Support Systems, 32*(1), 53-69.

Kasper, G. M. (1996). A theory of decision support system design for user calibration. *Information Systems Research, 7*(2), 215-232.

Koutsabasis, P., Darzentas, J. S., Spyrou, T., & Darzentas, J. (1999). *Facilitating user-system interaction: The GAIA interaction agent.* Paper presented at the 32nd Hawaii International Conference on System Sciences, Hawaii. Maui, Hawaii (January 5-8).

Lang, K. R., & Whinston, A. B. (1999). A design of a DSS intermediary for electronic markets, decision support systems. *Decision Support Systems, 25*(3), 193-214.

Limayem, M., & DeSanctis, G. (2000). Providing decisional guidance for multicriteria decision making in groups. *Information Systems Research, 11*(4), 386-401.

Maes, P., Guttman, R. H., & Moukas, A. G. (1999). Agents that buy and sell. *Communications of the ACM, 42*(3), 81-87.

Malhotra, M. K., Sharma, S., & Nair, S. S. (1999). Decision making using multiple models. *European Journal of Operations Research, 114*, 1-14.

Manheim, M. (1988). *An architecture for active DSS.* Paper presented at the 21st Hawaiian International Conference on Systems Sciences. Kailua Kona, Hawaii. (January 5-8).

March, S., Hevner, A., & Ram, S. (2000). Research commentary: An agenda for information technology research in heterogeneous and distributed environments. *Information Systems Research, 11*(4), 327-341.

McDonald, J., & Tobin, J. (1998). Customer empowerment in the digital economy. In A. Lowy & D. Ticoll (Eds.), *Blueprint to the digital economy: Creating wealth in the era of e-business* (pp. 202-220). New York: McGraw-Hill.

Montazemi, A. R., Wang, F., Nainar, K. S. M., & Bart, C. K. (1996). On the effectiveness of decisional guidance. *Decision Support Systems, 18*, 181-198.

Negroponte, N. (1997). Agents: From direct manipulation to delegation. In J. M. Bradshaw (Ed.), *Software agents* (pp. 57-66) Cambridge, MA: MIT Press.

Nissen, M. E. (2000). *Supply chain process and agent design for E-Commerce.* Paper presented at the 33rd Hawaii International Conference on System Sciences. Maui, Hawaii (January 4-7).

Nunes-Suarez, J., O'Sullivan, D., Brouchoud, H., Cros, P., Moore, C., & Byrne, C. (2000, June). *Experiences in the use of FIPA agent technologies for the development of a personal travel application.* Paper presented at the Fourth International Conference on Autonomous Agents, Barcelona, Spain.

O'Connor, R., Cochran, R., & Moynihan, T. (2000, June). *Prompter - A project planning assistant.* Paper presented at the International Conference on Software Engineering, Limerick, Ireland.

Pinson, S. D., Louca, J. A., & Moraitis, P. (1997). A distributed decision support system for strategic planning. *Decision Support Systems, 20*(1), 35-51.

Pring, M. J. (1991). *Technical analysis explained: The successful investor's guide to spotting investment trends and turning points.* New York: McGraw-Hill.

Raghavan, S. A. (1991). JANUS: A paradigm for active decision support. *Decision Support Systems, 7*, 379-395.

Rao, H. R., Sridhar, R., & Narain, S. (1994). An active intelligent decision support system. *Decision Support Systems, 12*(1), 79-91.

Sen, S., & Hernandez, K. (2000, June). *A buyer's agent.* Paper presented at the Fourth International Conference on Autonomous Agents, Barcelona, Spain.

Shaw, M., & Fox, M. (1993). Distributed artificial intelligence for group decision support. Integration of problem solving, coordination and learning. *Decision Support Systems, 9*, 349-367.

Shaw, M., J., Gardner, D., M., & Thomas, H. (1997). Research opportunities in electronic commerce. *Decision Support Systems, 21*, 149-156.

Shaw, N. G., Mian, A., & Yadav, S. B. (2002). A comprehensive agent-based architecture for intelligent information retrieval in a distributed heterogeneous environment. *Decision Support Systems, 32*(4), 401-415.

Shoham, Y. (1993). Agent-oriented programming. *Artificial Intelligence, 60*, 51-92.

Silver, M. (1991). *Systems that support decision makers: Description and analysis.* New York: Wiley.

Silverman, B. G. (1992). *Critiquing human error: A knowledge based human-computer collaboration approach.* London: Academic Press.

Simon, H. A. (1960). *The new science of management decision.* New York: Harper.

Sprague, R. H. J., & Carlson, E. D. (1982). *Building effective decision support systems.* Englewood Cliffs, NJ: Prentice-Hall.

Sycara, K. P., & Zeng, D. (1996). *Multi-agent integration of information gathering and decision support.* Paper presented at the European Conference on Artificial Intelligence. Budapest, Hungary (August 12-16).

Sycara, K. P., Decker, K., & Zeng, D. (1997). Intelligent agents in portfolio management. Jennings, R. & Wooldridge, M. (Eds.), *Agent technology: Foundations, applications, and markets* (pp. 267-282). Heidelberg, Germany: Springer Verlag.

Tennenhouse, D. (2000). Proactive computing. *Communications of the ACM, 43*(5), 43-50.

Tseng, C.-C., & Gmytrasiewicz, P. J. (2002, January). *A real time decision support system for portfolio management.* Paper presented at the 35th Annual Hawaii International Conference on System Sciences, Big Island, Hawaii.

Vahidov, R. (2000). *A framework for multi-agent DSS.* Unpublished doctoral dissertation, Georgia State University, Atlanta.

Vahidov, R. (2002, January). *A notion for a situated DSS.* Paper presented at the 35th Hawaii International Conference on System Sciences, Big Island, Hawaii.

Vahidov, R., & Elrod, R. (1999). Incorporating critique and argumentation in DSS. *Decision Support Systems, 26*(3), 249-258.

Wooldridge, M., & Jennings, N. (1995). Intelligent agents: Theory and practice. *Knowledge Engineering Review, 10*(2), 115-152.

Yen, J. (2000). Special issue of DSS - Intelligent agents and digital community. *Decision Support Systems, 28*, 217-218.

Chapter XIII

Mining Message Board Content on the World Wide Web for Organizational Information

Cheryl Aasheim
Georgia Southern University, USA

Gary J. Koehler
University of Florida, USA

ABSTRACT

This chapter proposes a methodology to scan, analyze and classify the content of primarily text-based Web documents to aid an organization in gathering information. The representation and classification of the document is based on the popular vector space model and linear discriminant analysis, respectively. The methodology is developed and demonstrated using real chat room discussions about a publicly traded company collected over a 12-day period. The purpose of this chapter is to develop and demonstrate a methodology used to aid an organization in its environmental scanning efforts, in light of the vast quantities of information available via the Internet.

INTRODUCTION

Data and knowledge derived from data is critical to an organization. The amount of data available to an organization for possible analysis via sources both internal and external is vast. Processing, interpreting, using and managing data is paramount to an organization's success. One source of information is the World Wide Web (WWW). There are many documents of primarily text-based data available on the WWW including documents from chat rooms, message boards and news documents. Content analysis of such documents can provide an organization with useful information for decision-making. One corporation, Opion, is making use of Web documents to obtain useful information for an organization by monitoring chat rooms (Wakefield, 2001).

The purpose of this paper is to provide a process to scan, analyze and classify the content of Web documents in an automated manner, in order to provide useful information to an organization for the purpose of decision-making. The Web documents analyzed are text-based messages from chat rooms or message boards that are written about various organizations. The content of message boards can be used to detect possible future changes in the stock returns or trading volume for an organization, its key vendors, distributors and/or competitors. This chapter will outline how such documents could be organized, analyzed and used by an organization to gain valuable information.

The process developed in this chapter combines many areas of research including the vector space model (VSM) introduced by Salton (1968), linear discriminant analysis introduced by Fisher (1936), environmental scanning (Aguilar, 1967) and text classification methods (for examples, see Hayes & Weinstein, 1990; Lewis & Ringuette, 1994; Apte, Damerau & Weiss, 1994; Wiener, Pedersen & Weigend, 1995; Lewis, Schapire, Callan & Papka, 1996; Cohen & Singer, 1996; Moulinier, Raskins & Ganascia, 1996; Yang, 1994; Vapnik, 1995; Cortes & Vapnik, 1995). First, a brief review of each of the areas of research is provided. Next, we describe the process used to analyze the Web documents and provide an example. The chapter concludes with a discussion of the implications of our process in practice.

LITERATURE REVIEW

Environmental scanning is a process that involves gathering and using information from an organization's environment to aide management in decision-making (Aguilar, 1967; Choo & Auster, 1993; Lester & Waters, 1989). Aguilar (1967) was the first to classify the types of search an organization uses to scan the environment. The categories he developed are undirected viewing, conditioned viewing, informal search and formal search. Choo (1995) provides a framework for examining the environmental scanning literature prior to 1995. He organizes the literature into the following research categories: information needs as the focus of environmental scanning, information seeking use and preferences, information seeking through scanning methods and information use. He reviews the major contributions in each area.

Several studies have found a link between organizational performance and scanning activity (Miller & Friesen, 1977; Newgren, Rasher & LaRoe, 1984; Dollinger, 1984; West, 1988; Daft, Sormunen & Parks, 1988; Subramanian, Fernandes & Harper, 1993;

Subramanian, Kumar & Yauger, 1994; Murphy, 1987; Ptaszynski, 1989). In addition, the development of the Internet has provided organizations with a vast amount of information. "Companies of all shapes and sizes are finding that the Internet provides new opportunities for competitive advantage" (Cronin, 1993, pp. 40-43). Pawar and Sharda (1997) warn that unsystematic gathering of information via the Internet can be costly and time consuming. They say that an Internet-based scanning system can provide benefits, including the timeliness, low-cost and quantity of the information available, but can also have high search costs. Drucker (1998) claims that the development of information technology has had little or no impact on strategic decision-making. Others support this by noting some of the drawbacks of the quantity and quality of information. For example, Denton (2001) states that organizations are drowning in too much information and claims that the Internet should be used to concentrate on critical information to simplify decision-making. Hence, there is a need for a Web-based scanning system to organize and classify information available on the Internet via primarily text-based Web pages in an automated manner with minimal search costs to aide an organization in decision-making.

Often the end result of environmental scanning is to determine various signals. For example, will the economy go up or down over the next period? Will a competitor introduce a new product in the next period, and so on. We seek a method that takes large amounts of text data from the Internet and produces signals of interest in an automated fashion. This method must scale well for large amounts of data.

Many data mining, knowledge-extraction and machine-learning methods are available for reducing observed data into knowledge of some sort but all such methods start with several assumptions. A taxonomy of these methods would partition on the nature of the independent and dependent variables (nominal, ordinal, etc.), the hypothesis space of possible results (e.g., decision trees, discriminant functions, neural nets, etc.) and a host of other factors. Here, we start with text data and wish to produce a categorical signal. Decision trees (see Quinlan, 1993) are often used to represent rules, where the attribute partitions lead to leaf nodes providing a classification. They scale well for large amounts of data and have been used successfully in many areas. However, decision trees are not well suited for text-based attributes primarily due to the rapid growth in independent variables (a variable for each word). Neural-nets (e.g., Fausett, 1994) have had great successes in financial areas, pattern recognition and other applications but are generally hard to train especially with large amounts of data. Discriminant functions (Fisher, 1936) are determined by methods that scale well for large data sets and have been used widely in loan approval and other applications. However, linear discriminant functions work best with real-valued attributes. We start with a discussion of methods used to reduce text to real-valued attributes.

The problem of analyzing the content of text-based documents for classification purposes is not new. The purpose of text categorization is to classify each document in a document collection into zero to multiple categories, based on a predefined set of categories. Many algorithms have been written for the text classification problem including CONSTRUE (Hayes & Weinstein, 1990), DTree (Lewis & Ringuette, 1994), NaiveBayes (Lewis & Ringuette, 1994), SWAP-1 (Apte et al., 1994), Nnets (Wiener et al., 1995), Rocchio (Lewis et al., 1996), k-NN (Hayes & Weinstein, 1990) and support vector machines (SVM) introduced by Vapnik (1995) and Cortes and Vapnick (1995). Many of the algorithms are based on statistical learning methods and some are based on the VSM

(Salton, 1968). The process discussed in the next section is based on the VSM (Salton, 1968) in accordance with the most popular text categorization algorithm, Rocchio (Lewis et al., 1996), also based on the VSM.

The first problem encountered in text categorization is how to represent the documents. Salton (1968) developed the VSM to represent documents and queries issued by users as vectors. Using vectors to represent documents provides a quantitative approach to the problems of information retrieval and text categorization. The basic idea in the VSM is to convert documents to vectors by first converting each word in the document to its word stem and then constructing the document vector by counting the frequency of each word stem in that document.

After a suitable document representation has been decided, the next problem in text classification is the method of categorization. As the VSM provides a linear representation of documents, it is natural to categorize the documents via linear discriminant analysis (LDA) or natural generalizations, such as support vector machines (Vapnik, 1995; Cortes & Vapnik, 1995). This is in contrast to the categorization method used in the Rocchio (Lewis et al., 1996) algorithm. In Rocchio, each document vector is categorized according to a set of prototype vectors. Each predefined category has a prototype vector constructed based on a training set of documents. Each document is ranked according to a similarity measure comparison between the document vector and each prototype category vector.

In LDA (Fisher, 1936), one or more discriminant functions are determined based on a training set of documents, and each document is categorized according to its score in the discriminant function. The goal of LDA is to find the discriminant functions that best separate observations into classes by minimizing the number of misclassifications of observations or some surrogate criterion (Koehler & Erenguc, 1990). Due to several restrictive assumptions in Fisher's LDA (1936), such as multivariate normality, Mangasarian (1965) and Rosen (1965) proposed mathematical programming methods for discriminant analysis. Later, Hand (1981) and Freed and Glover (1981a, b) examined the linear programming (LP) approach to LDA in greater depth. Ragsdale and Stam (1991) reviewed the various LP approaches developed to date and their problems. Additionally, they offered two simplified formulations based on the classification gap called the epsilon minimize the maximum deviations (EMMD) model and the epsilon minimize the sum of deviations (EMSD) model.

As stated, the purpose of this paper is to combine the aforementioned areas of research to develop a process that scans, analyzes and classifies the content of chat-room discussions about an organization to detect and/or predict changes in the trading volume of the organization's stock or changes in the organization's stock returns. The process involves four main steps: (1) collecting Web documents, (2) representing documents via the vector space model, (3) separating a training set of documents using two-group linear discriminant analysis and (4) using the discriminant function determined by LDA to classify new documents.

In order to collect documents, predetermined chat-room Web sites need to be identified and monitored regularly. The text-based content of the Web sites is put into vector format by (1) eliminating stop words, (2) representing each word in the document collection with word stems, (3) computing the frequency of each distinct word stem in each document, called the term frequency (tf), (4) including only word stems with frequencies of more than four, (5) scaling each term frequency with the inverse document frequency (idf) as suggested in the information retrieval literature (Salton and Buckley, 1988) and (6) normalizing each document vector.

Once the documents are represented as vectors, a training set of document vectors is used to determine the discriminant function. The training set is first classified as group 1 or group 2. Documents appearing the day before an increase in trading volume are classified as group 1 documents. Documents appearing before a decrease or no change in trading volume are classified as group 2 documents. The discriminant function is found via linear discriminant analysis (Fisher, 1936). The combination of the VSM and LDA to classify the text-based documents is in contrast to Rocchio (Lewis et al., 1996), in that a discriminant function is found to classify documents as opposed to measuring the similarity between documents and prototype category vector. Finally, new documents collected from message boards are used to predict changes in the next-day's trading volume.

PROCESS OUTLINE

As previously mentioned, the Web-based scanning process developed in this paper involves four steps. In this chapter, each of these is described in detail. Additionally, the application setting is discussed.

Application Setting and Document Collection

The information that is gained via chat room or message board discussions can be quite valuable. Opion, a consulting company that profits from gathering and analyzing such information for publicly traded corporations, examines the relationship between the content of chat room discussions and stock returns (Wakefield, 2001). Additionally, the relationship between stock returns and news is a hot topic in the financial literature, with several very recent papers in the financial literature examining this relationship (Huberman & Regev, 2001; Chan, 2001; Daniel & Titman, 2001). The purpose of this chapter is to outline a process that can be used to explore the relationship between the content of message board discussions about publicly traded companies and the corresponding changes in trading volume.

As mentioned previously, the chat room or message board sites that are monitored for a particular company will be predetermined. On a daily basis, the content of the message board discussions will be downloaded for analysis. Initially, message board discussions and trading volume for a company are collected for a period of time, to be used as a training set for the calculation of the linear discriminant function via LDA. In the training set, the message board content is represented via the VSM, then LDA is used to separate the message board discussions, based on changes in trading volume in the next period following the appearance of the message board discussion. Based on the use of LDA as the classification tool, two research questions are:

RQ1: How well does the process classify or group the training set of documents based on changes in trading volume?

RQ2: Does the process predict the correct change in trading volume better than random guessing?

Document Representation

For a given company, **k** message board discussions will be collected to determine if the text or terms in the discussion indicate whether the company's trading volume will increase or decrease in the target period following the discussion. Once the discussions or documents are collected, a set of **n** index terms needs to be determined. Let $\mathbf{t}_1, \dots, \mathbf{t}_n$ for $\mathbf{t}_i \in \Re^n$, be the vectors corresponding to the **n** index terms. The term vectors form a vector space. When the terms are linearly independent, the dimensionality of the vector space is **n**. For a summary of the notation, see Table 1.

With full dimensionality, each document can be written as a linear combination of term vectors. Documents are represented by vectors, $\mathbf{d}_r$. For the collection of **k** documents or message board discussions about a company, an $\mathbf{n} \times \mathbf{k}$ document by term matrix **D** can be constructed with the document vectors, where each column of the document matrix corresponds to a document vector $\mathbf{d}_r$.

$$\mathbf{d}_r = \sum_{i=1}^{n} a_{i,r} \mathbf{t}_i = \mathbf{T}\mathbf{a}_r \tag{1}$$

$$\mathbf{d}_r = \mathbf{D}\mathbf{e}_r = \mathbf{T}\mathbf{A}\mathbf{e}_r \quad r = 1,\dots,k \tag{2}$$

The elements of $\mathbf{d}_r$ are the term weights, when the terms are orthogonal, which can be confirmed by $\mathbf{t}_i'\mathbf{d}_r = a_{i,r}$.

The set of terms, $\mathbf{t}_1, \dots, \mathbf{t}_n$, used to represent the document collection and the term weights, $\mathbf{a}_r$, for the terms in document **r** are determined by an indexing operation (Salton, 1989). The first step in indexing is eliminating stop words and html formatting in the document collection. Next, each word in the document is replaced with its corresponding word stem. Then, the frequency of each distinct word stem in each document $\mathbf{d}_r$ is computed. This is called the term frequency, $\mathbf{tf}_{i,r}$. To avoid large term vectors, only word stems with term frequencies above four are used. For each of the remaining terms in document $\mathbf{d}_r$, the set of term weights for the document are computed by:

$$a_{i,r} = \mathrm{tf}_{i,r} \cdot \log\left(k \middle/ \mathrm{df}_i \right), \tag{3}$$

where $\mathbf{tf}_{i,r}$ is the term frequency, **k** is the number of documents in the collection and $\mathbf{df}_i$ is the number of documents in the collection that contain term **i**. The second term in the right-hand side of Equation 3 is an idf. Each document $\mathbf{d}_r$ is represented, according to Equation 1. Finally, each of the document vectors $\mathbf{d}_r$ is normalized.

Document Classification

Once the training set of documents have the above representation for each company, each document needs to be classified as first appearing a day prior to the trading volume increasing or as first appearing a day prior to the trading volume decreasing. All the documents that correspond to an increase in the company's trading volume are group 1 documents, π_1, and the documents that correspond to a decrease or no change in trading volume are group 2 documents, π_2. Hence, all documents are classified as $\mathbf{d}_i, i=1$, if $\mathbf{d}_r \in \pi_1$ and $i=2$ if $\mathbf{d}_r \in \pi_2$. Let k_1 be the number of group 1 documents,

Table 1. Variable Definition

Variable	Meaning
k	Number of documents
k_i	Number of documents in group i, i = 1, 2, k = k_1 + k_2
n	Number of terms
t_i	n × 1 term vector representing term I
T	n × n term matrix where t_i's are the columns
d_r	n × 1 vector for document r, $d_r = De_r$
D	n × k matrix where d_r's are the columns
D_i	n × k_i matrix where d_r's in group i are the columns, i = 1, 2
A	n × k term document matrix where $a_{i,r}$ is the weight of term i in document r
a_r	n × 1 term weight vector for document r, $a_r = Ae_r$
π_i	Documents in group i, i = 1, 2
z	Cutting score for Fisher discriminant analysis
q_i	k_i × 1 vector of distances for documents in group i, i = 1, 2
1_i	Column vector N_i × 1 of ones, i = 1, 2
w	Vector of discriminant weights
w_0	Intercept of discriminant function

so that $k_2 = k - k_1$ is the number of group 2 documents. Let $d_1, ... , d_{k_1}$ be the group 1 documents and $d_{k_1+1}, ... , d_{k_1}$ be the group 2 documents.

Discriminant analysis is then used to derive a variate, $w'd_r$, that best discriminates between the groups. In the classic Fisher approach, the elements of w are weights that are determined by maximizing the between group variance relative to the within group variance. The discriminant score, z_r, is calculated for each document by $z_r = w'd_r$. The score is used to predict whether the document is in group 1 or group 2, according to the cutting score z by:

$$w'd_r \geq z \quad d_r \in \pi_1$$
$$w'd_r \leq z \quad d_r \in \pi_2. \tag{4}$$

Once the discriminant function has been determined, based on the training set of documents, new message board documents can be classified according to content. The new documents are represented according to the index term set, and the discriminant score is calculated by $z_r = w'd_r$ for each document. On a given day, more than one document may be collected. The average discriminant score, $\bar{z}_r$, for documents collected on a given day is calculated. If the average discriminant score is above the cutting score, the message board discussions for that day indicate an increase in trading volume in the next period. Otherwise, the discussions signal no change or a decrease in trading volume.

EXAMPLE

Message board content for E.I. Du Pont De Nemours & Co. (DuPont) was downloaded at Yahoo! Finance for 12 days. The total number of messages or documents was

$k = 188$. The messages on a given day were classified as appearing prior to an increase in DuPont's trading volume at the close of the next business day, and added to π_1, or as appearing prior to a decrease or no change in trading volume, and added to π_2. The trading volumes for the days collected in our sample and corresponding group memberships are given in Table 2. The total number of documents in π_1 was $k_1 = 78$ and the number in π_2 was $k_2 = 110$.

The content of each message was cleaned and then stemmed as discussed earlier. For stemming, we used the Porter stemming algorithm (Porter, 1980). The java code for the Porter stemming algorithm was obtained from http://www.tartarus.org/~martin/ PorterStemmer/java.txt. The number of distinct word stems in the entire document collection after cleaning and stemming was 2,159. Only word stems with frequencies in the entire document collection above four were actually used, to avoid large term vectors and reducing the number of distinct word stems to 323.

The document frequency, df_i, was calculated for each of the 323 remaining terms or word stems in the document collection. For each term in each document collection, the term weight was calculated by Equation 3. For example, the word stem "account" occurred in the entire document collection six times. Therefore, "account" was in the final set of 323 terms. The inverse document frequency, the second term in the right-hand side of Equation 3, is $\log\left(\frac{188}{6}\right) = 1.496$. This term occurred once in the second document collected on the first day. Therefore, the term weight for "account" in that document was $a_{i,r} = 1.496$.

Now, each document is represented by a 323×1 vector of term weights. Group membership for each document is known. Linear discriminant analysis was performed on the document collection via SPSS version 10.0.5. The group mean or centroid of the canonical discriminant functions for π_1 is $z_1 = 1.622$. The group centroid for π_2 is $z_2 = -1.150$.

Table 2. Trading Volume and Group Membership for DuPont*

Date	Volume	Group
March 20	2623000	2
March 19	2627400	1
March 18	2028600	2
March 15	4444000	1
March 14	2416800	1
March 13	2287500	2
March 12	2321800	2
March 11	2680100	1
March 8	2407000	2
March 7	2857600	2
March 6	4321200	1
March 5	4027700	2
March 4	4260500	

* *Source: http://table.finance.yahoo.com/k?s=dd&g=d*

As the groups are not of equal size, a weighted average is used to compute the cutting score z. Hence, the cutting score, assuming equal costs of misclassification, is $z = (k_2 z_1 + k_1 z_2)/(k_1 + k_2) = 0.472$ (Hair, Anderson, Tatham & Black, 1998). Documents that have discriminant function values above this cutting score are classified as belonging to π_1 and as belonging to π_2, otherwise. The classification matrix for the training set of documents is given in Table 3. The number of correct classifications is 171 or 91 percent. This percentage is quite high compared to two criteria for judging classification accuracy in Hair et al. (1998). The first criterion is to compare the classification accuracy percentage to a value 25 percent higher than would be obtained by simply classifying all documents in the group with the higher number of documents, 73.1 percent. The second criterion, the proportional chance criterion, is based on a comparison to the proportion of cases that would be correctly classified by chance. With unequal group sizes, this value is $((78/188)^2 + (110/188)^2)*100 = 51.4$ percent. As the classification accuracy of our data is significantly higher than the percentages suggested by these two criteria, our classification accuracy is quite high. Additionally, Wilks' lambda (Hair et al., 1998), another criterion that is used to assess the significance level of the discriminant function's discriminatory power, is 0.346 with a level of significance of 0.12.

Cross validation of the training set of documents was performed using the standard jackknife procedure. The cross-validation classification matrix is given in Table 4. The number of correct classifications is 104 or 55.3 percent. This percentage is higher than the proportional chance criterion of 51.4 percent, previously mentioned. Press's Q is a statistical measure of predictive accuracy, based on the chi-square distribution with one degree of freedom (Hair et al., 1998). Press's Q is given by:

$$\text{Press's} Q = \frac{(N - nK)^2}{N(K-1)},$$
(5)

where N is the number of discriminant cases, K is the number of groups in the classification and n is the number of cases classified correctly. For the cross validation given, Press's Q is 2.13, which is not statistically significant at 0.10.

The calculated discriminant function and cutting score can be used to predict changes in trading volume, based on new message board discussions. Periodically, the

Table 3. LDA Classification Matrix

| | | Predicted Group Membership | | Total |
		π_1	π_2	
Original Count	π_1	62	16	78
	π_2	1	109	110
Total		63	125	188

discriminant function and cutting score should be updated as new documents are collected and trading volumes are monitored.

DISCUSSION: CONCLUSION AND FUTURE RESEARCH

The purpose of this chapter was to outline a process to scan, analyze and classify the content of primarily text-based Web documents to aid an organization in gathering information. A key advantage of the process described in this chapter is that it can be automated.

The example given in this chapter uses the content of message boards for DuPont to classify documents, according to changes in trading volume. The process can be used for other applications as well. The relationship between news and stock returns and between chat room discussions and stock returns was previously mentioned. The process discussed in this chapter can easily be adapted to classify news documents and chat room discussion documents according to stock returns. Non-financial applications are easily imagined, too. For example, chat room discussions, critic reviews and press releases for movies are documents that can be classified according to the success of a movie. As new movies are released, their success can be predicted based on the content of the aforementioned documents. Another example is political in nature. The text from chat room discussions, news articles, campaign releases and expert analysis can be used to predict the outcome of an election.

The cross-validation results presented in the previous section show promise, as the percent of correctly classified documents is higher than the proportional chance criterion. However, Press's Q statistic is not statistically significant in the cross-validation procedure. The authors believe that one reason for the weak results is the small scale of the study. Another reason for the weak results from a statistical standpoint is the ratio of documents to variables. There are 188 documents with 323 independent variables. Hair et al. (1998) suggests a 5:1 ratio of observations to variables. This reinforces the need for a larger scale study. The ratio of observations to variables problem can also be solved by putting a limit on the number of variables included in the discriminant procedure. This limit can be imposed through a step-wise linear discriminant procedure, with a maximum number of entering variables. Another way to improve the

Table 4. Cross Validation Classification Matrix

		Predicted Group Membership		Total
		π_1	π_2	
Cross-Validated Count	π_1	32	46	78
	π_2	38	72	110
Total		70	118	188

results is to use linear programming approaches to solve the discriminant analysis problem and to ameliorate departures from the assumptions made by the Fisher model. Finally, in a larger scale study, the linear discriminant function, computed with the use of the training set, needs to be updated periodically as the trading volume for the holdout sample becomes known. The authors believe that updating the linear discriminant function periodically will improve results.

There are several, potentially enhancing additions that can be made to the process. Variables can be added to include information about the nature and reliability of the source of message board discussion, news article or chat room discussion. Techniques to reduce the dimension of the document vectors can be added to the process, such as Latent Semantic Indexing introduced by Deerwester, Dumais, Furnas, Landauer and Harshman (1990). The use of linear programming approaches to the discriminant analysis problem should be investigated to ameliorate the departures from assumptions made by the Fisher model. The dependent variable, changes in trading volume, can be changed to classify documents according to the level of trading volume as opposed to whether volume has increased or decreased as compared to the previous day. Previously, classification, based on changes in stock returns, was mentioned. In the future, a trading strategy can be developed and tested based on the linear discriminant function determined by using stock return as the classification mechanism.

This study presents a small illustrative example and, not surprisingly, did not produce significantly better results than chance alone. Larger studies are needed to test the predictive power of the methodology and to bring to light factors that may not scale for practical implementations.

REFERENCES

Aguilar, F. J. (1967). *Scanning the business environment.* New York: Macmillan.

Apte, C., Damerau, F., & Weiss, S. (1994). Towards language independent automated learning of text categorization models. *Proceedings of the 17th Annual ACM/SIGIR Conference.* Dublin, Ireland (July).

Chan, W. S. (2001). *Stock price reaction to news and no-news: Drift and reversal after headlines.* Working paper, Massachusetts Institute of Technology. Cambridge, MA.

Choo, C. W. (1995). *Information management for the intelligent organization: The art of scanning the environment.* Medford, NJ: Information Today, Inc.

Choo, C. W., & Auster, E. (1993). Scanning the business environment: Acquisition and use of information by managers. In M. E. Williams (Ed.), *Annual review of information science and technology.* Medford, NJ: Learned Information, Inc.

Cohen, W. W., & Singer, Y. (1996). Context-sensitive learning methods for text categorization. *SIGIR '96: Proceedings of the 19th Annual International ACM SIGIR Conference on Research and Development in Information Retrieval,* (pp. 307-315). Zurich, Switzerland (August).

Cortes, C., & Vapnik, V. (1995). Support-vector networks. *Machine Learning, 20,* 273-297.

Cronin, M. J. (1993, November/December). What's my motivation? Why businesses are turning to the Internet. *Internet World,* 4(9), 40-43.

Daft, R. L., Sormunen, J., & Parks, D. (1988). Chief executive scanning, environmental characteristics, and company performance: An empirical Study. *Strategic Management Journal, 9*(2), 123-139.

Daniel, K., & Titman, S. (2001). *Market reactions to tangible and intangible information*. Working paper, Northwestern University. Evanston, IL.

Deerwester, S., Dumais, S. T., Furnas, G. W., Landauer, T. K., & Harshman, R. A. (1990). Indexing by latent semantic analysis. *Journal of the American Society for Information Science, 41*(6), 391-407.

Denton, D. K. (2001). Better decisions with less information. *Industrial Management, 43,* 21-25.

Dollinger, M. J. (1984). Environmental boundary spanning and information processing effects on organizational performance. *Academy of Management Journal, 27* (2), 351-368.

Drucker, P. E. (1998, August 24). The next information revolution. *Forbes,* 46-53.

Fausett, L. (1994). *Fundamentals of neural networks*. New York: Prentice Hall.

Fisher, R. A. (1936). The use of multiple measurements in taxonomic problems. *Annals of Eugenics, 7,* 179-188.

Freed, N., & Glover, F. (1981a). A linear programming approach to the discriminant problem. *Decision Sciences, 12,* 68-74.

Freed, N., & Glover, F. (1981b). Simple but powerful goal programming formulations for the discriminant problem. *European Journal of Operational Research, 7,* 44-60.

Hair, J. F., Anderson, R. E., Tatham, R. L., & Black, W. C. (1998). *Multivariate data analysis*. Upper Saddle River, NJ: Prentice Hall, Inc.

Hand, D.J. (1981). *Discrimination and classification*. New York: John Wiley & Sons.

Hayes, P.J., & Weinstein, S.P. (1990). Construe/tis: A system for content-based indexing of a database of news stories. *Proceedings of the Second Annual Conference on Innovative Applications of Artificial Intelligence* (pp. 1-5) Georgetown, Washington, DC.

Huberman, G., & Regev, T. (2001). Contagious speculation and a cure for cancer: A non-event that made stock prices soar. *Journal of Finance, 56,* 387-396.

Koehler, G. J., & Erenguc, S.S. (1990). Minimizing misclassifications in linear discriminant analysis. *Decision Sciences, 2,* 63-85.

Lester, R., & Waters, J. (1989). *Environmental scanning and business strategy*. London: British Library, Research and Development Department.

Lewis, D. D., & Ringuette, M. (1994). Comparison of two learning algorithms for text categorization. *Proceedings of the Third Annual Symposium on Document Analysis and Information Retrieval*. Las Vegas, NV (April).

Lewis, D. D., Schapire, R. E., Callan, J. P., & Papka, R. (1996). Training algorithms for linear text classifiers. *Proceedings of the 19th Annual International ACM SIGIR Conference on Research and Development in Information Retrieval,* (pp. 298-306). Las Vegas, NV (April).

Mangasarian, O. L. (1965). Linear and nonlinear separation of patterns by linear programming. *Operations Research, 13,* 444-452.

Miller, D., & Friesen, P. H. (1977). Strategy-making in context: Ten empirical archetypes. *Journal of Management Studies, 14*(3), 253-280.

Moulinier, I., Raskins, G., & Ganascia, J. (1996). Text categorization: A symbolic approach. *Proceedings of the Fifth Annual Symposium on Document Analysis and Information Retrieval.*

Murphy, M. F. (1987). Environmental scanning: A case study in higher education. Unpublished doctoral dissertation, University of Georgia, Athens, GA.

Newgren, K. E., Rasher, A. A., & LaRoe, M. E. (1984). An empirical investigation of the relationship between environmental assessment and corporate performance. *Proceedings of the 44th Annual Meeting of the Academy of Management* (August, pp. 352-356). Washington, DC.

Pawar, B., & Sharda, R. (1997). Obtaining business intelligence on the Internet. *Long Range Planning, 30,* 110-121.

Porter, M. F. (1980). An algorithm for suffix stripping. *Program, 14*(3), 130-137.

Ptaszynski, J. G. (1989). Ed quest as an organizational development activity: Evaluating the benefits of environmental scanning. Unpublished doctoral dissertation, The University of North Carolina at Chapel Hill.

Quinlan, J. R. (1993). *C4.5: Programs for Machine Learning.* San Francisco, CA: Morgan Kauffman.

Ragsdale, C. T., & Stam, A. (1991). Mathematical programming formulations for the discriminant problem: an old dog does new tricks. *Decision Sciences, 22,* 296-307.

Rosen, J. B. (1965). Pattern separation by convex programming. *Journal of Mathematical Analysis and Applications, 10,* 123-134.

Salton, G. (1968). *Automatic information organization and retrieval.* New York: McGraw-Hill Book Co.

Salton, G. (1989). *Automatic text processing.* Reading, MA: Addison-Wesley Publishing Co., Inc.

Salton, G., & Buckley, C. (1988). Term weighting approaches in automatic text retrieval. *Information Processing and Management, 24* (5),513-523.

Subramanian, R., Fernandes, N., & Harper, E. (1993). Environmental scanning in US companies: Their nature and their relationship to performance. *Management International Review, 33* (3), 271-286.

Subramanian, R., Kumar, K., & Yauger, C. (1994). The scanning of task environments in hospitals: An empirical study. *Journal of Applied Business Research, 10* (4), 104-115.

Vapnik, V. N. (1995). *The nature of statistical learning theory.* New York: Springer Verlag.

Wakefield, J. (2001, November). Catching a buzz. *Scientific American,* 285(5), 30-32.

West, J. J. (1988). Environmental scanning, and their effect upon firm performance: An exploratory study of the food service industry. Unpublished doctoral dissertation, Virginia Polytechnic Institute and State University. Blacksburg, VA.

Wiener, E., Pedersen, J. O., & Weigend, A. S. (1995). A neural network approach to topic spotting. *Proceedings of the Fourth Annual Symposium on Document analysis and Information Retrieval.* Las Vegas, NV (April).

Yang, Y. (1994). Expert network: Effective and efficient learning from human decisions in text categorization and retrieval. *Proceedings of the 17th Annual International ACM SIGIR Conference on Research and Development in Information Retrieval,* 13-22. Dublin, Ireland (July).

Section IV

Industrial ODM Applications

Chapter XIV

Data Warehousing: The 3M Experience

Hugh J. Watson
University of Georgia, USA

Barbara H. Wixom
University of Virginia, USA

Dale L. Goodhue
University of Georgia, USA

ABSTRACT

Data warehouses are helping resolve a major problem that has plagued decision support applications over the years — a lack of good data. Top management at 3M realized that the company had to move from being product-centric to being customer savvy. In response, 3M built a terabyte data warehouse (global enterprise data warehouse) that provides thousands of 3M employees with real-time access to accurate, global, detailed information. The data warehouse underlies new Web-based customer services that are dynamically generated based on warehouse information. There are useful lessons that were learned at 3M during their years of developing the data warehouse.

INTRODUCTION

The information systems field has a long history of using computers to support decision making. The 1960s saw management reporting systems, the 1970s witnessed decision support systems (DSS) and the 1980s saw executive information systems (EIS). Throughout the 1990s and continuing on to today, there is great interest in online analytical processing (OLAP), data mining, customer relationship management (CRM) and other decision-support applications.

While there have been many successes with these applications, there have also been many failures. A frequent reason for failure has been the absence of a solid data infrastructure to support the applications. System developers simply could not access the data that was needed to support the applications. The data was often "locked up" in operational systems, either because of data ownership issues or the technical difficulties of accessing needed data. Even when the data could be accessed, it was typically "dirty." Data was missing; dummy values were in fields (e.g., 999-99-9999 as a SSN); fields were used for multiple purposes; primary keys were reused; business rules were violated (e.g., a loan rate lower than the lowest rate) and so on. Then there was the problem of integrating the data from multiple source systems. Either there were nonunique identifiers (e.g., multiple account numbers) or the absence of an appropriate primary key. Developers knew how to build the applications, but, without a solid data infrastructure in place, they were doomed to failure.

A response to the data infrastructure problem emerged in the late 1980s (Inmon, 1992). A few leading-edge firms in the telecommunications, retail and financial services industries developed data warehouses — large repositories of data created to support decision making. These firms wanted to use their customer data as a basis for competing in the marketplace. By knowing their customer well, they hoped to maintain and enhance customer relationships, better meet customers' needs and wants, and increase revenues and profits. Over the next decade, most large- and many medium-sized firms began data warehousing initiatives. At the turn of the century, data warehousing had become one of the top two or three strategic initiatives (along with e-commerce) in the information systems field (Eckerson, 1998).

Data warehouses are built because they promise to provide organizational benefits. They can generate cost saving through the consolidation of multiple, disparate decision-support platforms; provide time savings for information technology professionals and end users by making data easier to access and use; improve the quality of data that is available to decision makers; support the redesign of business processes and enable new business initiatives and strategies (Haley, Watson, & Goodhue, 1999). Data warehouses are challenging undertakings for both organizational and technical reasons (Crofts, 1998). On the organizational side, there must be executive sponsorship, management support and participation, effective handling of data ownership issues and user participation in determining data requirements. On the technical side, new hardware and software must be selected and implemented; data from source systems must be understood, extracted, transformed and loaded into the warehouse; appropriate data models must be developed and implemented and users must be trained and supported on data access tools. In the following section, the architecture for data warehousing is discussed.

In order to illustrate data warehousing in practice, a case study is presented. It describes 3M and the business and systems drivers for the global enterprise data warehouse (GEDW) that was developed. Next, the development of GEDW and its architecture are described. The case concludes with benefits of the data warehouse and the lessons that 3M has learned along the way. The case illustrates many of the organizational and technical issues associated with data warehousing.

THE ARCHITECTURE FOR DATA WAREHOUSING

The architecture for data warehousing includes the component parts and the relationships among the parts. Figure 1 shows a typical, comprehensive architecture for data warehousing.

The left-hand side of the figure shows the various data sources. Much of the data comes from transactional (i.e., operational) systems — production, accounting, marketing, etc. Data may also come from an enterprise resource planning (ERP) such as SAP or PeopleSoft. Web data in the form of Web logs may also be fed into the data warehouse. And finally, external data, such as the U.S. census data, may be used. These data sources often use different hardware and software, and a mixture of hierarchical, network and relational data models for storing the data. It is not unusual for a data warehouse to draw upon more than 100 source systems.

The data are extracted from the source systems using custom-written software (such as COBOL routines) or extraction, transformation and loading (ETL) software. The data is then feed into a staging area (e.g., an Oracle database), where it is transformed. Special-purpose software may be used to facilitate data cleansing processes. The processed data may then be used to support an operational data store. The data is then also ready for loading into the data warehouse.

The data warehouse provides the repository of data used for decision support. Subsets of the data may be used to create dependent data marts that support specific

Figure 1. A Comprehensive Data Warehousing Architecture

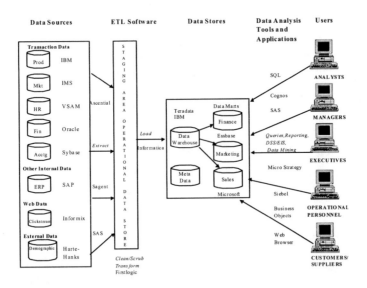

kinds of users, such as financial analysts or quality control specialists. Typically, the dependent marts provide a multidimensional view of the data, such as by customer, by product, by location and over time. A multidimensional database, such as Essbase, that is designed to represent data multidimensionally and provide fast response times may be used. Metadata about the data in the warehouse (e.g., where and when the data are extracted and the scheduled reports for users) are maintained so that it can be accessed by information technology (IT) personnel and users.

A variety of users access the warehouse using data access tools and applications that are appropriate for their needs. Power users (e.g., analysts), who understand the underlying data model for the warehouse and how to write structured query language (SQL) queries, may write their own SQL queries. Many users (e.g., analysts, managers) employ a managed query environment (e.g., Business Objects, Cognos) to access data. These products provide a Windows-like interface for designing queries, which then automatically generate the needed SQL code. Specially trained analysts may also perform data mining using warehouse data (either within the warehouse, downloaded to a server or on the desktop). The data warehouse may also be used to support specific DSS and EIS applications. Products, like DSS Agent from MicroStrategy and Holos from Seagate Software, are used for these purposes. The warehouse is also used with specific application software (e.g., Seibel), such as for customer relationship management. A recent development is to give customers and suppliers access to warehouse data. A Web browser is normally the client of choice for this purpose. In general, a Web browser is being used to access data warehouse data by a wide variety of users for many different purposes.

3M MOVES TO A CUSTOMER FOCUS USING A GLOBAL DATA WAREHOUSE

In 1995, 3M Chairman and CEO L. D. DeSimone, along with his top management team, recognized that the focus of 3M had to change. For nearly 100 years, 3M manufactured products to make life easier, safer, healthier and more productive for people in nearly 200 countries. In the excitement of creating innovative products, however, 3M was ignoring its customer relationships.

Until that point, 3M was organized into 50 autonomous, product-centric divisions, each with its own IT group, its own strategy, products and markets. Innovation was the driving force of 3M's decentralized organization, and each division focused on selling its own unique suite of products, which resulted in $15.7 billion in sales in U.S. and abroad in 1999 (3M Annual Report, 1999).

Unfortunately this approach confused customers who often had to interact with a host of 3M divisions to meet a wide range of needs. Under DeSimone's leadership, 3M was restructured into seven market segments: Industrial, Transportation, Health Care, Graphics and Safety, Consumer and Office, Electro and Communications and Specialty Material. Each segment was charged with serving customers better and efficiently meeting their needs.

Changing a large Fortune 100 company like 3M is not easy. It requires shifts in mindsets, work processes and the information that is needed to run the business. To address the latter need, 3M began a significant initiative to create GEDW. Before the

GEDW, aggregate information was available only on division- or country-specific monthly reports at a fairly high level of aggregation. With GEDW, thousands of 3M employees now have real-time access to accurate, global, detailed information about sales, orders, customers, and products down to the stock number (SKU) level of detail. The GEDW also underlies new Web-based customer services that are dynamically generated based on warehouse information.

GEDW has created a number of benefits for 3M, the most important being the capability to understand 3M's customer relationships by providing a customer-centric view of the business. The data warehouse has enabled 3M personnel and processes to become more customer-focused, and it serves as the foundation for CRM initiatives throughout the organization.

COMPANY BACKGROUND

Minnesota Mining and Manufacturing (3M) is a $15.7 billion manufacturer with 70,000 employees selling 50,000 products that comprise 500,000 SKUs. The products are diverse, ranging from office supplies and industrial supplies to healthcare products and telecommunications and electronics components. 3M is a global company, with operations in more than 60 countries, manufacturing in 41 countries, research in 29 countries and sales in 200 countries (52 percent of sales come from outside the U.S.). 3M strives to be the preferred supplier to its channel partners (e.g., K-Mart, Target, Office Depot) and customers, and focuses on customer loyalty, supply chain excellence and new product innovation.

Until 1995, 3M's divisions were autonomous. Because of a major emphasis on product innovation throughout its history (30 percent of 3M's sales each year come from products introduced within the previous four years), 3M divisions were good at sharing research and development knowledge throughout the corporation. However, there was little sharing of information about customers and markets across divisions. Most divisions also had their own IT group and decision-support strategy. Before the recent reorganization, there were 25 IT groups supporting the divisions and 60 IT groups supporting non-U.S. countries.

Several times in recent years, 3M reorganized the middle layer between divisions and top management; however, these business groups were focused around technologies. In 1995, top management at 3M realized that the company needed to become more customer and market focused and that to do so would require dramatic changes in corporate culture and information systems. At this time, 3M grouped its divisions into six market centers, and 3,000 IT personnel were shifted from their division and country IT groups into the market centers, with only small IT staffs of up to three people left at divisions.

THE BUSINESS AND TECHNICAL DRIVERS BEHIND THE WAREHOUSING INITIATIVE

The need for GEDW became clear when the move to market centers was announced. The GEDW business drivers included what we call CRM today: the need to understand customers, what they buy globally; and global pricing, sales and customer information.

Ron Mitch, the assistant chairman of the board, was a key driver of the move to market centers. Mitch complained that he was tearing his hair out because when he visited key customers, information systems (ISs) could not tell him what the customers bought from 3M — he had to ask the customers. There were 30 data marts across the company, but they were all organized differently and developed by different groups for different purposes. How could 3M increase customer penetration when it could not identify sales by customer? How could 3M track global pricing to prevent 3M from competing against itself, when pricing information was split between business unit specific systems? As Mitch reorganized the company around market centers, it became clear that the existing information systems could not provide the information needed to support the new focus.

During this time, Al Messerli, a veteran IS manager who managed the advanced IS technologies group, began a crusade to move from decentralized DSS to a single global data warehouse, supporting 3M's decision-support needs. Messerli argued that a data warehouse would be the only way to generate the necessary data to support the new market focus. Specifically, 3M needed global direct and indirect customer sales, the ability to track product pricing globally, customer and market profitability, demand planning and new product tracking. Current systems could not provide this information.

In addition, if the GEDW were installed, all of the division-specific decision-support platforms and their antiquated systems could be removed, for a savings of many millions of dollars. All reporting and decision-support applications could be driven from a single, consistent source of data.

Messerli and his group began a major effort to sell the concept of the GEDW from the CIO to the top of the organization, and out to the division VPs. Eventually, the dual arguments of access to global data and reduced costs for decision support succeeded. By mid-1996, Messerli's group was given funding and corporate approval for Phase 1, and they started implementing GEDW for the U.S. sales data.

GEDW

Getting Business Support

Three parallel efforts laid the groundwork for GEDW. The first effort involved selling the concept to top and division management. To succeed at this, 3M needed a champion with broad business knowledge, an understanding of the role of data within key business processes and knowledge of organizational politics. Most database administrators cannot connect at that level; however, Messerli had credibility with high-level business managers, because of his long tenure at 3M and his proven ability to deliver valuable systems to the business. Messerli began selling the idea up the chain of command to senior management, even creating videos of quotes from executives who supported the idea. However, the sector vice president to whom IT reported insisted that before the operating committee would approve the GEDW, Messerli had to gain approval from the 50 divisions.

This was a significant and time-consuming challenge. However, Messerli had been at 3M for 30 years, and he understood that there was a balance of power between the divisions and the country subsidiaries. The division VPs were hungry for global data so they could be more effective in managing globally. According to Messerli, "I knew what the business unit people wanted." Messerli spent a year selling the divisions on GEDW.

That yearlong detour likely was a key to the success of GEDW. It created two important outcomes. First, getting division VPs on board gave the GEDW effort strong buy in. Second, the process showed that sharing data on a global scale would require a nontrivial shift in corporate culture around data ownership. 3M had a culture of sharing information about product technologies, but this had not been the case with information about markets and customers. For example, if there was a breakthrough with a new customer, there was no mechanism for sharing this information with other divisions. Similarly, there was no process to share contact information. Before GEDW could be implemented, it would require corporate approval to share sales, profitability, margin, service, inventory, customer and product data across the business units. This decision to share information ultimately was supported by the CEO and the senior VPs (i.e., the highest level of sponsorship).

Benchmarking

The second process that moved the GEDW project forward was benchmarking the data warehouse technology platform. Messerli's group spent several million dollars benchmarking five different platforms and databases. This was critical because the financial justification for the warehouse included replacing existing decision-support applications. If the intended technology could not support the load and replace the old systems, the team could not justify the expense.

Messerli's group provided benchmark tests to the vendors; the hardware had to be $2M or less, configured any way the vendor desired; 3M would provide the data to fill what would normally be considered a fairly small data warehouse database (i.e., 200 gigs) and the systems would have to respond to specific queries. The process included (1) load the database and see how long it takes, (2) run the queries and see how long it takes and (3) scale up the number of users from one to 200. 3M benchmarked five different platforms and most crashed as the number of users increased. NCR's Teradata was the only platform that completed the entire benchmark test.

Gathering Requirements

The third effort in moving forward with GEDW was developing an understanding of the business needs and systems requirements for the data warehouse. Messerli's group interviewed 250 mid-level managers to set priorities and specify requirements, working from the general down to specific subject areas and detailed data.

Understanding the business and the data was critical in developing the requirements and specifying the data definitions for the data warehouse. Although a separate global data standards group at 3M had been working on global definitions for some time, Messerli found that their data definitions were useless. For example, the data definitions for the global order subject area were based on the way orders were handled in the U.S. system. This was less advanced than the European order model and made it almost impossible to link the pieces of an order back together once it was processed.

The problem was that the people who wrote the data definitions were low-level employees who had little understanding of the order fulfillment process and how the data was used. Messerli assembled a team of people who had strong business knowledge and knowledge of the IS applications. The team also included people who understood the global and U.S. businesses. "If you are going to build a global solution you have to have global participation."

Messerli's team built the data model and the data standards according to what was needed for the future 3M organization, not according to what was currently done. "We went for what we should have, not what exists already." This meant that often there was not an exact match between the existing systems and the data model for the GEDW; however, the effort positioned the GEDW for meeting long-term needs. Now that GEDW data standards exist, 3M finds that when new operational systems are designed, the GEDW data standards are used as the basis for data within the new systems. The data management team spent more than 20 people years standardizing data globally. They created more than 1,000 tables and 3,000 data elements.

Developing GEDW

3M built the GEDW with minimal help from outside consultants, relying on a strong core of IT and business personnel, who had an excellent understanding of the business and its data. Messerli controlled the project within 3M, doing project management and design and installing and managing the data warehouse platform. He was skeptical about the ability of system integration consultants to add value, but he noted that they did receive helpful knowledge transfer from the platform vendor, NCR Teradata. Managing the platform within the project team was important, Messerli felt, to ensure the effort got off the ground. Once the platform was in place, it was transferred to the 3M IT infrastructure group.

Interestingly, the strongest resistance to the GEDW came from the IT groups, who were losing control of their data. Although the IT personnel from the old division IT groups had been centralized into market centers, they still had to cooperate with the GEDW project to shift decision-support applications away from the legacy platforms. Often, the IT personnel were resistant to change, even though the savings from making this shift were significant and the data was of higher quality. The GEDW project team pushed the IT folks hard to switch over, and, at the same time, they sold the warehouse to marketers, sales representatives, business-unit analysts and functional area managers.

Cost savings was an important selling point. For example, in one division, there was a $2 million savings by moving off of legacy systems. A GEDW analyst explained, "[Some IT folks] weren't looking at the overall picture. They were just looking at here and now. They do data loads and queries against this old horrible data from the '70s. It is very inefficient, and the programs are horrible. And, it is costing a lot of money to maintain it." The data charges and the computer time for loading and accessing data were about $180,000, and the cost of several people hired to maintain the applications was another $400,000. Savings totaled several million dollars over a year and half.

A big issue in switching to GEDW was that GEDW reports often did not match existing reports. Initially, users reacted by criticizing the GEDW information, but the GEDW team responded by showing users the reasons for discrepancies. Now the GEDW team is able to take the stance that the GEDW data is right, and the legacy applications are wrong. After a year of development, the project team has moved from selling the warehouse, to feeling secure in its existence and to facing almost too much demand for new projects because users want so much from the warehouse.

The Phase 1 GEDW (U.S. sales data only) was deployed in April 1997. In 1998, the team justified Phase 2 by rolling out the business intelligence portion to the rest of the world (except North America and Europe). By that time, the need to share information with channel partners (85 percent of 3M's business is with office distributors, industrial wholesalers and health care distributors), the public and customers was obvious. The Internet was emerging, and customers were demanding more and better product information. Also, it was clear that 3M needed point of scale (POS) information from its channel partners to understand the end customers.

In 1999, the project team began Phase 3, which was implementing e-business supported by the GEDW. Phase 3 included putting multimedia product information on the Web and dynamically generating Web pages based on GEDW content. This application was called Data Express, and it was used to push product information to channel partners, who traditionally have had poor information about 3M products. Data Express pushes current, accurate, quality data into the channel partners Web sites and makes catalogs and marketing literature available online. This has moved the marketing groups at 3M towards a data manager/data trustee focus and saved millions of dollars a year in publishing costs.

THE WAREHOUSE ARCHITECTURE

GEDW is deployed as a three-tier architecture that includes database servers, application servers and user desktop browsers. The database technology is NCR's Teradata RDBMS and WorldMark massively parallel processing (MPP) servers. The primary database server consists of 20 5150 nodes with 80 200-mhz processors and eight 4800 nodes with 32 550-mhz processors. A secondary database server is a six-node MPP 5100 with 24 Pentium 200-mhz processors. The system has a total of 10.3 TB NCR/LSI Raid storage, across two different physical platforms. Though each platform has five terabytes of storage, the current warehouse is one terabyte. MPP architecture provides the linear scalability required to support the growth of data and users for internal and external access.

High availability is essential for this mission critical system. It has 7x24, 99.9 percent availability for global business intelligence and external public access. Continuous "follow-the-sun" loading is accomplished with ping-pong loading processes and replication of the critical application access layer and data to two physical platforms in two buildings. The ping-pong loading process assures that one machine is always available for queries. Data is loaded into a highly normalized foundation data layer organized by subject areas (e.g., product, customer, order, genneral ledger (GL)). Above that sits an application access layer (e.g., metadata from the toolset, a de-normalized star schema database, etc.). The team makes upgrades to this weekly without affecting applications running off of the warehouse.

Primary access to the database engine is provided via a high speed, ATM network infrastructure. MVS and VM mainframe systems are direct connected to the data warehouse with multiple, high speed ESCON channels. On a daily basis, Teradata software utilities use these channels to extract, transform and load source data into the warehouse. Data is also sourced from NT and UNIX operational systems.

A variety of NT and UNIX application servers are used to access the Teradata RDBMS. The primary application tool set for internal business intelligence is Computer Associate's MyEureka! suite, which facilitates high performance and mass deployment of analysis, query, enterprise reporting and portal capabilities. The primary tool set for dynamic Web publishing of multimedia product information from the GEDW on 3M.com and extranet sites is ATG's Dynamo.

Use of standard Microsoft or Netscape browsers on user desktops minimizes maintenance and support. The GEDW homepage provides a common interface to all GEDW capabilities, and this is supplemented by personalized portals for many users, which simplify access to the reports, queries or analysis applications that they commonly use.

The GEDW includes data for every 3M order, shipment, customer and product. Direct sales, indirect sales (POS), price, gross margin, service metrics, demand, forecasts, inventory, supply plans, procurement, vendor and financial data are all included. In addition to 3M legacy systems, a key source of data is Dun & Bradstreet WorldBase, which contains 50+ million company sites for understanding customer organizations. For disparate legacy systems that cannot be easily linked directly into the GEDW (primarily non-U.S. systems), the "Green Book" provides a convenient way to facilitate data feeds. This is a standard format for information on shipments, orders, invoice, product and customer data.

Ultimately the GEDW team compromised on forcing all data into a set of completely standardized global tables. They now allow local users to put some of their own local tables in the warehouse to better meet local needs. The GEDW staff reviews requests for these local tables to confirm that they do not fit within the global data model. In addition, local temporary files of a limited size are allowed with no supervision of the GEDW project team.

GEDW AND THE
GLOBAL CRM ARCHITECTURE

Although there are quite a few applications focused on developing and supporting customer relationships with 3M, many of these have been driven by local business needs and local perspectives, in keeping with the long time innovative and autonomous culture of 3M. While there continues to be a significant focus on local management, it is now clear that customers, markets and the competitive business environment are converging on the need for global decision support and global CRM. "That's were we have to be!" said one CRM manager. To support this global CRM capability, 3M is in the process of implementing a packaged CRM application from Siebel Systems.

Though there is currently no direct link between GEDW and the Seibel Systems CRM package, GEDW figures prominently in 3M's long-term architecture for CRM. The GEDW will be the source for additional data not contained in Seibel. This data will be drawn upon as necessary by the Siebel CRM package. Thus, the GEDW will provide two important capabilities in the overall CRM architecture.

First, it will be the decision-support tool for the corporation. GEDW is the storage area for data (an absolute necessity) and the source for analysis tools. It provides not only sales reporting but also sophisticated analytical tools. Decision support is obviously critical to the management of products, markets and customer relationships. GEDW provides better information than the old local decision-support platforms because it provides more information. In addition, it has much more powerful decision-support tools. Where before the typical product of an information request was a paper report, now it is possible for management to take an initial result and follow up with drill-down analysis or other related analyses.

Secondly, GEDW is seen as providing the mechanism for integrating transaction processing across multiple (previously separate) systems, including the Seibel CRM package. GEDW is a single source for a wide variety of information pertinent to a given transaction and accessing that information requires only a single interface.

THE GEDW TODAY

Since its inception in 1996 through mid-2000, 3M has made a $30 million capital investment in the GEDW, including hardware, software and major applications. Ongoing maintenance costs (e.g., hardware, operating system, database management system), analysis software, query and reporting tools and portal software total $2.6 million per year.

The current data warehousing team includes data management, common applications development, digital media and e-business. The total team has 40 full-time 3M employees and 40 professional services people in St Paul, Minn. More than 100 IT, business unit and subsidiary users globally create queries, analyses and reports. GEDW initiatives are ongoing, and additional users and applications are continually added. A GEDW steering committee oversees ongoing GEDW efforts. The group includes IT managers and directors from the market centers and functional area representatives.

An important role of the GEDW project team is to encourage users to take advantage of the capabilities of the warehouse. Every month the group demonstrates interesting applications or shares examples of the benefits from using the systems.

Training has focused on the use of the applications — what the applications can do, how to use them, how to navigate and the benefits. The GEDW team is now shifting from application training to more general global data warehouse training. The latter training includes information about the warehouse, the data within the warehouse and the various ways to access information. Last year the project team trained 400 IT and business people on GEDW.

APPLICATIONS AND USE OF WAREHOUSE DATA

GEDW can handle hundreds of concurrent users, and as of June 2000, there were over 10,000 employee and channel partner users, in addition to public access via 3M.com. By the end of 2000, there were to be 20,000 registered, secured users and millions of public users. By the end of 2001, there were to be 30,000 registered, secured users, and daily access of public information is expected to reach 15 million database hits.

Employees, customers, distributors, suppliers and the public worldwide can access one centralized information source via the Internet, intranet or extranet with a Web browser. Users view data by product, customer, market, channel, site, account, geographic area, organizational unit or time dimensions, at any level of detail from total 3M to the individual SKU level. There is a collection of fixed hierarchies included in the reporting schemes, but business units can build specific ones for specific needs.

Business intelligence content is pushed to desktops or pulled on demand with interactive drill down to detail. There are alerts, which notify users of reports or exceptions. Users get information when they need it, in a personalized format meaningful to them via their personal portal.

Some specific GEDW applications include:

- **"One Face, One Voice" digitization:** a corporate process to digitize and load all product information — images, text, structured data, video, and other data types — into the GEDW.

- **GEDW Data Express:** quality of product data for channel partners is now greatly enhanced by the ability to push digital information about products to channel partners. In the past, 3M channel partners have had incomplete, inaccurate, inconsistent and often obsolete product information. The GEDW Data Express application assures current and accurate daily, weekly or monthly updates, automatically triggered by any content change for any range of selected products. The information is transmitted in formats that include EDI, proprietary formats, or URLs, which enable direct real-time links from a channel partner Web site to the GEDW.

- **Products on the Web! (PoW!):** dynamically produces Web pages on demand. It enables employees, channel partners, customers and the public to navigate 3M product information, drilling down via market, product line, product family, product and item (SKU) to get the information needed to buy. The GEDW is the focal point in 3M's new global electronic commerce architecture, providing an integrated shopping and buying experience for channel partners and customers, and making it easier to do business with the manufacturer.

- **D&B WorldBase:** data that is used to match 3M customer account records from all 3M subsidiaries globally to provide visibility of customer hierarchies and accurate summarization of customer data, and, thus, a complete picture of global customers not previously available. Accurate global sales, profitability and price reporting is now possible for multinational customers, eliminating unsuccessful manual attempts to do this.

THE BENEFITS OF THE WAREHOUSING INITIATIVE

The GEDW has achieved a variety of quantitative and qualitative. The warehouse was justified based on:

- IT savings from eliminating dozens of independent data marts;
- re-engineering sales reporting processes and reducing the people resources required to report sales and reward sales forces;
- value of understanding customers and markets across all 3M business units globally;

- improving sales force and customer service productivity;
- reducing 3M and channel partner cost of providing product information to customers (marketing communications cost);
- speeding the product commercialization process; and
- improving growth and profits by increasing customer satisfaction.

Based on these and other hard benefits, the GEDW return on investment is 56 percent, substantially exceeding 3M's investment threshold.

Since the investment in the GEDW has been quite sufficiently justified by the cost savings from phasing out the decentralized decision-support platforms, the GEDW group has not focused on developing a concerted and complete assessment of the value of the business benefits. However, during the summer of 2000, the GEDW group sponsored a contest for business units to report quantifiable savings or business benefits, with $100 prizes going to the most compelling entries. From the entries in the contest and from additional anecdotal evidence, the following picture emerges of the ways in which GEDW is helping the business develop customer relationships.

Customer service: Prior to GEDW, when customers would call about electronics parts, the service representative would search through a 900-page report to find them. Now they search the Web-enabled GEDW, and they are off the phone with a happy customer in much less time. In addition, in the past when customers inquired about order status, customer reps had to copy information from paper reports, put it into spread sheets and send it out to the customer. Now that information flows through to the customer on the Web, without any involvement from the customer rep.

Sales force automation: Sales representatives are paid to manage their territories; however, they used to receive information from monthly reports, including a sales report and a rebate report. Because of problems and complexity in the rebate system, the reports often did not match. In order to reconcile the various reports and make sure they were getting proper credit for their sales, reps typically spent about five hours a month manually checking multiple paper reports. Now all the reports are based on the GEDW, and all of them always match. The reduction in reconciliation time is estimated to result in a $2 million dollar savings in just one business unit, and extended corporate wide should be approximately $20 million a year.

In addition, since the reports are daily and online, sales representatives have begun to monitor how close their customers are to qualifying for rebates, based on current orders, and to work with those customers who are very near to qualifying. They point out what additional orders are needed to get the rebate, and often get the additional sales.

Quality control: 3M recently decided that it would no longer produce Scotch-Guard. Its long half-life was considered a potential product liability problem, even though there had been no indication of trouble. 3M needed to know the buyers of Scotch-Guard and alert them to the fact that the product was being discontinued. The GEDW provided this information.

Cross-selling: Some groups now analyze sales data to recognize when a customer buys one product from 3M without buying related products from them. The analysis identifies sales opportunities for the related products.

Understand the end customer: In the past, POS data from channel partners has not been gathered in a centralized or standard way. Now the obvious resting place for the

POS data is the warehouse. There is movement towards a coordinated effort to assemble all the POS data on the warehouse for the analysis of the end customer.

Sales tracking and analysis: Because the tax department was able to easily to identify shipments outside of the U.S. that 3M should not be paying taxes on, they saved $5 million last year.

LESSONS LEARNED

There are a number of lessons that 3M has learned during its years of developing GEDW. In this section, some of the company's most important lessons are presented.

Selling the warehouse to the organization takes more than DBMS skills and experience. If you do not have business credibility at high levels, you will need to partner with someone who does. Key people, who are located throughout the organizational hierarchy, especially at high levels, will be critical to move the company from a traditional way of thinking to a focus on customer relationships.

Designing a data warehouse requires very good people who understand the data and the business. Data models and data definitions designed by people who do not meet this requirement will be useless or counterproductive. An IT/business hybrid also is the best kind of person to design the new way to support the future business as opposed to the old way of doing things.

A substantial savings can be achieved by creating a single, well-managed platform that serves as the single source of data for reporting and decision support. Typically, decentralized organizations have a wide array of legacy systems that have high maintenance costs associated with them. Eliminating these systems reduces costs, while improving the access to consistent, high quality information throughout the organization.

Do not underestimate the resistance to change. IT personnel can be the hardest to convert to new systems strategies. A combination of tangible cost savings and benefits and support from business users likely will be necessary to drive IT personnel to a centralized data warehouse strategy.

Do an extensive benchmark. If your data warehouse size or end user base is large, it is critical to benchmark a variety of technology platforms, before choosing a vendor partner. Otherwise you may discover, when it is too late, that your hardware cannot scale to meet future growth.

CONCLUSION

A large organization can change direction as well as an ocean liner moving at full-speed on the open seas. You can expect great shudders, confusion and tremendous pull in the wrong direction. As companies focus increasingly on customer relationships, they cannot underestimate the systems changes that will need to occur to support new information requirements. Often, a data warehouse is the way to meet those needs, and 3M illustrates the effort of a large Fortune 100 company that experienced a successful warehouse implementation.

The 3M case offers hope for large companies that have operated under a decentralized structure and now need to gain a comprehensive view of their customers. It shows the importance of first creating a robust data infrastructure and laying the groundwork that can support customer relationship management in the future. The definition of CRM continues to evolve, but 3M considers its infrastructure good enough to keep pace with change.

REFERENCES

Crofts, S. (1998). Twenty steps to data warehousing success. *Journal of Data Warehousing, 3*(2), 19-23.

Eckerson, W. W. (1998). Post-chasm warehousing. *Journal of Data Warehousing, 3*(3), 38-45.

Haley, B. J., Watson, H. J., & Goodhue, D. L. (1999). The benefits of data warehousing at Whirlpool. *Annuals of Cases in Information Technology Applications and Management in Organizations, 1,* 14-25.

Inmon, W. H. (1992). *Building the data warehouse.* New York: Wiley.

Sections of this chapter were adapted from Harnessing Customer Information for Strategic Advantage: Technical Challenges and Business Solutions. *Seattle, WA: The Data Warehousing Institute, 2000.*

Chapter XV

Data Mining in Franchise Organizations

Ye-Sho Chen
Louisiana State University, USA

Robert Justis
Louisiana State University, USA

P. Pete Chong
University of Houston-Downtown, USA

ABSTRACT

Franchising has been used by businesses as a growth strategy. Based on the authors' cumulative research and experience in the industry, this paper describes a comprehensive framework that describes both the franchise environment — from customer services to internal operations — and the pertinent data items in the system. The authors identify the most important aspects of a franchising business, the role of online analytical processing (OLAP) and data mining play and the data items that data mining should focus on to ensure its success.

INTRODUCTION

Franchising has been popular as a growth strategy for businesses (Justis & Judd, 2002), and its popularity continues to increase in today's e-commerce-centered global economy. Take Entrepreneur.com, for example. In early 2001, the company included a category called Tech Businesses into its Franchise Zone that contains subcategories of Internet Businesses, Tech Training and Miscellaneous Tech Businesses. At the time of the writing, 27 companies are on the list of the Web site of Entrepreneur.com.

A recent Jupiter Report (2001) recommends using strategic partnerships, such as joint ventures and franchises, to enter e-commerce. A good demonstration of this type of strategic partnership is the online bank, where Juniper's customers may deposit checks at the franchise chain Mail Boxes Etc. (Porter, 2001). Leaders of other industries also recognize the benefits of such cooperation or symbiosis. For instance, Gates (1999) believes that information technology and business are becoming inextricably interwoven. This nature of integration/interaction among businesses and technologies is especially pertinent in franchise organizations. For example, McDonald's real moneymaking engine is its little-known real estate business, Franchise Realty Corp. (Love, 1995). This ability to leverage the assets, real estate in this case, of franchise operations, into profitable products or services is at the heart of a successful franchise. Thus, any effort to obtain "meaningful" information in franchise organizations must take this lesson to heart, and a tool for recognizing these meaningful patterns from both internal and external data source can give those in charge the ability to see the big picture without being sidetracked by the tedious process of sifting through mountains of data.

Leveraging franchise assets must be built upon sound fundamental practices. Among the many fundamental practices for franchise growth, developing a good relationship between the franchisor and the franchisee is believed to be the most important one (Justis & Judd, 2002). This relationship is developed during the time when a franchisee learns how the business operates. Since all of these elements are learned from working knowledge, thus working knowledge becomes the base of the franchise "family" relationship; and, through the learning process, working knowledge is disseminated throughout the system.

The working knowledge is generally accumulated from information that is deciphered from data analyses. In this paper, based on the concept of Digital Nervous system (DNS) suggested by Gates (1999), we propose a framework for leveraging franchise organizational data, information and knowledge assets to acquire and maintain a competitive advantage. This framework is the culmination of the authors' years of research and experience in the franchising industry.

MANAGING FRANCHISE ORGANIZATIONAL DATA

According to Gates (1999, p. xviii), a DNS is the digital equivalent of the human nervous system and in corporation that provides information to the right part of the organization at the right time. A DNS "consists of the digital processes that enable a company to perceive and react to its environment, to sense competitor challenges and customer needs, and to organize timely responses," and "it's distinguished from a mere network of computers by the accuracy, immediacy, and richness of the information it brings to knowledge workers and the insight and collaboration made possible by the information." The development of a DNS goes through three phases: (1) Empowerment and Collaboration Phase, (2) Business Intelligence and Knowledge Management Phase, and (3) High Business Value Creation and Implementation Phase. Specifically, the following questions need to be addressed in the franchise industry:

1.   How is franchise organizational data being collected, used, renewed, stored, retrieved, transmitted and shared in the Empowerment and Collaboration Phase?

2. How is the franchise organizational information deciphered from data analyses, i.e., OLAP analyses and data mining, in the Business Intelligence and Knowledge Management Phase?

3. How is franchise organizational knowledge being leveraged to acquire and maintain a competitive advantage in the High Business Value Creation and Implementation Phase?

4. What are the implications for companies using franchising as an e-commerce growth strategy in the global market?

Any nervous system has many contact points with its environment; in business, these contact points are sometimes called "touchpoints." Based on the Customer Service Life Cycle (CSLC) model developed by Ives and his colleagues (Ives & Learmonth, 1984; Ives & Mason, 1990), Chen, Chong and Justis (2002) proposed a framework (Table 1) to harness the Internet to serve the customers in the franchising industry.

The 11 substages in Table 1 are based on two well-known franchising books by Justis and Judd (2002) and Thomas and Seid (2000). The model in Table 1 may be used as a comprehensive guide for a franchise system to develop its Web site, especially at the stages of Requirements and Acquisition. Among these substages, "Building the Relationship between the Franchisor and the Franchisee" has drawn the most attention in the franchising literature. Schreuder, Krige, and Parker (2000) propose a Franchisee Lifecycle Concept (FLC) as a new paradigm in managing the franchisor/franchisee relationship. The four phases in FLC — Courting, "We," "Me" and Rebel — are shown as bullets in Table 1.

In the Courting phase, the franchisee is new to the system and is eager to learn all the ins and outs related to the franchise business, thus there is a strong desire to maintain a good relationship with the franchisor, especially in the first year of the franchise

Table 1. The Customer-Service-Life-Cycle Model in Franchising

CSLC	Sub-stages	Example: Quik Internet (www.quik.com)
Requirements	Understanding How Franchising Works	
	Investigating Franchise Opportunities	• How It Works • Quik Internet Products • Business Is Booming • Operational Support • Your Opinion Counts • Marketing • Communication • Markets Served • Testimonials • Franchise Fee • FAQs • Executive Staff • Quik Internet Press Room • Franchise Opportunities • In USA • International and Master
	Obtaining Franchisee Prospectus	• The Next Step • Print Information
	Making the Choice	• Territory Availability
Acquisition	Preparing Business Plan	
	Financing the Franchised Business	
	Signing the Contract	

Table 1. The Customer-Service-Life-Cycle Model in Franchising (Continued)

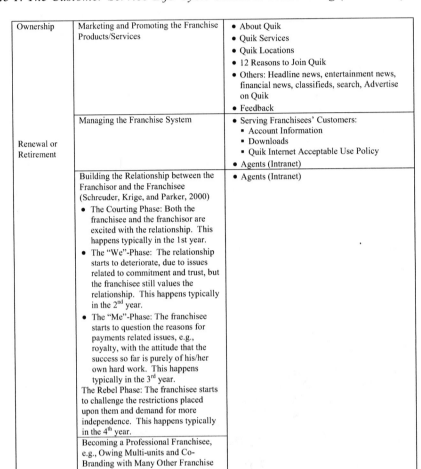

Ownership	Marketing and Promoting the Franchise Products/Services	• About Quik • Quik Services • Quik Locations • 12 Reasons to Join Quik • Others: Headline news, entertainment news, financial news, classifieds, search, Advertise on Quik • Feedback
	Managing the Franchise System	• Serving Franchisees' Customers: ▪ Account Information ▪ Downloads ▪ Quik Internet Acceptable Use Policy • Agents (Intranet)
Renewal or Retirement	Building the Relationship between the Franchisor and the Franchisee (Schreuder, Krige, and Parker, 2000) • The Courting Phase: Both the franchisee and the franchisor are excited with the relationship. This happens typically in the 1st year. • The "We"-Phase: The relationship starts to deteriorate, due to issues related to commitment and trust, but the franchisee still values the relationship. This happens typically in the 2nd year. • The "Me"-Phase: The franchisee starts to question the reasons for payments related issues, e.g., royalty, with the attitude that the success so far is purely of his/her own hard work. This happens typically in the 3rd year. The Rebel Phase: The franchisee starts to challenge the restrictions placed upon them and demand for more independence. This happens typically in the 4th year.	• Agents (Intranet)
	Becoming a Professional Franchisee, e.g., Owing Multi-units and Co-Branding with Many Other Franchise Products, or Retiring from the Franchise System	

contract. In the "We" phase, the franchisee has learned most of the rules in the business environment and is relying less on the franchisor; thus, the relationship starts to deteriorate, but the franchisee still values the relationship. This phase typically happens in the second year of the contract. In the third year, the franchisee moves into the "Me" phase, when the franchisee starts to question the reasons for payments and related issues, e.g., ongoing royalty and marketing fees, with the attitude that the success so far is purely of his/her own hard work. The relationship gets worse in the Rebel phase, happening typically in the fourth year, when the franchisee starts to challenge the restrictions placed upon them and demand more independence.

A franchise faces its biggest crisis when many franchisees move from the Ownership phase into the Rebel phase. The major challenge is to move them further from the Rebel phase into the Renewal phase, where they can continue to be a productive "Professional" in the system. Although granting multi-units in certain territories (Lafontaine & Sun, 2001; Azoulay & Shane, 2001; Shane & Foo, 1999) and providing various cobranding opportunities to maximize the return of the outlet investment (Justis & Judd, 2002) are two common ways to cool down the "rebellious" attitude of the franchisee, more innovative approaches of asset leveraging are often needed to continue the "family" relationship for the expansion and growth of the franchise system. The Franchise Realty Corp. of McDonald's mentioned previously is an example.

Thus, Table 1 also is a comprehensive framework for a franchise organization to model the data needed to serve its customers, i.e., franchisees and their customers. A well-designed Digital Nervous System (DNS) in the Empowerment and Collaboration Phase empowers the franchisor and the franchisees to collect, use, renew, store, retrieve, transmit and share the organizational data needed to do the collaborative work in different phases of the CSLC model. Specifically, three types of data are needed:

- Operational data: the daily activities at (1) the franchisor headquarters, including six major entity types: employees, business outlets owned by franchisees or companies, prospective franchisees, product development, suppliers (e.g., marketing agents, accountants, insurance providers, attorneys, real estate agents) and government offices (e.g., taxes and worker compensation) and (2) the franchisee business outlet, including six major entity types: customers, employees, contacts with the headquarters, product inventory, suppliers and government offices.

- External data: the relationship management activities in the franchise community, including three major entity types: the relationship with customers, the relationship with partners and suppliers, and the performance benchmarks in the industry.

- Legacy data: the activities that have been working well or gradually adapted since the franchise system came into existence. Examples include (1) rewarding activities to the top performers among the franchisees, (2) efficient procedural activities for the employees at the headquarters supporting the franchisees and (3) effective and friendly face-to-face activities for the field representatives to serve the franchisees at their outlets.

TURNING FRANCHISE ORGANIZATIONAL DATA INTO INFORMATION

A franchise system generates voluminous data every day. Consider the "Managing the Franchise System" substage as an example. The end of each business transaction, billing, customer tracking, inventory control and labor all generate enormous amounts of operational data. At the end of the day, a sale report is sent through the telecommunication system to the franchisor headquarters to summarize the daily business transactions, such as total sale, total cost of raw materials and total cost of labor. If the report is not received after a predetermined time, a message is triggered to request prompt actions by the franchisee. Once the daily sale reports are received from all the business outlets, they are converted into information, using various analytical methods. These statistical data analyses also help generate many business intelligence reports. For example, a business outlet will typically receive its performance ranking report with respect to the franchise system, along with the top 10 business outlets having the best sale reports. A rewarding system can be built into the information generation process,

Figure 1. The Four Levels of Turning Franchise Organizational Data into Information

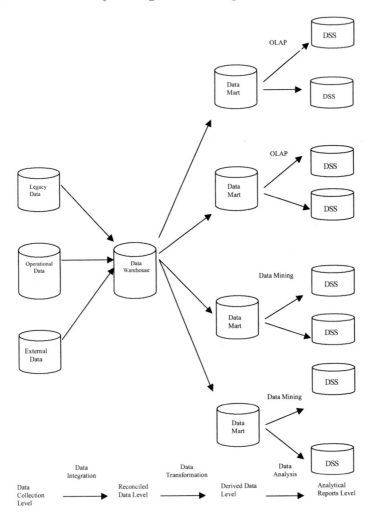

e.g., the owner of the winning franchisee outlet may receive a free trip to Hawaii if she/he has been among the top 10 lists for a number of consecutive time periods.

Adapted from Inmon (1996), the information generation process can be presented in four levels as is shown in Figure 1. To move from the data collection level to the reconciled data level, data integration is needed. This process involves activities, such as cleansing, extracting, filtering, conditioning, scrubbing and loading, and is very time consuming. To move from the reconciled data level to the derived data level, data transformation is needed that involves activities, such as replication, propagation, summary, aggregate and metadata. To move from the derived data level to the analytical reporting level, data analysis is needed that involves two major activities — OLAP and data mining.

Table 2. Franchisees' Customers Data Mining Using the CSLC Approach

CSLC	Explanation	Data Mining Activities

Requirements	Finding and reaching the customers	• Lead Generation
		  • Market Analysis & Segmentation
		  • Mining Web Site Visitors
		  • Text Mining Usenet Newsgroups

Acquisition	Selling to the customers	• Customer Acquisition Profiling
		  • Customer Segmentation Strategy
		  • Online Shopping Tracking
		  • Pricing Strategy
		  • Customer-centric Selling
		  • Text Mining Contact E-Mails
		  • Scenario Notification

Ownership	Satisfying the customers after the sales	• Customer Service
		  • Inquiry Routing
		  • Text Mining E-Mails & Inquiries
		  • Scenario Notification
		  • Staffing Level Prediction

Retirement or Renewing	Retaining the customers so that you can continue coming back	• Customer Retention
		  • Sharper Customer Focus through Loyalty Program
		  • Detecting Customer Complaints through Text Mining
		  • Detecting Inappropriate Customer Services
		  • Individual Customer Profiles
		  • Scenario Notification

A typical OLAP analysis is composed of predefined, multidimensional queries (Kimball, 1996). Some examples are shown below:

- Show the gross margin by product category and by franchise outlets from Thanksgiving to Christmas in the last five years.
- Which franchise outlets are increasing in sales and which are decreasing?
- Which kinds of customers place the same orders on a regular basis at certain franchise outlets?
- How many franchisees did we lose during the last quarter of 2001, compared to 2000, 1999 and 1998?

Other OLAP activities include spreadsheet analysis, data visualization and a variety of statistical data modeling methods. Data mining, on the other hand, is used to identify hidden patterns in the data residing in the data marts, which are derived based on criteria such as frequent customers and products of high profits. Typical data mining modeling techniques for analytical reporting include decision tree analysis, cluster analysis, market segmentation analysis, cross-sell analysis, association analysis, neural network and genetic algorithm. Table 2, adapted from Delmater and Hancock (2001), shows that data mining techniques can be used to help serve franchisees' customers at the different stages of the CSLC model.

As we can see, the Four Levels architecture depicted in Figure 1 shows how the franchise organizational information is deciphered from data analyses, i.e., OLAP analyses and data mining. The valuable information contained in the business intelligence reports becomes the foundation upon which the working knowledge of the franchise system may be built. Thus, a well-designed DNS in the Business Intelligence and Knowledge Management Phase empowers the franchisor and the franchisees (e.g., through the use of mobile and wireless information technologies) to turn the valuable information into actions in real time.

LEVERAGING FRANCHISE ORGANIZATIONAL KNOWLEDGE

As mentioned earlier, developing the good "family" relationship between the franchisor and the franchisee is the most important. Justis and Judd (2002) examine the relationship issues in various franchise systems and identify the key for building the "family" relationship in the franchise organizational learning. They also find that there are five vital factors for a successful learning program in franchise organizations: (1) working knowledge — proven abilities of expanding the franchise system profitably; (2) positive attitude — constructive ways of presenting and sharing the working knowledge; (3) good motivation — providing incentives for learning or teaching the working knowledge; (4) positive individual behavior — understanding and leveraging the strengths of the participants to learn and enhance the working knowledge — and (5) collaborative group behavior — having the team spirit to find the best way to collect, dissimilate and manage the hard-earned working knowledge. Through this "family" learning program, both the franchisor and the franchisee will progress gradually along the following five stages of growth: (1) Beginner — learning how to do it; (2) Novice — practicing doing it; (3) Advanced — doing it; (4) Master — teaching others to do it; and (5) Professional — becoming the best that you can be.

It is quite clear that working knowledge is the real foundation of a successful franchise "family" relationship. The working knowledge is structured in many forms of profiles that are embedded in the operational manuals of the franchise business processes. Table 3 gives some examples of those working knowledge profiles with respect to the CSLC business processes associated with the substages in Table 1. A working knowledge profile is developed when a certain task of the CSLC process is repeated many times with good results. Consider the Site Profile used at the "Marketing & Promoting the Franchise Products/Services" substage in Table 3. The Site Profile is used to help the new franchisee find a good business site, and, typically, it is the real estate department at the franchisor headquarters who is responsible in developing the profile. The Site Profile is continuously tested and enhanced. Various analytical reports monitoring the performance of sites are generated at the Analytical Reports Level, shown in Figure 1. Based on those reports, real estate experts and their teams are able to fine tune the attributes and the parameters within the Site Profile. Most often, the corresponding data collection procedures in the CSLC substage also need to be revised and perfected so that better report score cards can be generated.

This process of enhancing the working knowledge profile will achieve its highest peak when both the franchisor and the franchisees arrive at the Professional stage of growth. The significance of being a Professional franchisor or franchisee is his or her ability to leverage the assets of the hard-earned working knowledge profiles into dynamic capabilities and high-business-value-creation completive-advantage strategies. The

Table 3. The Customer-Service-Life-Cycle Model of Franchise Working Knowledge

CSLC	Sub-stages	Examples of Working Knowledge Profiles
Requirements	Understanding How Franchising Works	• Lead Generation Profile
	Investigating Franchise Opportunities	• Benchmark Profile
	Obtaining Franchisee Prospectus	• Prospectus Profile
	Making the Choice	• Competitor Profile
Acquisition	Preparing Business Plan	• Business Plan Profile
	Financing the Franchised Business	• Financing Institute Profile
	Signing the Contract	• Franchisee Profile
Ownership	Marketing & Promoting the Franchise Products/Services	• Site Profile • Customer Profile • Product Profile
	Managing the Franchise System	• Support Team Profile • Employee Profile • Supplier Profile
	Building the Relationship between the Franchisor and the Franchisee	• Event Management Profile • Best Practices Profile • Crisis Management Profile
Renewal or Retirement	Becoming a Professional Franchisee or Retiring from the Franchise System	• Multi-unit Franchisee Profile • Co-branding Profile • Opportunities Profile

new products or services coming out of the process of leveraging the working knowledge profiles may transform the franchise business into a more, sometimes surprisingly, profitable enterprise. Consider, as an example, the site selection working knowledge at McDonald's as was mentioned previously. The Franchise Realty Corp. real estate business, a result of site selection asset leveraging, is the real moneymaking engine at McDonald's. A most recent high-business-value-creation strategy based on these real estate capabilities is the so-called Greenberg's law (Samuels, 1996, p. 46), named after McDonald's chairman and chief executive officer: "The more stores McDonald's puts in a city, the greater the overall number of transactions per capita in that market." As we can see, McDonald's can execute this Greenberg's law for market penetration strategy because of its strong capabilities of real estate.

To cultivate the working knowledge profiles so that the "Professional" franchisor and franchisees can continuously leverage valuable assets, we propose an Intranet-based Franchise Working Knowledge Repository as is shown in Table 4. The Repository provides a framework on which a franchise system may transform itself into a more profitable learning organization. It consists of two important classifications: (1) user skill levels, including Beginner, Novice, Advanced, Master and Professional — the five stages of growth of the franchisor and the franchisees; and (2) working knowledge level for the collaborative team, the franchisee outlet, the franchisor headquarters and the franchise community — the environment where the franchisor and the franchisees learn. Note that Knowledge, Attitude, Motivation, Individual Behavior and Group Behavior are the fundamentals for perfecting the working knowledge profiles, so their major principles

Table 4. An Intranet-Based Franchise Working Knowledge Repository

		User Skill Levels				
		Beginner	Novice	Advanced	Master	Professional
Working Knowledge Levels	Collaborative Team	Beginner guide to knowledge, attitude, motivation, individual behavior, and group behavior	Practicing knowledge, attitude, motivation, individual behavior, and group behavior	Doing knowledge, attitude, motivation, individual behavior, and group behavior	Teaching others knowledge, attitude, motivation, individual behavior, and group behavior	Improving and leveraging the value of knowledge, attitude, motivation, individual behavior, and group behavior
	Franchisee Outlet	Beginner guide to working knowledge profiles for running the Franchisee Outlet	Practicing working knowledge profiles for running the Franchisee Outlet	Doing working knowledge profiles for running the Franchisee Outlet	Teaching others working knowledge profiles for running the Franchisee Outlet	Improving and leveraging the value of working knowledge profiles for running the Franchisee Outlet
	Franchisor Headquarters	Beginner guide to working knowledge profiles for running the Headquarters	Practicing working knowledge profiles for running the Headquarters	Doing working knowledge profiles for running the Headquarters	Teaching others working knowledge profiles for running the Headquarters	Improving and leveraging the value of working knowledge profiles for running the Headquarters
	Franchise Community	Beginner guide to working knowledge profiles for relationship management with the community	Practicing working knowledge profiles for relationship management with the community	Doing working knowledge profiles for relationship management with the community	Teaching others working knowledge profiles for relationship management with the community	Improving and leveraging the value of working knowledge profiles for relationship management with the community

shall be learned first. The working knowledge profiles in Table 4 can be modularized according to the user's level. A curriculum of working knowledge modules can then be designed to effectively train the user. The goal is to provide an efficient and effective learning environment so that the franchisor and the franchisees can speed up their growth process to become the "Professional" innovators and make the franchise system more profitable and competitive.

In summary, a well-designed DNS in the High Business Value Creation and Implementation Phase incorporates the Intranet-based Franchise Working Knowledge Repository framework depicted in Table 4, since it enables a franchise organization to leverage its working knowledge to acquire and maintain a competitive advantage in the market.

IMPACTS OF USING FRANCHISING AS A GROWTH STRATEGY

As was mentioned in the Introduction, there is a growing trend of using franchising as the growth strategy in the global e-commerce market. Consider Eastman Kodak as another example. Kodak knows quite well the importance of the Chinese market, as can be seen from the quote of its former Chairman George Fisher: "To be the leader in the world, you have to be the leader in China" (Matthews, 2002, p. 31). Although Kodak has no franchise outlets in its home country (U.S.), Kodak realizes franchising is a very effective solution to deal with the so-called "three mountains" major obstacles of e-commerce in China (Chen, 2000): (1) online payment, (2) certificate authority and (3) product distribution. Kodak's e-commerce/franchising strategy in China can be seen from the Chinese-style Kodak China Web site (www.kodak.com.cn) and the successful Kodak Express franchise outlets (Alon, 2001): "Revenues of China's operation in 1999 grew 36 percent while profits mushroomed 58 percent, which compares favorably with Kodak's global growth of 5 percent and 13 percent, respectively. Kodak is the best selling film in China, with a 40 percent market share. Kodak Express with 5,500 outlets in 500 cities is the largest retail chain in China ... Kodak signs up entrepreneurs at the rate of three per day and is planning to grow its franchising system to 8,000 outlets by 2001" (Swift, 1999, p. 1). Another very important reason for the success of Kodak in China is its ability to help solve the unemployment problem, a burning issue in China, through the joint franchise loan program with the Industrial and Commercial Bank of China's Shanghai branch (China Online, 2000) and the Bank of China (China Online, 2002). Through the help of the loan, Chinese entrepreneurs, including unemployed workers, can start up with their own Kodak Express franchises.

Using China as an example, we can see that a sound growth strategy for multinational companies that do e-commerce in developing countries is to have a Host-Country-Language Web presence globally and franchisee/company brick-and-mortar outlets present locally. When the franchisor starts international franchising, many barriers demand changes and adaptations of the franchise system (Sherman, 1999), including language, culture, laws, marketing and employment. Among the many ways of international franchising, establishing a master franchisee is the most frequently used approach (Justis & Judd, 2002). The master franchisee, assuming the role of the franchisor, will work closely with the franchisor to develop the following areas in the host country (Thomas & Seid, 2000): franchisee recruiting, site selection, marketing, training, standards enforcement and office management. Once the franchise system in the host country is up and running, it is usually up to the master franchisee to deal with issues related to data, information and knowledge development and leveraging. As the master franchisee will be busy on expanding the franchise system in the local market, those important issues are usually dealt with loosely.

As the franchise system continues growing in the host country, more and more franchisees will be in the Rebel phase of the franchisee life cycle shown in Table 1; and the same challenging questions as in the home country will occur again and again, such as "I have learned all you have taught me?"; "Why should I continue paying you the royalty fee?" If the master franchisee doesn't deal carefully with the franchisor on foreseeing this challenge wisely, the whole franchise chain may disappear totally from the host country (Thomas & Seid, 2000). Bud Hadfield, the founder of Kwik Kopy franchise and the International Center of Entrepreneurial Development (www.iced.net) said it the best: "Obviously, one of the satisfactions of expanding overseas is the fact that you can now be sued in different languages" (Hadfield, 1995, p. 151). Thus, a formal, rigorous and timely approach to transforming the working knowledge profiles repository, such as the one shown in Table 4, from the home country to the host country is not just a strategy for the franchise to grow and expand, it also is a necessity for the franchise system to survive.

CONCLUSION

In this paper we studied organizational data mining in the franchising industry with the DNS framework proposed by Gates (1999). Specifically, we discussed the following topics:

- How the franchise organizational data is managed in the Empowerment and Collaboration Phase of the DNS.

- How the franchise organizational information is deciphered from the customer-centered data in the Business Intelligence and Knowledge Management Phase of the DNS. OLAP and data mining are the two analytical techniques that can be used to decipher the franchise organizational data.

- How the franchise organizational knowledge assets are leveraged in the High Business Value Creation and Implementation Phase of the DNS. We showed in Table 3 the importance of organizing the working knowledge profiles with respect to the Customer Service Life Cycle. We also explained that building an Intranet-based Franchise Working Knowledge Repository, similar to the one in Table 4, will enable the franchisor and the franchisees to become "Professional" innovators so that they can continue leveraging the organizational knowledge assets. This is what a franchise business is about.

Since the Franchise Working Knowledge Repository is the most important intellectual capital of the company, we recommended it be managed within the franchise system. Finally, realizing the increasing popularity of using franchising as a growth strategy in the global e-commerce market, we also discussed the implications of the study for companies considering international franchising as a competitive strategy for the growth of their global e-commerce markets.

REFERENCES

Alon, I. (2001, February). International franchising in China: an interview with Kodak. *Proceedings of the 15th Annual International Society of Franchising Conference*, 15(1), 70-90.

Azoulay, P., & Shane, S. (2001, March). Entrepreneurs, contracts, and the failure of young firms. *Management Science*, 47(3), 337-358.

Chen, G. (2000, January). E-commerce with Chinese characteristics. *China Online*. Available online at http://www.chinaonline.com/commentary_analysis/internet/currentnews/secure/c00012719-ss.asp.

Chen, Y.S., Chong, P. P. & Justis, R. T. (2002, February). E-business strategy in franchising: A customer-service-life-cycle approach. *Proceedings to the 15th Annual International Society of Franchising Conference*, 16(1), 251-272.

Delmater, R., & Hancock, M. (2001). *Data mining explained: A manager's guide to customer-centric business intelligence*. Boston, MA: Digital Press.

Gates, B. (1999). *Business@the speed of thought*. New York: Warner Books.

Hadfield, B. (1995). *Wealth within reach*. Cypress, TX: Cypress Publishing.

Inmon, W. H. (1996). *Building the data warehouse* (2 ed.). New York: John Wiley & Sons.

Ives, B., & Learmonth, G. P. (1984, December). The information system as a competitive weapon. *Communications of the ACM, 27,* 1193-1201.

Ives, B., & Mason, R. O. (1990). Can Information technology revitalize your customer service? *Academy of Management Executive, 4,* 52- 69.

Jupiter Report. (2001, January 11). *Asia Pacific to outpace US online population by 2005, but US sites turn blind eye toward globalization.* Retrieved June 6, 2002 from http://www.businesswire.com/cgi-bin/f_headline.cgi?bw.011101/210112033&ticker=JMXI.

Justis, R. T. & Judd, R. J. (2002). *Franchising* (2 ed.). Thomson Learning, OH: DAME.

Kimball, R. (1996). *The data warehouse toolkit: Practical Techniques for building dimensional data warehouses.* John Wiley & Sons.

Lafontaine, F., & Sun, S. (2001, February). The effect of macroeconomic conditions on US franchisor entry and survival. *Proceedings of the 15th Annual International Society of Franchising Conference,* 15(1), 120-140.

Love, J. (1995). *McDonald's: Behind the arches.* New York: Bantam Books.

Matthews, M. (2002). *Why China, always a seemingly alluring investment site, often stumps investors.* Chicopee: Barrons.

Paswan, A. K., Young, J. A., & Kantamneni, S. P. (2001, February). Public opinion about franchising in an emerging market: an exploratory investigation involving Indian consumers. *Proceedings of the 15th Annual International Society of Franchising Conference,* 15(1), 182-201.

Porter, M. E. (2001, March). Strategy and the Internet. *Harvard Business Review,* (79), 63-78.

Samuels, G. (1996, November). Golden arches galore. *Forbes.* Retrieved June 6, 2002 from http://www.mcspotlight.org/media/press/forbes_4nov96.html.

Schreuder, A. N., Krige, L., & Parker, E. (2000, February). The franchisee lifecycle concept – A new paradigm in managing the franchisee-franchisor relationship. *Proceedings of the 14th Annual International Society of Franchising Conference,* 14(1), 69-83.

Shane, S., & Foo, M. (1999). New firm survival: Institutional explanations for new franchisor mortality. *Management Science,* 45(2), 142-159.

Sherman, A. J. (1999). *Franchising & licensing* (2 ed.). New York: AMACOM.

Thomas, D., & Seid, M. (2000). *Franchising for dummies.* Foster City, CA: IDG Books.

Chapter XVI

The Use of Fuzzy Logic and Expert Reasoning for Knowledge Management and Discovery of Financial Reporting Fraud

Mary Jane Lenard
University of North Carolina at Greensboro, USA

Pervaiz Alam
Kent State University, USA

ABSTRACT

This chapter examines the use of fuzzy clustering and expert reasoning for the identification of firms whose financial statements are affected by fraudulent financial reporting. For this purpose, we developed a database consisting of financial and nonfinancial variables that evaluated the risk of fraud. The variables were developed using fuzzy logic, which clusters the information into various risk areas. Expert reasoning, implemented in an Excel spreadsheet model, is then used as a form of knowledge management to access the information and develop the variables continuously over the life of the company. At the conclusion of the chapter, the authors discuss emerging trends and future research opportunities. The combination of fuzzy logic, expert reasoning and a statistical tool is an innovative method to evaluate the risk of fraudulent financial reporting.

INTRODUCTION

In the light of recent reporting of the alleged financial reporting abuses in some of the major publicly-held companies in the U.S. (e.g., Enron and WorldCom), it has become increasingly important that management, auditors, analysts and regulators be able to assess and identify fraudulent financial reporting. This chapter is an attempt to use some of the latest statistical methods, expert reasoning and data mining techniques to achieve this objective.

Knowledge management can be used to a company's advantage in day-to-day decision-making. From a financial standpoint, a company must accumulate and disclose information to its employees, customers and investors. This information database can enable a company to support and maintain a competitive position. For instance, one way that a company can justify its financial health is by developing a knowledge management database of financial and nonfinancial variables to evaluate the risk of employee and financial reporting fraud. Collecting data using information processing and organizing the data through knowledge management can create a database for fraud detection and facilitate organizational data mining. Such a database can assist in knowledge discovery and help a company acquire and develop variables useful for the detection of fraud. The database can consist of historical data about the company as well as data for other companies in the industry. This database may be used by banks for lending decisions, by audit firms in an audit or by the company's management to gather and assess new information. These variables could also be evaluated to determine if the company has reached a stress level susceptible to fraud or for identifying fraud indicators.

The auditor's responsibility for detecting financial statement fraud is described in SAS No. 82, Consideration of Fraud in a Financial Statement Audit (American Institute of Certified Public Accountants (AICPA), 1997). Because fraud detection often involves an auditor's judgment in an unstructured environment, there is a possibility that the auditor may enhance the decision-making process with the assistance of a decision model. Using publicly available information, models can be designed to aid an auditor in detecting and evaluating financial statement fraud. Previous studies have focused on the examination of "red flags," or fraud risk factors, as likely indicators of fraud (Bell & Carcello, 2000; Pincus, 1989). Today, the auditor has the responsibility for detecting financial-statement fraud along with the audit of the company's financial statements.

This chapter presents a description, testing and summary of methods of analysis used in fraud determination. First, it is shown how financial and nonfinancial statement data (data based on analysis of company annual reports) can be used to develop membership coefficients that are evaluated in a fuzzy logic approach to data analysis. The fuzzy logic analysis applied to fraud detection is used to cluster the information into various risk areas. The cluster approach also identifies variables that can be used in a logistic regression (logit) model for fraud determination. Expert reasoning can then be applied to "mine" new information and develop the variables continuously over the life of the company. In this chapter, we also discuss the use of an additional fuzzy model for comparison purposes and to assess model accuracy. The chapter contributes to the fraud literature by incorporating a nonfinancial fuzzy logic variable in a statistical model.

The following sections of the chapter provide the background of fraud modeling and of fuzzy logic, and the methodology used to develop the study, including a description of the sample firms. The sample description is followed by a discussion of the financial variables that are developed and used in the models presented in the chapter. The discussion of variables includes a description of the research procedure that identifies nonfinancial variables used in the fuzzy logic clustering method. The next section presents results and analysis of the models. The last part of the chapter discusses emerging trends and future opportunities in this line of research, along with a conclusion.

LITERATURE REVIEW

Fraud Detection

When investigating financial reporting fraud, the auditor looks for "red flags" that might indicate a problem with the financial statements. Lists of questions that an auditor or an analyst should consider asking the client that may help raise red flags have been included in SAS No. 82 (AICPA, 1997), identified in previous studies and have been gathered for this chapter in consultation with auditing experts. SAS No. 82 provides over 30 red flags that may be used to detect fraud in financial statements, but it does not give any guidance of how these factors could be combined to detect fraud. Loebbecke, Eining and Willingham (1989) divided their list into low-, medium- and high-risk indicators of fraud.

Prior research shows that various kinds of decision aids may be used to assist the auditor in detecting financial reporting fraud. Pincus (1989) used a questionnaire and gathered data to predict the presence of management fraud. She found that subjects without the decision aid outperformed those who had the decision aid. Bell, Szykowny and Willingham (1993) used bivariate and cascaded logit to assess the likelihood of management fraud. Their model achieved within-sample correct classification of 97 percent on the fraud observations and 75 percent on the nonfraud observations. Hansen, McDonald, Messier and Bell (1996) used a generalized qualitative response model to predict management fraud. They reported 89.3 percent predictive accuracy over 20 trials. When they adjusted their model for asymmetric misclassifications costs, the model's accuracy dropped to 85.5 percent but, at the same time, the rate of type II errors, or failure to predict fraud when it was present, decreased considerably. Bell and Carcello (2000) also developed a logistic regression model as a decision aid to assist in the auditor's fraud decision.

More recently, studies have shown the effect of the company's internal auditors, auditor tenure and auditor judgment in suggesting reasons for financial reporting failures. Church, McMillan and Schneider (2001) found that internal auditors assign a higher likelihood of fraud when income is greater than expected, and when there is a combination of restrictive debt covenants that impose high costs for additional borrowing and an earnings-based bonus plan for management. In research focused on a company's external auditors, Geiger and Raghunandan (2002) looked for an association between auditor tenure and audit reporting failures. They found significantly more audit reporting failures in the earlier years of an auditor's tenure, perhaps indicating a temptation to appease new clients or a lack of knowledge regarding specific tasks associated with a new client (Geiger & Raghunandan, 2002). Other research has examined factors affecting the generation of financial reporting alternatives in a setting where a client uses aggressive financial reporting. Johnstone, Bedard and Biggs (2002) found that auditors with high understanding of accounting rules are better able to negotiate with clients interested in aggressive financial reporting. By proposing various alternatives to a complex accounting issue, an auditor is able to convince the client to use a more conservative financial accounting alternative, thus minimizing the possibilities of a future litigation. These studies show that the auditor's knowledge of the task or the ability to accumulate knowledge of the task is of utmost importance in the ability to detect fraudulent financial reporting.

Auditors may also use expert systems as a decision aid to assist in fraud determination. Eining, Jones and Loebbecke (1997) examined the effect that the use of an expert system has on auditor decision-making ability in detecting fraud. Their research showed that in allowing the interaction between the auditor and the system, the expert systems that have been used to assist auditors in complex decision processes often give results that are more accurate and consistent. Similarly, Whitecotton and Butler (1998) found that allowing decision makers to select information for the decision aid increases decision aid reliance.

Fuzzy Clustering

When data does not suggest a precise answer, decision makers often recognize patterns or can form groups in the data in order to make a decision (Alam, Booth, Lee & Thordarson, 2000). While discriminant and logit analysis assign observations to groups that were defined in advance, cluster analysis is the art of finding groups in data (Kaufman & Rousseeuw, 1990). Fuzzy set theory, introduced by Zadeh (1965), attempts to classify subjective reasoning (e.g., a human description of "good," "very good" or "not so good") and assigns degrees of possibility in reaching conclusions (Lenard, Alam & Booth, 2000). As opposed to hard clustering, where there is a clear-cut decision for each object, fuzzy clustering allows for ambiguity in the data, by showing where a solution is not clearly represented in any one category or cluster. Fuzzy clustering shows the degree to which (in terms of a percentage) an item "belongs" to a cluster of data. In other words, a data item may belong "partially" in each of several categories. The strength of fuzzy analysis is this ability to model partial categorization.

Lau, Wong and Pun (1999) used neural networks and fuzzy modeling to control a plastic injection-molding machine. They suggested that the neural network and fuzzy technology complement each other and offset the pitfalls of computationally intelligent technologies. Alam et al., (2000) also used a combination of fuzzy clustering and self-organizing neural networks, and were successful in identifying potentially failing banks. Ahn, Cho, and Kim (2000) reported results using these technologies to predict business failure, and stressed the importance of these predictions as useful in aiding decision makers. Lenard, Alam and Booth (2000) used fuzzy clustering to identify two different categories of bankruptcy. Companies placed in the second bankruptcy category exhibited more extreme values in terms of the financial ratios used in the study. Companies either showed much better results (such as a high current ratio) than would be expected for a company facing bankruptcy, or the companies showed very poor results, such as a much higher debt ratio than any of the other bankrupt companies in the data sample. Nolan (1998) used expert fuzzy classification and found that fuzzy technology enables one to perform approximate reasoning (e.g., as when a student assignment is graded as "very good" or "not so good") and improves performance in three ways. First, performance is improved through efficient numerical representation of vague terms, because the fuzzy technology can numerically show representation of a data item in a particular category. The second way performance is enhanced is through increased range of operation in ill-defined environments, which is the way that fuzzy methodology can show partial membership of data elements in one or more categories that may not be clearly defined in traditional analysis. Finally, performance is increased, because the fuzzy technology has decreased sensitivity to "noisy" data, or outliers. Ammar, Wright and Selden (2000) used a multilevel fuzzy rule-based system to rank state financial management. The authors used fuzzy set theory to represent imprecision in evaluated information and judgments.

METHODOLOGY

Sample

The sample of fraud firms was identified using the Wall Street Journal Index for the time period 1992 through 1997. Financial statement data for 30 fraud firms was matched with data from 30 healthy firms, for a total sample of 60 firms. The sample was then randomly divided into a training data set of 15 fraud firms and 15 healthy firms. The remaining 30 firms comprise the test data set on which the predicted results are evaluated. The data for the firms in the study were obtained from the 1998 Compustat tape.

Fuzzy and Logit Models

The fuzzy clustering procedure used here is called FANNY (Kaufman & Rousseeuw, 1990). The program FANNY uses "fuzziness" to partition objects by avoiding "hard" decisions, or clustering into fixed, definite categories. For each item in the data set, the algorithm provides k+1 pieces of information, where k is the number of clusters that are used in the clustering algorithm. The k+1 pieces of information are: U_{iv}, the membership coefficient of item i in cluster v, v = 1 ... k, and S_i, the silhouette coefficient of item i. A higher value of U_{iv} indicates a stronger association of item i and cluster v. The silhouette coefficients satisfy the constraints $-1 \leq S_i \leq 1$ and indicate how a well-clustered object uses average distances from its own cluster to the closest neighboring clusters. The closer S_i is to 1 the better the clustering of an individual item. A value of S_i close to -1 indicates that an item may be assigned to more than one cluster (Alam et al., 2000). The Euclidean distance measure is used to compute distances between objects and to quantify the degree of similarity for each object. The degree of similarity for each object i and j is computed as:

$$d(i,j) = \sqrt{(x_{i1} - x_{j1})^2 + (x_{i2} - x_{j2})^2 + ... + (x_{ip} - x_{jp})^2} \quad , \tag{1}$$

where the pth measurement of the ith object is given by x_{ip} and $d(i,j)$ is the actual distance between objects i and j.

For the testing of variables in this chapter, we used a logit model to determine whether a company is likely to commit financial reporting fraud. Our SPSS procedure, which runs the logit model, accepted a variable for entry into the model, if it had a probability of 0.05 or above.

Variables

Various financial accounting textbooks recommend using financial ratios from the three areas representing liquidity, leverage and profitability to evaluate the financial health of a firm (e.g., Meigs, Williams, Haka & Bettner, 2001). Bankruptcy studies recommend similar financial ratios for assessing the financial health of a firm (Altman, 1968; Ohlson, 1980; Mutchler, Hopwood & McKeown, 1997). Additional studies recommend that these variables use logistic regression or discriminant models to predict whether the auditor should modify the audit report to reflect that the firm may not continue as a going concern (Mutchler, 1986; Chen & Church, 1992; Lenard, Alam & Madey, 1995; Nogler, 1995). Person (1997) has suggested the use of a sales variable, or sales weighted by total assets (SATA), to identify what may be fictitious trends in growth. Because we have a relatively small sample size of 30 items each in the training data set and the test data set, we believe that a selection of three to five variables is appropriate. As a result, we have used one financial variable from each financial health assessment category of liquidity, leverage and profitability, based on the most frequently used and successful variables from previous studies. We have also used a second liquidity variable, representing cash flow from operations, because of the reliance on cash in fraud schemes as implied by the high-risk categories featured in the fraud questionnaire reported in this chapter. Therefore, the financial statement variables that are considered in our preliminary analysis of fraud assessment are: (1) CACL: current assets divided by current liabilities; (2) TLTA: total liabilities divided by total assets; (3) NITA: net income divided by total assets; and (4) CFOTL: cash flow from operations divided by total liabilities. CACL and CFOTL are liquidity variables. Healthy firms would have higher values of these variables than a stressed or an unhealthy firm. TLTA determines a company's leverage. A healthy firm would have a lower percentage of total liabilities divided by total assets than a stressed or an unhealthy firm. NITA is a profitability variable, generally referred to as return on assets. In summary, it is expected that for fraud firms the variables CACL, CFOTL and NITA will be relatively small than for healthier firms. On the other hand, the TLTA variable will be relatively large for fraud firms than for healthier firms.

Research Procedure

The first step in defining the nonfinancial variables is to develop a decision table based on all possible answers to a list of fraud questions ("Yes" answers equal high or medium risk; "No" answers equal low risk) as input into the fuzzy logic program. The list of fraud questions appears in Figure 1. These questions were gathered from SAS No. 82 (AICPA, 1997), and modified in consultation with an auditing expert, a manager at a "Big Five" accounting firm. This method of expert system development follows Gal (1985), who used one expert for knowledge acquisition and validation. The four risk categories, described in the questionnaire, are cash risk, earnings risk, industry risk and operations risk. All possible combinations of the answers to the fraud questions are then coded as input into the fuzzy clustering program. For example, cash risk can be low (score of 0) or high (score of 1). Each of the other categories can have low or medium risk — our expert felt that the cash risk was the only category that warranted a high risk. As a result, the risk of fraud is considered high for cash transactions and where fiduciary responsibility exists. Fraud risk can be low or medium in the area of earnings management, where specific industry conditions are indicated, or because of operational characteristics. The score for medium risk in the earnings risk or industry risk categories can range from 0.4 to 0.7. Medium risk for operations is scored as 0.5, if any one of the questions is answered "yes," otherwise risk is low (scored as 0). Again, the expert we consulted felt that any one "yes" answer reflected medium risk in the operations category. So a possible score combination could be a 0 (low) for cash risk, 0.4 (medium risk) for earnings risk, 0.4 (medium risk) for industry risk and 0.5 (medium risk) for operations risk.

The systematic coding of all the possible combinations resulted in 84 observations. These observations represent the database that is used for data mining. Based on membership coefficients of clusters produced by the fuzzy run, each decision situation

Figure 1. Excel Spreadsheet — Implementation of the Fraud Questionnaire

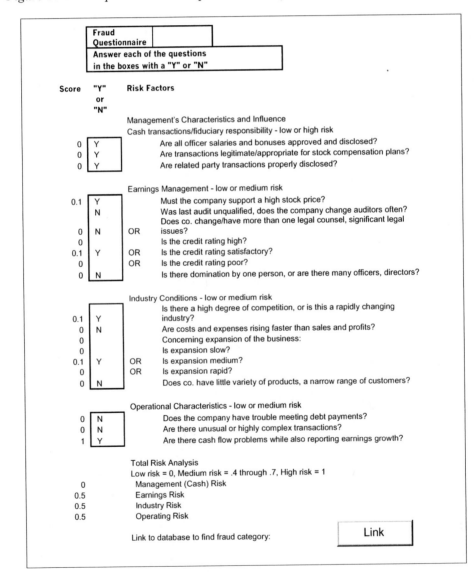

(combination of high-, medium- and low-risk values for the fraud questions) is then assigned a fraud variable, one variable for each of the clusters produced by the fuzzy clustering program. Once the fraud questions are answered for a company in our data set, the particular observation from the knowledge base is retrieved, and the values of each fraud variable can be entered into the logit model. The logit model predicts the probability of fraud, and the fuzzy model is operationalized in an expert system rule-base or in an Excel spreadsheet, using the spreadsheet's logic capabilities. The logit model accomplishes the prediction of fraud using the financial statement variables and one or more of the fuzzy cluster variables.

RESULTS

We ran the fuzzy clustering program for the red flag indicators, using 2 through 6 clusters. For our variable choices, we used the fuzzy clustering run with four clusters (see Table 1). Table 1 shows the membership coefficients for the four closest hard clustering of each of the data items. The fuzzy clustering program computes Dunn's

Table 1. Fuzzy Clustering Membership Coefficients — "Red Flag" Statements

	1	2	3	4
001	.3510	.2819	.1913	.1758
002	.4003	.2834	.1653	.1509
003	.4038	.2837	.1633	.1493
004	.3995	.2849	.1646	.1509
005	.3886	.2868	.1690	.1556
006	.4003	.2834	.1653	.1509
007	.4038	.2837	.1633	.1493
008	.3995	.2849	.1646	.1509
009	.3886	.2868	.1690	.1556
010	.2934	.3329	.1827	.1910
011	.6119	.2143	.0913	.0825
012	.6513	.1952	.0805	.0729
013	.6260	.2084	.0868	.0789
014	.5555	.2419	.1059	.0967
015	.6513	.1952	.0805	.0729
016	.7057	.1673	.0666	.0604
017	.6733	.1847	.0743	.0676
018	.5832	.2299	.0976	.0893
019	.6260	.2084	.0868	.0789
020	.6733	.1847	.0743	.0676
021	.6452	.1996	.0811	.0741
022	.5653	.2388	.1021	.0938
023	.5555	.2419	.1059	.0967
024	.5832	.2299	.0976	.0893
025	.5653	.2388	.1021	.0938
026	.5136	.2614	.1170	.1080
027	.2223	.5874	.0909	.0994
028	.1966	.6381	.0788	.0865
029	.1999	.6289	.0815	.0897
030	.2270	.5684	.0975	.1072
031	.1966	.6381	.0788	.0865
032	.1587	.7106	.0622	.0686
033	.1644	.6974	.0656	.0725
034	.2052	.6128	.0865	.0955
035	.1999	.6289	.0815	.0897
036	.1644	.6974	.0656	.0725
037	.1695	.6855	.0688	.0762
038	.2074	.6056	.0888	.0982
039	.2270	.5684	.0975	.1072
040	.2052	.6128	.0865	.0955
041	.2074	.6056	.0888	.0982
042	.2299	.5531	.1031	.1140
043	.1913	.1758	.3510	.2819
044	.1653	.1509	.4004	.2834
045	.1633	.1493	.4038	.2837

Table 1.   Fuzzy Clustering Membership Coefficients — "Red Flag" Statements (Continued)

	1	2	3	4
046	.1646	.1509	.3995	.2849
047	.1690	.1556	.3886	.2868
048	.1653	.1509	.4004	.2834
049	.1633	.1493	.4038	.2837
050	.1646	.1509	.3995	.2849
051	.1690	.1556	.3886	.2868
052	.1827	.1910	.2934	.3329
053	.0913	.0825	.6119	.2143
054	.0805	.0729	.6514	.1952
055	.0868	.0789	.6260	.2083
056	.1059	.0967	.5555	.2419
057	.0805	.0729	.6514	.1952
058	.0666	.0604	.7058	.1672
059	.0743	.0676	.6734	.1847
060	.0975	.0893	.5833	.2299
061	.0868	.0789	.6260	.2083
062	.0743	.0676	.6734	.1847
063	.0811	.0741	.6453	.1996
064	.1021	.0938	.5654	.2387
065	.1059	.0967	.5555	.2419
066	.0975	.0893	.5833	.2299
067	.1021	.0938	.5654	.2387
068	.1170	.1080	.5137	.2613
069	.0909	.0994	.2223	.5874
070	.0788	.0865	.1966	.6381
071	.0815	.0897	.1999	.6289
072	.0975	.1072	.2269	.5684
073	.0788	.0865	.1966	.6381
074	.0622	.0685	.1587	.7106
075	.0656	.0725	.1644	.6975
076	.0865	.0955	.2052	.6129
077	.0815	.0897	.1999	.6290
078	.0656	.0725	.1644	.6975
079	.0688	.0761	.1695	.6856
080	.0888	.0982	.2074	.6057
081	.0975	.1072	.2269	.5684
082	.0865	.0955	.2052	.6129
083	.0888	.0982	.2074	.6057
084	.1031	.1139	.2299	.5531

```
PARTITION COEFFICIENT OF DUNN =    .41
ITS NORMALIZED VERSION         =    .21
```

Note: The membership coefficients represent the degree to which an observation belongs to a cluster. For instance, for observation 1, 35% belongs to cluster 1, 28% to cluster 2, 19% to cluster 3, and 18% to cluster 4. The combined "belonging" percent adds up to 100%.

partition coefficient (Kaufman & Rousseeuw, 1990), which is the sum of the squares of all the membership coefficients divided by the number of objects. The normalized version of the Dunn's coefficient falls between 0 and 1, with a coefficient of 0 being completely fuzzy clustering and a coefficient of 1 being completely hard clustering. The normalized value of the coefficient for our model with four clusters was 0.21, which suggests a fuzzy clustering. The membership coefficient values show the portion to which the observation belongs to a cluster.

As noted above, the fuzzy run identified four clusters or variables. We introduced these four variables along with the four financial statement variables in a logit run. We achieved the highest prediction when only one of the fuzzy variables, FR_1, and the four financial statement variables were used. Results of the logit run, containing five variables and using the training set of 30 firms, appear in Table 2, Panel A. The dependent variable is coded as 1 for fraud firms and 0 for healthy firms. The classification accuracy of the model in the training set is 80.0 percent and the fraud variable is significant. Overall accuracy rate in the test data set is 86.7 percent (see Table 2, Panel B). It is interesting to note in Table 2, Panel A that the sign of the coefficient of the variable CACL is not in the anticipated direction for firms reporting financial reporting fraud. But this variable is one that a company would want to disguise, if they were trying to commit fraud. In addition, by including the fuzzy variable (FR_1), we have operationalized the use of fuzzy logic, which is also the significant variable in our logit regression. The negative sign of the FR_1 coefficient indicates that the probability of fraud is low, when the value of the FR_1 variable is high. Companies with higher values of this variable have lower cash and operating risk. An important component of this analysis is that the auditor or the analyst still gets to apply judgment in responding to fraud questions (see Figure 1), but now has quantitative support for the decision about whether there is fraud in the financial statements.

Sensitivity Analysis

Logit Results

Since the logit model presents its results in terms of a probability, we can analyze the model based on the likelihood estimate of fraud occurrence. In our model represented in Table 2, we used a cutoff point of 0.5, meaning that a probability of 0.5 or above predicts a "fraud" company. In order to analyze the value of a cutoff point in determining the fraud prediction, we followed the approach of Bell and Carcello (2000) and assessed prediction

Table 2. Panel A — Results of Logistic Regression for Fraud vs. Healthy Companies with Selected Financial Variables and a Fraud Variable

Variable	Expected Sign	Coefficient	T-Value
TLTA	+	1.3402	0.8966
CFOTL	-	- 7.0083	- 0.9811
NITA	-	- 0.3639	- 0.0275
FR_1	-	- 4.6858	- 1.6471 *
CACL	-	0.8308	0.6138
Constant		- 1.6537	- 0.2861

❑   * Significant at 0.10 level, two-sided test
❑   Overall prediction accuracy in training set 80%
❑   Cox & Snell R-square = 0.404

Table 2. Panel B — Prediction Accuracy of Logistic Regression Model on Test Dataset to Predict Fraud

	Predicted Fraud --	No	Yes	Total	Percent correct
Actual	No	11	4	15	73.3%
Fraud	Yes	0	15	15	100.0%
	Total	11	19	30	´86.7%[a]

[a](11 correctly predicted "No" + 15 correctly predicted "Yes") / 30 total = 86.7%

Table 3. Analysis of Classification Accuracy for Logit Model

Predicted Probability of Fraud	% of Observations Fraud	Correctly Classified Non-fraud
.95	33	93
.90	33	87
.85	47	87
.80	66	87
.75	80	87
.70	80	87
.65	87	87
.60	93	73
.55	100	73
.50	100	73
.45	100	73
.40	100	73
.35	100	60
.30	100	47
.25	100	47
.20	100	40
.15	100	27
.10	100	27
.05	100	27

accuracy for a range of cutoff points from 0.05 to 0.95 (see Table 3). The results show that the logit model is quite sensitive to fraud prediction because the highest accuracy is when the cutoff point for fraud is 0.65 or above. Using this cutoff point, 87 percent of fraud companies and 87 percent of nonfraud companies are correctly classified. That means there are still two nonfraud companies that exhibit fraud characteristics in our test data set. However, that also means the remainder of the fraud companies are correctly classified. We represent this analysis graphically in Figure 2. If we use four subjective fraud categories, representing the risk of fraud as low, moderate, high or very high, according to cutoffs of 0-0.14, 0.15-0.29, 0.30-0.64 and 0.65-1.0, respectively, we see that 87 percent of the fraud companies in the sample are in the very high category. But 40 percent of the nonfraud companies are still in a high-risk category, with a fraud prediction between 30 percent and 64 percent. However, this is possible for companies that have complex transactions that should be looked at more closely.

Figure 2. Graphical Categorization of Classification Accuracy for Logit Model in Various Risk Categories

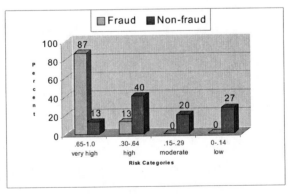

Fuzzy Clustering

Fuzzy clustering can also be used on the test data set itself, using the variables previously defined in our analysis. This is done for comparison purposes to assess the accuracy of our logit model and also to gain more knowledge about whether a company belongs in a fraud or nonfraud category. As mentioned earlier, fuzzy clustering finds groups in data, instead of assigning data to groups that were defined in advance. The variables that achieve a definitive analysis for fuzzy clustering are the financial statement variables SATA, TLTA, CFOTL and NITA and the fraud variable, FR_1. Again, we have maintained the CFOTL variable for liquidity analysis, the TLTA variable to represent leverage and the NITA variable to analyze profitability, along with the SATA variable for firm size. When the test data set is grouped into three clusters, there is a group representing fraud companies, a group representing healthy companies and a mixed group (see Table 4).

The fraud group (cluster 2) has one misclassified firm and the nonfraud group (cluster 3) has two misclassified firms, for a total classification accuracy of 27/30 = 90.0 percent. In the mixed group (cluster 1), the healthy firms that are included are firms 17,

Table 4. Fuzzy Clustering with Selected Financial Statement Variables and a Fraud Variable

	1	2	3
001	.3383	.3376	.3241
002	.3575	.3574	.2851
003	.3638	.3641	.2721
004	.3654	.3655	.2691
005	.3782	.3797	.2420
006	.3523	.3520	.2957
007	.3168	.3163	.3670
008	.3524	.3530	.2946
009	.3340	.3340	.3320
010	.3603	.3609	.2788
011	.3002	.2994	.4003
012	.3501	.3506	.2993
013	.3683	.3694	.2623
014	.3701	.3713	.2586
015	.3581	.3589	.2830
016	.2762	.2753	.4484
017	.3442	.3440	.3118
018	.2817	.2807	.4376
019	.3328	.3323	.3348
020	.3051	.3041	.3908
021	.3560	.3560	.2881
022	.3390	.3384	.3226
023	.3687	.3693	.2620
024	.2738	.2728	.4534
025	.2943	.2936	.4121
026	.3449	.3449	.3102
027	.2853	.2845	.4302
028	.3210	.3205	.3585
029	.2718	.2710	.4572
030	.2860	.2852	.4288

PARTITION COEFFICIENT OF DUNN = .34
ITS NORMALIZED VERSION   = .01

Table 4. Fuzzy Clustering with Selected Financial Statement Variables and a Fraud Variable (Continued)

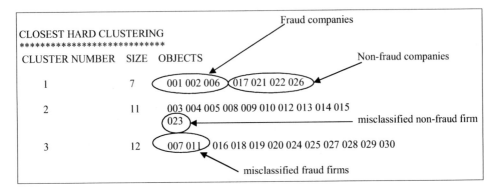

21, 22 and 26. These firms are also classified as marginal firms or fraudulent firms by the logit model. Using the logit model from Table 2 and the analysis of Figure 2, firm 17 has a predicted probability of 0.39, which is in the high-risk group. Similarly, firm 22 has a predicted probability of 0.63, also in the high-risk group. Firm 21, with a predicted probability of 0.98, is in the very high-risk group, while firm 26 is in the moderate-risk group, with a probability of 0.16. For those fraud firms in the mixed group, firm 2 has a predicted probability of fraud of 0.64, which is in the high-risk group. Firms 1 and 6, with predicted probabilities of 0.78 and 0.96, respectively, are in the high-risk group but share similar characteristics to those of the nonfraud companies in the mixed group. So the fuzzy clustering provides additional support for our logit analysis, by creating a separate cluster that includes nonfraud firms that are uncharacteristic of other nonfraud firms and may require closer scrutiny.

Implementation of the Data Mining Application

The determination of the fraud variable, FR_1, for inclusion in the logit model is implemented in an Excel spreadsheet. The spreadsheet runs like an application, with the components of the application linked by macros. A flowchart of the process is depicted in Figure 3.

Figure 3 indicates that the process starts with the questionnaire, which uses the logic features of Excel to build a rule-base and compute a score for fraud analysis (see Figure 1). As stated previously and shown in Figure 1, the cash risk (or management risk), can have low risk (a score of 0) or high risk (a score of 1). Each of the other three categories (earnings risk, industry risk and operations risk) can have low or medium risk. The medium-risk scores for earnings risk and industry risk can range from 0.4 (a "yes" answer to one risk question) to 0.7 (four "yes" answers). The medium-risk score for operations risk is 0.5 (a "yes" answer to any of the risk questions). When the spreadsheet has displayed the score for each risk factor, the user presses the "Link" button to progress to the data-mining feature and is instructed through the process that will result in a match of one of the 84 fraud combinations (see Figure 4).

Figure 3. Flowchart — Implementation of the Data Mining Application

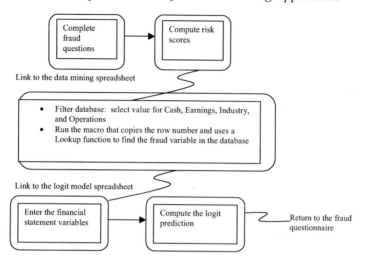

Once the fraud combination has been retrieved, or "mined," from the database, the fraud variable that has been derived for that situation from the fuzzy clustering run can be located. Then the user can link to the model page and enter the fraud variable and the financial statement variables into the spreadsheet. In each cell that is requesting a financial statement variable, the user can double click and see a definition of the variable, described using Excel's "Note" feature. The spreadsheet is programmed with the logit equation and automatically computes a prediction (see Figure 5). This prediction is the probability that a company fits the characteristics of a fraud firm.

Figure 4. Excel Spreadsheet with Data Mining Capability

Fraud worksheet:		Questionnaire results:			
		Cash	Earnings	Industry	Operations
		0	0.5	0.5	0.5
Steps:	1	Filter database as follows:			
	2	Click on the arrow by "Cash" and select the value of your questionnaire result.			
	3	Click on the arrow by "Earnings" and select the value of your questionnaire result.			
	4	Click on the arrow by "Industry" and select the value of your questionnaire result.			
	5	Click on the arrow by "Operations" and select the value of your questionnaire result.			
	6	Run macro to copy row number:			

Copy_row

	Row number:	32	Fraud1 variable:	0.1587

Click on the menus "Data" "Filter" "Show All" to
7 reset.

8 Then link to logit model to find fraud prediction:

Link

	Cash	Earnings	Industry	Operations
32	0	0.5	0.5	0.5

Using the "Auto Filter" feature of Excel, the above figure shows that for this particular example, with cash risk of 0, earnings risk of .5, industry risk of .5, and operations risk of .5, the row in the database that matches this score is line 32, and the value of the fraud variable, FR_1, at this location is .1587.

Figure 5. Excel Spreadsheet Implementation of the Logit Model

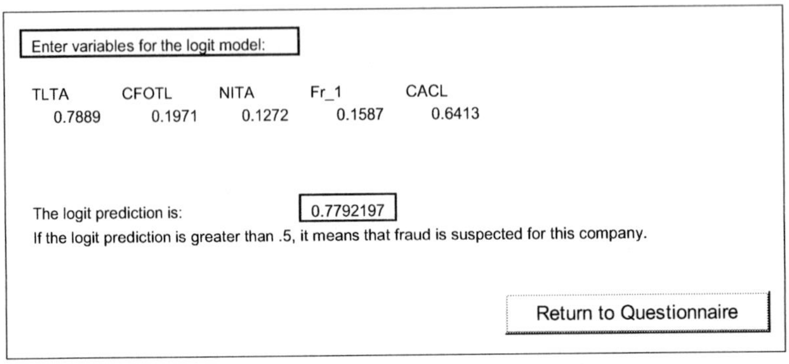

Enter variables for the logit model:

TLTA	CFOTL	NITA	Fr_1	CACL
0.7889	0.1971	0.1272	0.1587	0.6413

The logit prediction is: 0.7792197
If the logit prediction is greater than .5, it means that fraud is suspected for this company.

Return to Questionnaire

On this page of the spreadsheet application, each of the variables is explained using the "note" feature of Excel (not visible in this reproduction). TLTA is total liabilities divided by total assets, CFOTL is cash flow from operations divided by total liabilities, NITA is net income divided by total assets, FR1 is the fraud variable derived on the previous page with the data mining feature, and CACL is current assets divided by current liabilities. We make our recommendation of whether to suspect fraud based on the convention used by the logit model, which is that a value or "prediction" of .5 or above from the logit equation is an indication of fraud.

CONCLUSION

This chapter has introduced a procedure, implemented through the use of fuzzy logic, to show that red flags in a company's annual audit do contribute to the information that is available to assist in the decision about whether the company may commit financial statement fraud. By using the fuzzy logic model to develop clusters for different statements representing red flags in the detection of fraud, nonfinancial data can be operationalized and included with financial statement variables as a database for knowledge management and discovery of fraud.

Emerging Trends

Financial statement information is used by management, employees, outside analysts, investors and creditors to assess the health of publicly traded companies. Just as this information is now readily available through the Internet and online financial services, so should tools that help in the analysis of that information be readily available or easily obtainable. Although the data mining application described in this chapter is a research model, its implementation through the use of an Excel spreadsheet emphasizes its portability. The application can easily be downloaded for individual use, and the database can be easily updated. It then becomes an important tool for all users.

Future Research Opportunities

The data mining model in this study has been used on a limited basis with a relatively small sample of firms. Further study in fraud research could result in a larger database that involves a more detailed questionnaire. This approach can also be applied to other unstructured decisions. Specifically, in the field of auditing, there is the auditor's decision, reflected in the audit report, about whether the company can continue as a going concern. The auditor uses the analysis of financial variables and a framework of questions to make this judgment. The auditor also applies judgment in the consideration of materiality. Materiality judgment is closely linked to the analysis of fraud, because the auditor must decide the extent to which a discrepancy will affect the financial statements. These decisions can be supported by the use of data mining tools and provide a continuing demand for the development of knowledge management.

ACKNOWLEDGMENTS

We are thankful to D. Dennis for helpful comments and suggestions, and to Casey Harrington for the research work. Earlier versions of this chapter were presented at the 2000 Decision Science Institute, Southeast regional meeting and at the 2001 Ohio regional meeting of the American Accounting Association.

REFERENCES

Ahn, B. S., Cho, S. S., & Kim, C. Y. (2000). The integrated methodology of rough set theory and artificial neural network for business failure prediction. *Expert Systems with Applications, 18,* 65-74.

Alam, P., Booth, D., Lee, K., & Thordarson, T. (2000). The use of fuzzy clustering and self-organizing neural networks for identifying potentially failing banks: An experimental study. *Expert Systems with Applications, 18,* 185-199.

Altman, E. I. (1968, September). Financial ratios, discriminant analysis and the prediction of corporate bankruptcy. *The Journal of Finance, 23,* 589-609.

American Institute of Certified Public Accountants (AICPA). (1997). Consideration of fraud in a financial statement audit. *Statement on Auditing Standards No. 82.* New York: AICPA.

Ammar, S., Wright, R., & Selden, S. (2000). Ranking state financial management: A multilevel fuzzy rule-based system. *Decision Sciences, 31*(2), 449-481.

Bell, T. B., & Carcello, J. V. (2000). A decision aid for assessing the likelihood of fraudulent financial reporting. *Auditing: A Journal of Practice & Theory, 19*(1), 169-184.

Bell, T. B., Szykowny, S., & Willingham, J. J. (1993). *Assessing the likelihood of fraudulent financial reporting: A cascaded logit approach.* Working paper, KPMG Peat Marwick, Montvale, NJ.

Chen, K. C. W., & Church, B. K. (1992). Default on debt obligations and the issuance of going-concern opinions. *Auditing: A Journal of Practice & Theory, 11*(2), 30-49.

Church, B. K., McMillan, J. J., & Schneider, A. (2001). Factors affecting internal auditors' consideration of fraudulent financial reporting during analytical procedures. *Auditing: A Journal of Practice & Theory, 20*(1), 65-80.

Eining, M., Jones, D. R., & Loebbecke, J. K. (1997). Reliance on decision aids: An examination of auditors' assessment of management fraud. *Auditing: A Journal of Practice & Theory, 16*(2), 1-19.

Gal, G. (1985). *Using auditor knowledge to formulate data model constraints: An expert system for internal control evaluation.* Unpublished doctoral dissertation, Michigan State University, Lansing, Michigan.

Geiger, M. A., & Raghunandan, K. (2002). Auditor tenure and audit reporting failures. *Auditing: A Journal of Practice & Theory, 21*(1), 67-78.

Hansen, J. V., McDonald, J. B., Messier Jr., W. F., & Bell, T. B. (1996). A generalized qualitative-response model and the analysis of management fraud. *Management Science, 42*(7), 1022-1032.

Johnstone, K. M., Bedard, J. C., & Biggs, S. F. (2002). Aggressive client reporting: Factors affecting auditors' generation of financial reporting alternatives. *Auditing: A Journal of Practice & Theory, 21*(1), 47-65.

Kaufman, L., & Rousseeuw, P. T. (1990). Finding groups in data: An introduction to cluster analysis. New York: John Wiley & Sons.

Lau, H. C. W., Wong, T. T., & Pun, K. F. (1999). Neural-fuzzy modeling of plastic injection molding machine for intelligent control. *Expert Systems with Applications, 17,* 33-43.

Lenard, M. J., Alam, P., & Booth, D. (2000). An analysis of fuzzy clustering and a hybrid model for the auditor's going concern assessment. *Decision Sciences, 31*(4), 861-864.

Lenard, M. J., Alam, P., & Madey, G. R. (1995). The application of neural networks and a qualitative response model to the auditor's going concern uncertainty decision. *Decision Sciences, 26*(2), 209-227.

Loebbecke, J. K., Eining, M. M., & Willingham, J. J. (1989). Auditors' experience with material irregularities: Frequency, nature, and detectability. *Auditing: A Journal of Practice & Theory, 9*(2), 1-28.

Meigs, R. F., Williams, J. R., Haka, S. F., & Bettner, M. S. (2001). *Financial accounting* (10th ed.). Boston, MA: Irwin/McGraw-Hill.

Mutchler, J. F. (1986, Fall). Empirical evidence regarding the auditor's going-concern opinion decision. *Auditing: A Journal of Practice & Theory, 6,* 148-163.

Mutchler, J. F., Hopwood, W., & McKeown, J. M. (1997). The influence of contrary information and mitigating factors on audit opinion decisions on bankrupt companies. *Journal of Accounting Research, 35,* 295-310.

Nogler, G. E. (1995). The resolution of auditor going concern opinions. Auditing: *A Journal of Practice & Theory, 14*(2), 54-73.

Nolan, J. R. (1998). An expert fuzzy classification system for supporting the grading of student writing samples. *Expert Systems with Applications, 15,* 59-68.

Ohlson, J. A. (1980). Financial ratios and the probabilistic prediction of bankruptcy. *Journal of Accounting Research, 18,* 109-131.

Person, O. S. (1997). Using financial statement data to identify factors associated with fraudulent financial reporting. *Journal of Applied Business Research, 11*(3), 38-46.

Pincus, K. (1989). The efficacy of a red flags questionnaire for assessing the possibility of fraud. *Accounting, Organization and Society, 14,* 153-163.

Whitecotton, S. M., & Butler, S. A. (1998, Supplement). Influencing decision aid reliance through involvement in information choice. *Behavioral Research in Accounting, 10,* 182-201.

Zadeh, L. A. (1965). Fuzzy sets. *Information and Control, 8,* 338-353.

Chapter XVII

Gaining Strategic Advantage Through Bibliomining: Data Mining for Management Decisions in Corporate, Special, Digital, and Traditional Libraries

Scott Nicholson
Syracuse University, USA

Jeffrey Stanton
Syracuse University, USA

ABSTRACT

Library and information services in corporations, schools, universities and communities capture information about their users, circulation history, resources in the collection and search patterns (Koenig, 1985). Unfortunately, few libraries have taken advantage of these data as a way to improve customer service, manage acquisition budgets or influence strategic decision making about uses of information in their organizations. In this chapter, we present a global view of the data generated in libraries, and the variety of decisions that those data can inform. We describe ways in which library and information managers can use data mining in their libraries, i.e., bibliomining, to understand patterns of behavior among library users and staff members and patterns of information resource use throughout the institution. The chapter examines data sources and possible applications of data mining techniques in the library.

INTRODUCTION

For several decades, library and information services in corporations, schools, universities and communities have had the ability to capture information about users, circulation history, resources in the collection, and search patterns (Koenig, 1985). Collectively, these data can provide library managers more information about common patterns of user behavior to aid in decision-making processes. Unfortunately, few libraries have taken advantage of these data as a way to improve customer service, manage acquisition budgets or influence strategic decision making about uses of information in their organizations. The application of advanced statistical and data mining techniques to these kinds of data may provide useful ways of supporting decision making at any library where user, cataloging, searching and circulation interfaces are automated.

Use of data mining to examine library data records might be aptly termed bibliomining. With widespread adoption of computerized catalogs and search facilities over the past quarter century, library and information scientists have often used bibliometric methods (e.g., the discovery of patterns in authorship and citation within a field) to explore patterns in bibliographic information. During the same period, various researchers have developed and tested data mining techniques — advanced statistical and visualization methods to locate nontrivial patterns in large data sets. Bibliomining refers to the use of these techniques to plumb the enormous quantities of data generated by the typical automated library.

Forward-thinking authors in the field of library science began to explore sophisticated uses of library data some years before the concept of data mining was popularized. Nutter (1987) explored library data sources to support decision making, but lamented that "the ability to collect, organize, and manipulate data far outstrips the ability to interpret and to apply them" (p. 143). Johnston and Weckert (1990) developed a data-driven expert system to help select library materials, and Vizine-Goetz, Weibel and Oskins (1990) developed a system for automated cataloging based on book titles (also, see Morris, 1991; Aluri & Riggs, 1990). A special section of Library Administration and Management ("Mining your automated system") included articles on extracting data to support system management decisions (Mancini, 1996), extracting frequencies to assist in collection decision making (Atkins, 1996) and examining transaction logs to support collection management (Peters, 1996).

More recently, Banerjeree (1998) focused on describing how data mining works and ways of using it to provide better access to the collection. Guenther (2000) discussed data sources and bibliomining applications, but focused on the problems with heterogeneous data formats. Doszkocs (n.d.) discussed the potential for applying neural networks to library data to uncover possible associations between documents, indexing terms, classification codes and queries. Liddy (2000) combined natural language processing with text mining to discover information in "digital library" collections. Lawrence, Giles and Bollacker (1999) created a system to retrieve and index citations from works in digital libraries. Gutwin, Paynter, Witten, Nevill-Manning and Frank (1999) used text mining to support resource discovery.

These projects all shared a common focus on improving and automating two of the core functions of a library — acquisitions and collection management. What these projects did not discuss was the use of library data to support strategic management decisions for libraries and their host institutions. A few authors have recently begun to address this need by focusing on understanding library users. Schulman (1998) discussed using data mining to examine changing trends in library user behavior. Sallis, Hill, Janee, Lovette and Masi (1999) created a neural network that clusters digital library users, and Chau (2000) discussed the application of Web mining to personalize services in electronic reference. In this chapter, we extend these efforts by taking a more global view of the data generated in libraries, and the variety of decisions that those data can inform. Thus, the focus of this chapter is on describing ways in which library and information managers can use data mining to understand patterns of behavior among library users and staff, as well as patterns of information resource use throughout the institution. We assume throughout that readers have access to material on the technical aspects of data mining, based on other chapters in this volume and outside sources. Thus, we focus here on the unique data sources and applications available within library environments. Additionally, we explore the unique legal and ethical implications of bibliomining that result from the ability of librarians to access and, potentially use, patron data.

DATA MINING IN LIBRARY AND INFORMATION SERVICES

Background

Most people think of libraries as the little brick building in the heart of their community or the big brick building in the center of a campus. These notions greatly oversimplify the world of libraries, however. Most large commercial organizations have dedicated in-house library operations, as do schools, nongovernmental organizations, as well as local, state and federal governments. With the increasing use of the Internet and the World Wide Web, digital libraries have burgeoned, and these serve a large variety of different user audiences, e.g., people interested in health and medicine, industry and world news, law and business. With this expanded view of libraries, two key insights arise. First, libraries are nearly always embedded within larger institutions. Corporate libraries serve their corporations, academic libraries serve their universities and public libraries serve taxpaying communities. Second, libraries play a pivotal role within their institutions as repositories and providers of information resources. In the provider role, libraries represent in microcosm the intellectual, learning, and knowledge management activities of the people who comprise the institution.

This fact provides the basis for the strategic importance of library data mining. By ascertaining what users need to know and how well those needs are served, bibliomining can reveal insights that have meaning in the context of the library's host institution. Using bibliomining, libraries can ascertain what their constituencies want to learn, whether they find the information they seek and whether that information satisfies their learning and knowledge needs. In corporate libraries, which serve the knowledge needs of commercial organizations, such insights can help to develop and maintain a competitive, cutting-edge workforce. In special libraries, which support the research needs of government and nongovernmental organizations, these insights can influence the success of policies and programs that are informed by research. In academic organizations, accurate insights into faculty and student knowledge needs can enhance the viability of the whole institution. Finally, in public libraries, clear understanding of patron information needs can support the effectiveness of regional community and political processes. Understanding libraries can help achieve these insights and, thus, help enhance the effectiveness of the host organizations or communities. It is important to understand the workflow and associated dataflows that occur within a prototypical library.

Overview of Library Workflow

Because some readers may not have a detailed sense of the behind-the-scenes activities in contemporary libraries, we begin by providing a data-focused overview of their internal workings. Workflow in a traditional "bricks and mortar" library creates a number of data sources appropriate for bibliomining. Before a library obtains new information resources (e.g., books, databases, reference tools, electronic access, etc.), a librarian assesses the needs of the existing collection in light of available and upcoming publications. Next, acquisitions personnel obtain the information resources specified from this needs assessment. Once the library obtains requested new resources, cataloging personnel either create or purchase a catalog record for the new resource. The circulation department then makes the resource available to end users. Depending upon the size of the library and the scope of its operations, these activities fall within the purview of one, a dozen or possibly hundreds of different employees organized into specialized departments.

After an information resource appears in the library's collection, users locate it using catalog search systems and bibliographic databases. Although little uniformity exists with regard to the specifics of the user interfaces for these systems, most catalogs and bibliographic databases support a standard Web browser client as the user interface. Increasingly, catalogs and databases are crosslinked, and each user's search record and traversal of links appears in log files. When users find resources that they wish to borrow, the circulation department records their selection in a database that tracks the location of each resource owned by the library. As this overview suggests, all functional processes of the library — collection assessment, acquisition, cataloging, end-user searching, and circulation — generate large reserves of available data that document information resource acquisition and use. Library information systems frequently use large relational databases to store user information, resource information, circulation information and, possibly, bibliographic search logs.

Although the processes outlined above adequately describe the traditional library with its physical infrastructure and tangible resources (e.g., books, maps, etc.), an increasing proportion of libraries offer many or most of their information resources in digital form over local or wide-area networks. These "digital libraries" do, however, employ many similar techniques for selecting and acquiring information as those described above. While the personnel involved may have different titles and slightly different roles, the activities remain the same: identify resources needed for the collection, acquire the resources, make the resource available to users and assist users in locating the resource through electronic and virtual reference aids. Most digital libraries do not have a circulation function; if users need something, they just save it or print it to their own equipment. Unlike the traditional library, the information systems of a digital library can track and log the entire visit of a user to a digital library.

The vast data stored in the databases of traditional and digital libraries represent the behavioral patterns of two important constituencies: library staff and library users. In the case of library staff, mining available acquisitions and bibliographic data could provide important clues to understanding and enhancing the effectiveness of the library's own internal functions. Perhaps more importantly, however, mining user data for knowledge about what information library users are seeking, whether they find what they need and whether their questions are answered could provide critical insights useful in customer relations and knowledge management. Whether the library users are the public in a local community or the internal staff of a large corporation, understanding their search, borrowing and related behavioral patterns can indicate whether they have obtained the information resources they need, what information resources they find most useful and insights into their future needs. These kinds of information can have strategic utility within the larger organization in which the library is situated.

As a closing note, many companies have information services that are not explicitly called digital libraries but can nonetheless be analyzed using some of the techniques listed here. These sources may be called knowledge bases and are commonly associated with customer service applications. These services function similarly to digital libraries in that they have a collection, i.e., the set of searchable documents gathered to allow users to help themselves, and a virtual reference service, i.e., the mechanism provided to connect users with employees to aid in the resolution of problems. The reference service may produce another collection of previous questions and answers. Once distinction between a help desk and most virtual reference services is that the help desk attempts to resolve the problem directly, while the virtual reference points the user to some resource that may help solve the problem.

Integrated Library Systems and Data Warehouses

Although the system used in most parts of the library is commonly known as an Integrated Library System (ILS), very few ILS vendors facilitate access to the data generated by the system in an integrated fashion. Instead, most librarians conceptualize their system as a set of separate data sources. While a relational database stands at the heart of most ILS systems, few system vendors provide sophisticated analytical tools that would promote useful access to this raw data. Instead, vendors encourage library staff to use prebuilt front ends to access their ILS databases; these front ends typically have no features that allow exploration of patterns or findings across multiple data sets. As a first step, most managers, who wish to explore bibliomining, will need to work with the technical staff of their ILS vendors to gain access to the databases that underlie their system.

Once the vendor has revealed the location and format of key databases, the next step in bibliomining is the creation of a data warehouse. As with most data mining tasks, the cleaning and preprocessing of the data can absorb a significant amount of time and effort. A truly useful data warehouse requires integration methods to permit queries and matches across multiple heterogeneous data sources. Only by combining and linking different data sources can managers uncover the hidden patterns that can help the understanding of library operations and users. Two studies have documented the processes needed here. The first was at the University of Florida library system, where a relational database was created for analysis by gathering information directly from screen images on the integrated system, because the underlying database was inaccessible. While the authors documented traditional library statistics gathered from this data, they also discussed a scenario for data mining with a neural network (Su & Needamangala, 2000). Another study in this area occurred at Kansas State University where researchers presented a prototype for a decision support system based on library automation data (Bleyberg, Zhu, Cole, Bates & Zhan, 1999).

Once the data warehouse is set up, it can be used for not only traditional SQL-based question-answering, but also online analytical processing (OLAP) and data mining. Figure 1 provides a schematic overview of the complete process from the collection of the data, through creation of the data warehouse to the application of various analysis techniques. Multidimensional analysis tools for OLAP (e.g., Cognos) would allow library managers to explore their traditional frequency-based data in new ways, by looking at statistics along easily changeable dimensions. The same data warehouse that supports OLAP also sets the stage for data mining. This data warehouse will lower the cost of each bibliomining project, which will improve the cost/benefit ratio for these projects. The remainder of this chapter builds on the assumption that this data warehouse is available.

Bibliomining Applications

By going beyond standard frequency-based reports provided by vendors, managers can learn much more about the needs and behaviors of those involved in staffing and using the library. Bibliomining can provide deeper understanding of the individual

Figure 1. Typical Data Flow for Bibliomining Applications

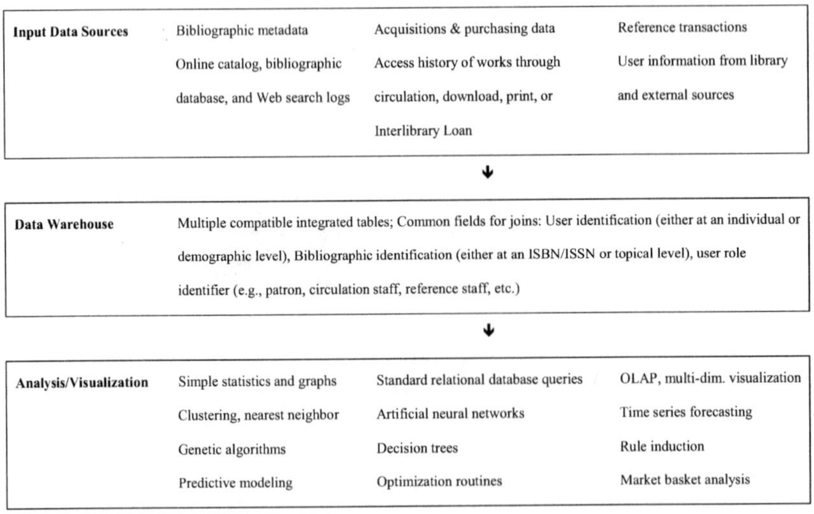

Input Data Sources	Bibliographic metadata	Acquisitions & purchasing data	Reference transactions
	Online catalog, bibliographic database, and Web search logs	Access history of works through circulation, download, print, or Interlibrary Loan	User information from library and external sources

↓

Data Warehouse	Multiple compatible integrated tables; Common fields for joins: User identification (either at an individual or demographic level), Bibliographic identification (either at an ISBN/ISSN or topical level), user role identifier (e.g., patron, circulation staff, reference staff, etc.)

↓

Analysis/Visualization	Simple statistics and graphs	Standard relational database queries	OLAP, multi-dim. visualization
	Clustering, nearest neighbor	Artificial neural networks	Time series forecasting
	Genetic algorithms	Decision trees	Rule induction
	Predictive modeling	Optimization routines	Market basket analysis

sources listed above; however, much more information can be discovered when sources are used in conjunction with one another. Most of these data sources contain fields that can be used to link them to other sources. This is where a data warehouse may prove useful; as it stands, many databases in a library system are optimized for searching and tracking, instead of reporting and mining. Each bibliomining analysis can reveal a pattern of activity within the library. Uncovering and reporting these patterns may have potential benefits at three nested levels: benefits for individuals through improved library services, benefits for library management through the provision of improved decision-making information and benefits for the institution that the library serves through reporting of relevant patterns of user behavior. Additionally, by providing information on the performance and utility of the library as a unit, bibliomining can provide justification for continued financial and institutional support for library operations. These levels serve to structure our presentation of bibliomining opportunities and applications.

Bibliomining to Improve Library Services

The users of library services are one of the most important constituencies in most library organizations. Most libraries exist to serve the information needs of users, and, therefore, understanding those needs is crucial to a library's success. Examining individual user's behavior may aid in understanding that individual, but it tells librarians very little about the larger audience of users. Examining the behaviors of a large group of users for regular patterns can allow the library personnel to have a better idea of the information needs of their user base and, therefore, better customize the library services to meet those needs.

For many decades libraries have provided reader's advisory services with the help of librarians who know the collection well enough to help a user choose a work similar to other works. Market basket analysis can provide the same function by examining circulation histories to locate related works. In addition, this information could be provided to the library systems, to allow users to see similar works to one they have selected, based upon circulation histories. While it is technically possible to build a profile for users based on their own circulation history (see Amazon.com, for example), it may be legally and ethically questionable to do this without a user's permission. Nonetheless, by obtaining and using anonymous data from a large number of users, one can obtain similar results.

In order to locate works in the library, users rely on the library systems. Librarians often examine user comments and surveys to assess user satisfaction with these tools. However, these comments can be deceptive. Applegate (1993) found that users often report satisfaction with a system even when they receive poor results, and Hildreth (2001) confirmed these results on Web-based library systems. Therefore, librarians may wish to examine the artifacts of those searches for problem areas, instead of relying on user comments and surveys in order to improve the user experience. When upgrading or changing library system interfaces, librarians can explore these patterns of common mistakes in order to make informed decisions about system improvements.

Bibliomining can also be used to predict future user needs. By looking for patterns in high-use items, librarians can better predict the demand for new items, in order to determine how many copies of a work to order. To prevent inventory loss, predictive modeling can be used to look for patterns commonly associated with lost/stolen books and high user fees. Once these patterns have been discovered, appropriate policies can be put in place to reduce inventory losses. In addition, fraud models can be used to determine the appropriate course of action for users who are chronically late in returning materials. The library can also better serve their user audience by determining areas of deficiency in the collection. The reference desk and the library systems are two sources of data that can aid in solving problems with the collection. If the topics of questions asked at the reference desk are recorded along with the perceived outcome of the interaction, then patterns can be discovered to guide librarians to areas that need attention in the collection. Increased use of virtual reference services (in which the text of every inquiry is recorded) can help to facilitate this process. In addition, library system searches that produce no results can be analyzed to document deficiencies.

With electronic information resources, the same work may be offered by a number of different vendors in different packages. Sometimes these resources are unavailable, and other times the resource is difficult to find on a vendor's site, even if it is available. In addition, when a vendor changes the layout of the Web resource, links from the online catalog to the resource may become invalid. By looking at the access paths by users to electronic resources, libraries can detect repeated patterns of failure with a vendor or a resource. Instead of waiting for user complaints, librarians can be notified when a problem exists and can work to resolve the problem.

Digital libraries, as well as libraries with Web-based services, can use different techniques and tools to examine common patterns in the path taken through their Web site. This could give the library ideas of problem areas of its Web site, good places to post important messages, areas where more guidance is needed and opportunities to keep people from leaving the site. Just as library managers must observe a physical library for signage needs, digital libraries must also be examined for appropriate areas for guidance. In addition, predictive modeling could be used to present users with the information they are seeking with fewer clicks. Research in the analysis of Web logs is fairly well established for nonlibrary situations, one example of which is research by Zaïane, Xin and Han (1998), who applied data mining and OLAP to Web logs to discover trends.

Bibliomining for Organizational Decision Making Within the Library

Bibliomining can be used to aid library managers in monitoring their organizations and making decisions. Just as the user behavior is captured within the ILS, one can examine regularities in the behavior of library staff by connecting various databases. The ILS can provide information about the number of relevant transactions that staff complete per unit time (e.g., by examining orders to vendors), but, perhaps more importantly, can connect particular actions (e.g., the acquisition of a particular resource) to relevant outcomes, such as patron utilization. In short, the ILS can provide snapshots of staff behavior that can, in turn, connect with relevant organizational outcomes. While monitoring staff through their performance records may be an uncomfortable concept for many librarians, tighter budgets and demands for justification require thoughtful and careful tracking of performance. In addition, research has shown that incorporating clear, objective measures into performance evaluations can actually improve the fairness and effectiveness of those evaluations (Stanton, 2000). The concepts suggested here are not intended to replace more typical methods of library staff performance measurement; rather, they can help to quantitatively justify statements and bring possible problem areas to light. Bibliomining can also aid in more general questions of staffing allocation. If the ILS captures reference question transaction events, for example, these can be used to build patterns of user load at the circulation desk. By looking at these patterns, library managers can optimize the number of staff members needed at the circulation desk. In addition, by looking at the time and frequency of different types of reference interactions for patterns, reference desk schedules can be optimized.

If items that are not circulated or used are considered to be an inappropriate expenditure, then bibliomining may provide insight as to how those items got into the library. By looking for correlations between low-use items and subject headings, publisher, vendor, approval plan, date, format, acquisitions librarian, collection development librarian, library location and other items in the data warehouse, managers might discover problem areas in the collection or organization. Low-use statistics for a work may indicate a problem in the cataloging process. By seeking patterns in low-use statistics with the library staff responsible for that work, possible issues could be unearthed. Along these lines, looking at the associations between assigned subject headings, call numbers and keywords, along with the responsible party for the catalog record, may lead to a discovery of "default" subject heading terms or call numbers that library staff members or the outsourcing organization are assigning inappropriately.

Interlibrary loan (ILL) departments are frequently asked to justify and reduce their costs. Bibliomining can aid the ILL manager in refining policies for lender selection. In interlibrary loan, a library usually participates in a number of consortium and reciprocal agreements. In addition, there are a number of suppliers that offer their services for fees. The higher-cost ILL services are often more convenient and less difficult to use than lower-cost methods. To complicate the matter, other institutions borrow from the library and may or may not return works in a timely fashion. Bibliomining is a tool that will allow ILL librarians to look within these complicated relationships for patterns that are either favorable or unfavorable and create appropriate policies. In addition, these techniques can justify policies and standards by discovering the appropriate patterns to support policies.

In acquisitions, vendor selection and price can be examined in a similar fashion. If a staff member consistently uses a more expensive vendor, when cheaper alternatives are available, the acquisitions librarian may need to get involved with clearer policies about vendor selection. Seeking patterns in the time it takes between the receipt of a book and the placement of that work on the shelf may bring to light some areas that need attention. This is difficult to track using normal means, as different types of works require different processes in preparing them for use. Bibliomining can be used to look for patterns in the complexity, and allow the clustering of types of works by the average time it takes to prepare them for the shelf. This can then be used to set policies for expected turnaround time for preparing works.

Most libraries acquire works both through individual orders and automated ordering plans that are configured to fit the size and type of that library. Outside vendors provide automated ordering plans, for a fee, as a way of reducing the collection assessment and acquisition workload within the library. While these automated plans do simplify the selection process, if some or many of the works they recommend go unused, then the plan might not be cost effective. Therefore, merging the acquisitions and circulation databases and seeking patterns that predict low use can aid in appropriate selection of vendors and plans. The library also has the option of outsourcing particular subsets of acquisitions and cataloging processes. If the acquisitions database contains details about this outsourcing that can be tied into a file that records changes to bibliographic records, library managers can then look for patterns of problems with different types of outsourcing. One example of this involves the process of copy cataloging, where a library purchases or accesses a catalog record from an outside source, copies it into the bibliographic database and changes it as needed. If some measure of the changes is tracked, either by the number of characters that are changed or time taken to make the change, then it could be matched up with the record sources. By looking for and eliminating problematic sources, copy catalogers could streamline their workflow.

As a closing note, data mining works optimally on very large data sets. As with most bibliomining projects, obtaining more information can allow for discovery of more meaningful patterns. This consideration argues for the formation of data sharing consortia, particularly among smaller libraries whose transaction volumes may not be high. Data sharing consortia among libraries that have similar functions and that they serve similar constituencies can help to join together the large data sets needed for effective bibliomining.

Bibliomining for External Reporting and Justification

Most libraries do not exist independently but rather answer to a parent organization or are embedded within a larger community. Thus, using bibliomining, a library may be able to offer insights to the parent organization or community about its user base. In addition, library managers are often called upon to justify the funding for their library, when budgets are tight. Likewise, managers must sometimes defend their expenditures on knowledge resources and services, particularly when faced with budgetary restrictions or user/customer complaints. Bibliomining can provide data to support the anecdotal evidence usually used for such arguments.

Bibliomining of circulation data can provide a number of insights about the groups who use the library. By clustering the users by materials circulated and tying demographic information into each cluster, the library can develop conceptual "user groups" that provide a model of the important constituencies of the institution's user base. If the library has collected usage data, even more can be ascertained about user group usage patterns. Digital libraries can use Web log information for similar patterns, but care should be taken as to the importance given to these patterns, as it takes much less effort to follow a link than it does to check out a book. In either case, the user group concept can fulfill some common organizational needs for understanding where common interests and expertise reside in the user community. By helping to identify groups of individuals with common interest and/or expertise in a topic, bibliomining can support a key component of knowledge management systems. This capability may be particularly valuable within large organizations where research and development efforts are dispersed over multiple locations.

The searches employed and reference questions asked by users can be mined for patterns. This has been an area explored by researchers (Harter & Hert, 1997), although few advanced data mining tools have been applied to such data. Clustering techniques could be used to explore common search topics in order to help determine instructional or training needs. This strategy would be particularly appropriate in commercial organizations, where training needs assessment is a critical element in developing and maintaining a skilled workforce. Tracking the frequency of questions on these topics before and after training can also allow library managers to justify the cost for training courses or instructional materials.

In reviewing organizational strategies for purchasing information resources and services, managers can also use bibliomining to explore the appropriateness of current approaches. Seeking patterns in circulation time, renewals and holds in conjunction with format, user classification, topic and other variables may help library managers set circulation policies, information access privileges and resource allocations that better match the information needs of users to current budgetary constraints. Because users can access information in a variety of formats — print, electronic, microform, ILL — and because these formats all have different costs associated with them, mining these transactions for patterns of use can help library managers make more appropriate resource acquisition decisions. Perhaps equally important, bibliomining may support managers in justifying their resource acquisitions to their funding bodies.

In the future, organizations that fund digital libraries can look to text mining to greatly improve access to materials beyond the current cataloging/metadata solutions. The quality and speed of text mining continues to improve. Liddy (2000) has researched the extraction of information from digital texts, and implementing these technologies can allow a digital library to move from suggesting texts that might contain the answer to just providing the answer, extracted from the appropriate text or texts. The use of such tools risks taking textual material out of context and also provides few hints about the quality of the material, but, if these extractions were links directly into the texts, then context could emerge along with an answer. This could provide a substantial asset to organizations that maintain large bodies of technical texts, because it would promote rapid, universal access to previously scattered and/or uncataloged materials.

LEGAL AND ETHICAL IMPLICATIONS OF BIBLIOMINING

To close the chapter, we discuss the legal and ethical implications of bibliomining. User privacy may present a somewhat less thorny legal problem in corporate and special libraries, but, in many states, strict regulations govern the privacy of user records for publicly funded libraries. In fact, many automation systems hide or discard circulation records after the material has been returned for precisely this reason. Organizations must strike a careful balance between discovering patterns and connecting those patterns to particular individuals in the system.

Legal Issues

User information used to be unprotected. For example, library circulation cards used to list the names of those who had checked out a book (Estabrook, 1996). In the 1940s, FBI director J. Edgar Hoover initiated the Library Awareness program, an FBI program that monitored the circulation records of library users. This activity continued on through to the 1980s, when library records were opened further as several states passed open record laws, making the records of the state government (and, therefore, libraries that were part of this system) open to the public (Seaman, 2001). The American Library Association (ALA) reacted and librarians across the country lobbied for laws that would protect user records in the libraries. Now, all 50 states have some type of law protecting library records (Seaman, 2001). These laws vary in their scope and protection; however, internal use of user information for library management is usually permitted. Libraries can use patron records to support the mission of the library but third parties are usually proscribed from reviewing this information.

This stipulation causes difficulty when groups of libraries work together, as is commonly done through consortium agreements. Library consortium groups can concentrate large amounts of information about behavior, far beyond what any individual library can collect, but if state laws prohibit the sharing of user information with a third party, then sharing consortium information is also prohibited. Laws may specify particular types of protected data. For example, data from acquisitions and bibliographic catalogs can usually be shared freely, but data connected to a user's behavior must remain protected. When a consortium crosses state lines, the problem compounds, and each library must only share information allowed in their state.

Restrictions may also govern the granularity of analysis and distribution of analytical results. Illinois' state law, for example, allows library managers to create and share reports about library records as long as no individuals can be identified from the reports (Library Records Confidentiality Act, 1983). Conversely, Virginia's regulations for public libraries state that after the user returns an item, the record of that transaction is deleted. The record noting the occurrence of a transaction may stay attached to an item, however, until no circulation of that item has taken place for a year (Library of Virginia Records Management Division, 1996). These laws may extend beyond public libraries, as well, into any library that is open to the public. Many university libraries participate in a Government Documents program; they may fall under similar legal restrictions as public libraries. Where these kinds of complex and occasionally contradictory regulations exist, libraries cannot take full advantage of the potential offered by circulation information. If bibliomining becomes more popular in libraries, it is possible that librarians, libraries and their host organizations may seek common federal legislation to rationalize the governance of these activities and provide an appropriate balance between user protections and management needs. For the present, before engaging in bibliomining, librarians must ensure that their data collection and analyses fit within the legal framework of their home states.

Ethical Issues

The code of ethics for the American Library Association (1995, Code III, ¶ 1) states, "We protect each library user's right to privacy and confidentiality with respect to information sought or received and resources consulted, borrowed, acquired, or transmitted." This statement provides the basic ethical principle that all bibliomining efforts must respect. Libraries are known as a place to conduct research privately. Librarians have kept third parties away from user circulation records for years. As previously mentioned, librarians spearheaded the counterattack against Hoover's intrusive Library Awareness program. Users conduct research in the library with a sense of security that their research will not be scrutinized. Nonetheless, while working within the bounds of this principle, librarians can still ethically examine the behavior of library users. In order to track in-house use, library employees scurry around behind users, tracking which books were used during a library visit. Researchers have explored library system searching logs for decades. Today, libraries keep Web logs, proxy records and other artifacts left behind from a user's visit (Pace, 2001). To collect and analyze these data ethically, it is important to work from established guidelines and policies that ensure the privacy of user records and the confidentiality of individual users. As a general basis for such guidelines, we recommend the Code of Fair Information Practices (U.S. Department of Health, Education and Welfare (HEW), 1973), which specifies principles and practices for the ethical handling of personally identifiable data about people. Appendix A provides a list of the five principles described in the code.

In the past, librarians had to depend upon surveys for gathering user information, but, with bibliomining, they can discover similar patterns without wasting the user's time or the taxpayer's money on surveys (Estabrook, 1996). In order to do this ethically, however, libraries should develop, implement and disseminate a privacy policy. The library must inform users of the intended use of the records, and, at the very least, have a procedure available where users can opt out of the analysis. It would be more appropriate to get the permission of users before using their circulation records. It would take some time and money to gather the permissions through mail, the telephone or in person, but would help to make the public aware of what is happening and ensure that only those users that wish to participate in the analysis are used. In addition, it would avoid potentially costly legal action that might ensue, if users felt that their rights were infringed in the analysis of their behaviors. Research on monitoring of user behavior has consistently shown the importance of "choice" and the ability to opt out in users' judgments of the fairness of monitoring (Stanton, 2000).

Another option, and perhaps a safer path on which to start, is to not examine any information that ties a particular user to a circulation history. This would, of course, reduce the power and the personalization available from bibliomining but may be worthwhile to avoid ethical and legal breaches. Public institutions may find that this is the only solution, while private libraries may have more flexibility in what they can do. Each library must balance their legal and ethical situation with the desire to better manage their library and better serve their users.

CONCLUSION

Libraries have gathered data about their collections and users for years but have rarely used those data for better decision-making. By taking a more active approach based on applications of data mining, data visualization and statistics, information organizations can get a clearer picture of their information delivery and management needs. At the same time, libraries must continue to protect their users and employees from misuse of personally identifiable data records. In "Sacred trust or competitive opportunity: Using user records," Estabrook (1996) discussed this moral dilemma. She pointed out that librarians must balance information protection with the need to create new library services (e.g., personalization functions). Now that libraries must compete against online booksellers, downloadable audio books and the vast supply of "free" information of varying quality from the Internet, librarians must begin to take the initiative in using their systems and data for competitive advantage and to justify continued support and funding of libraries.

The process of using library data more effectively begins by discovering ways to connect the disparate sources of data most libraries create. Connecting these disparate sources in data warehouses can facilitate systematic exploration with different tools to discover behavioral patterns of the libraries primary constituencies. These patterns can help enhance the library experience for the user, can assist library management in making decisions and setting policies and can assist the parent organizations or communities to understand information needs of their members.

Information discovered through the application of bibliomining techniques has the potential to save money, provide more appropriate programs, meet more of the user's information needs, become aware of gaps and strengths in information resource collections and serve as a more effective information source for users. Bibliomining can provide the data to justify the difficult decisions and funding requests library managers must make. Finally, bibliomining can inform the processes and products of knowledge management that have grown in importance within contemporary organizations.

REFERENCES

Aluri, R. & Riggs, D. (1990). *Expert Systems in Libraries*. Norwood, NJ: Ablex Publishing Corporation.

American Library Association. (1995). *Code of ethics of the American Library Association*. Retrieved January 27, 2002, from http://www.ala.org/alaorg/oif/ethics.html.

Applegate, R. (1993). Models of user satisfaction: understanding false positives. *RQ, 32*(4), 525-539.

Atkins, S. (1996). Mining automated systems for collection management. *Library Administration & Management, 10*(1), 16-19.

Banerjee, K. (1998). Is data mining right for your library? *Computers in Libraries, 18*(10), 28-31.

Bleyberg, M. Z., Zhu, D., Cole, K., Bates, D., & Zhan, W. (1999). Developing an integrated library decision support warehouse. *Proceedings of the IEEE International Conference on Systems, Man, and Cybernetics, Piscataway, NJ, 2*, 546-551.

Chau, M. Y. (2000). Mediating off-site electronic reference services: Human-computer interactions between libraries and Web mining technology. *Proceedings of the Fourth International Conference on Knowledge-Based Intelligent Engineering Systems & Allied Technologies, Piscataway, NJ, 2*, 695-699.

Doszkocs, T. E. (n.d.). *Neural networks in libraries: The potential of a new information technology*. Retrieved October 24, 2001, from http://web.simmons.edu/~chen/nit/NIT%2791/027~dos.htm.

Estabrook, L. (1996). Sacred trust or competitive opportunity: Using patron records. *Library Journal, 121*(2), 48-49.

Guenther, K. (2000). Applying data mining principles to library data collection. *Computers in Libraries, 20*(4), 60-63.

Gutwin, C., Paynter, G., Witten, I., Nevill-Manning, C., & Frank, E. (1999). Improving browsing in digital libraries with keyphrase indexes. *Decision Support Systems 21*, 81-104.

Harter, S. P., & Hert, C. A. (1997). Evaluation of information retrieval systems: Approaches, issues, and methods. In M. E. Williams (Ed.), *Annual review of information science and technology* (vol. 32, pp. 3-94). Medford, NJ: Information Today.

Hildreth, C. (2001). Accounting for users' inflated assessments of on-line catalogue search performance and usefulness: An experimental study. *Information Research, 6*(2). Retrieved January 25, 2002, from http://InformationR.net/ir/6-2/paper101.html.

Johnston, M., & Weckert, J. (1990). Selection advisor: an expert system for collection development. *Information Technology and Libraries, 9*(3), 219-225.

Koenig, M. E. D. (1985). Bibliographic information retrieval systems and database management systems. *Information Technology and Libraries, 4,* 247-272.

Lawrence, S., Giles, C. L., & Bollacker, K. (1999). Digital libraries and autonomous citation indexing. *IEEE Computer, 32*(6), 67-71.

Library of Virginia Records Management Division. (1996). *General schedule no. 22.* Retrieved January 27, 2002, from http://www.lva.lib.va.us/state/records/schedule/gs%2D22.htm.

Library Records Confidentiality Act, 75 Illinois Compiled Statutes §70 (1983).

Liddy, L. (2000). Text mining. *Bulletin of the American Society for Information Science, 27*(1), 13-14.

Mancini, D. D. (1996). Mining your automated system for system-wide decision making. *Library Administration & Management, 10*(1), 11-15.

Morris, A. (Ed.). (1991). *Application of expert systems in library and information centers.* London: Bowker-Saur.

Nutter, S. K. (1987). Online systems and the management of collections: Use and implications. *Advances in Library Automation Networking, 1,* 125-149.

Pace, A. K. (2001). It's a matter of privacy. *Computers in Libraries, 21*(6), 50-52.

Peters, T. (1996). Using transaction log analysis for library management information. *Library Administration & Management 10*(1), 20-25.

Sallis, P., Hill, L., Janee, G., Lovette, K., & Masi, C. (1999). A methodology for profiling users of large interactive systems incorporating neural network data mining techniques. *Proceedings of the 1999 Information Resources Management Association International Conference* (pp. 994-998). Hershey, PA: Idea Group Publishing.

Schulman, S. (1998). Data mining: Life after report generators. *Information Today, 15*(3), 52.

Seaman, S. (2001, October 27). *Confidentiality of library records.* Presentation at the Colorado Library Association Annual Meeting. Retrieved January 27, 2002 from http://spot.colorado.edu/~seaman/confidentialitylaws.htm.

Sprain, M. (2001). Confidentiality in libraries. *Colorado Libraries, 27*(1), 36-38.

Stanton, J. M. (2000). Reactions to employee performance monitoring: Framework, review, and research directions. *Human Performance, 13,* 85-113.

Su, S., & Needamangala, A. (2000). Harvesting information from a library data warehouse. *Information Technology and Libraries, 19*(1), 17-28.

U.S. Department of Health, Education and Welfare (HEW). (1973). Secretary's advisory committee on automated personal data systems, records, computers, and the rights of citizens. Washington, D.C.: Government Printing Office.

Vizine-Goetz, D., Weibel, S. & Oskins, M. (1990). Automating descriptive cataloging. In R. Aluri & D. Riggs (Eds.), *Expert Systems in Libraries* (pp. 123-134). Norwood, NJ: Ablex Publishing Corporation.

Zaïane, O., Xin, M., & Han, J. (1998). Discovering Web access patterns and trends by applying OLAP and data mining technology on Web logs. *Proceedings of the IEEE Advances in Digital Libraries* (pp. 19-29). Los Alamitos, CA: IEEE Computer Society.

APPENDIX

Principles from the code of fair information practices (HEW, 1973)

1. There must be no personal data record-keeping systems whose very existence is secret.

2. There must be a way for a person to find out what information about the person is in a record and how it is used.

3. There must be a way for a person to prevent information about the person that was obtained for one purpose from being used or made available for other purposes without the person's consent.

4. There must be a way for a person to correct or amend a record of identifiable information about the person.

5. Any organization creating, maintaining, using, or disseminating records of identifiable personal data must assure the reliability of the data for their intended use and must take precautions to prevent misuses of the data.

Chapter XVIII

Translating Advances in Data Mining to Business Operations: The Art of Data Mining in Retailing

Henry Dillon
Independent Consultant, UK

Beverley Hope
Victoria University of Wellington, New Zealand

ABSTRACT

Knowledge discovery in databases (KDD) is a field of research that studies the development and use of various data analysis tools and techniques. KDD research has produced an array of models, theories, functions and methodologies for producing knowledge from data. However, despite these advances, nearly two thirds of information technology (IT) managers say that data mining products are too difficult to use in a business context. This chapter discusses how advances in data mining translate into the business context. It highlights the art of business implementation rather than the science of KDD.

INTRODUCTION

In the past, high storage and processing costs meant that businesses had to be selective about what data they stored. Today, this restriction has been removed as costs of data storage plummet. In addition, there are now more opportunities for capturing detailed data, particularly with the increase in e-commerce activities, where detailed business transactions can be traced (Kimball & Merz, 2000). As the volume and detail of stored data increases, the demand for effective and efficient analysis tools also increases (Brachman, Khabaza, Kloesgen, Piatetsky-Shapiro & Simoudis, 1996).

KDD has been rigorously researched, particularly in the area of data mining (Fayyad, Piatetsky-Shapiro, Smyth & Uthurusamy, 1996). This has resulted in an array of models, theories, functions and methodologies for producing knowledge from data. Despite these advances, nearly two thirds of IT managers say that data mining products are too difficult to use in a business context (Foley & Russell, 1998). This is because, along with the scientific aspects of KDD, a business needs the artistic application of KDD to business (Kimball & Merz, 2000). While it is possible to propose strategies and methods for best practice in applying data mining to a business context (Brachman et al., 1996), this would be from an academic perspective. This chapter does not seek to do this. Instead, we focus on the pragmatic issue of how advances in data mining can be used in the business world, using action research in an energy firm to demonstrate the potential. We first present a review of the relevant academic literature and then apply this knowledge to a business case study in a major gas service station corporation.

BACKGROUND

The purpose of this section is to provide an understanding of the concepts of data mining to be used in discussing the case study. Here, we briefly address three concepts: data warehousing, KDD and data mining.

Data Warehousing

In 1990, William Inmon coined the term "data warehousing" (Sakaguchi & Frolick, 1997). The new concept differed from previous data storage concepts by incorporating data extracted from a variety of production databases, rather than focusing on the storage of raw production data from individual sources (Inmon, 1996). The intent was to construct an architecture that improved data analysis and decision support. Inmon identified four properties of a data warehouse:

- **Subject Oriented:** In the data warehouse, there is a shift from application-oriented data to decision-support data. If designed well, subject-oriented data will provide a stable image of business processes, capturing the basic nature of the business environment.
- **Integrated:** The warehouse consolidates application data from different legacy systems and eliminates data inconsistencies.
- **Time-Variant:** Each data point is associated with a point in time. Warehoused data can be compared along a time axis, unlike transactional data, which capture a moment in time.
- **Non-Volatile:** The database absorbs new data, integrating it with previous data, that is, new data is appended rather than substituted.

Data warehouses provide an abundance of data for analysis. However as data warehouses grow in size, users encounter information overload issues and find that their traditional applications are inadequate to access and analyze the data. Advances in KDD seek to remedy this problem.

KDD

KDD is a way of better exploiting the potential of data warehouses through improved analysis. It has been defined as "The non-trivial process of identifying valid, novel, potentially useful and ultimately understandable patterns in data" (Fayyad, 1996, p. 21).

A key point to draw from this definition is the concept of process. KDD is not a technique or method, rather it is an elaborate methodology, of which data mining is one part. Fayyad et al.'s, (1996) classic five-step process for drawing knowledge from data is shown in Figure 1. Each step of the process is imperative, but data mining has received the most attention. The steps are:

1. Select data for a specific target.
2. Preprocess the data.
3. Transform the data into a form for data mining.
4. Mine the transformed data to identify patterns.
5. Interpret and evaluate the patterns found to produce knowledge.

Data Mining

There are two key objectives in any data mining application: description and prediction. To achieve these, analysts may employ one or more of the six common data mining methods: classification, regression, clustering, summarization, dependency modeling and deviation detection (Fayyad et al., 1996).

Classification involves the mapping of data values into classes using a derived function. This provides a class representation of past trends enabling predictions based on classification dependencies. For example, banks could use classification to influence decisions in loan approval. This could be achieved by constructing a function that determines risk categories based on applicant characteristics.

Regression is similar to classification in that it uses a function to provide grounded predictions. It differs in that, instead of using classes, regression measures the correlation between two variables. This can be translated to the business context through applications, such as predicting future sales over a time series. For example, a bank might use regression to determine the strength of relationship between income and demand for financial services. What is the strength of correlation between an account holder's income and his demand for online share trading facilities?

Clustering is a descriptive tool used to group common data instances. The concept has classic applications in the marketing discipline, where customers with common attributes are grouped in the process of "segmentation" (Guiltinan, Paul & Madden,

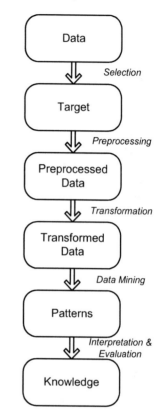

Figure 1.   KDD Process Overview (Fayyad et al., 1996)

1997). For example, banks might use clustering to identify customers who are heavy users of particular services.

Summarization uses an array of techniques to describe data. Simple techniques include tabulation of aggregates or averages. Advanced techniques stretch to summary rules, functional relationships or associations derived from a data source (Argawal, Mannila, Srikant, Toivonen & Verkamo, 1996). For example, a bank may use summarization to determine the mean and standard deviation of overdraft account balances.

Dependency modeling incorporates probability and uncertainty into a model to determine the significance of dependency between variables. It offers strong grounds for predicting uncertain outcomes, such as human behavior. For example, banks with loyalty programs could develop a dependency model to determine the probability of a customer visiting three retail outlets in the coming month.

Deviation detection examines the comparative dynamics of patterns in data, usually over a time series. This delivers both a predictive and descriptive benefit (Berndt & Clifford, 1996). The description of past data trends can highlight seasonality or periodic market characteristics. It may then be possible for the business to predict and prepare for changes. For example, a bank could identify trends in home loan applications. By identifying new application seasons, banks could schedule advertising to maximize their opportunities.

The science of data mining has advanced rapidly over recent years. The added complexity has allowed scientists to predict and describe reality in a richer form. Our interest is in how these complex advances can be applied to the business context. We sought to determine this through a case study in the gas service station industry.

CASE METHODOLOGY

This research uses a single organization as a case study to demonstrate the application of data mining techniques to a business context. Data were collected through interviews, observations and document examination. Among these, interviews provided the main source of data.

- **Interviews:** Semistructured interviews were conducted with selected employees at three levels — operational, tactical and strategic — with interviews tailored to each level.
- **Observation:** During the project, the principal researcher had a specialist technical role within the firm, which gave him an opportunity to observe and reflect on events in context. A journal of these observations was kept. This captured the unexpected aspects outside of formal interactions.
- **Documentation:** Material, such as newspaper articles, public documents and industry literature, were used to supplement and validate data gained in interviews.

Data from all sources were interpreted to generate a story. Through reflection, chunks of meaning were identified across data sources, branded and then compared to findings in the academic literature. This analytic method is consistent with good practice (Yin, 1990; McCracken, 1988; Creswell, 1994).

A NEW ZEALAND CASE EXAMPLE
The Organization

The selected company, which we will call EnergyCo, is a global energy company with retail operations in 125 countries. It has revenues of $65.9 billion and average investment spending of $4.9 billion a year over the last five years. More than 15,000 company-branded retail outlets operate internationally. In New Zealand, the company owns 70 service stations and supplies hundreds of independent outlets. Just prior to the study, a new entrant to the local industry triggered a price war on wet-stock product (gas, diesel and alternative fuels). Throughout this price war, unprofitable wet-stock margins were sustained, resulting in heavy dependence on alternative profit centers, such as dry-stock merchandising (automotive supplies, groceries and fast foods) to maintain profitability.

Within EnergyCo, the Retail Stores Marketing department is responsible for decision making regarding dry-stock merchandising. The department can be divided into three managerial levels based on the nature of decision-making: operational, tactical and strategic. The relationships between levels are shown in Figure 2. The lowest level of merchandising decision making, operational, is the responsibility of site managers at local service stations. Site staff have the closest relationship with customers, consequently, they are given some autonomy in decision making to ensure the needs of local customers are met. Supporting the site mangers are staff in the Resale Stores Marketing group. Decisions made at this tactical level are less site specific. Here, nationwide tactics are designed with the intention of increasing profitability and volume for the organization as a whole. Guiding the direction of the group's efforts is senior management. Decisions at this strategic level range from corporate visions to specific quantifiable goals.

Figure 2. Organizational Structure

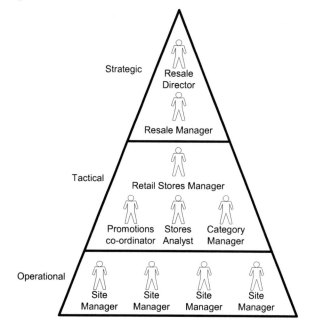

The Opportunity for Change

Prior to the wet-stock price war, the company had few strategies for effective dry-stock merchandising; the primary business concern had been wet-stock volumes. The price war forced management to focus on dry-stock sales and to adopt better merchandising practices. The weaknesses, and consequent opportunities, of the old practices are shown in Table 1.

A key weakness was the bloated nationwide product range. Over time, sites had accumulated a large and differentiated range of products and this weakened profitability. This damage to profitability was explained by:

1.   Sites choosing to stock inappropriate or unprofitable products;
2.   Failure of some sites to stock market leader products or flavors; and
3.   Head Office unable to negotiate nationwide product ranging deals at special rates.

Other weaknesses included the lack of sales information about individual sites caused by localized decision-making and difficulty in executing Head Office decisions regarding sites. Reasons for the lack of centralized control were many, including: poor communication, decisions being undermined by rival political opinions and site negligence.

Management sought to overcome these problems by centralizing management of merchandising operations. The objective was to increase site uniformity, thereby creating opportunities to leverage deals with suppliers and to employ advanced merchandising practices. The effectiveness of centralized decision making depended upon two key objectives: improved Head Office knowledge about sites and customers and improved execution of Head Office decisions. These were to be achieved through the initiation of the data warehouse project and the Category Management System (CMS) Project.

Table 1. Merchandising Weaknesses and Opportunities

Weaknesses	Opportunities
• Large range of products stocked across the country • Site rather than Head Office control over product ranges • Limited company-wide sales information	• Centralized Management of Merchandising operations • Ability to leverage deals from suppliers • Advanced merchandising practices, such as dynamic advertising

The Data Warehouse Project

Centralized decision making required centralized data. The initial objective of the data warehouse project was to provide information to allow product rationalization; the longer term objective was to facilitate tactical and strategic decision making. The data warehouse would help meet the first objective by improving Head Office knowledge about sites, customers and sales patterns. However, it did not address the second objective, improved execution of Head Office decisions. To address this, management implemented a new digital communication infrastructure to automatically implement Head Office decisions. This was the CMS project.

The CMS Project

One of the roles of the Merchandising group at the Head Office is to leverage special deals and negotiate promotions for sites. However, the execution of, and compliance with, these plans at the site was never absolute. The promotions coordinator in Head Office noted that, although the data warehouse would provide crucial, timely information to support decisions, it would be worthless if decisions were not executed at site. CMS was designed to effect Head Office decisions.

Figure 3 illustrates how the two projects fit together. Sales information from sites is electronically retrieved and loaded into the central data warehouse. Head Office merchandising personnel then make decisions based on knowledge mined from the warehouse. Changes required at sites as a result of the merchandising decision are stored on CMS, which updates the stock lists and order requirements for each store. Site managers are able to view any changes CMS makes. Subsequent changes are automatically made to the site computer and point-of-sale units. Metaphorically speaking, the data warehouse acts as the company's eyes and ears for observing reality, while CMS acts as the arms and legs for reacting to the observations.

During the writing of this case, both the data warehouse and CMS projects were stalled due to complications in contract negotiations with the software supplier. A temporary data mart solution, called Thomas, was developed to meet the information requirements of the Head Office Merchandising staff. Thomas did not provide the data mining techniques planned for with the use of the data warehouse, but it did provide substantial insight into sales information.

Figure 3. The New Merchandising Opportunity

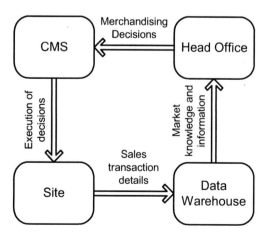

RESULTS

Case study data from respondents were analyzed with respect to the grand tour question, namely, "How do today's advances in data mining translate to business operations?" To answer this question, we examined the past data analysis function within the Stores marketing department, and compared these to the new developments, such as the proposed data warehouse project and Thomas, the substituted data mart.

Past Data Analysis Infrastructure

Prior to the new initiatives, data analysis processes at Head Office were limited. Information came from a variety of sources including a leading market research firm, suppliers and internal departments. However, the data were not in a form suitable for mining. The market research firm supplied detailed market performance information about product sales on a monthly basis for the entire retail network, rather than on a site basis. Supplier information and internally generated information were highly variable in their level of detail and generally came from disparate sources making integration difficult.

Under the old regime, four factors hindered data analysis at Head Office: limited access to data, inadequate detail, unacceptable latency and inaccuracy. Although the technology at sites was capable of capturing rich data, the communications infrastructure and storage capabilities at the Head Office did not support accessibility. The Stores Marketing Manager at the Head Office commented:

> *Retail business is all about having access to information and using it. Because we were decentralized, the stores themselves had access to a sophisticated system that provided quite a bit of information to make their own decisions. However, centrally, ... I had no access to detailed data; I only had access to department, or aggregated level data, through [our market research firm]. Consequently, until we really started to get access to the summary information through suppliers, we weren't able to make rational decisions, and as a consequence we didn't make any. Autonomy was seen to best reside with the site manager.*

Figure 4. Past Data Analysis Information Sources

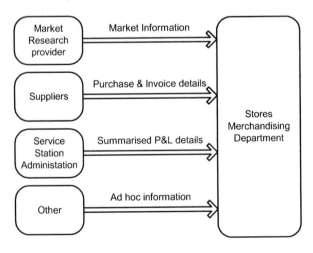

The lack of detail in data meant that only high-level summarization and limited-trend analysis could be used to examine field information. Information was used for periodic profit and loss measurement and understanding tactical positioning and performance. Latency was another problem. Information was collected and presented on a monthly basis, which was, in many cases, too late. The promotions coordinator at the Head Office pointed out that, since a standard promotion duration was four weeks, no feedback could be gained regarding the success or failure of a promotion before the promotion was already completed. Ad hoc information collection from sites was possible, however this required considerable time and resources and, consequently, was requested in only special cases. Finally, information accuracy and completeness under the old system was questionable. It is common KDD practice to expect data to be "unclean" and consequently to undertake a scrubbing process. However, such processes for field data were absent from the previous information infrastructure. As a result of these inadequacies in data quality, tactical staff were often forced to make uninformed or gut-feeling decisions.

The reader will recall that one of the objectives of this research was to understand how the science of KDD could be applied to the art of retailing. We found that this was not an easy task. We first had to educate the users on the nature of each data mining technique. Only after this was done could we complete interviews and analyze them to identify common retail principles and situations that were amenable to particular data mining techniques. Each technique was assessed in terms of how it could be applied within the business, and the value it might contribute to achieving business goals. Because we were interested in the art of implementation, our grounds for determining value were respondent's perceptions, rather than heuristics or interviewer expertise. Perceived value was measured using three levels of granularity: high, medium and low (Table 2).

Table 2. Summary of Data Mining Techniques Applied in the Case Study

Data Mining Technique	Application Example	Value
Dependency Modeling	Provides grounds for the cross merchandising of products	High
Deviation Detection	Discovering seasonal or unique sales trends	High
Clustering	Provides a model for rationalizing product ranging and pricing	High
Summarization	Supplies a more detailed understanding of the market reality	Medium
Regression and Classification	Determining price elasticity and evaluating product cost/benefit	Low
High:	Respondents identified a well-defined business application with clearly valuable returns.	
Medium:	The technique could be applied to a business context with reasonable associated value.	
Low:	Business applications were difficult to articulate or no clear value could be foreseen.	

Dependency Modeling

A number of respondents saw the retail concept of cross merchandising as a sound application of dependency modeling. Cross merchandising is the bundling or grouping of different individual products together at a special or exclusive price. The rationale for doing this is to maximize the total gross profit dollars per customer. The Stores Marketing Manager at Head Office explains:

> *The opportunity, or the times, that [a customer] visits you with a particular product in mind won't produce volumes large enough to make merchandising profitable. Instead, [merchandisers] rely on the fact that humans are relatively impulsive. As a result, we must be able to gauge how this impulsion can be controlled or manipulated. The fundamental objective is to increase the basket amount or gross profit dollars per customer.*

Dependency modeling can give merchandising analysts valuable information regarding the probability of given product combinations. This provides a grounded understanding of potential impulse buying triggers, and allows merchandising analysts to prepare marketing tactics for firing these triggers.

Deviation Detection

Respondents identified a number of business applications, which could use deviation detection techniques. These included discovery of new trends, monitoring of current and past performance and prediction of future trends. Cyclical or seasonal surges in demand are largely unresearched at a microlevel, however these can be valuable for managers serving impulsive consumers in a convenience market. A Stores Analyst at the Head Office recalls one such gem:

> *In the week before Christmas, we will always see an enormous lift in the number of battery sales. And do you know why? It's because people buy their kids presents but forget the batteries. So they rush out to one of our sites and buy some. Because we know and understand this trend, we can prepare for this sales lift and increase our returns.*

The promotions coordinator also commented on the potential significance of deviation detection in determining the effectiveness of promotions. Throughout a promotion period, all sites should experience some lift in sales. If this isn't the case, then investigation and explanation are required. For example, Have they got the signage up?; Is the promotion at the right price?; and Is the promotion receiving good placement relative to foot traffic? The promotions coordinator explained that many sites lose opportunities for higher profits due to failure to comply with promotion guidelines. Deviation detection can supply microlevel analysis of both past history and future trends. This can allow analysts to make grounded decisions on time-based site information.

Clustering

Respondents identified a variety of hypothetical merchandising applications appropriate for the clustering technique. Previously, many of these were infeasible due to limited information on environmental dimensions, such as customer demographics,

Figure 5. Two-Dimensional Clustering from Thomas, the Data Mart

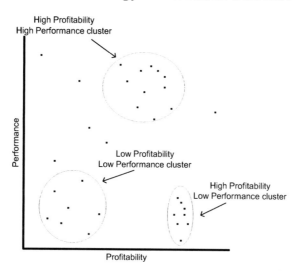

psychographics or geographic location. A potential application of clustering identified by respondents was product performance vs. profitability. Thomas already delivered a simple two-dimensional cluster analysis (Figure 5), but data mining will allow more detailed analysis by enabling inclusion of additional factors. Cluster analysis can provide rational grounds for product ranging and pricing. For example, management may decide to expand the Asian foods range at sites identified as high performers in this food category.

Respondents had difficulty discriminating between clustering and dependency modeling. This is understandable given that they can have applications that cross over. For example, clustering can provide good initial grounds for determining and describing product bundles appropriate for cross merchandising, and dependency modeling can provide a predictive element, allowing analysts to determine the probability of a customer buying product X, if they also bought Y.

Summarization

Prior to the new initiatives, Thomas enabled basic summarization analysis to be performed, for example, means analysis and standard deviations for site figures. More advanced summarization, such as summary rule definition, could provide a sound grounding for understanding the dynamics of merchandising reality. Suppose, for example, an analyst identified a number of variables that influenced the sales performance of a site (Figure 6). Summary rules could provide analysts with information to better understand reality and use this understanding to justify or rationalize future decisions.

Summary rules have limitations when applied to social behavior phenomena because of the enormous number of variables present in the "real world." This complexity impacts on the ability to formulate stores merchandising summary rules. The example in Figure 6 shows only a few of the variables that can affect sales performance and fails to consider variables, such as weather, customer psychographics and culture. This complexity issue reduced the perceived value of summarization for respondents.

Figure 6. Summary Rule Concept

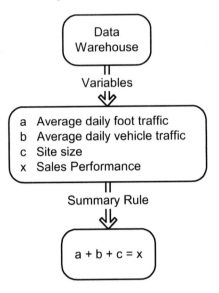

Regression and Classification

Of all the data mining techniques, regression and classification received the least respondent interest. Many respondents had difficulty understanding the concepts, and, consequently, they had difficulty applying them. One respondent suggested price elasticity and classification of product cost and benefit. These could result in models of customer responsiveness to price changes, and an ability to predict the likely outcome of new product ranging decisions. Despite these applications the availability of such information had limited appeal. Perhaps this limited appeal was due to the lack of understanding of the technique.

The majority of data mining techniques discussed have shown application value to merchandising operation, particularly Dependency Modeling, Deviation Detection and Clustering. Most examples given to us related to tactical activities within the organization and did not address the strategic relevance of data mining. The following section addresses this issue.

STRATEGIES ENABLED BY DATA MINING

Data mining enables innovative strategies to be justified by providing analysis based on large data stores. Management at EnergyCo is still underutilizing the data sources at their disposal. At the time of writing, no new strategies had been implemented with respect to the information provided by Thomas the data mart. Despite this, many respondents recognized potential strategies enabled by data mined information.

One significant strategy is the discovery of cross-merchandisable products using dependency analysis. This might be used to justify a strategy to install service stations without fuel. There are many costs and risks involved in the resale of fuels, so, if data showed that showroom sales were not dependent of fuel sales, management might consider constructing sites that didn't sell fuel.

Another strategy suggested by respondents was dynamic on-site advertising. Throughout the day, sites serve a range of customers with differing characteristics. By changing site advertising to suit current audience and demand, sites could improve the on-site advertising effectiveness. For example, suppose we could establish sales volumes trends for two different products over a daily time frame. Such a trend could be represented as in Figure 7. Notice that Product X achieves peak sales volume around midday, whereas Product Y has higher sales volume in the late afternoon and early evening. Using this information, site staff could change signage to match expected volume fluctuations and hopefully trigger, persuade and motivate more customers to purchase the advertised product.

Data mining will inevitably enable new strategies. This section presented just two of the possibilities. There is great potential: the only limitation is managerial creativity.

Future Trends

A number of implications have emerged from this study. These include implications for practitioners and for further research into KDD.

Implications for Practitioners

Data mining initiative at EnergyCo had most relevance at the tactical level. Operational level decision makers had limited use for mined information because of the decentralized and territorial nature of their responsibilities. This resulted from three factors. First, because of their frontline involvement, site managers considered they already had a good understanding of customer patterns. Second, individual sites are small-scale operations with low data volumes unsuitable for data mining tools. Third, operational managers often lacked the expertise to understand data mining techniques

Figure 7. Product Performance by Daily Time Series

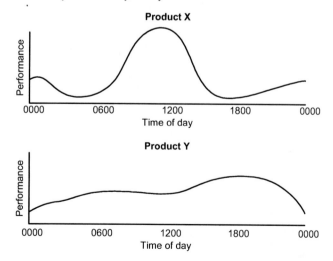

and, hence, were unable to perceive its value. Data mining may have the potential to support strategic decision making, but it was not evidenced in this study. The findings of this study suggest that practitioners should first target data mining efforts at the tactical level and, after success is experienced there, target the strategic level of their business.

A critical issue facing practitioners is the complexity of the KDD science. Respondents in this study had difficulty understanding the concepts and techniques associated with data mining. In several cases, respondents' understanding was generic or oversimplified, that is, they understood data mining to be a "black box" solution that returned valuable information without any requirement for direction or instruction. This observation highlights the disparity of understanding between the science and art of data mining. To resolve this gap, more intensive training of analytic skills is needed to improve understanding of the results delivered by data mining. This is particularly important for tactical and strategic decision makers, where data mining deliverables seem to be most relevant.

A transactional data store does not supply the richness of data required for modern decision making. Environmental information, such as customer demographics and geographic characteristics, must also be fed into the data warehouse to supply richer knowledge nuggets. Customer loyalty programs are one means by which businesses can gain supplementary information to add the desired richness to customer profiles.

Implications for Research

Advances in KDD research have resulted in improved methods of using data warehouses to describe and predict phenomena of interest. The majority of KDD literature focuses on the scientific perspective of KDD, that is, the development of new processes and techniques for discovering knowledge. While scientific studies have undoubtedly added value to the field, little academic work has been directed toward the application of KDD to commercial reality. Areas for future research include:

1.   Modes of information presentation to decision makers,
2.   Education of analysts and decision makers in data mining methods, and
3.   Managing organizational change toward a data aware culture.

Better modes of presenting mined information are required. Data mining techniques can lead to abstract presentations of results (Fayyad et al., 1996), which are difficult for practitioners to understand, interpret and act upon. Research into better presentation styles and aids is already expanding into a field known as Data Visualization, however, further work is required, if it is to become practical.

There is also a need to improve analysts' understanding and knowledge of the KDD process. Data mining, in particular, requires a special set of skills to allow analysts to exploit the potential of large data stores. Without at least a base understanding of the process and techniques, the benefits of conducting a data mining operation are severely reduced. Research needs to identify the data mining skills relevant to business and offer some suggestion as to how organizations should approach this training issue.

To facilitate the change, from a traditional mindset to data mining mindset, requires a supportive organizational culture. Research into factors that foster or inhibit acceptance of KDD within organizations will assist the uptake of data mining in organizations.

Managing culture change is particularly relevant in the new environment, where the analyst's role moves beyond information to knowledge and assisting knowledge workers.

CONCLUSION

In this study, we sought to determine how advances in data mining could be applied to modern business operations. To do this we conducted a case study. Our analysis showed that not all data mining techniques are applicable at all business levels. There is particular value in applying KDD at the tactical level and potential value at the strategic level. The applicability of each technique is likely to differ across businesses and industries, and businesses must train analysts and users in the KDD process and data mining techniques, while also allowing them the freedom for creativity in its application. Once users are familiar with data mining techniques, finding business applications should not be difficult.

The research findings clearly indicate the need for further work in this growing field. Issues regarding tactical worker training and evolution of an organizational mindset to support KDD need to be addressed to ensure data mining benefits are maximized. The next logical step from this research would be an examination of the new skills and understanding required by knowledge workers of the future.

REFERENCES

Argawal, R., Mannila, H., Srikant, R., Toivonen, H., & Verkamo, A. (1996). Fast discovery of association rules. In U. M. Fayyad, G. Piatetsky-Sharpiro, P. Smyth, & R. Uthurusamy (Eds.), *Advances in knowledge discovery and data mining* (pp. 307-328). MA: MIT Press.

Berndt, D. J., & Clifford, J. (1996). Finding patterns in time series: A dynamic programming approach. In U. M. Fayyad, G. Piatetsky-Sharpiro, P. Smyth, & R. Uthurusamy (Eds.), *Advances in knowledge discovery and data mining* (pp. 229-248). MA: MIT Press.

Brachman, R. J., Khabaza, T., Kloesgen, W., Piatetsky-Shapiro, G., & Simoudis, E. (1996). Mining business databases. *Communications of the ACM, 39*(11), 42-48.

Creswell, J. W. (1994). *Research design: Qualitative and quantitative approaches.* Thousand Oaks, CA: Sage.

Fayyad, U. M. (1996). Data mining and knowledge discovery: making sense out of data. *IEEE Expert, 11*(5), 20-25.

Fayyad, U. M., Piatetsky-Sharpiro, G., Smyth, P., & Uthurusamy, R. (1996). *Advances in knowledge discovery and data mining.* MA: MIT Press.

Foley, J., & Russell, J. (1998, March). Mining your own business [Electronic version]. *InformationWeek.*

Guiltinan, J., Paul, G., & Madden, T. (1997). *Marketing management: strategies and programs.* New York: McGraw-Hill.

Hall, O. P. (2001). Mining the store. *The Journal of Business Strategy, 22*(2), 24-27.

Inmon, W. H. (1996). The data warehouse and data mining. *Communications of the ACM, 39*(11), 49-50.

Kimball, R., & Merz, R. (2000). *The Data Webhouse Toolkit: Building the Web-enabled Data Warehouse*. New York: John Wiley & Sons.

McCracken, G. (1988). *The long interview*. Beverley Hills, CA: Sage.

Sakaguchi, T., & Frolick, M. A. (1997). Review of the data warehousing literature. *Journal of Data Warehousing, 2*(1), 34-54.

Yin, R. K. (1990). *Case study research: Design and methods*. Newbury Park, CA: Sage.

Section V

ODM Challenges and Opportunities

Chapter XIX

Impediments to Exploratory Data Mining Success

Jeff Zeanah
Z Solutions, Inc., USA

ABSTRACT

This chapter discusses impediments to exploratory data mining success. These impediments were identified based on anecdotal observations from multiple projects either reviewed or undertaken by the author and are classified into four main areas: data quality; lack of secondary or supporting data; insufficient analysis manpower; lack of openness to new results. Each is explained, and recommendations are made to prevent the impediment from interfering with the organization's data mining efforts. The intent of the chapter is to provide an organization with a structure to anticipate these problems and to prevent the occurrence of these problems.

INTRODUCTION

Organizations of all kinds are experimenting with the application of data mining techniques. They may refer to these projects as data warehousing applications, market research or data mining. Regardless of the terminology, data mining applications are intended to provide an organization with a better understanding of the environment or market in which they operate.

There are two general types of data mining undertakings. Relatively well understood are the traditional scoring applications in which observations are scored to determine if they met certain criteria. In these projects, an organization typically will apply a set of tools to a large database, such as a mailing list. For example, a charity which is considering a mailing to solicit donations will score its list to determine the most likely candidates to be solicited. By using data mining to examine the characteristics of individuals who donated in the past, the charity can reduce a mailing list of 2 million households to a list of the 200,000 households most likely to donate. Soliciting this smaller list will be more profitable than "wasting" a mailing to the 1.8 million households that are very unlikely to respond. In this effort, there is not a great need to understand why the households were selected, only whether or not the refinement of the list leads to a higher response rate and increases the profitability of the mailing.

Conversely, exploratory data mining is designed to provide strategic insights from the data and guidance for future strategic or operational decision-making. Consider the following example. A consumer products manufacturer is interested in characteristics of consumers who buy its products, rather than its competitor's. Are these customers younger or older? Are they married or single? What is their ethnicity? Are their household incomes higher or lower? Simple queries of the company's data warehouse can be used to answer most of these questions. If the data is available, the average household income of the company's customers easily may be compared to the average household income of a competitor's customers. This is exploratory data mining. And for many organizations, the ability to read the databases and perform these queries is the extent of their data mining activities. In fact, for very large databases, this can be nontrivial, requiring substantial effort.

Simple queries may not provide all the answers the company needs. For example, the company discovers that its customers have higher household incomes than the competitor's customers have, are older and are more likely to be married. The organization realizes that many married families have higher incomes than do single households (two incomes versus one), and many older households have higher incomes than do the younger beginning households. The company wonders: "Are the customers who prefer our product older and happen to be married at a higher percentage or are our customers married and happen to be older?" Or are they just higher income people? Whatever the relationship, is this the same as it was five years ago? And most important, what will they be like five years from now? If the overall population ages, will that help the company sales? Will it help the company's sales only if the aging population stays married? Is the company not seeing a hidden trend that may change the company's strategic direction? These questions are not going to be answered through simple methods. The solution will be found only through causal predictive modeling and similar investigations.

Many organizations lack the ability to answer these difficult questions. When they began collecting data in their data warehouse, they expected that they would be able to resolve some of these difficult strategic puzzles. Their exploratory findings are less than they had hoped. They can identify what has happened, but have a more difficult time answering why it happened.

This chapter discusses reasons for these shortcomings. Anecdotal observations of actual projects are used as the basis for these findings. These observations are based on projects reviewed by the author, supplemented by discussions with more than 100 data mining professionals. Based on these observations, four impediments to exploratory success have been identified. Conditions leading to the impediments are discussed and solutions presented. The four impediments are:

- data quality,
- lack of secondary or supporting data,
- insufficient analysis manpower, and
- lack of openness to new results.

The projects that provided the foundations for these conclusions are proprietary efforts from private corporations and public sector organizations that are seeking to improve their understanding of their environments. Because of the proprietary nature of the projects, specific situations and data details are not presented, but are discussed in general terms.

IMPEDIMENT 1: DATA QUALITY

Lack of data quality is an obvious impediment to successful exploratory data mining. However, the root causes of the problems are not obvious. Given the obvious requirement for data quality, why are so many organizations surprised to discover the data collected turns out to be less than anticipated? Certainly data quality is not an oversight. Therefore, what leads to bad data?

There are, of course, examples of gross errors, such as faulty data entry programs or faulty metering and storage issues. However, there are things an organization or manager seeking to improve data should look for. The manager should consider two general trends when reviewing data collection plans: does the data contain a financial transaction or is it close to a financial transaction and what are the incentives or disincentives to collecting accurate data.

Experience has shown that data quality is in direct proportion to the closeness to a financial transaction. As demonstrated in Figure 1, the further away from the transaction, the greater the concern should be for data quality. Organizations are usually very successful in keeping track of the flow of money. The record keeping of a financial transaction is usually quite accurate. However the further the data is from the transaction, the lesser the data quality. Consider the example of a company that provides settlement of workers' compensation claims. When analyzing these claims to find patterns concerning the value of claims, the amount of workers' compensation payment was found to be reliable. This is expected. If the organization did not keep track of payments, the company would not be in business long. Further work with the data reveals that the recipients of the payments were reliable to a lesser degree. There was more uncertainty in some of these data fields. The name might be correct, but the address of

Figure 1. A Simple Transaction: Relationship of Transaction to Data

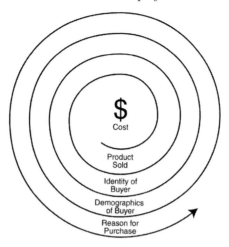

$

Cost

Product
Sold

Identity of
Buyer

Demographics
of Buyer

Reason for
Purchase

the person might be missing or the zip code incorrect. Or perhaps the name was misspelled making it impossible to match the record with other files. The individual identifier information is further away from the financial transaction and did not have a high degree of data quality. Other necessary information for the completion of the study included the type of injury leading to the claim. This information was actually not necessary for the financial transaction. The company found this data was the lowest quality data. Often the data was missing or apparently inaccurate. For example, it is difficult to explain the loss of work of six months for a minor sprained ankle. Other unrecorded mitigating factors had to be in play.

The second corrective action for data quality is to recognize that "what gets rewarded, gets done." In the above example, the field agents had a data entry system to collect information and return that information to the corporate office. However, the field agents were compensated for the number of claims handled. The implementing and structuring of compensation packages is well beyond the scope of this discussion. However, the impact on data quality of this situation is intuitive.

In most organizations the sales staff is compensated with sales commissions. There is an obvious incentive to complete the information on the volume of each sale. However, if there is an expectation that the sales staff is to collect demographic information and the collection of that information is not rewarded, then the results will be obvious. The quality of the demographic information will not be as high as the volume of sales. If data is to be a value to the organization, then collecting that data has to be of value to the employees. Data quality needs to be measured and made an organizational goal.

The electric utility industry provides a classic example of this problem. When a new commercial or industrial facility is planned, the marketing representatives of the utility meet with the customer to determine the electrical needs of the new facility. Through this process, the total amount of each type of load is recorded. The process is easy to understand by considering the total lighting load, i.e., the total lighting requirements measured in kilowatt demand. The total lighting requirement is equal to the number of bulbs multiplied by the wattage of the bulbs multiplied by the likelihood that the bulbs are on at the time of maximum facility usage. Other loads, such as the cooling load, space heating load, water heating load and cooking load, are a little more difficult to estimate, but the concept is the same. Based on the information the marketing representative collects, the company's distribution engineers size the service requirements, including the size of the transformer needed to serve the building. If the total requirements are overestimated, then the transformer is oversized, resulting in additional cost to the company. If the total requirements are underestimated, then the transformer is under-sized, resulting in a reduced economic life of the transformer. This can cause the transformer to "blow" from overheating.

The marketing representative is focused on what are called the competitive loads. These loads — water heating, space heating and cooking — can be provided by electricity or natural gas. Therefore, the marketing representatives are offered incentives to sell those loads. One can be assured that if the customer is convinced to install electric appliances to provide heating or cooking, the total provided is certainly not undercounted. However, the same cannot be said for the total lighting load — the marketing representative does not have the same incentive to get that information correct.

Trivial as this might seem, the effect can easily be seen through a review of data. The marketing representative may have the best of intentions by entering the competitive loads first and intending to go back and enter the other data later. However, workload or a typical daily work emergency interferes, and the representative forgets to go back and enter that data. The engineer working on the job recognizes the information is missing and adds his own estimates to continue his work; the result is that the database is not complete. What is the worth of the data to the company? Potentially, it is worth a great deal. The total investment in distribution to serve individual customers through trans-formers can be quite high. If the utility underestimates the requirements, the result is a reduced life of a transformer. If the load exceeds the transformer capacity, the transformer overheats, reducing the transformers service life. However, an oversized transformer (capacity is greater than needed) represents a stranded and underutilized investment. If the utility does not have good records of the total requirements of the customer, they do not know if they are routinely over-sizing or under-sizing the transformers and cannot improve their processes.

IMPROVING DATA QUALITY

Situations like the above are rampant in most organization. Frequently there is an acceptance of the data quality situation as, "that is just the way it is." Through downsizing and reorganizations, workloads are increased in most organizations. Certainly, there are economic benefits from the resulting efficiencies, but frequently something has to slip as a result. Frequently that something is data quality. Many of the following issues are present in the typical organization:

- No one is giving the data a thorough evaluation on an ongoing basis.
- There is an assumption that the data is better than it is.
- Systems to access the data are limited. There is little in the way of comparative reports or graphics to quickly visualize the data.
- Older data is archived, therefore difficult to work with or compare with new data.

- More attention (and money) is put on storage equipment (hardware and software), than to the actual data itself.
- Little screening is being done to test data and tolerances when the data is entered.

Raising the Issue of Data Quality

What is the cost of reduced data quality? It is hard to know. Organizationally, it becomes difficult to present the issue. Even as presented here, it sounds like a petty whine — not the type of thing to get broad organizational or upper management support.

To raise the issue of data quality above a whine, the implications of bad data must be shown. But first the nature of the cost of bad data must be understood. In most cases, poor data quality represents a lost opportunity cost — not a direct cost but limited opportunity. In the above example, incorrectly estimating the total electric requirements of a new customer may be a direct cost, but not having accurate data to analyze and improve the process is a missed-opportunity cost. In a marketing example, the lost opportunity is missed sales.

Improving data quality depends on understanding and utilizing one simple fact. Bad data is usually not going to get the organization's attention, but bad decisions will. Demonstrating the cost of bad decisions or the potential of a future bad decision will make the point. From a practical point of view, it is difficult, if not impossible, to calculate the Return on Investment (ROI) implications of bad data, however you can calculate the ROI implications of a bad decision.

The Time Component of Data Quality

Typically there is a delay between the collection of data and when it is analyzed. Problems developed in data collection can remain unrecognized for an extended period of time. An example of this is a direct marketing company recording catalog sales. The company has instituted a new plan to send certain mailings to certain addresses. In this program, 90 percent of the catalog is the same for each recipient; however, the cover and a few internal pages may change. A certain demographic will receive a cover highlighting some of the company's active wear, showing models involved in outdoor activities. Other recipients will receive the catalog showing a model relaxing, wearing a sweater in a comfortable chair in front of a fireplace. The direct mailing company has used demographics available on their mailing list to determine which address gets which catalog. Because this is a new program for the company, the data on individual customers purchases is not available to the detail desired. When catalogs are sent out, only summary data is collected. The company knows the total number of catalogs mailed out and total sales, but details behind those sales are not available. Therefore, the plan is to estimate the missing information as best as possible, institute the program, validate the economics of the program and improve the program over time.

Most direct sales follow certain patterns. Most sales occur during the Christmas season. However, two other patterns are seen throughout the year. Spring sales are higher as the weather warms up. In the late summer and early fall, back to school activity also increases sales. If the company wants to analyze the economic impact of a new program to better target future mailings, then a complete year of data is needed. One could argue that it would be enough to look at the impact on the Christmas season, when most of the company's sales take place. However, an equally convincing case can be made for the evaluation of sales at other times of the year. If people buy less in the spring than at Christmas, then spring is the time for the better target marketing to have an effect — turning a nonbuyer into a buyer. This may be considered a more meaningful marketing accomplishment. Which point of view is correct? A year of mailings and purchases should be considered to answer the organization's questions.

The company starts data collection in the early summer and data collection continues into Christmas. However, after Christmas some initial review of the data begins. At this time, it is clear that there are data collection problems. Some detail is not recorded or is recorded incorrectly. At this point, it is too late to do anything about the situation: another Christmas season must pass before the program can be fully analyzed. The effectiveness of the program cannot be evaluated, and, more importantly, the program cannot be refined for one more full year.

To prevent this problem an initial analysis should be performed at the end of the summer. The early summer data is insignificant relative to the other seasons of the year. But it is the best time to perform the initial analysis of the data, including:

- Initial screening of the data, including graphical analysis. This review gives indications of data quality and completeness. Is the correct data being collected? Can the products being featured be identified for the special analysis?
- Gathering and merging of secondary data with the primary data. This assures that the necessary data is available and meets the needs of the analysis and the organization. (Secondary data is discussed in detail below.)
- Performing the initial analysis and developing conclusions. A complete analysis ensures that the data and processes are available to address the organization's issues and questions.

This complete initial analysis ensures that the data is being collected and the analysis is being performed. The analysis will remove all doubt that data is being collected correctly and will be available when needed. Beginning preliminary analyses before all data is collected, even if the process to be analyzed is still incomplete, is the only certain corrective action that can be recommended to improve the data quality.

IMPEDIMENT 2: SECONDARY OR SUPPORTING DATA

Organizational data mining is not just the analysis of data warehouses and large databases or analysis of customer databases. It is an evaluation of an organization's entire operations including the environment in which the organization operates. Figure 2 presents a simple Operational Schematic describing a manufacturing company. The company makes decisions such as: what product lines will be offered; how the products are manufactured and product pricing. The decisions are implemented through the company's operations and, lastly, there is an interface with the customer — the customer purchases and uses the product. This total operation takes place in an operating environment affected by economic conditions, competitor actions and other factors not in control of the company. The interaction between the customer and the company is the

Figure 2. Operational Schematic Describing a Manufacturing Company

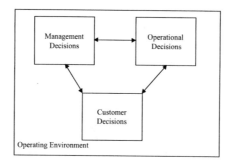

focus of most data mining activities, which try to understand customer decisions by asking questions, such as what and how much does a customer purchase? The answers to such questions are usually the primary focus of the activity, when data warehousing activities are discussed in an organization. However, data mining activities do not have to be limited to the interaction between the company and the customer. In fact, data from each of the areas in the operational schematic can have impact on the customer/company interaction. This data is usually not voluminous information that belongs in data warehouses. It is smaller — sometimes only a few hundred records. This data can be thought of as secondary or supporting data. It is not the primary requirement of a data warehouse, but it is the data that makes the primary data (the focus of the expensive development) valuable.

This concept is not new. Supporting data is frequently brought into an analysis, without much recognition. A typical example is when a company is analyzing product sales over a period of years. Often included in this analysis is data related to economic conditions, such as Gross National Product, interest rates and unemployment. The organization determines their sales performance based on general economic conditions. Therefore, some downturn in sales can be attributed to economic conditions, not to a lack of success of the company related to their competitors. The company may be using a large database of product sales, which resides in the company data warehouse. However, the company does not keep track of economic data and is fortunate that others keep this data for it.

Using external secondary data to improve an analysis is common. But, unfortunately, when there is a need for secondary and supporting data from internal sources, we can have an altogether different story. This secondary data does not get the attention of the data warehouse data, but it can be as or more important. The following examples will demonstrate our point and may sound familiar to some organizations.

A large electric utility company has for years kept detailed information on customer outages — the loss of electrical power. Outages are usually caused by severe weather but can be minimized through maintenance and the engineering of the electrical system. In addition to the inconvenience and cost to customers, reconnecting service is a major cost to the company. The electric utility in question had performed a number of projects to minimize outages including tree trimming (cutting tree limbs away from wires) and re-engineering the system and animal protection (providing guards to make it difficult for squirrels and other animals to get on the wires). The company desired to evaluate the cost effectiveness of the different efforts and to determine where future efforts should be made. An extensive exploratory data mining project was undertaken. The company developed a comprehensive predictive model designed to predict outages for a given geographical region on a given day. The number of customers affected in a geographic region on a given day was dependent on weather (rain, snow, wind, lighting, temperature, relative humidity, barometric pressure), the customer density, the type of customer (industrial, commercial, residential) and forestation (the amount and type of trees in the area). The modeling effort was designed to take into account that some geographic areas are more prone to outages than others, and all are ultimately dependent on the weather. For example, a utility may have a relatively high number of outages in the summer of 1998, then perform all reasonable corrective actions before the summer of 1999, and still have a greater number of outages. If the number of electrical storms (by far the greatest cause of outages) in 1999 was significantly greater than in 1998, then the number of outages will be greater. This is true even if the corrective actions (maintenance, etc.) were effective. The outages may be lower than they would have otherwise (without corrective action) but still higher than they were in 1998. Therefore, a simple query of outages in 1999 compared to 1998 would not show that the actions were effective. The predictive model was created to handle this problem. The model could predict the outages given the mild weather conditions and the extreme weather conditions. By controlling for the different weather conditions, the effect of the system improvements could then be determined.

The company's large data set of outages was in good shape. The customer data was accurately recorded. All the major data needs from the company were available and the data quality was excellent. External secondary data collected by U.S. government agencies was used. The weather data was available from the National Oceanic & Atmospheric Administration (NOAA). Forestation data from the United States Geological Survey was far better than expected.

However, there was a problem. The information detailing which outage reduction actions were installed and where they were installed was missing. Decisions concerning which areas received tree trimming, which areas received reengineering and which received animal protection were made on the division level. The record keeping was not complete. Some divisional managers kept paper records, some kept electronic records on spreadsheets and several managers had retired with a company-wide early retirement program. It was never determined how the records from many of the retired managers were kept and what happened to them. As a result, the study was limited to a small geographic section of the company — the division in which the records were stored on a spreadsheet. Because of the lack of secondary data, which would have been approximately 300 to 500 observations, the usefulness of the study to judge the cost effectiveness of the different measures was significantly less than expected.

A consumer electric products manufacturer had a similar situation. After years of producing high quality products, the company was experiencing a high number of returns for repair. The product in question had a five-year warranty, and products were coming back for repairs long after manufacturing. Not only were the repairs an inconvenience for the customers, the cost of the repairs were affecting the company's profits. In order to solve this problem, the company examined the data collected during manufacturing for any indication of the future problems. This data mining process considered all of the components of the operational schematic presented in Figure 2. The company had collected information from the customers on product use. The company also had information about product testing during manufacture, including test per unit and periodic detailed testing of production "batches." There was also information related to the process — how the product is assembled, etc. An analysis was initiated covering most of the operational schematic. Because the product was under a five-year warranty, the manufacturing data needed for this analysis covered history from five and one-half years back to the last six months.

Initial results were not very good. There was little predictability of future problems. However, some patterns began to emerge. Continued exploratory evaluations revealed that what predictability there was of future problems was based on the specific subcomponents used in the product. These subcomponents were produced by outside vendors. It became clear that many of the repairs were caused by problems in the subcomponents, and that no meaningful evaluations could be done to predict future problems without understanding what might be happening to the subcomponents.

Further interviews with the company revealed that these subcomponents were not tested in the manufacturing line. They were tested independently by the organization in charge of purchasing the subcomponents. The results of this testing were kept by one of the engineers. This very encouraging news quickly turned into disappointment when the engineer keeping the data revealed that the data was only recorded on his hard drive of his personal computer, and he had recently erased it. After all he had collected and stored the information for five years, and no one had asked about it.

This project wasn't a complete failure. Internally there had been great debate about whether or not the company had been collecting sufficient data to predict future problems and take corrective action. It was now clear they had not.

IMPROVING SECONDARY OR SUPPORTING DATA

Not having the necessary secondary or supporting data can be an impediment that can stop a data mining activity very quickly. The corrective actions for this problem are twofold. Simple in concept, these corrective actions require diligence to implement.

Recognition

The first corrective action is recognizing that the secondary data is important to the process. In the development of data warehouses the concentration cannot be limited to just voluminous data. The organization must remember the issue of smaller databases. This will greatly increase the likelihood that the data will be available when needed.

Anticipation

The second corrective action is a widespread use of personal databases throughout the organizations. Most office software suites come available with a database programs. Making these products available throughout the organization and providing training and support for these products can provide unexpected dividends.

Obviously providing backups of these personal databases would be additional insurance. As recommended above in the discussion of data quality, undertaking preliminary analyses can insure that the proper data is being collected and if not, then corrective action can be implemented.

IMPEDIMENT 3:
ANALYTICAL MANPOWER

Stories are common of data warehousing projects that have exceeded time and budget expectations. Significant executive support and guidance are usually needed to complete these projects. Staffing of Information Technology (IT) organizations is increased for the development or outside consultants are used. These projects stretch the resources of the organizations involved both in terms of financial resources and the internal political capital needed to keep the project alive through setbacks and inevitable delays. Frequently, these same projects do not follow with additional emphasis on using the data. The last thing the organization wants to hear at the end of such a project is, "It is now time to add additional resources and staff to analyze this data."

A recent search of Monster.com shows anecdotal evidence of this difference in emphasis. A search on the term "data warehouse" returns 1,002 possible job opportunities in the United States, while a search on the term "data mining" produces 258 possible jobs.

Frequently, the thought is that the analytical staff in place is going to be able to use the information. If it is marketing data that is being collected, then the present marketing staff will analyze this information. If it is manufacturing data, then the production engineers are going to use it. This plan is faulty: more data requires more time to analyze. Furthermore, exploratory data mining is an extremely complicated task, requiring several specific skills including programming, statistics and predictive modeling, such as neural networks; database processing (queries, structure, etc.) and presentation skills including graphical display of information and written presentation. In addition to the above skill set, a successful exploratory data miner must have a good understanding of the business problem or the organization's mission, must know how to apply the information from the data to the problem and must understand the meaning of the information. The key to understanding the manpower impediment is to understand the following axiom.

Chances are that if a person exists presently in an organization who has the broad range of technical capabilities to perform exploratory data mining and that person has the experience and knowledge in the organization to apply the information to be gathered from the data, then that person is likely overworked now. He is already overtaxed, and having new data does not mean he will have time to fully utilize it.

In many organizations a lack of manpower is the primary impediment to meaningful investigative analyses. It is estimated that data collection and storage is increasing at a rate of 130 percent annually. Yet only two percent of this data is ever analyzed (Nachtwey, 2000).

REMOVING THE
MANPOWER IMPEDIMENT

The key to removing this impediment is to recognize the need for manpower and to plan ahead. The organization should plan for the analysis and recognize that additional data means additional effort.

Estimating required manpower and the cost effectiveness of additional manpower is case specific. There is no general rule of thumb that can be applied to each situation. A careful review of the steps and processes needed for data mining can be reviewed and will provide a foundation for manpower estimates. The review should follow along the lines of the following major categories of effort:

- Data maintenance,
- General queries,
- Data preprocessing,
- Data analysis,
- Developing conclusions, and
- Presenting results.

As the organization contemplates the impending effort, it should first think of foundation systems. Foundation systems are the basic software systems and customized code needed to provide the tools to answer most requests. The work on these foundation systems has to be completed before the data can be analyzed in a timely manner. Through the addition of staff (or undertaking staff augmentation through consulting services) these foundation systems are required.

As the organization considers its review, they should consider each of the major categories of effort in terms of both foundation systems and on-going efforts. Foundation systems should be considered the minimum requirements to access and analyze data.

Data Maintenance

Even in the best data warehouses, there will be data maintenance activities that are required before data analysis activities. Three examples of data maintenance activities: reviewing the quality of data entry, handling changes in the data over time and adding or dealing with missing data.

As discussed above in the data quality section, periodic reviews of data are required. This will include reviews of human data entries and automated systems, such as: "Did the staff in the field get the appropriate directions?" and "are they entering data correctly?" Automatic metering devices need calibration and review. And, lastly, online data collection must insure that the correct data forms are mapped to the correct data fields in the company's databases. As a system operates over time, minor changes to the online programming can create problems where they did not exist before. All of these are issues needing periodic review.

Many interesting data mining projects analyze patterns over time. Changing consumer purchasing habits are a common example. Studying these changing habits requires data collected over multiple years. Typically, this data cannot be analyzed without some intervention to correct for changing definitions or classifications. An example can be found in the United States Census data. For the year 2000 census, respondents were allowed for the first time to check more than one ethnicity (U.S. Census Bureau, 2000). Most consumer surveys are designed to be consistent with the census ethnicity question in order to compare populations of customers to the general population. Therefore, this change requires a rethinking of how future data will be collected and how past data was collected and stored.

Lastly, in every data analysis effort, there is a problem of missing data. There is always some effort needed to handle missing data for the analysis. It is generally considered a good practice to store missing data as missing data in the data warehouse. This practice is preferred to as storing data with some estimate of the missing value because changing conditions may invalidate an estimate.

As a general rule, when performing data mining, each variable in the analysis has to be evaluated to determine how to handle missing data. In some instances, the observation should be dropped, others a replacement value estimated and, in others, particularly nominal variables (such as ethnicity, gender, region), a new category "missing" can be added. Often, meaningful results are obtained through replacing the missing value with an estimate of the missing value generated from other variables.

Regardless of the method of handling missing data in analysis, standard acceptable methods will need to be developed that will be used by the organization. These methods must be in place before analysis.

General Queries

Much of the work with the new data will be answering simple general queries like "What percentage of our customers are women under 30 years of age?" Simple descriptive statistics can answer many questions. While the experienced data miner does not generally find it difficult to get such answers, these issues can be problematic if the appropriate software and connections are not made with the database. The foundation systems will need hardware and software for automating (as much as possible) the most common tasks. If the foundation systems are not in place, the available manpower will find much of their precious time is spent handling these simple requests.

Data Preprocessing

Although this topic is less exciting than other aspects of data mining (such as predictive modeling techniques), data preprocessing is where the data mining manpower will be spending much of their time. It is not unusual to spend upwards to 90 percent of the analysis time on this. Few organizations starting a data mining effort recognize this need and plan for the time requirements necessary.

Data preprocessing consists of any of a number of tasks that are required before a successful analysis may be performed. These tasks convert data from storage format to analysis format and include any of the data maintenance tasks mentioned above, in addition to case-specific modifications of the data to make the data more meaningful.

Data storage considerations are not consistent with analytical considerations, nor should they be. Data storage systems of any significant size are more concerned with efficiency of storage space, of updating records and of retrieval. This has significant implications for analysis.

Consider the example of an international airline. At any given time, only one record of hundreds of thousands of records recording the flight of a customer may be required for retrieval. Accessing this information quickly one record at a time from hundreds of thousands of records can make the difference between a high level of customer satisfaction or the airline going out of business. Therefore, rapid access is the primary concern when storing this information. However, this storage priority doesn't help analysis. For example, the airline stores each customer's flight reservation as an individual record. Although this is the appropriate way to store this information for retrieval and updating, data analysis will require developing observations and organizing the observations in a different way. Suppose the analyst has been asked to answer the following question:

Most frequent air travelers fly less in the summer than other periods of the year. What distinguishes those frequent travelers that do not reduce their travel throughout the summer?

The answer to this question will require creating a record of the total number of flights taken by the customer and of the revenue produced. This record would be created by combining all the customer's records into one record.

Mathematical Transformations

In addition to record transformations, the data may require mathematical transformations. Various modifications to the data will allow the exploratory tools to find more information in the data. An experienced analyst will spend a great deal of time working with the data and will look at various methods of presenting the information to the exploratory analysis tool.

Data Analysis

The data analysis, the analytical processes applied to reveal the exploratory findings, can encompass a number of techniques and capabilities. As the amount of data that is being collected grows and the questions that are being considered increase in complexity, the complexity of the analytical techniques should also increase. The responsibilities of the analytical staff also increase both in terms of time and abilities.

In general, it should be expected that new exploratory findings would be related to looking at the data in new or multiple dimensions. That is, considering more factors simultaneously, revealing a deeper look at the organization's problems. However, these efforts come at a cost.

Recall the example from the beginning of the chapter in which a sample look at the data reveals that customers who buy a company's products have higher household incomes than the competitor's customers. However, deeper thinking about the problem leads to questions concerning whether or not the issue is their marital status or age. The true understanding of the customers is only revealed through a multidimensional analysis taking into account all factors simultaneously. It takes more effort and time than a simple query to find the determining characteristic.

Presenting Results

The multidimensioned exploratory findings are not easy to sell across an organization. Generally, we are used to thinking of problems and reviewing graphs in two dimensions. Rarely do we review a three-dimensional chart and, even more rarely, information in a higher dimension. Therefore, higher dimensioned results must be processed and prepared in order to be presented to an outside audience. Again the deeper meaning comes at a cost of manpower resources.

Summary

Organizations hope to find new insights into their efforts through exploratory data mining. The insights may be in the data, but they are not going to be revealed unless significant manpower is applied to the issue. The justification of the manpower is difficult, because a direct cost benefit analysis cannot usually be applied. The above discussion presents some of the issues faced and provides an outline to estimate and justify the manpower requirements.

IMPEDIMENT 4: LACK OF OPENNESS TO NEW RESULTS

The last impediment to the organization fully utilizing the value of exploratory data mining is referred to as a "lack of openness." The opposite of this lack is a "sense of openness." At the heart of this sense of openness is the recognition that the value of exploratory data mining is the ability to discover what the organization presently doesn't know and, the more difficult task, to correct incorrect beliefs. The exploratory data miner's greatest success is a change in organizational thinking. But change is difficult.

Dr. Jonah Folkman of Children's Hospital of Boston is a leading cancer researcher. His ideas include developing treatments to effectively starve cancer growths by limiting their blood supply. His theory, which he called angiogenesis, was based on the fact that tumors secrete a factor that stimulates new blood vessels to form, supporting the tumor with a private blood supply. Starving the tumors instead of trying to kill the cancer has the potential to change, not only how we treat cancer, but also how we view cancer. In the beginning, his work was not well accepted, but Dr. Folkman persevered. He explained his doggedness this way, "We've always said there is a fine line between persistence and obstinacy in research and you never know when you have crossed that line" (All Things Considered, 2001). But his persistence in taking a risk and working in a direction at odds with the mainstream establishment has revolutionary potential. Exploratory findings that may have a significant impact on an organization must have an environment in which they can develop. An organization with a sense of openness allows an exploratory data miner the ability to be persistent.

Three requirements are needed to create the sense of openness. They are executive sponsorship, a reduction in the emphasis on statistical accuracy and for the data miner to present exploratory findings with good documentation and support.

Executive Sponsorship

Dr. Robert Kriegel (Kriegel & Brandt, 1996), a leading writer and lecturer on organizational change, believes resistance to change is personal. In his book "Sacred Cows Make the Best Burgers," he lists four personal resistance drivers:

- Fear — "What if... I lose my job, look stupid, can't adapt," etc.
- Feeling Powerless — "No one asked me!"
- Inertia — "It's too much effort, too uncomfortable."
- Absence of Self-Interest — "What's in it for me?" (Kriegel & Brandt, 1996, p. 195)

Dealing with these personal resistance drivers is an organizational issue, but they do impact the completion of data mining projects. A manager's fear that his understanding of the marketplace, developed over 30 years, no longer applies is powerful. In addition to the fears identified by Kriegel, we can add the fear of "What if I am wrong?" Feeling powerless, left out, when new techniques are used that you do not understand is an equally strong deterrent to change. The same can be said for inertia. When a product is at the top of a cycle of market share, who wants to say, "Now is the time to make changes?" Even though, we all know that products have life cycles and sales go up and sales go down. And we have all seen great products, once unstoppable, reduced in significance. It makes an organization very uncomfortable to discuss a potential change from this lofty position. The desire to believe that the present situation will continue provides inertia that is hard to overcome. For new exploratory findings to have a significant impact, these personal and organizational issues must be understood and addressed.

Although executive sponsorship is cited as the requirement for most organizational accomplishments, ranging from human resource programs to recycling programs, rarely are we told exactly how to apply it. However, the requirement here is clear. An acknowledgment is required that an effort is underway to investigate information to reveal what is not presently known or what is incorrect. Presently held beliefs can be questioned. Furthermore, it is still acceptable to continue the research, when it is revealed the initial questioning was incorrect.

The importance of this executive sponsorship of new thinking becomes apparent when it is recognized that the nature of exploratory findings are additive. Usually there is not an "eureka" moment; new exploratory findings are the result of cumulative efforts. A requirement of a "sense of openness" is the freedom to speculate. The first findings from exploratory analyses must be able to be presented as initial speculations to be discussed and considered before further research — even if the researchers are not sure of the speculations and cannot presently "prove" their points. The freedom to speculate recognizes that some of the speculations (initial findings) will later be proven wrong, but can be presented and discussed without the loss of support of the total project.

As discussed in the previous section, a data miner must have a large set of skills and extensive knowledge of techniques and of the organization's operating conditions in order to accomplish its goals. Adding the complexities of organizational management and change management to that list overloads the researchers. That is the job of the organization's executives.

Heresy: Ignore Statistical Accuracy

This section is intentionally mislabeled to make a point — to state clearly what we are not saying before the point can be misrepresented. The recommendation is not to ignore statistical accuracy, rather it is to temporarily drop or reduce the requirements of statistical accuracy.

In most projects, we analyze a sample of a larger population. Analysts work from a representative sample of the population, drawn randomly. Therefore, there can be variation in the results — leading to the need to understand the variation and determine if the sample is accurate.

Our society has become accustomed to statistical accuracy. For example, consider the following quote:

> "His job approval rating is 60 percent, which is similar to that of his father, George Bush, and Bill Clinton in the opening months of their presidencies. ... The nationwide telephone poll of 1,105 adults was conducted March 8-12 and has a margin of sampling error of plus or minus three percentage points" (Berke & Elder, 2001).

The general populace is accustomed to seeing this type of result. They have the basic understanding that if the margin of error was plus or minus six percentage points, the poll is less accurate. The general populace understands this even if they don't have an understanding of how these calculations are made. What the quote is saying is (in practical terms), we couldn't ask all of the population because it is impractical, but, if we did, our sample is telling us it would be within plus or minus three percentage points of 60 percent. The sample is used to estimate the total population. Statistical accuracy is almost always the appropriate consideration when producing final results. But statistical accuracy becomes a detriment when it stands in the way of an otherwise useful preliminary analysis.

The exploratory data miner's job is to find new relationships; relationships we don't know exist. Often these relationships are found outside the main view of the organization. For example a company may make a product that has been traditionally sold to middle-aged single family home buyers. Therefore, the company has traditionally focused their market research on those markets. From census data, the company recognizes their markets by zip code. The census data can reveal less dense suburban (single family housing) areas.

A clever researcher may decide to analyze the zip codes of the newest customers looking at the population density of the zip code region based on census data. The researcher notices a greater percentage of the new customers living in the more dense population areas (multifamily housing as opposed to single family housing). With a redevelopment of many urban centers, a new market is emerging. More upscale in-town housing is changing the market. These customers represent a growing customer base.

The researcher reviews the existing market research data, looking for customers living in the densely populated urban areas. Because previous research did not focus on these areas, but on single-family suburban areas, the researcher finds a very limited number of observations. He knows the subsample is not statistically valid — in fact, he knows he does not have enough observations to make any definitive statements. The researcher now has a dilemma: Withhold this potential change in new customers, because he cannot "prove" it, or report the new discovery and begin speculations about the new customers based on the research of the small subsample. In the organization with a sense of openness, the speculation will open new discussions about the marketplace. The discussion will suggest new areas of research to be explored to answer the questions the speculation raises. Even if some of the statistically questionable initial ideas later prove wrong, the organization will benefit from the focus on the new market. In the organization with the sense of openness, the researcher is confident that his speculations will be used appropriately. They will not be confused with research findings, but the speculations will instead be the foundation of potential new knowledge. In an organization with a sense of openness, the result of an analytical project may be a series of speculations and questions, not proven relationships — through statistics. One of the foundations of a sense of openness is that new ideas may be floated, may be speculated on, without the fear that these new ideas will be abused. These speculations form a foundation for later research. In this case, research focusing on the dense urban market.

Presenting Exploratory Findings

For speculations to be treated as speculations, then it must be clear what an exploratory result, or finding, must be. These final results of the exploratory analyses should be properly documented and circulated throughout the organization.

The goal of exploratory data mining is finding relationships and trends that are not readily apparent. In order to show these difficult findings, the researcher must clearly and completely articulate what has been discovered and offer supporting documentation for the discovery. It should be stated clearly to what the results apply. In order to differentiate these findings from speculations, a format for presenting results, such as the following, should be used.

Finding: Women under 25 who buy product X are three times more likely to report that they are interested in using the product for "fun," than women under 25 who buy products Y and Z.

Support:
1.   Customer surveys from 1998-2001 used for the analysis. Of the women under 25 that responded, there were 98 responses from purchasers of product X and 154 responses from purchasers of products Y and Z. Of the product X responses, 54 percent listed "fun" as a reason for purchase; of the product Y and Z responses, 17 percent mentioned "fun."
2.   Women of all other age groups did not show the same emphasis on "fun." Of those responses, 16 percent listed "fun," if they purchased product X, and 18 percent listed "fun," if they bought products Y and Z.

The finding states clearly what the exploratory finding is about — the reason for buying the product. The statement also makes very clear the dimensionality of the problem and what region of the data the finding related to: gender is a dimension, age is a dimension and product preference is a dimension. The supporting statement gives the statistics behind the statement and even alludes to another dimension, the time period.

The format that the organization uses can vary, but the components above should be used. The finding states clearly what population is being discussed. Depending on the audience, it is not necessary to give specific statistical information in the finding. However, the supporting information should give the details. Notice the supporting information also clarifies why this finding is important. In this case, it is because this population is different from other women.

The same approach is required for graphical presentation of data. Standards should be developed and used to make very clear what is being presented and what region of the data is being presented. To present the data using two- or three-dimension representations, then other dimensions are being held constant. For example, if graphing the above data, only women are presented, thereby, reducing the gender dimension.

For exploratory data mining, it is paramount that the organization is comfortable with presenting multidimensioned information. Edward Tufte, Yale professor and leading lecturer and author on clearly presenting graphical data, reminds us that"…all the interesting worlds (physical, biological, imaginary, human) that we seek to understand are inevitably and happily multivariate in nature" (Tufte, 1990, p. 13).

MOVING FORWARD

Writing in The Atlantic, author Jonathan Rauch (2001) presents the concept of the "New Old Economy" to explain the recent impact of IT on the economy. The New Old Economy refers to the impact of IT on old-line businesses that have existed for decades, using basically the same processes but with greater efficiency thanks to improvements from IT capabilities.

The United States economy grew at an unprecedented rate in the 1990s. The economy produced a higher rate of growth of real output per worker in that decade than in the previous decade. Throughout the late 80s and into the 90s, organizations operating in the "old economy" were investing in personal computers and the basic software (spreadsheets and word processing packages) to perform the old-economy tasks. At first, the uses of those innovations were a convenience at best and a difficult-to-use nuisance at worse. Gradually as the organizations learned to apply spreadsheets and word processing (the new technology of the time), software and hardware technology showed gains in efficiency. Now those techniques are considered basic to these Old Economy businesses, hence, the term New Old Economy. Eventually, the convenience of the then new, now commonplace, tools (spreadsheets and word processing) made them more viable than the old mainframe systems that cost hundreds of thousands of dollars. They are now so seamlessly integrated into the company's old-economy businesses that they receive little attention as opposed to the attention given the Internet and e-commerce activities. As Rauch (2001) states, the impact of these basic technologies is unquantified and perhaps unquantifiable. However, it is certain that we can see it in today's workplace.

The parallel to the growth of the use of PCs in the 80s and 90s is today's use of data mining software and databases. As in the past, there is an organizational learning curve (as well as individual learning curve) in applying the new technology. The organization must understand new large databases and learn how to apply what is available. That process will occur in countless gradual steps and some great leaps in data, software and techniques. A necessary first step is to remove present organizational impediments to the use of exploratory data mining so that these techniques become basic to the process. As Lyndon Johnson once advised the country, "We must change to master change" (Johnson, 1966).

REFERENCES

All things considered. (2001, May 2) [Radio broadcast]. Linda Wertheimer, Reporter, Washington, D.C., National Public Radio.

Berke R. L., & Elder, J. (2001, March 14). 60% in poll favor bush, but economy is a major concern. *The New York Times,* p. A1.

Johnson, L. B. (1966). State of the Union message. Retrieved on March 31, 2003 from http://www.janda.org/politxts/State%20of%20Union%20Addresses/1964-1969%20Johnson/LBJ.66.html.

Kriegel, R., & Brandt, D. (1996). *Sacred cows make the best burgers.* New York, NY: Warner Books.

Nachtwey, D. (2000, March 20). Accuracy wins. *Intelligent Enterprise, 3*(5), 45-49.

Rauch J. (2001, January). The New Old Economy: Oil, computers, and the reinvention of the Earth. *The Atlantic Monthly, 287*(1), 35-50.

Tufte, E. R. (1990). *Envisioning Information.* Cheshire, CT: Graphics Press.

U.S. Census Bureau. (2000). *Racial and ethnic classifications used in census 2000 and beyond.* Retrieved on July 30, 2002 from http://www.census.gov/population/www/socdemo/race/racefactcb.html.

Chapter XX

Towards Constructionist Organizational Data Mining (ODM): Changing the Focus from Technology to Social Construction of Knowledge

Isabel Ramos
Universidade do Minho, Portugal

João Álvaro Carvalho
Universidade do Minho, Portugal

ABSTRACT

This chapter addresses the definition of organizational data mining (ODM) practices that leverage knowledge creation in organizations. It argues that knowledge resides in human minds and it is created by the continuous action and interaction happening in specific social contexts. Knowledge has a rational and an emotional foundation. When represented, knowledge becomes information that shapes the action and interaction by which individuals and communities create their specific knowledge. The purpose of this chapter is to highlight the advantages of adopting a constructionist approach and to present some constructionist guidelines to assist the definition of ODM practices that leverage knowledge creation in organizations.

INTRODUCTION

The creation of scientific and organizational knowledge is guided by the assumptions its creator holds about the nature of the studied reality, the validity of knowledge and the methods and techniques to be used to assist the process.

Traditionally, it has been assumed that an organization and the business in which it is engaged have an objective existence that can be known from an independent and neutral viewpoint. Knowledge is created to assist the decision-making, the definition of strategies and the organizational change. Nevertheless, organizations can also be understood as socially constructed realities. They are, then, seen as subjective in nature, since they do not exist apart from their members and other stakeholders.

Attached to these ontological perspectives on organizations are specific epistemological and methodological assumptions that provide different ways of creating knowledge about organizational phenomena. The next section explores two perspectives on knowledge creation, presenting the advantages and drawbacks of adopting either one of them.

Whatever the paradigm used to guide the creation of knowledge, the process unfolds at two levels: individual and social. At the individual level, the intending knower, through processes such as cognition, action, interaction and emotion, actively creates knowledge. At the social level, people develop shared knowledge, when they are actively involved in the construction of something external and sharable. This chapter details these two levels of knowledge creation.

In the last two sections of the chapter, the constructionist perspective on knowledge creation is used to highlight some problems associated with the current practices in ODM, and some constructionist guidelines to assist the definition of ODM practices that leverage knowledge creation in organizations are presented.

The chapter is structured with the aim of challenging the much advanced idea that knowledge can be elicited from organizational actors and stored in repositories, assuming an independent existence from those who create it. This idea, true or false, is assumed by most existing frameworks for software and requirements engineering (Finkelstein, 2000).

In this chapter, we argue that knowledge resides in human minds, and it is created by the continuous action and interaction happening in specific social contexts. Knowledge has a rational and an emotional foundation. It has an inherently tacit nature and is made explicit in language, through the myriad of linguistic artifacts at the disposal of organizational actors. When represented, knowledge becomes information that shapes the action and interaction by which individuals and communities create their specific knowledge. We also argue that ODM can be designed to assist the social construction of knowledge.

THE PROCESS OF KNOWLEDGE CREATION

Scientific or organizational knowledge creation has been addressed from different perspectives along the history of science and, in particular, of social sciences. The process is guided by the set of values, beliefs and norms shared by the members of the community to which the creator of this knowledge belongs, that is, it is guided by the adopted paradigm (Lincoln & Guba, 2000). The adopted paradigm determines how the nature of the studied reality is understood, the criteria that will be used to assess the validity of the created knowledge and the construction and selection of methods and techniques to structure and support the creation of knowledge. This set of ontological, epistemological and methodological assumptions that characterize the paradigm one implicitly or explicitly uses to make sense of the surrounding reality is the cultural root of the intellectual enterprises. Those assumptions constrain the accomplishment of activities, such as construction of theories, definition of inquiry strategies, interpretation of perceived phenomena and dissemination of knowledge (Schwandt, 2000).

The Objective Reality

Traditionally, social realities have been assumed to have an objective nature. Assuming this viewpoint, the knowledge we possess about things, processes or events that occur regularly under definite circumstances should be an adequate representation of them. Knowledge is the result of a meticulous, quantitative and objective study of the phenomenon of interest. Its aim is to understand the phenomenon in order to be able to anticipate its occurrence and to control it.

In this sense, knowledge is discovered and developed by successive testing of new hypotheses. Truth is a matter of verifying or refuting the hypotheses, adequately applying the right method to guide the study of things, processes or events. Thus, developed knowledge is independent of the knower. When developed explanations are empirically tested, and, if they prove effective in predicting the occurrence of phenomena in other settings, they can be generalized to all situations in which the phenomenon occurs under similar circumstances.

The above paragraphs summarize the core assumptions guiding the discovery of scientific knowledge in the last four centuries of human history and Western culture. The creation and management of organizational and business knowledge is also strongly influenced by this paradigm.

The expressions "knowledge discovery" and "knowledge capture" are often used in the literature addressing the issues relevant to organizational knowledge management. These expressions are rooted in the assumption that an organization and the business in which it is engaged have an objective existence that can be known from an independent and neutral standing point. In order to understand organizations and businesses, the intending knower creates models of processes, resources, events and their interconnections. These models are empirically tested, and, then, they are used to support the decision-making, the definition of strategies and the organizational change. Facts, models, best practices and the results of decisions, strategies and social change can be stored for future use, informing new decisions, plans and changes (Sekaran, 1992; Palmer & Hardy, 2000).

All this means that knowledge is viewed as independent of the knower and of the organizational or business reality that it represents. It is understood as an invaluable organizational resource that can be extracted from the knower and made available to others. It provides strategic advantage, when it is delivered in time to people that need it. Another aspect that emerges from this perspective is that knowledge is understood as fairly stable and consensual, so it can be stored to be used later on by different organizational actors in different situations.

Based on these assumptions, information technologies have been used to develop knowledge management tools that should support effective creation, capture, storage and delivery of knowledge (Nemati, Steiger, Iyer & Herschel, 2002).

Limitations of Objectivism

This objectivist view of knowledge and its creation has some limitations:

a) It assumes that when presented with facts, organizational actors will reach consensual interpretations and views. However, it may very well be that "…we can only see what fits into our mental space, and all description includes interpretations as well as sensory reporting" (Gould, 1998, p. 72). This accounts well for the difficulty in reaching consensus in organizations, even when confronted with the same information about events or processes (Sparrow, 1998). Our mental spaces are constructed and reconstructed along stages of socialization that occur in childhood, in learning role-specific knowledge and the professional language associated with it and in interactions with others. Our mental constructs define what we see as reality. Because individuals have different life experiences, it is not surprising that different organizational actors see different realities. When a common view of the reality is developed, this may not be related with some intrinsic meaning of the available information, but because individuals who interact for some time and extensively in similar social contexts, as is the case of people working in the same organization, develop similar mental constructs and end up seeing similar things. However, this is not true for situations such as when new organizational members interpret the stored information, when people subjected to recent or restricted learning interpret the information or when the stored information is interpreted in the ever-changing contexts of some organizations.

b) It assumes that knowledge has a stable nature. However, stable knowledge creates stable ways of understanding realities, and stable, unchanging understanding could be highly problematic for organizations operating in turbulent environments. In order to implement concepts, such as flexibility, creativity and continuous learning, organizational actors must value the challenge of established knowledge and foster pluralism of perspectives in assessing complex realities and problems.

c) It assumes that organizational actors understand the value of sharing knowledge and are motivated to contribute with their own knowledge. However, knowledge is power in organizations. Individuals compete for access to resources, promotion, wages, etc. Knowledge helps to make informed decisions, to be more effective and to be creative. These are aspects for which organizational actors get rewarded. In order to promote knowledge sharing, a balance between competition and collaboration must be cultivated for each organization and trust must be built upon ethical concerns about human action and interaction (Parker & Wall, 1998).

d) It assumes that a complete account of specialized knowledge is possible. However, even if we feel motivated to externalize our specialized knowledge, a complete account of it is impossible. All knowledge we possess about a concept, thing, process, event or behavior is inherently tacit. It can be expressed in order to become explicit. However, no matter how much we try and how good are the tools we use to externalize our knowledge, there is always a part that we cannot express. Tacit knowledge includes the knowledge that is related with personal emotions involved in knowing, the practice we gained manipulating and experimenting with the object of interest but we are not able to verbalize and the unconscious processes involved in knowing.

e)   It assumes that the knowledge of managers and for management is the most important, when approaching knowledge management in organizations. This approach is founded on bureaucratic (Weber, 1947) and Tayloristic (Taylor, 1911) views of organizations, which propose a clear distinction between management and operation. Managers are seen as the elite that hold the responsibility of guiding the organization through the path that leads to its success. The employees have the obligation to comply with work rules and procedures. However, this perspective does not fit the internal and external complexity and uncertainty faced by current organizations. Moreover, information technologies enable decisions to be made closer to operations, thus empowering employees, flattening the organizational structure and rendering the resolution of problems and the reformulation of work practices more effective.

The Socially Constructed Reality

Organizations can instead be understood as socially constructed realities. As such, they are subjective in nature, since they do not exist apart from the organizational actors and other stakeholders. The stable patterns of action and interaction occurring internally and with the exterior of the organization are responsible for the impression of an objective existence.

The paradigm behind this view of the organization is called constructivism (Piaget, 1954) and, in a later development, called constructionism (Papert, 1990). Constructivism refers to the theory that defines human beings as active constructors of their own learning and development. Constructionism refers to the theory that adds to constructivism the idea that learning and development of human knowledge happen more effectively when individuals are involved in the construction of something external, something that can be shared or both. In the rest of this chapter, we refer to the constructionist paradigm, since it integrates the theory we find useful in supporting the ideas presented here.

Viewing reality as socially constructed implies several epistemological and methodological assumptions, including (Schwandt, 2000; Arbnor & Bjerke, 1997):

1.   Reality is constructed through purposeful human action and interaction.
2.   The aim of knowledge creation is to understand the individual and shared meanings that define the purpose of human action.
3.   Knowledge creation is informed by a variety of social, intellectual and theoretical explorations. Tools and techniques used to support this activity should foster such explorations.
4.   Valid knowledge arises from the interactions between the members of some stakeholder community. Agreements on validity may be the subject of community negotiations regarding what will be accepted as truth.
5.   To make our experience of the world meaningful, we invent concepts, models and schemes, and we continually test and modify these constructions in the light of new experience. This construction is historically and socio-culturally informed.
6.   Our interpretations of phenomena are constructed upon shared understandings, practices and language.

7. The meaning of knowledge representations is intimately connected with the authors' and the readers' historical and social contexts.
8. Representations are useful if they emerge out of the process of questioning the status quo, in order to create a genuinely new way of thinking and acting.

The social construction of reality emerges from four main social processes: subjectification, externalization, objectification and internalization (Arbnor & Bjerke, 1997).

Subjectification is the process by which an individual creates her own experiences. How an individual interprets what is happening is related to the reality she perceives. This reality is shaped by her subjective conceptual structures of meaning.

Externalization is the process by which people communicate their subjectifications to others, through a common language. By making something externally available, we enable others to react to our previously subjective experiences and thoughts. By means of this communication, humans may transform the original content of a thought and formulate another that is new, refined, changed or developed. The mutual relation with others is dialectical and leads to continuous reinterpretation and change of meanings. Surrounding reality is created by externalization.

Objectification is the process by which an externalized human act might attain the characteristic of objectivity. Objectification happens after several reflections, reinterpretations and changes in the original subjective thoughts, when the environment has generally started to accept the externalization as meaningful. This process can be divided into two phases: institutionalization and legitimization.

Internalization is the process by which humans become members of the society. It is a dialectic process that enables humans to take over the world in which others already live. Internalization is achieved through socialization occurring during childhood, and in learning role-specific knowledge and the professional language associated with it.

This way of understanding and assisting human action in organizations holds some important advantages. By viewing organizations as social constructions, their members and external entities interested in them can assume the responsibility for their own decisions, for the visions they create for the organization and for the work performed there. The defined goals, objectives, strategies and plans emerge, then, as mechanisms to structure human action for as long as internal and external circumstances keep stable. The organization assumes a contextual objective nature, i.e., concerns about its identity are matched with constant assessment of historical and socio-cultural circumstances that justify keeping that identity or demand its reconstruction.

The clear division between managerial activities and operational activities loses its meaning. The organization is all its members. There is no privileged knowledge, since organizational knowledge is constructed upon the shared experiences of its members, plus all tacit knowledge held by all of them. Managerial and operational activities are interconnected. Thinking and doing are emerging at all levels of the organization as a result of human action and interaction.

Thus, the organization appears as a flexible, albeit complex, social construct where learning occurs spontaneously from the social processes of transformation happening continuously. It does not mean that the learning processes should not be intentionally designed in order to increase their effectiveness. This can be done by understanding how knowledge is socially constructed, fostering the challenge of the status quo and taking care that the means exist to create genuinely new ways of thinking and acting.

Limitations of Constructionism

Nevertheless, the constructionist perspective contains some risks associated with extreme interpretations of some of its assumptions. It may sound like organizational actors have free choice relating to the future of the organization and the design of work environments. In fact, they are inserted in contexts that are made stable by the action of wider communities of practice. This action is founded in common values and beliefs, historically and socio-culturally rooted. These values and beliefs are responsible for patterns of action that constrain the choices of organizational actors.

Another aspect that should be considered is the consequences of extreme pluralism. Although pluralism of perspectives and practices is important to keep the organization flexible and able to learn from experience, it must be balanced with the need for cohesion, shared goals and common interests (Wallace, 2000). For this reason, processes of negotiation, power, sense making and socialization interact to keep individual and group freedom inside of certain boundaries (Buchanan & Badham, 1999).

Since the constructionist perspective endorses that all social constructions are based on specific historical or socio-cultural circumstances, it may seem that these constructions can not be judged or arbitrary criteria can be used as long as the community making the assessment believed the criteria of judgement fair. By understanding our reality as objective and stable, we may lose the capacity to critically analyze the values, beliefs and emotions upon which the reality is based. The community whose interaction gives rise to a social construction, such as an organization, must continuously question and negotiate the ethical and moral foundations for the criteria that are used to judge the validity of its practices.

THE RATIONAL AND EMOTIONAL NATURE OF PERSONAL KNOWLEDGE

Knowledge is not simply transmitted from a knower to a learner. It is actively constructed by the mind of the learner (Kafai & Resnick, 1996).

We make ideas instead of simply getting them from an external source. Idea making happens more effectively when the learner is engaged in designing and constructing an external artifact, which is meaningful for the learner, and she can reflect upon it and share it with others. From this constructionist description of the learning process, we can emphasize several elements associated with the creation of knowledge, namely, cognition, introspection, action, interaction and emotion.

Through cognitive processes, humans construct mental representations of their external realities. Human cognitive functions, such as language, memory, reasoning and attention, interact to produce and sustain symbols, schemas, images, ideas and other forms of mental representation (Damásio, 1999; Wallace, 2000). Cognitive knowledge is the result of the use and interconnection of these objects of knowledge, i.e., mental constructs, to make sense of the world and our action in it.

Introspection is a specific type of cognition that permits the personal inquiry into subjective mental phenomena, such as sensory experiences, feelings, emotions and mental images. Through introspection, we can see ourselves in action and observe the dialectic relations we establish with the external objects.

Through action and interaction, we create the experiences of the world we live in. These experiences construct or reconstruct our mental constructs, which in turn are responsible for a new understanding of the external reality. In this way, knowledge and experience are inseparable and influence each other.

The effective construction of personal knowledge requires the building of relationships between concepts and other mental constructs, in profoundly meaningful experiences (Shaw, 1996). All human experience is mediated by emotions, which drive our attention and concentration in order to help us process external stimuli and communicate with others. According to Damásio (1999), there are three types of emotions: primary emotions, background emotions and social emotions. Primary emotions include joy, sadness, fear, anger, surprise and aversion. Background emotions include the sensations of well-being and malaise, calmness and tension, pain and pleasure, and enthusiasm and depression. The social emotions include shame, jealousy, guilt and pride.

All knowledge and actions are associated with experiences that trigger negative and positive emotions. Specific kinds of objects or events tend to be more systematically associated with specific kinds of emotion than others. This creates consistent patterns of emotion, either at the level of the individual or the group sharing the same socio-cultural antecedents.

In accordance with the previous paragraphs, we can define meaningful experiences as those in which positive primary, background and social emotions flow easily, either as drivers or consequences of the experiences. In this sense, knowledge construction is more than cognition and action, it is also affection towards the ideas we construct and the actions we perform (Kafai & Resnick, 1996).

In the learning of new skills, concepts or practices needed to adapt to new organizational situations, emotions, such as calmness, trust, enthusiasm, pleasure, pride and self-esteem, play an important role. Because our mental constructs define the reality we see and the understanding of our place in the world, to reformulate them means to navigate for a while in ambiguity, uncertainty and risk. Those circumstances inherent to organizational change bring about emotional responses. These may be positive or negative responses. Positive emotions connect us to the new knowledge and favor its stabilization; negative emotions may lead to rejecting the new mental constructs or the process of constructing them. Thus, in effective learning environments, emotions cannot be ignored, but must be taken care of in environments that foster mutual trust.

THE HISTORICAL AND SOCIO-CULTURAL CONTEXT OF KNOWLEDGE

A social reality is a construction in continuous reformulation that occurs whenever social actors develop social constructions that are external and sharable. Those actors are active constructors of:

1. Social relationships, such as friendships, familial relationships, partnerships, and all other associations that people actively develop and maintain in their social setting;
2. Social events, which are activities that happen because people come together under some organized manner; they have a well-defined duration and may happen regularly;
3. Shared physical artifacts, such as things and physical spaces that people build, or maintain through their own efforts and expense;
4. Shared social goals and projects, which are those goals upon which the community agreed upon and is motivated to achieve, and which are those projects in which members of the community actively participate in order to achieve the social goals;
5. Shared cultural norms and traditions, which are things, such as shared dialects, music, styles of interacting and dressing, identity and organizational processes, with which people are comfortable (Shaw, 1996, p. 181).

Social constructors need materials for their constructions. It is the surrounding culture that provides those materials. If these materials exist in abundance, constructive learning is facilitated. If these materials are scarce, learning becomes difficult. Yet, in some situations, the surrounding culture may provide the materials in abundance but block their use. This latter situation may happen, for example, in social settings marked by fractured or limited social activity, in situations where conflicts are kept too high or are suppressed, when people do not have at their disposal enough time to experiment with new concepts, practices, etc.

As a general assumption, constructionism proposes that by the mere fact that people interact, influencing each other's mental constructs, social reality is in constant reconstruction. As mentioned before, the processes of subjectification, externalization, objectification and internalization exist in a constant interplay to create and recreate the social reality. In this context, learning of new concepts and practices is happening continuously, either intentionally or unintentionally.

The main conclusion about learning that emerges from what has been said in this section is that learning happens inside specific mental and social spaces, meaning that what a group can learn is influenced by:

1. The concepts, schemata, values, beliefs and other mental constructs shared by the group. What does not fit our mental spaces may never be seen, experienced, internalized or shared. Only what we can understand molds our interactions and helps define our position in relation to the external world that we are able to see.
2. All knowledge we create about external things, events and relationships is based on and constrained by our mental constructs. The richness of our perspective of the world depends on the diversity, complexity, depth and intensity of our own mental constructs, which in turn can be developed only by growing in connection with the reality that surrounds us.
3. The creation of knowledge is founded on the historical and socio-cultural context of its creators, providing a shared basis for the interaction inside a group. The continuous interaction of the group members, happening in a common environment, leads to similar mental constructs, a common interpretation of events and the

creation of shared meaning structures and external constructions. These common meaning structures and external constructions are responsible for the stable reality that all members of the group experience. If these meanings are never challenged, they imprison the group in taken-for-granted concepts and practices.

4.   There is no viewpoint outside human subjectivity or historical and socio-cultural circumstances from which to study phenomena and to judge the inquiry process and the knowledge produced. Even if we decide to study, for example, how an application of IT is used in an organization other than ours, we will always be constrained by our mental space, and the broader historical and socio-cultural circumstances that render that use meaningful to the studied organizational actors.

The above considerations highlight the point that there are many truths about social realities, each one derived from specific mental, historical and socio-cultural circumstances. It is not possible to establish definitively that the knowledge that one individual or group creates in a disciplined and honest way is preferable to the knowledge created by another individual or group. Moreover, knowledge created in the past that brought great advantages to a community, often later became inadequate to deal with new social circumstances.

If there is no privileged perspective from which to produce knowledge that is intrinsically true, a pluralistic and multidimensional perspective should be encouraged, whenever a solution must be envisioned, a decision must be made or an intervention must be carried out. The active participation of individuals and groups subjected to different constraints can contribute to the enlargement of each other's mental space and to the enrichment of the knowledge representations and social constructions produced while making a decision or performing a social intervention.

Of course, in reality, human relationships and interests are not as consensual and passive as the above paragraphs may imply. That is why political and symbolic processes are so important in keeping conflicts to acceptable limits, in supporting the negotiation of interests and helping create and use symbols to foster group cohesion and meaning.

Accepting relativism and pluralism as relevant assumptions in reshaping social realities and creating knowledge, the next important step is to determine how knowledge claims should be judged by a community of practice. Constructionist assumptions propose that those claims (Lincoln & Guba, 2000):

- are plausible for those who were involved in the process of creating them,
- can be related to the individual and shared interpretations from which they emerged,
- express the views, perspectives, claims, concerns and voices of all stakeholders,
- raise awareness of one's own and others' mental constructs,
- question the status quo and unfair social arrangements,
- prompt action on the part of people involved in the process of knowledge creation, and
- empower that action.

ODM AND KNOWLEDGE CREATION: PROBLEMS AND OPPORTUNITIES

The previous sections offered the context for knowledge creation, viewed as an individual and collective effort to make sense of the social realities that we actively construct and reconstruct. The reasoning developed in the previous sections is applied to the reconstruction of the concepts of knowledge and information. These two concepts are central in applying the constructionist paradigm to discuss current ODM practices and to propose some guidelines to reconstruct the practices in order to enhance their effectiveness.

The facts, events, things, procedures, rules, concepts, models, ideas registered and stored outside a human mind cannot be considered knowledge, since knowledge can reside only in human minds continuously growing in connection with the inner and outer worlds. What we register, store and manipulate with specific tools is some part of the human knowledge that has been expressed in some form of language. In this chapter, we call those externalized items of knowledge, knowledge representations or information. All meaningful information, which fits our mental or social spaces, has the potential of creating new knowledge through the processes of cognition, feeling and interaction.

Based on the notions of information, knowledge, and the process of knowledge creation, we are going now to present and then deconstruct the discourse usually associated with ODM. Table 1 summarizes the discourse to be deconstructed.

Knowledge discovery in data repositories has been defined as the process of analyzing organizational data from different perspectives and summarizing it into useful information for organizational actors, who will use that information to increase revenues, reduce costs or achieve other relevant organizational goals and objectives (Fayyad, Piatetsky-Shapiro & Smyth, 1996; Matheus, Chan & Piatetsky-Shapiro, 1993).

Data mining is a subprocess of the knowledge discovery. It leads to the finding of models of consumer behavior that can be used to guide the action of organizational actors (Adriaans & Zantinge, 1996). The models are built upon the patterns found among data stored in large databases that are backed by statistical correlations among that data. Those patterns are extracted by specific mechanisms called data mining algorithms.

The algorithms integrating the available data mining tools increase the knowledge of organizational actors about consumer behavior or automate part of the decision-making process by defining the models that predict that behavior. Data mining tools

Table 1. ODM, Key Elements of a Discourse

Organizational Data Mining		
	Knowledge discovery in data repositories	**Data mining**
Purpose	To analyze organizational data from different perspectives and summarize it into useful information for organizational actors.	To produce statistically valid models of consumer behavior.
Input	Business knowledge and data from organizational repositories.	Selected data from the repository.
Tasks	Data selection and treatment; data mining and interpretation of results.	Classification, clustering, association, and/or sequencing.
Analysis approach	Qualitative/subjective.	Quantitative/objective.
Results	Valid, useful and possibly surprising patterns, correlations and models.	Patterns, correlations, and models with statistic significance.

analyze relationships and patterns in stored data based on open-ended queries. The relationships sought are of four types (Santos, 2001):

- **Classes.** Data are located in predetermined groups. These classes can then be used to predict the class to which a nonclassified record belongs.
- **Clusters.** Data items are grouped according to specific criteria that define metrics of similarity. The classes emerge from this process and are not predefined.
- **Associations.** The algorithm searches for relationships between data.
- **Sequential patterns.** Temporal relationships are identified in the data. These relationships help to anticipate behavior patterns and trends.

Data mining tools assist in performing different kinds of technical analysis on the stored data (Rainsford & Roddick, 1996; Adriaans & Zantinge, 1996):

- **Rule induction.** The extraction of statistically significant if-then rules from data. The rules are induced in a top-down or bottom-up process. Using the top-down strategy, the process begins with general concepts that describe the data. These concepts are then refined through a process of specialization. Using the bottom-up strategy, all records of the database are considered as rules, which the algorithm tries to generalize based on the data analyzed. This kind of analysis produces results that are usually considered easy to interpret.
- **Decision trees.** The algorithm produces tree structures that represent sets of decisions. The nodes show the attributes to be classified, the branches describe the values that the attribute can assume and the leaves represent the classes by which the records can be classified. The leaves can also represent a business rule associated with certain values of the attribute.
- **Neural networks.** These algorithms generate predictive models whose structure imitates live neural tissue built from separate neurons. These models can be made quite sophisticated through training in the execution of a specific task. The model is used to classify new records. The process of creating this structure is very complex and cannot be controlled in order to assure that the obtained model is really relevant.
- **Genetic algorithms.** The process of data analysis is founded on the concepts of genetic mutation and natural selection proposed by the theory of natural evolution of live organisms.
- **Nearest neighbor method.** This process of analysis leads to the forecast of a future situation or to a decision by finding the closest past analogs of the present situation and by choosing the same solutions that were the correct ones in those past situations.

The algorithms determine the statistical significance of the found patterns and correlations. This significance is considered an objective measure of the relevance of the produced models to support the decision-making, resolution of problems or any other management task.

The results of data mining (patterns, correlations and models) are usually referred to as knowledge, which is discovered in the analyzed data repository. This knowledge must then be subject to human interpretation. Organizational actors determine its qualitative significance according to their own knowledge of the business domain.

The interpretation of data mining results is considered the most subjective part of the whole process of knowledge discovery in data repositories. It depends on the individual and shared knowledge of the business, the interests that guide the interpretation, the cognitive and social circumstances that provide the context for that interpretation and the creativity of the interpreter.

Thus, the interpretation of patterns and models of consumer behavior may vary depending on who is the interpreter. That interpretation is qualitative in nature, and makes the interpreter a key element in the knowledge discovery process. This is believed to introduce some ambiguity and lack of rigor and control in the process.

A found pattern or model that does not fit the business expectations of the data mining system user is usually considered potentially very interesting. It is also interesting if it can be used to attain organizational interests. It must be valid when applied to new data.

We want to emphasize that the purpose of the above paragraphs about ODM is not to provide an extensive account of the relevant concepts, practices and tools. We also do not consider the consequences resulting from problems with the data in repositories, such as insufficient and corrupted data, which can lead to invalid data mining results. Our aim is to address the current discourse associated with this organizational process. In the sequel, we deconstruct this discourse by identifying the values, beliefs and meanings that support it.

The concepts of data, information and knowledge are closely linked with ODM. "Data" is often defined as facts, numbers or text that can be processed by the computer. There can be various kinds of data, namely, operational and transactional data, management data and metadata (data dictionary definitions are an example of metadata). Information is defined as the patterns, associations or relationships among the data. Information can be converted into knowledge about historical patterns and future trends of consumer behavior. This categorization seems to reflect the idea of growing sophistication and meaning. Information and knowledge result from computerized data processing.

However, when we analyze these concepts more closely, it emerges that patterns, associations, relationships and historical patterns and future trends could also be considered facts of varying degrees of complexity and certainty. They can also be subject to further computerized processing. Moreover, data, information and knowledge, as they are defined in the above paragraph, have no intrinsic meaning. They become a fact, a number, a pattern, a future trend and so on, only after a human interprets the symbols of a language. So, there is no significant basis for the separate use of the terms data, information and knowledge, other than some interest in separating knowledge representations before they are subjected to the process of computerized processing from the results of such processing.

In this chapter, we argue that the expression "knowledge representation" is better and more accurate than "data, information and knowledge," because:

- it avoids the use of three different terms to refer the same things;
- it avoids confusion with the much more complex concept of knowledge, which is inherently human;

- it links what exists in organizational repositories with the human capital of the organization and the historical, and socio-cultural circumstances that shape the organizational work realities;
- it emphasizes that organizational repositories are human constructions shaped by the shared values, beliefs, feelings and experiences, which were reinforced or reconstructed in the process of constructing and updating those repositories; and
- it addresses the importance of these repositories for the construction of individual and shared knowledge, having the potential of serving as support either for developmental activities or as the reinforcement of the status quo.

Attached to the discourse around the data mining tools, there is the idea that in the future, new and more powerful algorithms will be developed that will be able to find more valuable patterns and models, independent of human subjectivities and limitations. If it ever becomes possible to integrate the knowledge of the relevant business domain into the system, the algorithm would be able to decide the usefulness and validity of discovered patterns, correlations and models, as well as to grow in sophistication by integrating these models in its knowledge of the business. The decision-making process would become extensively automated and guided by the objective reasoning of clear and rational rules implemented in a computer-based system.

However, this view has several drawbacks related to the issues already addressed in the previous sections of this chapter, namely:

1. Since all human knowledge has a tacit and nonexpressible dimension, it will never be possible to integrate all relevant business knowledge in a repository to be analyzed by a data-mining algorithm.
2. The diversity of views about the business activities and their context is what allows for the emergence of organizational creativity and development and the challenging of taken-for-granted concepts and practices (Bolman & Deal, 1991; Morgan, 1997; Palmer & Hardy, 2000). The stored knowledge representations are those around which there is some degree of consensus. This is important for the stability of work concepts and practices and to support organizational cohesion. However, they may also trap organizational actors in those concepts and practices, even when evidence shows they are threatening organizational success.
3. The relevance of knowledge representations stored in organizational repositories changes according to changes in the socio-cultural circumstances that offer the context for making sense of the representations. Only the organizational actors can understand those contexts and are able to give meaning to knowledge representations.
4. It is still believed that decision-making is or should be an essentially rational process, guided by cognitive processes such as planning, resolution of problems, and creativity (Sparrow, 1998). However, recent experiments in neurobiology show that emotion is an integral part of reasoning and decision-making (Damásio, 1999). Thus, only organizational actors can make decisions. The full automation of the process is not a realistic objective.

Instead of the present focus on the technological side of ODM, it would be interesting to adopt a constructionist approach and to focus on the social process of knowledge construction that makes ODM meaningful. With this new focus on people and the way they create and share knowledge, the main concern would be to mobilize the knowledge of organizational actors so the whole organization can benefit from it. This concern is justified by the awareness that the organization, seen as a community, is more intelligent than each of its members, including any of its leaders.

As described in previous sections, knowledge construction and sharing is more successful, when individuals are involved in the construction of something external and/ or something that can be shared. Knowledge representations, organizational repositories and the results of data mining are external and sharable social artifacts. The use of data mining systems supports the building or reinforcement of social relationships, the achievement of shared goals and the accomplishment of shared projects.

All these social constructions help make ideas tangible, support the negotiation of meanings and facilitate the communication between organizational actors. Thus, the whole organization is involved in a developmental cycle each time social constructions are created or reconstructed. For the construction of individual and shared knowledge, as important as the shared artifacts, goals, projects, events, relationships and other constructions is the process of creating them is more important. In the next section, we present some constructionist guidelines to drive the ODM process to the goal of leveraging the social dynamics of knowledge creation in organizations.

DESIGNING THE ODM PROCESS TO LEVERAGE KNOWLEDGE CREATION IN ORGANIZATIONS: SOME CONSTRUCTIONIST GUIDELINES

A precondition to getting people naturally involved in the ongoing production of social constructions is the existence of social cohesion, a sense of belonging to a group and a sense of common purpose (Shaw, 1996). When the group is marked by fragmented and alienating relationships among its members, it will be very difficult for its members to engage in a joint effort to construct anything. In this way, organizational actors lose developmental opportunities.

The sense of common purpose is important to sustain interaction. It motivates organizational actors to come together as concerned parties to address common issues, and actively participate in decision-making and change. When actors get together to jointly construct something sharable, social relationships are established or reinforced. These relationships, along with cultural artifacts, provide the materials for further social construction, which will support new learning and creativity. In the process, the organization, in part or as a whole, is redefined.

With ODM there is a special focus on knowledge about consumer behavior to support decision and action. ODM assists the organization in knowing the preferences of its customers and in anticipating their needs and reactions. The construction of this knowledge must be guided by the specific purposes of the several communities of practice that constitute the organization.

ODM and the knowledge it helps to create are social constructions. Repositories, data mining tools and the resulting patterns, correlations and models are social artifacts that should be used to make ideas tangible, to negotiate meanings and to facilitate communication between organizational actors. As such, they may become catalysts for the development of shared knowledge about consumer behavior, when they are used in the contexts of meaningful projects.

Data mining systems may become empowering tools in the sense that they make viable the analysis of large organizational repositories of knowledge representations. These knowledge representations are social constructions that connect organizational actors to a common view of the business concepts and practices that shape their intentions and interactions. Problems in the performance of organizational tasks or in organizational adaptation to environmental changes may reside in the inappropriateness of knowledge representations or in the tools used to extract rules and patterns from them. Knowledge representations were created and stored under specific historical and socio-cultural circumstances of which their readers must be aware in order to be able to understand their relevance or inadequacy.

The patterns, correlations and models extracted from knowledge representations stored in organizational repositories become lenses, or assimilation frames, through which actors attribute meaning to others, the business, their action and interaction and the relationships with customers, suppliers and other relevant external entities. They can empower or impoverish an actor's decision-making and task performance. The risk of weakening action increases if organizational actors have no means of testing their interpretations of those patterns, correlation and models in practice, and if they are not given the opportunity of learning from their own mistaken interpretations or the mistakes of others. In order to support insight and creativity, organizational actors need time and opportunities to reflect upon those data mining results, to build mental relationships with their own previous mental objects of knowledge and to externalize their interpretations, i.e., talking about those interpretations and showing them to others allows each actor to influence and be influenced by the views of others.

Another important aspect to consider is that the patterns that are encountered in stored knowledge representations provide the means to reinterpret an actor's past experience and the past experience of others. Good formal and informal communication must exist in order to take advantage of this basis for the discussion of that experience in the light of the context in which it occurred in order to construct shared meanings. Thus, the meaning structures of the past are rearranged into new meaning structures.

Moreover, the rearrangement of meaning structures should be assisted with theoretical tools that critically analyze the old structures. Data mining tools can serve this aim, when they provide surprising patterns of behavior. Theoretical models, case studies and local explanations are examples of other means to support learning and the reconstruction of meaning by providing insights that do not fully overlap, or conflict with, individual and shared conceptual schemas.

In using data mining systems, the knowledge of the business domain assumes particular importance to define a user's goals and objectives, guiding the queries she defines and her interpretations of the results. The user's queries are used by the system to select the knowledge representations that are to be analyzed by data mining algorithms. Usually, this business knowledge is structurally and economically oriented; that is, it is focused on mission, strategy, objectives, tasks, processes, costs, profits, process and product quality, responsibilities, coordination and control of the activities, resources allocation, management levels, decision making, etc. These are assumed as

Table 2. Relevant Work Aspects (Adapted from the Work of Bolman & Deal, 1991; Morgan, 1997; Palmer & Hardy, 2000)

Structural Dimension	Social Dimension	Political Dimension	Symbolic Dimension
Definition of tasks;	Shared goals and objectives;	Individual interests: tasks, career, personal life;	Used symbols to reduce the uncertainty and ambiguity of organizational activities;
Formal roles;	Performance evaluation;	Conflict coming from the collision of interests;	
Coordination and control;	Criteria for the delivering of rewards and punishments;	Hierarchy of authority;	Shared values and beliefs and the way they influence and are influenced y the organizational structure;
Formal processes;		Control of the scarce resources;	
Objective, environmental and internal factors that determine the organizational structure;	Motivational factors;	Control of the organizational structure definition;	
	Informal roles and communication;		
	Professional recognition;	Actors with to restricted access to key knowledge and information;	Common language;
Authority;	Professional training;		Myths, stories, and metaphors;
Formal communication channels.	How well the organizational structure fits human needs and business constraints;	Control of boundaries;	Rituals and ceremonies;
		Control of core competencies needed to guarantee the quality of the production;	Messages to the entities that hold interest in the performed activities;
	Participation in the decision making process.	Coalitions and their specific interests;	
		Charismatic actors and their exerted influence;	Legitimized way of expressing emotions.
		Political processes which are responsible for the organizational structure.	

objectively identifiable aspects of work, and, therefore, they can be analyzed and measured.

However, to gain a deeper insight of the organization and its business, in order to better understand knowledge representations, stimulate creative interpretations of data mining results and to structure the ODM process in order to facilitate organizational learning, a diverse range of organizational aspects and of interests that support the use of the data mining system should be explored. Table 2 summarizes some key aspects of a multidimensional analysis of organizations.

The study of these organizational aspects helps to identify different venues for analyzing the stored knowledge representations by uncovering a diversity of useful applications of data mining results, which can function as materials for a wider range of social constructions. Patterns and models of consumer behavior can be searched and used:

- to support the achievement of organizational goals and the fulfillment of strategies, in accordance with the structural circumstances that sustain those goals and strategies;
- to develop shared purposes, to define performance criteria, to allow informal discussions of issues of common interest, to train newcomers and to support participation in decision-making processes;
- to further individual interests, to support the discussion and negotiation of interests, to empower the actors' action and to facilitate coalition building;
- to play the role of symbols that help reduce negative emotions triggered by the ambiguity and uncertainty resulting from turbulent markets, to help develop shared

Table 3. Constructionist Guidelines for ODM

Constructionist guidelines for ODM	
Creating rich learning environments	**Using data mining tools**
Work relationships must be strengthened in order to create the social cohesiveness needed for the ongoing production of shared constructions that engage the organization in developmental cycles.	Data mining results will support insight and creativity when organizational actors have enough time to reflect upon them and the opportunity to externalize and discuss their interpretations.
The construction of knowledge about customers' preferences and their future needs and reactions must be guided by the shared purposes of the specific communities of practice that constitute the organization.	Effective formal and informal communication must be fostered in order to become possible to discuss each other's interpretations of past experience in the light of the context in which it occurred.
Organizational repositories, data mining tools, and the results of data mining are social artifacts that should be used to make ideas tangible, to negotiate meanings, and to facilitate communication between organizational actors.	Theoretical tools, locally or externally developed, should be used to critically analyze the old meaning structures, facilitating the rearrangement of those structures.
Knowledge representations were created and stored under specific historical and socio-cultural circumstances of which their readers must be aware in order to be able to understand relevance or inadequacy of those representations.	The search and interpretation of patterns and models of consumer behavior should be guided by a multi-dimensional knowledge of the business domain, and work concepts and practices.

values and beliefs, to foster a common business language integrating the relevant concepts and practices and to design attractive messages for customers and public opinion.

Table 3 summarizes the guidelines presented in this section, grouping them in two categories:
1. guidelines that should be considered for the creation of rich learning environments in which data mining systems are used as social artifacts that leverage continuous learning and
2. guidelines that should be considered when using a specific data mining tool.

These guidelines are given from constructionist theories developed and applied in areas, such as psychology, education and organization theory.

An Illustrative Example

The following example is based on the implementation success story of an SAS solution (http://www.sas.com/news/success). This example serves to illustrate the concerns that would emerge from using the guidelines presented in this section. The set of concerns presented here include some abstract, albeit obvious, concerns since a more exhaustive set could be generated only in a detailed study of the organization, and the circumstances that provide the context and the meaning of the use of the data mining system.

An international supermarket chain has as its mission to provide the freshest food items and the best customer service possible. This supermarket chain has 170 stores spread across the country. The company has introduced a system that collects retail

Table 4.

Strengthening work relationships:	Data mining results in support of insight and creativity:
What can be done to capitalize on the eventual different interpretations about consumer behavior trends held by store managers and the head office buyers? Do buyers know the specifics of each store in order to better assess the supply orders and other relevant information? What events and common activities exist to relate the managers' work experiences with the buyers' experiences? How do friendship and other informal relationships between managers and buyers impact order fulfillment and purchasing decisions?	Do managers and buyers have opportunities to share their experiences, i.e., failures and successes, in using the system to support their tasks? Are the system users able to follow the consequences of their decisions? When needed, do users have time to seek the reasons for positive or negative consequences? How is failure to see relevant information in the reports acknowledged and, eventually, punished? Are individual and social factors considered in punishing or rewarding?
The construction of knowledge about customer's preferences and their future needs and reactions:	**Discussion of interpretations of data mining results:**
Do system users know how the system is supposed to support the company mission? What common projects, events, and artifacts have been developed by managers and buyers because of the existence of a data warehouse?	What happens when the intuition of a manager or a buyer goes against the findings of the system? Is the data mining system used to control work performance of the company staff, namely, salespeople? How are sudden drops in performance handled?
Making ideas tangible, negotiating meanings, and facilitating the communication:	**Critically analyzing meaning structures:**
Do managers and buyers understand each other's views better now that they use the same pool of information? Do users share a meaning for "effective system use"? What inter and intra store power imbalances does the system create?	Do managers use the database queries to highlight specific problems of the store? What are the feelings towards the system's support? What steps, if any, are being taken to reduce the impact of the system on the traditional ways of performing the tasks? Why? Can the resistance be stopped? Should it be stopped?
Historical and socio-cultural circumstances surrounding the creation of knowledge representations:	**Multi-dimensional knowledge of the business domain supporting interpretation of the data mining results:**
How are experiences communicated in order to provide the context for the sales figures in terms of product demand, demographic changes, specific characteristics of the store's costumer service, aspects of the organizational structure, specific skills and motivations, local consumer culture, etc.? Can managers and buyers save the reasons behind particularly risky decisions? If they can, are they motivated to do this?	With the support of the new system, do managers and buyers feel more confident in the quality of their decisions? How can the systems users be motivated to use the system to its full potential? Are unexpected uses accepted? Are external models of management and organizing used to discuss the improvement of sales and customer service?

sales data from every cash register in every store, and delivers analyzed sales figures to the head office in time for the next working day. In the morning, store managers and buyers at the head office get up-to-the minute information about daily sales, changes in stock and price change. Vital information relating to the company's performance through the use of critical success factors, traffic lighting and drill-down is displayed. The system helps the store managers order their supplies and helps the buyers to make purchases. With the system, the company's buyers can spot trends and adopt the best long-term buying strategies.

See Table 4 for a list of general concerns developed upon constructionist guidelines to leverage the knowledge creation.

CONCLUSION

According to the assumptions of the constructionist perspective, ODM should be designed to involve organizational actors in the social construction of something external and sharable. The designing of a marketing campaign, the making of a decision and the transformation of work concepts and practices are examples of social construction processes for which ODM could be viewed as relevant.

As a result of the process, the individual and shared knowledge will become more sophisticated, empowering the action of individuals and groups and facilitating interaction. In this way, organizational actors consciously create cohesive and pluralist work environments, more prone to deal with problems and difficult decisions associated with consumer behavior. This perspective is more realistic than the traditional view of ODM as a process of making knowledge neutral and independent of the knower and social contexts in which it was created, in order to support decision-making processes idealized as inherently rational.

The tools used to support ODM fundamentally shape and define the process. Lack of appropriate tools impoverishes a social setting and makes social construction difficult. Future research is needed to study if current data mining systems facilitate organizational developmental activities. It will also be important to create practical experiences of designing and implementing the ODM process in specific organizational settings, so that learning from a constructionist perspective can be supported.

We have planned a research project to understand the way Portuguese organizations view and do organizational data mining, and to study in specific settings, to what extent organizational data mining contributes to the organizational efficacy, according to the local definitions of efficacy and the historical, social and cultural circumstances in which that contribution is made and to define a conceptual framework to assist the design of the organizational data mining process.

REFERENCES

Ackermann, E. (1996). Perspective-taking and object construction: Two keys to learning. In Y. Kafai & M. Resnick (Eds.), *Constructionism in practice* (pp. 25-36). Mahwah, NJ: Lawrence Erlbaum Associates Publishers.

Adriaans, P., & Zantinge, D. (1996*). Data mining*. Harlow, UK: Addison Wesley .

Arbnor, I., & Bjerke, B. (1997). *Methodology for creating business knowledge*. SAGE Publications.

Bolman, L. G., & Deal, T. E. (1991). *Reframing Organizations: Artistry, choice, and leadership*. San Francisco, CA: Jossey-Bass Publishers.

Buchanan, D., & Badham, R. (1999). *Power, politics, and organizational change: Winning the turf game*. SAGE Publications.

Damásio, A. (1999). *The feeling of what happens: Body and emotion in the making of consciousness*. New York: Harcourt Brace.

Fayyad, U., Piatetsky-Shapiro, G., & Smyth, P. (1996). From data mining to knowledge discovery: An overview. In U. M. Fayyad, G. Piatetsky-Shapiro, P. Smyth, & R. Uthurusamy (Eds.), *Advances in knowledge discovery and data dining* (pp. 1-36). Cambridge, MA: The MIT Press.

Finkelstein, A. & Kramer, J. (2000, June). The future of software engineering roadmap. *Proceedings of 22nd International Conference on Software Engineering* (ICSE), Limerick, Ireland (pp. 3-22). New York: ACM Press

Gould, S. J. (1998). The sharp-eyed lynx, outfoxed by nature (part two). *Natural History, 107*(23-27), 63-73.

Kafai, Y., & Resnick, M. (Eds.) (1996). *Constructionism in practice: Designing, thinking, and learning in a digital world.* Mahwah, NJ: Lawrence Erlbaum Associates.

Lincoln, Y. S., & Guba, E. G. (2000). Paradigmatic controversies, contradictions, and emerging confluences. In N. K. Denzin & Y. S. Lincoln (Eds.), *Hanbook of qualitative research* (pp. 163-188). SAGE Publications.

Matheus, C. J., Chan, P. K., & Piatetsky-Shapiro, G. (1993). Systems for knowledge discovery in databases. *IEEE Transactions on Knowledge and Data Engineering, 5*(6), 903-913.

Morgan, G. (1997). *Images of Organization.* Thousand Oaks, CA: Sage Publications.

Nemati, H. R., Steiger, D. M., Iyer, L. S., & Herschel, R. T. (2002). Knowledge warehouse: An architectural integration of knowledge management, decision support, artificial intelligence and data warehousing. *Decision Support Systems, 33,* 143-161.

Palmer, I., & Hardy, C. (2000). *Thinking about management.* London: Sage Publications.

Papert S. (1990). Introduction. In I. Harel (Ed.), *Constructionist learning.* Cambridge, MA: MIT Media Laboratory.

Parker, S., & Wall, T. (1998). *Job and work design: Organizing work to promote well-being and effectiveness.* Thousand Oaks, CA: Sage Publications.

Piaget, J. (1954). *The construction of reality in the child.* New York: Ballantine Books.

Rainsford, C. P., & Roddick, J. F. (1996). *A survey of issues in data mining.* (Tech. Rep. CIS-96-006). University of South Australia, School of Computer and Information Science. Australia.

Santos, M. Y. C. A. (2001). *PADRÃO: um sistema de descoberta de conhecimento em bases de dados geo-referenciadas.* Unpublished thesis, Universidade do Minho, Portugal.

Schwandt, T. A. (2000). Three epistemological stances for qualitative inquiry: Interpretivism, hermeneutics, and social constructionism. In N. K. Denzin & Y. S. Lincoln (Eds.), *Handbook of Qualitative Research* (pp. 189-213). Thousand Oaks, CA: Sage Publications.

Sekaran, U. (1992). *Research methods for business: A skill-building approach.* New York: John Wiley & Sons Inc.

Shaw, A. (1996). Social constructionism and the inner city: designing environments for social development and urban renewal. In Y. Kafai & M. Resnick (Eds.), *Constructionism in practice* (pp. 175-206). Mahwah, NJ: Lawrence Erlbaum Associates Publishers.

Sparrow, J. (1998). *Knowledge in organizations: Access to thinking at work.* London: SAGE Publications.

Taylor, F. W. (1911). *Principles of scientific management.* New York: Harper & Row.

Wallace, B. A. (2000). *The taboo of subjectivity: Toward a new science of consciousness.* New York: Oxford University Press.

Weber, M. (1947). *The theory of social and economic organization.* New York: Free Press.

Chapter XXI

E-Commerce and Data Mining: Integration Issues and Challenges

Parviz Partow-Navid
California State University, Los Angeles, USA

Ludwig Slusky
California State University, Los Angeles, USA

ABSTRACT

Web mining is the application of data mining techniques to discover the usage patterns of Web data, in order to better serve the needs of Web site visitors. Web mining consists of three phases: data gathering, analysis and reporting. This chapter describes each of these phases in detail along with a discussion of electronic customer relationship management (eCRM). Several challenging research areas that need to be investigated for further enhancement of this field are also presented.

INTRODUCTION

For most companies, competitiveness in e-commerce (EC) demands a meaningful presence on the Web. Web pages are required to establish the company's image, to sell products and to offer customer support. The success of a Web site directly affects the success of the EC strategy of the company. EC is also emerging as one of the best application areas for data mining technology (Konrad, 2001).

Data dining (DM) technologies have been around for many years without notable success. While DM tools help in the identification of data patterns, DM applications are, for the most part, in the research area that focuses on high possible rewards along with high-risk business decisions. Having the following characteristics present in a DM application can help minimize the risk of business failure (Ansari, Kohavi, Mason & Zheng, 2002; Kohavi, 2001):

1. Data contained reach descriptions — For example, broad customer data combined with potentially useful data fields allow DM programs to look beyond plain correlations.
2. A substantial amount of analyzed data — Having many matching records guarantees the statistical significance of the found data patterns.
3. Controlled and reliable data collection procedures — Noisy and distorted data may fail to disclose patterns.
4. The ability to evaluate and track tangible results — Measurable return on investment can be very convincing.
5. Ease of integration of DM with existing operational processes — The operational system and the DM analysis system can be integrated into one closed-loop system.

EC is the ideal domain for DM. Many of the above characteristics are readily present in EC but rarely in legacy systems. Data are gathered electronically, rather than manually, thus less noise is introduced from manual processing. EC data are rich, containing information such as purchase history and demographic data. Also, some data that were difficult to gather before are now easily accessible. For instance, EC systems can keep track of the actions of the customer in the visual "shop," including what they review, what they place into their shopping carts, but do not purchase and so on. In the past, to gather such data, companies had to follow customers and record their activities, or had to conduct sophisticated analyses of store videos. Large amounts of data can be collected inexpensively in EC. To take full advantage of this process, DM must be integrated into EC systems. Such integration can significantly decrease the data preparation time. An integrated system can also offer users a standardized user interface and easy access to metadata. The goal of this chapter is to provide an overview of the challenges and issues in Web mining. We discuss Web mining phases and the inherent power in current eCRM solutions. Research areas that need to be examined for further enhancement of this area are also presented.

DM DEFINITION

DM can be defined (Berry & Linoff, 2000) as the process of exploration and analysis of large quantities of data in order to extract meaningful patterns and rules. DM tools identify patterns in data. These patterns can be used to help in the decision-making process and forecast the impact of these decisions. DM can decrease analysis time by directing attention to the most significant variables. The information resulting from DM falls into the following five categories:

*   **Classification.** This information identifies the main characteristics of a certain group (e.g., determining which telephone lines are used for Web access).
*   **Estimation.** This information helps forecast future values based on patterns within large sets of data (e.g., estimating a family's total income).
*   **Association.** This information determines the relationship between events that take place at one time (e.g., identifying what things go together in a shopping basket at the supermarket).

- **Clustering.** This information helps segment a diverse group into a number of more similar subgroups or clusters. What differentiates clustering from classification is that clustering does not depend on predefined classes. The data are grouped together according to self-similarity.
- **Description.** This information describes what is going on in a complex database in order to enhance our knowledge of the people, products or services that generated the data. For example, a simple statement such as "new immigrants support Democrats in greater numbers than Republicans," can generate further study on the part of journalists, sociologists, political scientists and candidates for public office.

WEB MINING

This section provides a model for an EC system integrated with DM. This model, as illustrated in Figure 1, is composed of three main components: Business Data Collection, Analysis and Reporting (Ansari et al., 2002; Analyzing Web Site Traffic, 2001).

Depending on how the data is collected, the data-gathering phase can be done using log files, packet sniffers or application server loggings. For the log file approach, this phase consists of parsing log files into a common format at scheduled intervals. The packet sniffer method consists of monitoring the network packets as they move across the network. And, finally, the application server logging adds modules to extend the Web server's functionality, which gathers the data in real time, before it is entered to the log file, and pass it along to the analysis component.

Once the data has been collected, it needs to be analyzed. During the data analysis phase, complex heuristic rules are applied to the data. For example, the results of this phase help organize the data into visits and page views instead of simply hits. The analysis might be based on the IP addresses of the visitor or on the information provided by the cookies. Once the data has been analyzed, it is stored in a database for processing in the final phase.

In the final phase of Web mining, reports are produced from the analyzed data. During this phase, the data in the database is converted into many different formats and reports, each responding to specific questions. For example, a report on what users have viewed on a Web site might include the top five pages that were accessed, how many

Figure 1. Integration Model

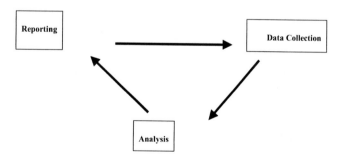

times each page has been viewed and how long, on average, users spent viewing each page. Graphs and charts are also generated during this stage. Let us review each of these phases (or procedural components of DM) in details.

Data Collection

This component keeps track of customers' transactions (e.g., purchases and returns) and logs customers' interaction, e.g., clickstream. The clickstream contains a log for every visitor to a given Web site. It is a record of every action each visitor makes (Kimball, 2000). There are various techniques for data collection and some of them are described below. It should be noted that the majority of the techniques presented below could also be easily applied to recording and analysis of other customer's touch points.

Web log analysis. When someone visits a Web page, he/she gets connected to a Web server that provides the files the customer has requested. In the process of providing access to the files, the Web server creates a log (clickstream), recording successful and unsuccessful sessions, identifying happy visitors and good prospects and discovering the elements of Web site that are useful at attracting and keeping visitors, such as file name, access date, time, etc. Log files are in a text format, and a record in the log file contains the following fields (Kimball, 2000):

- Date/time of page access along with IP address of the visitor;
- Page/object being accessed (the whole page or an object on the page);
- Form of request: "Get" or "Submit";
- Context from where the page request was made, i.e., referring page; and
- Type of browser accessing the Web site, usually Netscape or Explorer.

Figure 2 shows a portion of log file. A log file for a Web page with a low volume of traffic typically contains around 250,000 line of recording.

Employment of DM in Web applications and specifically in EC generally starts with Web server logs as the key source of data (Cooley, Mobasher & Sricastava, 1999; Kimball & Merz, 2000; Mirsky, 2001). However, log files are very large and contain detailed information for each file that has been processed. On the detail, table raw level they are practically worthless (Analyzing Web Site Traffic, 2001).

Figure 2. Small Portion of a Log File

```
165.24.63.78 - -   [02/Jul/2002:11:24:13 -0500]    "GET /images/lake.gif HTTP/1.0" 200 215 "http//www
165.24.63.78 - -   [02/Jul/2002:11:24:13 -0500]    "GET /images/collections.gif HTTP/1.0" 200 216 "http
165.24.63.78 - -   [02/Jul/2002:11:24:17 -0500]    "GET /images/education.gif HTTP/1.0" 200 205 "http:
165.24.63.78 - -   [02/Jul/2002:11:24:18 -0500]    "GET /images/library.gif HTTP/1.0" 200 168 "http:ww
165.24.63.78 - -   [02/Jul/2002:11:24:19 -0500]    "GET /images/lmembership.gif HTTP/1.0" 200 209 "h
165.24.63.78 - -   [02/Jul/2002:11:24:22 -0500]    "GET /images/shop.gif HTTP/1.0" 200 228 "http/www
165.24.63.78 - -   [02/Jul/2002:11:24:22 -0500]    "GET / HTTP/1.0" 200 0320 "HTTP://www.google.co
165.24.63.78 - -   [02/Jul/2002:11:24:24 -0500]    "GET /images/lnewsletter.gif HTTP/1.0" 200 209 "http
165.24.63.78 - -   [02/Jul/2002:11:24:26 -0500]    "GET /images/symposium.gif HTTP/1.0" 200 202 "http
165.24.63.78 - -   [02/Jul/2002:11:24:27 -0500]    "GET /images/feedback.gif HTTP/1.0" 200 208 "http://
165.24.63.78 - -   [02/Jul/2002:11:24:28 -0500]    "GET /images/on_homepage.gif HTTP/1.0" 200 204 "
165.24.63.78 - -   [02/Jul/2002:11:24:28 -0500]    "GET /images/home_exhibit.gif HTTP/1.0" 200 5318 "
165.24.63.78 - -   [02/Jul/2002:11:24:30 -0500]    "GET /images/home_education.gif HTTP/1.0" 543 "htt
```

Web log analysis software takes the raw log-file data and changes it into meaningful traffic information about the Web site. At a minimum, this comprises data produced by Microsoft Internet Information Server (IIS), Netscape SuiteSpot, Lotus Domino, Apache and O'Reilly Web site. The analysis is conducted largely to achieve a general understanding of the activities on a Web site. Log data can be, for example, helpful in tracking the results of specific marketing campaigns. This can be achieved by including information such as advertisement names, filters and virtual server data. Product managers and marketers need this information to provide answers to questions such as the following (Web Mining Whitepaper, 2001):

- How many hits, page views, visits and visitors is the Web site getting?
- What page is the most popular?
- What page is the least popular?
- From what sites are visitors being referred?

The choice seems logical since lots of sites use Web servers that support generating such logs. However, it also considerably restricts the type of data that is available and creates major obstacles when further information must be collected. Web server logs were designed to help debugging Web severs, not for DM. The following are some of the problems associated with using Web server logs for DM (Kohavi, 2001):

1. **User identification.** Web server logs are not capable of identifying sessions or users. The concept of a session is not present at the Web server level. Common techniques for user identification rely on cookies, IPs and browser user agents (Cooley et al., 1999; EMetrics Study, 2001). However, problems arise due to proxy caches, IP reassignment, browsers rejecting cookies, etc.

2. **Transactional data.** Web server logs need to be integrated with transactional data. Majority of organizations store transactional data in a database. However, combining the transactional data and Web server logs is a daunting task, requiring the identification of the clicks relevant to each transaction. For example, one of the most frequently requested reports for e-commerce pages is the sale proceeds attributed to the specific referring pages. Although the Web server logs can contain the referrer URL, computing this information requires both clickstream information and order information (Gomory, Hoch, Lee, Podlaseck & Schonberg, 1999).

3. **Events.** Critical events such as "put in cart," "remove from cart" or "change number of units" are absent from Web logs. Inferring these can be very difficult. For example, the log file can confirm that the user left the page with selection of six items for purchase and that the next page visited was the purchase cart. Did the user put an item in the cart or did he/she click on "show cart content"? One of the most valuable items for e-commerce is the worth of discarded shopping carts. However, these events are not available through Web logs.

4. **Web information.** When a visitor to a Web site fills out a form, for example, a search form, it is vital to be aware of the information entered. This will help companies to add synonyms and enhance their product mix. Web server logs do not gather Web form information.

5. **Web page information.** Web server logs contain URLs with no consideration for the contents of the page. For example, we need to know "What product is presented when a given URL is shown?"

6. **Dynamic content.** Web server logs do not have information for modern sites that generate dynamic content. Dynamic sites are designed on a small set of URL templates that are used over and over to display different information every time the user visiting the site. Which product was shown to the visitor? Did search succeed or fall short? How many results were returned? Did the number of results confuse the user?

7. **Flat files.** Web server logs are flat files on several file systems, most likely in various time zones. Larger sites usually are composed of many Web servers, each logging data into separate files. Knowing that the combined data must be stored in one time zone from Web servers physically located in different time zones, the problem is a complicated one. In addition, Web server logs are usually in ASCII format, which is an inefficient way to store large volume of structured data.

8. **Redundant information.** Web server logs often hold redundant information. Given the current DM technology and techniques, majority of entries in the Web log are of no value for mining. For example, they contain the requests for every image. Since a typical Web page contains multiple images and because the same page view usually contains the same images (with minor exceptions for personalization), 90 percent of the Web server logs is commonly deleted (Kohavi, 2001).

Packet sniffers. Packet sniffing is a technique whereby data sent out from the Web server to the client is monitored; it can be perceived as the Internet equivalent of telephone tapping. It provides a nonintrusive way to augment Web server logs with additional information. When a Web browser connects to a Web server, it uses the HTTP protocol to request and retrieve information. HTTP, along with other Internet application protocols, is transported across the Internet in a series of small TCP/IP packets. It is possible to "sniff" these packets as they travel across the network, in order to gather Web site traffic data. The approach is currently useful and more information is logged. One major advantage over the log files is that the data can be collected and analyzed in real time. It is also possible to gather network level information that is not present in log files. Information such as whether or not the user canceled the request by selecting the browser's Stop button.

Packet sniffing also has some major drawbacks and has many of the disadvantages listed in the previous section. Moreover, it is not appropriate for secure e-commerce sites. Packet sniffing does not work if traffic is encrypted, making the additional information unavailable at the most crucial times: registration and checkout (Analyzing Web Site Traffic, 2001; Kohavi, 2001).

Application server logging. Advanced Web site analysis solutions offer the option to use cookies to obtain more accurate user counts and the ability to analyze repeat users. A cookie is a small piece of information produced by the Web server and placed in the user's computer. When the user's browser requests a page from a Web server, the Web server will send back a response containing the requested Web page. The response is separated in two sections: the HTTP headers, which contain metadata about the document, and the document itself. Included in the HTTP header is the cookie that tags the user as unique visitor. When the user's browser requests another page from the same server, it will send the cookie back to the Web server to identify itself. Advanced Web site analysis techniques will capture this cookie information, and use it to identify new visitors compared to repeat visitors.

Collecting data at the application server level can clearly solve all the problems previously mentioned. The application server has full knowledge of the content being served. This is correct even when the content is dynamically generated or encoded for transmission. The application server controls sessions, user registration, login and logout. Thus, associating the user with a particular clickstream is easy. These can be directly logged and no heuristics are required. The application server can also be designed to gather information, such as pages that were aborted, local time of the user, speed of the user's connection and if the cookies are turned off. Redundancy of information is removed when the application server controls logging. For existing sites, however, re-architecting the whole system for application server logging may be too expensive (Ansari et al., 2002; Greening, 2000).

Business event logging. The data obtained from the application server has a significant amount of valuable information; however, further insight can be gained by considering the particular subsets of requests as one logical event or episode (Cooley et al., 1999; Osmar, Xin & Han, 1998). These aggregations of requests are called business events. Business events are also helpful in recognizing important user actions like sending an e-mail or searching (Schmitt, Manning, Yolanda & Tong, 1999).

Since the application server has the responsibility for maintaining the context of a user's session and related data, the application server is the rational choice for logging these business events. Business events can be used to track things like the content of discarded shopping carts, which are exceptionally hard to track using just request data. Business events also enable marketers to look past hit rates to microconversion rates (Gomory et al., 1999). A microconversion rate is referred to as the fraction of products that are successfully passed through to the next phase of purchasing process. Examples of microconversion rate include: the fraction of product views that ended up in the product being added to the shopping cart and the fraction of products in the shopping cart that successfully passed through each phase of the checkout process. The result is providing marketers the ability to look directly at product views and product sales that are far more powerful than just page views and click-throughs. Some interesting business events that help with the analysis phase are the following:

- Add/remove item to/from shopping cart,
- Initiate checkout,
- Finish checkout, and
- Search and register events.

Measuring personalization success. Including a rule engine that runs and personalizes the Web site can enhance the proposed model. Rules can be deployed for offering promotions to visitors and displaying specific products or content to a specific visitor. Following the firing of the rules, business events can be employed to identify the impact of deploying these rules. A business event can be logged each time that a rule is fired in personalization, and these events, along with the shopping-cart/checkout event, can provide an excellent estimate of the effectiveness of each rule (Ansari et al., 2002).

Similar data collection techniques can be employed for all the customer touch points. Examples include customer service representatives and wireless applications. Collecting the accurate data is crucial to effective analysis of an e-commerce operation.

Analysis

This section describes the analysis component of our model. We start with a discussion of data transformations, followed by analysis techniques.

The data warehouse is the source of data in this model. Many analyses require data transformation that converts the source data to a format friendlier to DM.

Since customers are the main focus of any e-commerce business, most DM analyses are at the customer level. That is, each record of a data set at the final stage of an analysis is a customer "signature," containing all the information about the customer. However, the majority of the data in the data warehouse is at other levels such as the order header level, the order item line level and the page request level. Each customer may have multiple rows at these levels. To make this detailed information useful for analyses at the customer level, aggregation transformation is necessary. Here are some examples of data items (attributes) that are useful:

- What percentage of each customer's orders used an American Express credit card?
- How much money does each customer spend on CDs?
- What is the total amount of each customer's five most recent purchases over $50?
- What is the frequency of each customer's purchase?

These attributes are very hard to construct using standard SQL statements, and they need powerful aggregation transformation. Model generation using DM algorithms is a key to the process. It reveals patterns about customers, their purchases, page views, etc. (EMetrics Study, 2001). By generating models, we can answer questions like the following:

- What characterizes heavy spenders?
- What characterizes customers who prefer promotion X over Y?
- What characterizes customers who accept cross sells and up sells?
- What characterizes customers who buy quickly?
- What characterizes visitors who do not buy?

Reporting

In an era of information overload, managers need to have quick access to information that impacts their business. Providing actionable information to mangers is very important in a complex and distributed environment. Reports should provide information about visitors' preferences and behavior, and the success of business initiatives. Typical outputs of Web mining systems include reports on marketing, advertising, technical analysis, long-term trends and management summaries. Reports can be simultaneously produced as HTML, Word or ASCII format (*A Buyer's Guide to eBusiness Intelligence,* 2001). A quality reporting system will include features, such as remote reporting, as well as drill-down features. Information is most useful when users can quickly drill down and examine attention-grabbing trends and anomalies. These features relieve system administrators from creating custom reports for each user, and provide managers with the information they need when they need it. Examples of questions that can be answered using reporting are:

- What are the top selling products?
- What are the worst selling products?
- What are the top viewed pages?
- What are the top failed searches?
- What are the conversion rates by brand?
- What are the top referrers by sales amount?

Given that humans are very good at identifying patterns from visualized data, visualization and online analytical processing (OLAP) tools can greatly help business users to gain insight into business problems, by complementing reporting tools and DM algorithms (EMetrics Study, 2001).

ECRM

Customer relationship management (CRM) is interested in managing the link between the business and the customer. Larger companies are recognizing the need for having full coordination between all customer-facing functions by integrating people, processes and technology to optimize relationships with all customers (Coldwell, 2002). With the advent of the Internet, the role of CRM within an organization is changing. eCRM is not just electronic CRM (CRM Community, 2002). It is about improving organizations' ability to effectively conduct Web-based campaigns, follow leads, translate leads into sales, provide responsive service and support internal and external customers and partners (Agrawal & Mittal, 2002).

Key success factors. The technologies that provide eCRM must support the following capabilities that determine the key success factors (Harvey, 2001; CRM, 2002):

- Gather customer data from all organizational data sources to assure a complete view of customer;
- Provide the right information about customers to selected employees who must have it, in the specific format they need and when they need it;
- Everyone throughout the enterprise must be able to see and understand the value of each customer's relationship;
- The analysis and insight must be accessible real time or near real time across the enterprise;
- The analysis must provide the foundation for taking proper steps for dealing with the customer, steps that build upon the present value and increase the future value of the relationships;
- The tools needed to implement these kinds of systems cannot be a one-size-fits-all solutions. Companies have a broad range of information needs, which varies from complex customer segmentation analysis to viewing customer account information over the Internet;
- Form an internal eCRM team that represents all facets of the business that will be using the new system;

- Determine the training required for the company to support the new system, i.e., system administration, development, DBA, etc.; and
- Roll out the eCRM system in phases.

One example of eCRM is Ernex Marketing Technologies, a subsidiary of the Royal Bank of Canada. It provides customer information to its clients in retail, hospitality and leisure industries — companies like Nike, Executive Inns, and Eddie Bauer. Ernex has to supply the right kind of insight to assist its clients to advertise and sell to their customers more profitably. To do so, Ernex gives its clients detailed reports about their customers' shopping activities and purchasing behaviors. Ernex collects customer information, in real time, from a variety of sources, including transactional and special discount cards (loyalty programs) data, and provides these data and its analysis of the data to clients through personalized Web portals. Thus, for example, during a sales transaction, when the special discount card is swiped, Ernex can deliver the insight needed to assist its client in determining how to deal with this particular customer. The client can use the information to suggest other products or offer further discounts. Ernex provides reports for its clients to help them better understand their customers' behavior, by keeping track of items such as average purchase, average purchase size and frequency of transactions by geography, demographics and time. From these reports, clients can drill into the multidimensional OLAP data cubes to investigate and examine their customer data and identify what's driving customer purchases (Harvey, 2001).

RESEARCH ISSUES

In this section, we describe several challenging problems in mining e-commerce data. The complexity and granularity of these problems differ and they are candidates for further research (Ansari et al., 2002; Kohavi, 2001):

1. Make DM models understandable to users — Users need to understand the results of DM. Summary reports and visualized data are easy to follow and usually not difficult to produce. Few DM models, however, are easy to understand. The challenge is to define more model types and ways of presenting them to decision makers. For example, how can one represent nearest neighbor models?

2. Make data transformation and model building accessible to users — The ability to provide an answer to a question asked by a user needs some data transformations and technical understanding of tools. Even commercial report designers and OLAP tools are too difficult for most users. Two possible solutions include: (a) Provide templates (e.g., reporting templates, OLAP cubes and recommended transformations for mining) for common questions. (b) Provide assistance through help desks and consultants. The challenge is to identify ways that users are able to find answers to their questions on their own.

3. Handle large amount of data — In December 1999, Yahoo had about 465 million page views per day (*CFO Magazine*, 2000). It is important to find techniques that will handle this volume of data.

4. Support and model external events — External events are events such as marketing promotions and media ads. The challenge is to be able to model these events.

5. Support slowly changing dimensions — Demographics of visitors change over a period of time (people get divorced, their children move out, they change job, etc.). With these changes, their needs, which are being modeled, change as well. Product attributes also change, such as new options may be available (e.g., new colors), packaging material or design modification may become available. These attributes that alter over time are often called as "slowly changing dimensions" (Kimball, 1996). The challenge is to follow these changes and offer support for such changes in the analyses.

6. Identify bots and crawlers — Bots and crawlers (artificial intelligence agents) can significantly change clickstream patterns at a Web site. For example, Keynote (www.keynote.com) offers site performance measurements. The Keynote bot can produce a request multiple times a minute, 24 hours a day, seven days a week, skewing the statistics about the number of sessions, page hits and exit pages (last page at each session). Also, search engines conduct breadth first scans of the site, generating many requests in short duration. These options create additional clickstreams and patterns. Spotting such bots to filter clickstreams is a nontrivial task, especially for bots that pretend to be real users.

7. Support multiple granularity levels — Data collected in a typical Web site holds records at various levels of granularity:

- Page views are at the lowest level with attributes such as product viewed and duration.

- Sessions contain attributes such as browser used, initiation time, referring site and cookie information. Each session may include multiple page views.

- Customer attributes include name, address and demographic information. Each customer may be part of multiple sessions.

The challenge is to develop algorithms that can handle multiple granularity levels appropriately.

· WEB MINING STATISTICS

Practitioners and researchers collected and analyzed a large volume of the Web mining statistics that can be helpful to developers of both e-commerce and Web mining applications. The following is a set of guidelines for Web mining development (Kohavi, 2001):

- Buyers and browsers are following quite different browsing models. The average visitor stays five minutes on the site and views eight to 10 pages. However, a buyer typically stays an average of 30 minutes at the site, viewing about 50 pages. These time and volume limitations should be considered when designing as effective Web site.

- About half of the sessions are less than one minute. And, about a third of sessions never going beyond the home page. The conclusion is that the designers of Web pages need to pay attention in making the home page appealing.

- Only a small percentage of visitors use the search feature. However, those that search buy more. Focusing on search capability and, if possible, capturing characteristics of the users who do the search will significantly increase the effectiveness of the Web site.

- Less than 0.5 percent of the visitors read the privacy policy. Nevertheless, its presence in the Web site is an important and reassuring factor.
- Approximately, one third of the shopping carts are dumped, so the capacity to maintain shopping carts should be increased by at least 50 percent over the projected number of the actual buyers.
- Be careful to identify crawlers and bots. On an average, 25-30 percent of traffic can come from crawlers and bots. This number may grow over a period of time and go as high as 70. It is a prudent strategy for a Web site developer to implement tools that can control and protect the Web site's traffic.

CONCLUSION

The World Wide Web is continuously growing and gathering all kinds of resources, text, applications, etc. Organizations that are serious about their online investment, must understand who is visiting their Web site and how the visitors are using it. Web sites can provide significant amount of data for mining. However, the simple approach of relying on Web logs is not acceptable and additional data must be collected and analyzed. Web mining can help to understand the user behavior. This information allows managers to make better business decisions by directing their marketing efforts toward their best customers. Sophisticated analysis can be performed easily and inexpensively with today's powerful Web mining software. In this chapter, we have provided detailed review of the three components of Web mining and eCRM along with research issues that need to be further addressed.

REFERENCES

A Buyer's Guide to eBusiness Intelligence. (2001). Retrieved from http://www.accrue.com.

Agrawal, V., & Mittal, M. (2002). Customer relationship management: The e11 way. *Data Business Review, 3*(1). Retrieved June 11, 2002 from http://www.gantthead.com/gantthead/departments/divisionpage/1,1518,148,00.html.

Analyzing Web Site Traffic. (2001). San Solutions, LLC. Retrieved June 15, 2002 from http://www.sane.com/products/nettracker/whitepapers.html.

Ansari, S., Kohavi, R., Mason, L., & Zheng, Z. (2002*). Integrating e-commerce and data mining: Architecture and challenges.* Retrieved April 15, 2002 from http://citeseer.nj.nec.com/update/353413.

Berry, M., & Linoff, G. (2000). *Mastering data mining.* New York: John Wiley & Sons.

CFO Magazine. (2000, April).

Coldwell, J. (2002). *Are you in a (customer) relationship?* Retrieved April 15, 2002 from http://www.crmcommunity.com/content/display/80E7971D-ADB1-4778-BFB3D505B9071FBC.pdf.

Cooley, R., Mobasher, B., & Sricastava, J. (1999). Data preparation for mining World Wide Web browsing patterns. *Knowledge and Information Systems, 1*(1), 5-32.

CRM Community. (2002). Retrieved April 15, 2002 from http://www.crm.community.com/library/fundamentals.cfm.

EMetrics Study. (2001). *Blue Martini Software*. Retrieved April 15, 2002 from http://developer.bluemartini.com/developer/articles/index/jsp.

Gomory, S., Hoch, R., Lee, J., Podlaseck, M., & Schonberg, E. (1999). Analysis and visualization of metrics for online merchandizing. *Proceedings of WEBKDD '99*. Retrieved November 15, 2001 from http://www.wiwi.hu-berlin.de/myra/WEBKDD99.

Greening, D. (2000) *Data mining on the Web: There's gold in that mountain of data*. Retrieved April 17, 2002 from http://www.webtechniques.com/archieves/2000/01/greeing.

Harvey, L. (2001). Building customer value across the enterprise. Retrieved November 16, 2001 from the Patricia Seybold Group at http://www.psgroup.com.

Kimball, R. (1996). *The Data Warehouse ToolKit: Practical techniques for building dimensional data warehouses*. New York: John Wiley & Sons.

Kimball, R. (2000). The special dimensions of the clickstream. *Intelligent Enterprise, 3*(2).

Kimball, R., & Merz, R. (2000). *The Data Webhouse Toolkit: Building the Web-enabled data warehouse*. New York: John Wiley & Sons.

Kohavi, R. (2001). Mining e-commerce data: The good, the bad, and the ugly. KDD 2001, San Francisco, CA.

Kohavi, R., & Provost, F. (2001). Applications of data mining to electronic commerce. *Data Mining and Knowledge Discovery, 5*(1/2), 1-7.

Konrad, R. (2001). *Will data mining revolutionize e-commerce?* Retrieved November 15, 2001 from http://news.com.com/2009-1017-252162.html?legacy=cnet&tag=lh.

Mirsky, D. (2001, May). *Tap your web site's log files to improve CRM*. Retrieved November 14, 2001 from the Customer Inter @ Ction Solutions Web site: http://www.tradepub.com/free/ccs/.

Myers, R. (2000, April). E-tailers and space invaders. *CFO Magazine*. Retrieved November 17, 2001 from http://www.cfo.com/issues/1,5457,345,00.html.

Osmar, R., Han, J., Li, Z., & Hou, J. (1998). *Mining multimedia data. Proceedings of CASCON '98: Meeting of Minds, Toronto, Canada*, 83-96. Retrieved November 14, 2001 from www.cs.ualberta.ca/~zaiane/htmldocs/publication.html.

Osmar R., Xin, M., & Han, J. (1998). *Discovering Web access patterns and trends by applying OLAP and data mining technology on Web logs. Proceedings of Advances in Digital Libraries '98, Santa Barbara, CA*. Retrieved November 14, 2001 from www.cs.ualberta.ca/~zaiane/htmldocs/publication.html.

Schmitt, E., Manning, H., Yolanda, P., & Tong, J. (1999). Measuring Web success. *Forrester Report*.

Web mining white paper. (2001). Retrieved from the Accrue Software Inc. Web site: www.accrue.com.

Chapter XXII

A Framework for Organizational Data Analysis and Organizational Data Mining

Bernd Knobloch
University of Bamberg, Germany

ABSTRACT

This chapter introduces a framework for organizational data analysis suited for data-driven and hypotheses-driven problems. It shows why knowledge discovery and hypothesis verification are complementary approaches and how they can be chained together. It presents a methodology for organizational data analysis including a comprehensive processing scheme. Employing a plug-in metaphor, data analysis process engineering is introduced as a way to set up data analysis processes based on taxonomies of tasks that have to be performed during data analysis and on the idea of re-using experience from past data analysis projects. The framework aims at increasing the benefits of data mining and other data analysis approaches, by allowing a wider range of business problems to be tackled and by providing the users with structured guidance for planning and running analyses.

INTRODUCTION

The way from raw data to business intelligence is often long and difficult to take, and, sometimes, it does not even lead to where you are heading. Since the time when data mining became popular, lots of methods and algorithms have been proposed, enabling efficient mining of large data sets. However, there are more steps to take than merely putting an algorithm to work on some data. The process embracing all these steps is known as knowledge discovery in databases (KDD). Some KDD tool vendors have covered process issues and provide features for defining sequences of processing steps tailored to meet the specific needs of individual mining cases. However, some, if not most of these approaches ignore conceptual questions, such as which business goal is to be pursued, which data are necessary for producing the desired information, which aspects of data organization have to be taken into account, etc. The need for a human-centered, process-oriented view on knowledge discovery has long been neglected. Analysts need more support in understanding how to do knowledge discovery (Brachman & Anand, 1996). As Smyth (2001) puts it, users "will almost certainly not say that they need a slightly more accurate decision tree algorithm, or a slightly faster association rule algorithm. Instead their most pressing problem is that of managing the whole process." It's well understood that methods are elementary, but they are of very limited use, if you don't know how to properly employ them to solve your business problems.

Moreover, discussion has almost always been restricted to data mining analyses. Data mining, however, is simply one of several approaches to data analysis. Focusing solely on data mining bears the risk of not applying the one analytical approach that fits the current business objective best. Why rule out the potentials of other approaches, if data mining is not the ultimate choice? Why not combine the strengths of different instruments for data analysis to obtain the best results possible? Why not think big and put the pieces of the puzzle together, constructing an overall framework for business intelligence?

This chapter introduces an organizational framework that helps mend some of the shortcomings mentioned above. That framework provides structured guidance to analysts for putting data analysis to work and covers different approaches to organizational data analysis. It may also serve as reference for documentation of project experience.

BACKGROUND

User support for data analysis is crucial in terms of efficiency. Data analysis is profitable only if the return gained from newly discovered insights is higher than the costs produced by the analysis effort. The efficiency issue has received surprisingly little attention from KDD research. However, some progress has been made.

Brachman and Anand (1996) investigate the interactions between humans and data during analysis, which are important for development of knowledge discovery support tools. Knobloch and Weidner (2000) have taken a problem-oriented approach to infer requirements for analysis tools that help reduce inefficient iterations in the analysis process.

Skalak (2001) suggests three areas for additional research in the data mining field to make data analysis processes more efficient. These areas are modeling the mining process, support for data preparation and automated model selection. Interestingly enough, these topics have already been addressed with considerable success. The Cross-Industry Standard Process for Data Mining (CRISP-DM) is a comprehensive model for analysis processes (Chapman, Clinton, Kerner, Khabaza, Reinartz, Shearer & Wirth, 2000) and may serve as recommendable reference. The European Mining Mart project deals with partially automated selection and configuration of preprocessing operations and data mining models. This is accomplished by employment of case-based reasoning to re-use best practices and by multistrategy learning methods for case adaptation (Mining Mart: Enabling End-User Data Warehouse Mining, 2002). In the MetaL project, a similar approach has been pursued, applying metaknowledge and metalevel learning to model selection and method combination (MetaL: A Meta-Learning Assistant for Providing User Support in Machine Learning and Data Mining, 2001). Both projects aim at development of user-oriented KDD support environments.

In spite of the considerable success delivered by these projects, further research is necessary. Still, emphasis lies on knowledge discovery, and other forms of data analysis are hardly addressed. The following sections intend to contribute further ideas to data analysis process research, enabling analysts to deploy data mining technology more efficiently and more effectively within organizations. To achieve that, some of the ideas outlined above are combined and extended to form a comprehensive framework for organizational data analysis.

DATA MINING, KNOWLEDGE DISCOVERY AND DATA ANALYSIS: THE BIG PICTURE

What is Data Mining?

Intuitively, one might think about data mining as a metaphor for the more scientific expression knowledge discovery: digging in large amounts of data on the quest for valuable pieces of knowledge. This analogy makes a good starting point. Klösgen and Zytkow (1996) brand data mining a "folklore term" for the application of low-level methods of data analysis. There is also a difference in meaning, though: Whereas data mining refers to extraction of patterns from data, knowledge discovery has a much broader scope, aiming at discovery not of mere patterns, but of valid and useful knowledge (Fayyad, Piatetsky-Shapiro & Smyth, 1996). In order to test whether the patterns identified in the data may be viewed as useful knowledge, they have to be verified and interpreted. Moreover, discovery of valid patterns is only possible if the data they are extracted from are of good enough quality, i.e., if the data have been accordingly preprocessed and if errors have been eliminated. This includes that the methods employed for pattern extraction need to be supplied with appropriately represented data, otherwise they may not properly work (Pyle, 1999). All these issues of data preparation, pattern extraction and evaluation are covered by the KDD process.

Summing up, knowledge discovery from databases is a special form of data analysis aiming at gaining new knowledge. Achievement of this goal requires a step of pattern extraction known as data mining along with further processing steps.

Knowledge Discovery and Hypothesis Verification

If KDD is a special form of data analysis, which other forms exist? Data analysis is performed in order to obtain answers to specific questions. One distinctive criterion to identify different types of data analysis is the role hypotheses play in the analysis. Hypotheses are statements that claim to be true, in terms of certain objects in a domain, and that can be tested against data or knowledge about these objects (Klösgen & Zytkow, 1996).

When you have a concrete idea about what you want to know by analyzing data, you have a hypothesis in mind. Typically, data analysis problems try to find answers to questions such as "What were the sales in Central Europe in 2001?" or "How many customers that bought diapers also bought beer?" In these cases, it is known rather well what to look for in the database, and analysis amounts to nothing more than retrieval and summary[1] (Pyle, 1999). The ideas guiding analysis are hypotheses in the broadest sense. In the second example, we suppose that there are at least some customers who bought both products together. Traditional statistics, SQL database queries or online analytical processing (OLAP) are typical approaches to that kind of problem.

If you don't have an exact idea about what to look for, then the questions you want to be answered will be less concrete and will often start with "How do I...?" or "Why is it that...?" (Pyle, 1999). Here, you demand ideas concerning a specific problem or domain. For example, you might want to know, "Which customers should I address in a target marketing campaign for upgrades of mobile phone contracts?" or "Which products are typically bought together in a shopping transaction?" As you do not yet have concrete ideas about what to do to solve your business problem, you will ask for suggestions based on patterns found in the data. These suggestions can be seen as hypotheses, as they still have to be evaluated in terms of utility and other criteria. This kind of analytical problem may be solved with data mining methods.

This discussion leads us to two basic types of data analysis. On the one hand, there are hypotheses-driven problems, aiming at verification or falsification of assumptions or "ideas" by inspecting the database. They are known as top-down approaches to data analysis, starting from business questions (hypotheses) to be answered by querying the data. On the other hand, there are data-driven problems, starting without concrete assumptions, and letting the data lead the way to discover new knowledge. These problems represent a bottom-up approach, autonomously searching the data for hypothetical patterns that might be of interest to the user and may constitute knowledge (Berry & Linoff, 1997; Knobloch, 2001).

The problem-oriented perspective on data analysis presented here allows for flexible mapping of analysis methods to problem types. Types of data analysis problems (especially data mining or KDD) are often defined in terms of methods or algorithms. However, this approach is problematic, since there is no consensus about which methods are data mining methods and which are not. To avoid confusion, we take the view that data analysis and its specializations are all tasks determined by certain problems. At this point, it is irrelevant how these tasks may be achieved (Knobloch, 2001). As Pyle (1999) states, the technologies themselves are not an answer, but simply tools to support the analyst with finding an answer.

Chaining Discovery and Verification Problems

Knowledge discovery is a bottom-up approach to data analysis that, in principle, does not require hypotheses to be tested, but comes up with new hypotheses in the form of patterns. More "classical" forms of analysis, by contrast, demand the definition of hypotheses to verify or to falsify it. Whereas top-down analyses can be executed stand alone, bottom-up analyses require some kind of follow-up evaluation or verification process, in order to assess the extracted patterns in terms of being new knowledge.

This suggests a combination of these two complementary forms of data analysis, making up a cycle of hypothesis generation and hypothesis testing chained together. First, when employing a bottom-up approach, we sift through the data producing hypothetical patterns. Second, in a top-down analysis, we inspect the database for proofs of these hypotheses (Adriaans & Zantinge, 1996). Comprehensive discovery may only take effect when this cycle as "the very heart of the discovery process" is implemented (Brachman & Anand, 1996). The cycle may be run through repeatedly, thus enabling complex search-and-test scenarios.

Case Study: Market Basket Analysis

To illustrate how our framework can guide organizational data analysis, we introduce a case study used throughout this chapter. It is taken from the retail domain and employs the popular problem of market basket analysis.

Suppose a supermarket chain wants to increase sales by improving advertisement. Management, therefore, needs to know the characteristics of typical shoppers in their stores, in order to gain knowledge about customer preferences. That knowledge can be used to set up campaigns tailored to selected customers' needs.

An initial problem inferable from the business objective of improving advertisement is to find customer groups with similar buying habits. That problem can be solved by database segmentation, representing a bottom-up approach. It generates hypotheses about what types of shoppers might exist, such as young, ecologically minded high-income families, etc. These hypotheses could need verification, suggesting top-down analysis on the same data, leading to a new analytical problem. If some of the identified segments can be confirmed, those of special interest can be selected to investigate their cross-selling behavior, i.e., which products they bought in one shopping transaction. This initiates another bottom-up problem of dependency detection within sets of

Figure 1. A Simple Scenario of an Organizational Data Analysis Cycle

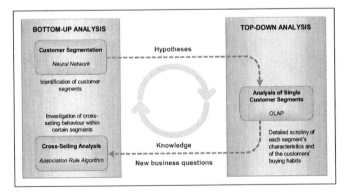

shopping items. The insights gained can serve as orientation for choosing products that should be advertised.

Figure 1 illustrates the resulting problem chain, showing how this data analysis cycle may be employed in a business context. Once the cycle has been completed, new analytical questions will arise, initiating a new cycle (Knobloch, 2001).

Organizational Data Analysis

What we have learned from the previous sections is that data analysis comes in several forms, and that chaining problems of different types can be of great use. When dealing with data mining, people often fail to recognize that there are other analytical approaches as well, and that data mining is not appropriate for solving every problem (Pyle, 1999). Many business questions can be answered better or equally well through top-down analysis. Engaging in complex knowledge discovery projects in cases where OLAP, for instance, would also do is an overshooting, not only time consuming and difficult, but also costly and inefficient.

In many situations, organizational data analysis problems can hardly be solved by means of a single analytical approach. Here, it is simply not sufficient to run a data mining analysis, or to use OLAP alone. On the contrary, the real potential of analyzing organizational data can only be exploited if various complementary approaches are combined. Any approach that may help to answer business questions or to come up with new actionable information can be of use, and it is highly recommendable to always employ the most suitable approach (Adriaans & Zantinge, 1996).

Obviously, we need to see the big picture. Data mining, or knowledge discovery, is simply one approach to data analysis, but there are others. Putting them together in an overall view of organizational data analysis is imperative if business value is to be produced. However, doing so further complicates the situation. Hence, we need support in terms of an overall methodology for organizational data analysis, providing structured guidance to the user.

A METHODOLOGY FOR ORGANIZATIONAL DATA ANALYSIS

Cases of Organizational Data Analysis

Organizational data analysis may be conceptualized into cases. A case describes the circumstances under which an analysis is carried out, and is defined by two elements: an analytical problem that has to be solved and a method suited for solving the problem. Analytical problems, in turn, are defined by their objectives and the subjects under study. Objectives are inferred from business questions and are needed for directing the analysis. Subjects provide the data to be analyzed[2]. This concept allows one problem to be solved by means of different methods, and methods to be used for solving different problems, making up different cases (cf. Ferstl, 1979).

Let's go into more details of the market basket analysis problem introduced above. What is it all about? As the wording suggests, it is about inspecting market baskets — nothing more is said. In particular, this analytical problem can be clearly characterized by its subject, namely the customers' market baskets, i.e., the sets of products they bought, and its objective, namely getting to know the customers' behavior in terms of buying habits. (As market baskets are hard to inspect physically, typically point-of-sale data from checkout systems are used as subjects, providing the same information, but being easier to analyze.) Consequently, there is no limitation to studying cross-selling phenomena, as often assumed. On the contrary, any question concerning customer behavior inferable from market baskets may be asked. This flexibility results from the definition of analytical problems as combinations of objectives and subjects. More precise specification of the initial objective leads to specialized analytical problems (such as cross-selling analysis or customer segmentation in our case study). Changing the subject (e.g., altering data selection criteria, moving to a different aggregation level, etc.) creates problem variations. Hence, market basket analysis can mean inspection of the products bought, i.e., the contents of the basket (embracing cross-selling behavior), as well as studying any descriptive features of a purchase, such as the grand total of the basket, the number of products bought, the share of products coming from a certain group of commodities (e.g., dairy products), transaction date and time, information about the weather and so on. The range of descriptive features may even be extended to demographic data about the customer who undertook the purchase, provided this information is available.

Now enter the methods. Usually, association rule inducers are used to investigate cross-selling potentials, and clustering algorithms can be applied to identify customer segments. In addition to these data mining approaches, top-down methods can be used for answering an equally wide range of questions concerning customer behavior. For instance, you can use OLAP reports to further analyze customer segments determined by data mining, as shown in Figure 1.

This conceptualization of analytical problems helps find new fields of analysis by studying different subjects for pursuing the same business objectives, or by defining different objectives for inspecting identical subjects. Each pair of objectives and subjects produces new analytical problems to solve. Considering different types of analyses and methods for a given problem results in a variety of thinkable studies. Each of them makes up a case, including a specific process.

A Scheme for Organizational Data Analysis Projects

In a business context, data analysis makes sense only if the insights gained from it may be converted into actions generating business value. The discovered knowledge must, therefore, be deployed in some way (Adriaans & Zantinge, 1996). After deployment, the effects of the actions taken have to be measured in order to see whether or not they were successful (Berry & Linoff, 1997). In case they fail, other actions may be inferred from the analytical results or new analyses may be performed.

Applying the concept of cases introduced above in an analysis project, we walk through a certain scheme of action that can be viewed as a generic process for organizational data analysis. This process comprises the following steps (Knobloch, 2001; cf. Berry & Linoff, 1997):

1. determine the analytical problem by defining the objective and finding an appropriate subject to study;
2. find suitable methods to solve the problem and conduct the analysis by applying at least one of these methods;
3. act on the information gained during the analysis step; and finally

4.   evaluate the project in terms of the objective pursued, the success of the actions taken and further analytical problems inferable from the results.

This scheme of action is applicable to all kinds of analyses in an organizational or business context.

Determine the Problem

Data analysis cannot produce business value unless there is a clear statement of a business problem to tackle. This includes definition of success criteria for the overall engagement. Business objectives, however, are not suited well for defining problems of data analysis. They have to be broken down to analytical objectives. The latter can be formulated as questions that are to be answered through data analysis and should be derived from the former. Business objectives already include deployment aspects of analytical results.

The business objective in our case study is to increase sales by improving advertisement. In order to accomplish that, it is necessary to know how this goal may be best achieved. Therefore, concrete questions must be identified, such as who are the customers buying at our shops and what kind of preferences do they have.

These questions may be answered by means of data analysis, which makes them suitable as analytical objectives (Pyle, 1999; Chapman et al., 2000). Problem determination should start from the user's interests and expectations and is essential for focusing the analysis (Klösgen & Zytkow, 1996).

The analytical problem includes specification of the data to be studied, i.e., the subject. Sometimes, available data can be the driver for problem determination. Once you have realized that some databases contain information about certain aspects of your business, this may instantly lead you to interesting analytical objectives you haven't thought of before (Knobloch, 2001). Imagine you find out that you have information about the weather and the outside temperature available for each day. Joining market basket data with this information, you are able to study the influence weather has on sales of certain products. It is, therefore, recommended that you provide the analyst with an overview of the information content available in the data stores.

Conduct Analysis

This is the main phase of the project, investigating available data to achieve the objectives specified. It will be covered in detail in the section Solving Organizational Data Analysis Problems. It is important to remember that any effort to produce business intelligence may be employed within that phase, from conducting marketing panels and customer surveys to evaluation of simple reports or from running statistics to OLAP queries and data mining analyses.

Deploy Results

Deployment of analytical results[3] may take several forms. The most desirable one is to directly take action, e.g., carrying out a target marketing campaign, based on the insight that a certain group of customers is most likely to respond to mailings. Another is to incorporate the newly gained knowledge into operative processes, such as implementing an online system for suggesting products to customers that they might be interested in, as is current practice in online book stores. A third — however, not very specific — way is to disseminate the results to interested persons without a specific action in mind, hoping that they might be of general use or gain value in some future context (Brachman & Anand, 1996; Knobloch, 2001).

Moreover, the deployment stage may consist of further analysis projects, if discovered hypotheses still need verification against other data. This is what we do in our case study, when investigating mined customer segments by means of OLAP reports (cf. Figure 1). Like this, one analysis project may incorporate others.

Evaluate the Project

Problem chaining may also take place within the evaluation stage, if project A's success is to be measured through a different analytical approach B. In this case, evaluation points back to the first project phase of problem determination (or, sometimes, if the problem specification is robust over time, to phase two), thus making up a continuous analytical cycle and creating a closed loop of control. Actions based on the outcome of data analysis are documented in transactional data, which, in turn, are analyzed, leading to new decisions and actions and so forth. Like this, data analysis itself becomes an operational process (Knobloch, 2001).

Project evaluation is often neglected (Berry & Linoff, 1997; Smyth, 2001), but it should become clear that it is elementary for knowing if your efforts have made sense and whether to make changes to your strategies, objectives, data, processes or actions.

SOLVING ORGANIZATIONAL DATA ANALYSIS PROBLEMS

Processes as Solutions to Data Analysis Problems

To solve an analytical problem, it is not sufficient to run an analysis algorithm on the data. Aspects such as data extraction, subsampling, preprocessing, analysis and interpretation of results are all crucial for an analysis project to become a success. Hence, a whole process made up from several single steps has to be executed[4]. From this perspective, the initial analytical problem incorporates a complex construction problem: finding the right process for a given analysis project. This process may be viewed as the overall method for solving the problem. Mining algorithms and the like represent only partial solutions applied as techniques within that process.

On a very abstract level, analysis processes may be divided up into three generic phases (Knobloch, 2001; cf. Bigus, 1996): (1) preprocessing the raw data, (2) analyzing the data, and (3) postprocessing the results.

Preprocessing the Raw Data

The preprocessing phase comprises such tasks as selection, extraction or sampling of data sets for analysis, as well as all efforts to minimize the effects of the "garbage in, garbage out" rule. This means that faulty data may produce erroneous or, at least, misleading results, and should, therefore, be avoided.

Thorough inspection of the data prior to analysis is highly recommended in order to prevent low-quality data from being fed into the algorithms. We refer to this task as data exploration, also known as data auditing or data surveying (Pyle, 1999). It is important to notice that the purpose of data exploration is not only to detect data quality problems, but also to get a feel for the data under study (Brachman & Anand, 1996). During exploration, the analyst gains knowledge about the content and applicability of the data, as well as ideas about how to use them for producing the best possible results.

The insights gained during exploration can be used to process the data so that they better address the problem to be solved. All the tasks dealing with enriching the data by additional variables or records, cleansing the data of bad records and fields, correcting false values or filling missing fields, removing inconsistencies and transforming inappropriate data representations are collectively called data manipulation (Knobloch, 2001).

Analyzing the Data

The actions to be taken during the analysis phase depend on the type of analysis to be conducted, which, in turn, depends on the desired results. As discussed before, there are top-down and bottom-up approaches to data analysis. Knowledge discovery tasks, e.g., are often specialized into data mining (dealing with structured data), text mining (unstructured data) and sometimes mining the Web. Data mining is generally further differentiated into generating predictive models, deviation detection, relationship detection and database segmentation (cf. Cabena, Hadjinian, Stadler, Verhees & Zanasi, 1997).

Postprocessing the Results

After analysis, the results produced must be evaluated to ensure that they are representative and valid. Findings that don't match defined criteria of significance and interestingness have to be filtered out, as they don't constitute new knowledge. Another elementary task on that stage is to interpret the results in order to make their statements actionable (Knobloch, 2001).

Appropriate presentation of new findings requires comprehensible output reports be produced (Brachman & Anand, 1996). This may involve application of visualization or presentation tools. Sometimes, it may be necessary to transform the results prior to presenting them to the user. Imagine neural networks, requiring numerical representation of the input data. To prevent the analyst from being confronted with the original network output (e.g., predicted target variables) in numerical format, it may be desirable to have the representation change undone, transforming the numerical values back into nominal ones (Pyle, 1999).

Another postprocessing task is automatic description of nonexplanatory black-box models, such as neural networks. That type of model hides the predictive knowledge it implicitly contains. For example, a neural scoring model delivers no explanation of why a customer is being assigned that very score. To remedy that defect, a follow-up analytical problem may be solved, such as generating decision rules based on the neural network's predictive logic, providing an explanation for customer scoring (cf. Saarenvirta, 1998).

Taxonomy of Tasks

For better orientation and clarity, tasks like the ones outlined in the previous sections can be organized in taxonomies (cf. Skalak, 2001), assigning tasks to problem

Figure 2. Parts of a Taxonomy of Tasks

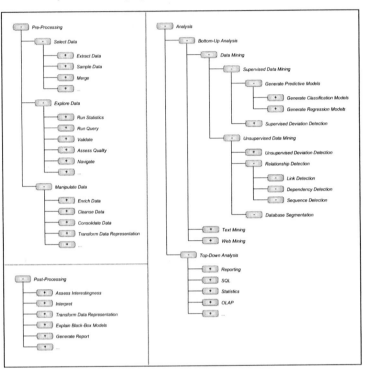

types. Each task may be recursively split up into more specialized tasks, incorporating more details of the analytical problem on hand. Figure 2 shows parts of a taxonomy of tasks. Similar individual taxonomies can easily be set up, thus enabling incorporation of different views and concerns. As for knowledge discovery, the CRISP-DM "step-by-step data mining guide" (Chapman et al., 2000) may serve as an orientation, but any other concept may be just as helpful.

General Structure of Analysis Processes

Generally, an analytical problem can be solved by running a process, executed by one or more actors. As introduced above, analytical problems are defined by an objective and the subject under study. The process constitutes the high-level method for tackling the problem.

Let's take a look at the inner structure of a process now, taking a problem-oriented view. In order to solve an analytical problem, one or more tasks have to be carried out. These tasks may be organized into schemes of action. A scheme of action is a sequence of tasks suited for solving either the analytical problem or a task on a higher level. Once assigned a method suitable to accomplish that task, a task becomes a step within a process. A step, therefore, is a specific method's application for fulfilment of a task. The methods are supplied by actors, such as software tools or users. The resulting sequence of steps constitutes the executable process for a specific data analysis project (Figure 3)[5]. If a scheme of action is generic, it is called a scheme template (or template for short).

Figure 3. Structure of Analysis Processes: Terminological Overview

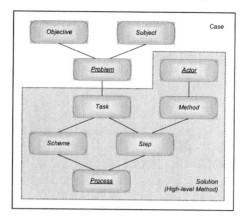

Then the sequence it defines is prototypical, serving as a proposal for the current context. Templates may be revised and adjusted as required.

The Complexity Problem: How to Set Up a Fitting Process?

Within the knowledge discovery context, many proposals have been made for what a typical KDD process might look like[6]. Since the specific conditions under which the projects have to be carried out differ strongly, it seems almost impossible to determine generic process schemes valid for any analytical problem, though. The situation worsens when lifting the restriction to data mining (data-driven analysis) and covering data analysis in general.

The elements of an analysis case determine how the process has to be set up: the requirements of the business context, the problem (objectives and data) and the methods and tools available must all be matched. Conceptually, this may sound easy. In practice, however, this is tiresome a task, not only time consuming, but also very demanding, requiring know how about analysis methods and databases, as well as business understanding (Kietz, Zücker & Vaduva, 2000). Analysts have to choose from a multitude of preprocessing operations, analytical approaches, algorithms, evaluation criteria, etc., and combine them in a feasible manner. The corresponding search space is characterized by a considerably high branching factor, imposing an enormously complex task on the analyst (Smyth, 2001).

Due to that complexity, real-life data analysis processes typically involve much trial and error, which makes them highly iterative. It is generally conceivable to imagine a return from any step to a previous one, making changes and then retracting the effects of tasks already performed (Skalak, 2001). Whenever the analyst realizes that he has failed to extract certain attributes from the data source, needs to make additional fixes to the data representation, or would better discretise a continuous variable to gain better results — he has to go back to previous process phases. Or having already completed preprocessing and started analyzing, he might end up with inappropriate mining results and find that he failed to recognize some problems and deficiencies in the data (Pyle,

1999). Consequently, he has to perform further manipulation tasks, inefficiently iterating over process parts.

All these difficulties are caused by strong interdependencies between process elements, i.e., tasks. The analytical problem determines which analytical approach is to be employed, pointing to suitable methods and to tools implementing them. These and the particular data sets on hand, in turn, influence how the data need to be prepared. For example, if rules are to be inferred, then a tool able to produce rules is needed, which might require special restructuring of the raw data (Pyle, 1999). The list of dependencies may be completed along the whole chain of preprocessing steps. While the more obvious interdependencies are comprehensible, this may not apply to all effects. The way in which a step affects others is often unclear, and some dependencies cannot be foreseen even theoretically (Skalak, 2001; Kietz et al., 2000). For example, the impact on the analytical outcome of including or omitting certain variables is often unknown (Krahl, Windheuser & Zick, 1998).

Hence, the phases suggested by idealistic process models usually cannot be walked through in a cascading, waterfall-like manner. A predefined sequence of actions can hardly be observed, except on a very abstract level. The three-step process model of preprocessing, analysis and postprocessing introduced above probably holds for most cases. However, it is doubtful whether such general schemes do really help much.

Process models can nevertheless be very handy for orientation. We prefer a task-oriented view to a process-oriented perspective, though. Taxonomies can help to structure tasks according to their contexts, and supplying lists of tasks that typically have to be accomplished in a certain context is less rigid than defining sequences. Imagine the high-level data manipulation task: As any other task on that level of abstraction, it may appear more than once in a process instance, and the single appearances need not be successive. Initial manipulations, such as joining multiple tables from different sources, along with some consolidation efforts, may take place right after extraction. After that, some data problems may be detected, necessitating further manipulation operations for tackling the defects. Initial results from subsequent modeling may suggest to discretise certain variables. Here, manipulation tasks are scattered over the whole process, intertwined with other tasks.

Data Analysis Process Engineering

The problem of designing data analysis processes aims at construction of a process able to solve a specified analytical problem. In other words, the desired behavior of the process (i.e., its ability to solve the problem) is the input to that design task, and the process structure is its output.

That design task can be formulated as an Artificial Intelligence (AI) planning problem (Skalak, 2001). If the task is to be carried out without a scientific planning tool at hand, it may best be done through trial and error, as is current practice (see above). A prototyping approach, iterative and incremental, as known from software development projects, generates functioning processes. Unfortunately, this approach does not score well enough in terms of efficiency (Knobloch & Weidner, 2000).

We believe that it is worthwhile to think about how at least some of the principles from engineering disciplines may be applied to process planning. You won't start building a house unless you know what it should exactly look like, breaking up rooms

already accomplished as you might find them unfitting to others you intend to build next
— will you? Seeing the big picture, defining requirements, selecting building blocks
appropriate to fulfil the requirements, and finally engineering the building blocks into a
fitting whole can make significant contributions to constructing effective processes
faster. "As the data mining process becomes better understood and more straightforward, it may be more efficient and more closely integrated into the business processes
of organizations" (Skalak, 2001).

Top-Down Process Planning: Stepwise Refinement

In engineering, abstraction is used as a tool to cope with the inherent complexity
of the systems that have to be designed (Ferstl, 1979). Abstraction means that mental or
explicit models[7] from systems are created that concentrate on components (and the
connections between them) that are crucial in the current context. Other components not
of interest are ignored for the time being.

Imagine a car. What constitutes a car — shock absorbers, camshaft and injection
nozzles? Certainly all of these are needed to build a modern car. But intuitively, when
thinking of a car, we will refer to more elementary components such as a chassis, an
engine, four wheels and so on. This is abstraction — focusing on the components of
interest in the current context. Abstraction is often used recursively, resulting in layers
of abstraction. A system consisting of components (A, B, C, D, E) may be viewed as a
more abstract system consisting of components (F, G), that, in turn, may be abstracted
to a single component H.

Generally, construction problems are solved by employing abstract representations of the system that is to be built and gradually refining them by concretization. The
ladder of abstraction is moved downward, getting more and more concrete. From a highly
abstract initial model, more detailed design models with decreasing abstraction are
derived, incorporating more and more functional requirements the system under design
has to fulfill. This process of concretization is repeated until an abstraction level
incorporating all of the relevant design features is reached (Ferstl, 1979). In the car
example, an engineer designing the engine will have to go deeper into the details of the
engine's structure, considering its parts and how they interact with another. The
engineer's view is the result of a concretization step from an abstract black-box engine.

Now let's employ this approach of stepwise refinement for structuring and planning
data analysis processes.

Suppose that we are planning an organizational data analysis project. In a first
concretization step, we can refine the black-box "data analysis project," according to the
scheme of action introduced in the section A Methodology for Organizational Data
Analysis, resulting in the four-task scheme 1 shown in Figure 4. As analytical problem,
we determine market basket analysis as discussed before, initially aiming at identification
of customer segments. Next, we are primarily interested in how to conduct the analysis.
Therefore, we may concretize the conduct analysis task within scheme 1 by identifying
three major subtasks: preprocessing, analysis and postprocessing (cf. section "Solving
Organizational Data Analysis Problems"). They need to be arranged in appropriate order,
constituting sequence 2. As the analysis phase is the "cornerstone" of an analysis
project (Brachman & Anand, 1996), we are advised to continue with detailing the
respective task. The type of analysis to be performed depends on the business objectives
specified in the determine problem step. As we decided to study customer groups

Figure 4. A Simplified Example Illustrating Methodology and Terminology

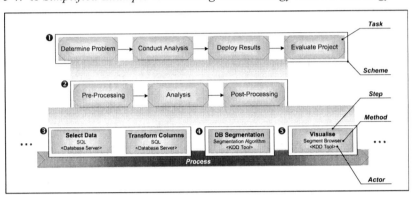

inferable from shopping transactions (data-driven database segmentation), we may choose an appropriate mining algorithm and a KDD tool implementing that method. At this level, we obtain an executable process step (4), since a method and an actor assigned to a task make up a step.

Knowing which data mining task to perform, we can now think about detailing the preprocessing task. Suppose for the moment that we know that there are two tasks to be accomplished in order to provide appropriate data for customer segmentation in our context. Here, these tasks are selecting some records from a database system and transforming representation of some data columns by SQL statements (data manipulation), resulting in scheme 3. To complete the process, we choose a visualization method for the postprocessing task (5). Associating methods and actors, we finally end up with a four-step executable process. The outcome of this hierarchical breakdown is a tree-like structure, as shown in Figure 4.

In order to methodically support the process of stepwise refinement of tasks onto a more detailed level of discourse and arranging them into schemes, taxonomies of tasks as proposed in Figure 2 may be taken into account. They can provide valuable orientation and can help with checking whether a process is complete in that it does not omit important steps, as well as a guideline for how deep we need to go into the details of a specific task. It is important to notice that the depth of the task tree constructed is not limited to a specific number of levels, and that the branches may feature different depths.

Since the initial tasks are inferred from the analytical problem, stepwise task refinement is often accompanied by simultaneous refinement of the problem statement. Refer to the section "Determine the Problem" for illustration of that aspect.

Figure 4 indicates another elementary aspect: differentiation between the level of applications and the level of methods (Knobloch, 2001; Ferstl & Sinz, 2001). As long as we are dealing with concepts such as objectives, subjects, tasks, and schemes, we act on an application-oriented level regardless of concrete implementations. Only on the lowest level within the task tree resulting from stepwise refinement do we take into account implementations of methods and corresponding actors. In other words, only the leaf nodes of the tree can be assigned actors. Actors may take two forms — human users or software tools. The latter allow the steps to be automated, the former demand nonautomated execution or human-computer interaction.

Bottom-Up Process Planning: Re-Using Past Experience

Top-down planning alone will not be sufficient. Remember that in the previous section, we mentioned that "we somehow know" that certain preprocessing tasks are necessary to provide the analysis tool with appropriate data. That kind of knowledge is not included in task taxonomies, containing mere structural information about is-a relationships between tasks. In data analysis, background knowledge of analytical issues as well as of the application domain is crucial (Brachman & Anand, 1996). Very often, analysis methods impose special restrictions concerning the representation of the input data. Neural networks, for instance, demand numerical data types. Method implementations through specific tools may have additional actor-specific requirements. There are many situations where analysis tasks necessitate special preprocessing operations, or generate new tasks to be included in the process. Thus, analysis processes cannot be planned without background knowledge of objectives, tasks, data, methods and tools. If that knowledge is not present prior to analysis, it has to be learned during the analysis project through trial and error, making the project inefficient and lengthy (Knobloch & Weidner, 2000).

To resolve this problem, we suggest complementary bottom-up planning. This means that analytical experience — be it generic or grounded on individual past analysis projects — can be retrieved and incorporated into the discovery process. To achieve that goal, a case-based reasoning (CBR) approach seems most promising (Kietz et al., 2000). Although the focus in CBR is on specific past experience that is represented as a case and can be adapted and re-used for solving a current problem (Aamodt & Plaza, 1994), we can also think of prototypical cases. For example, the case base may contain a case describing the fact that application of neural networks requires that the attributes of the input data be represented in numerical format. Other examples are cases that contain scheme templates for certain process tasks. The case base should include an additional number of cases representing concrete experiences from past projects. It is generally a good idea to store the heuristics that analysts use for solving problems (Skalak, 2001).

Supporting analysis process planning by CBR considerably eases the construction problem, and will lead to more efficient data analysis projects (Kietz et al., 2000). Since best practices and knowledge about optimized parameter sets for concrete methods and tools in specific contexts can be stored and re-used, analysis may also be more effective, i.e., results will tend to be more accurate.

Ideally, retrieved old cases can be directly re-executed as processes. CBR cases, however, need not include complete analytical cases. Referring to the general structure shown in Figure 3, CBR cases may contain project experience in whatever granularity needed. Besides complete processes, cases may represent single process steps, as well as tasks, schemes or problems. In general, any node of the task tree may be represented as a case in the case base, including or pointing to respective solution components, such as process parts or parameter sets for algorithms.

The knowledge represented in the taxonomy of tasks and the task tree can be used as indexing and selection criteria for case retrieval. Generally, a description of the business context and the analytical problem should be included in each CBR case, as well as more technical aspects, such as tasks, methods, actors, data characteristics, etc., depending on the scope of the case (Kietz et al., 2000). Like this, experience about individual data analysis projects may be recorded and re-used in the future.

A "Mining Kit" for Data Analysis Projects

The combination of the two complementary approaches to process planning introduced in the previous sections constitutes an orientation framework for organizational data analysis projects. Taking a problem-oriented perspective and starting at the top, then stepwise refinement of problems into tasks and of tasks into schemes leads to concrete steps of action that make up a process. This approach may be supplemented by a bottom-up approach, providing background knowledge and concrete experience from past cases that may be integrated into the structure where necessary (Kietz et al., 2000). Retrieved old cases may suggest appropriate discovery techniques (Brachman & Anand, 1996), tools, parameter settings, data specifications, data transformations and other processing steps, schemes, templates, problems and their solutions or whole analytical cases.

Like this, the whole variety of analytical cases, including all of their specializations can be structured in a methodological, but flexible manner. Facing a new problem, analysts can select the very process components they need to carry out an analysis, serving themselves from a kit of conceptual building blocks, and set up processes tailored to the specific needs of their project. The framework provides guidance to the user and copes with some of the inherent complexity of data analysis process planning by suggesting a modularization of processes. The "modules," i.e., tasks, schemes and steps, can first be fitted into the big picture as "black-boxes," before dealing with their inner structure. They can also be subject to documentation of analysis experience for later re-use. Generalizing conceptual elements and past experiences into modules, one can think of a flexible plug-in kit for data analysis problems, suited for hypotheses-driven and data-driven analysis problems, as well as for combinations thereof.

For each task on a certain level (within a "module"), the analyst has to decide whether it is necessary or feasible to refine it. In case he finds that a task needs further concretization, he may substitute it by a step, a scheme of action or a scheme template. This module is to be "plugged into" the task under consideration, creating a new level

Figure 5. The Basic Plug-In Idea

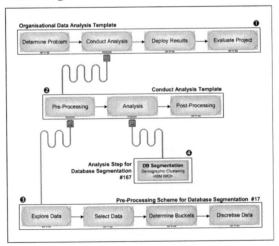

underneath, incorporating more details of the tasks to be performed, and, therefore, being less abstract.

Let's come back to our case study to see how we can employ the mining kit in this example (Figure 5). As before, we start with the organizational data analysis template (1) replacing the overall data analysis project. Within that scheme, we focus on the conduct analysis task, wondering how we can refine it. The mining kit generally presents us two alternatives. We can either navigate the task taxonomy in order to find a task or a set of tasks that can be substituted for the higher-level task. In case we want to plug in a set of tasks, we need to arrange them in appropriate order. This is the top-down approach. Alternatively, we can proceed bottom-up, asking the case base to suggest a module (a piece of generic knowledge or specific project experience) matching the current context. Sticking to the plug-in metaphor, we need a module fitting into the current task's socket. Suppose we can find an appropriate generic conduct analysis template (2) in the case base. We can retrieve this module and plug it into the respective task of scheme 1.

Figure 6. Case Study Process, Part 1

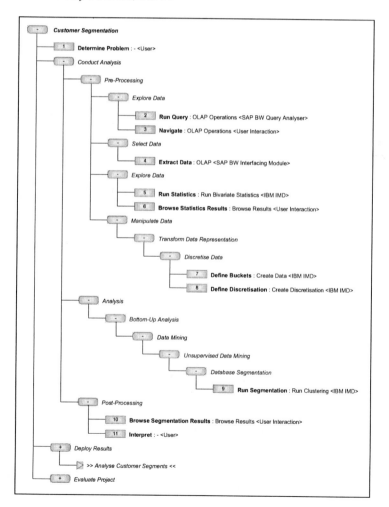

Figure 7. Case Study Process, Part 2

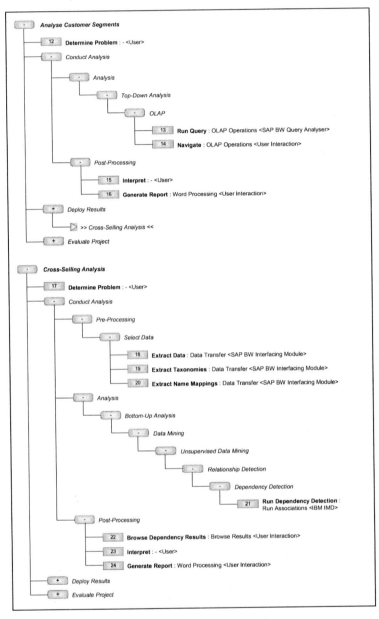

Stepping down on the newly created level, we concentrate on the analysis task, as our central goal is to do data analysis. In accordance with the objective of identifying customer segments, we could now browse the task taxonomy to end up with a specialized database segmentation task. As segmentation methods usually require a large number of parameters, we prefer to retrieve an old case from our repository, obtaining a proposal for method configuration. The associated parameter set may be re-used as is or adapted as needed. The executable processing step 4 is plugged into scheme 2.

The same plug-in idea applies to all the other tasks, on all levels of discourse. For the preprocessing task in scheme 2, we may decide to set up a new scheme based on the information from the task taxonomy, choosing four tasks and arranging them in a sequence (3). If the case base contained knowledge about a similar project, we could simply retrieve the respective case and plug the preprocessing scheme it contains into the process structure.

Complete process models for the chained analysis project introduced in Figure 1 are depicted in Figure 6 and Figure 7. These models include full context information from the taxonomy of tasks. The tree structures in the figures should be read top down. Rectangles symbolize executable process steps; triangles point to associated processes that are to be plugged in to accomplish the task. Each node in the tree constitutes a mining kit module (piece of knowledge) that may be substituted or refined. Modules representing executable process steps may include information about complete parameter sets. This way, the complicated task of variable discretisation may be supported by suggesting settings successfully applied in a past case. The same applies to configuration of the segmentation run and any other step in the process. The retrieved proposals may be revised and adjusted as required, and retained as new experience if proven feasible.

The case study is taken from a real-life project, employing a data warehouse system and a KDD tool[8] coupled by interfacing modules allowing for data and metadata transfers as described by Knobloch and Weidner (2000). Starting with consolidated data from a data warehouse, OLAP queries are used to select appropriate data sets for transfer to the KDD tool. Query results as shown on the OLAP worksheet can be directly transmitted to the KDD system together with their related metadata. The data are then explored by running univariate or bivariate statistics in order to get a feel for their structure and to determine buckets for the discretisation step. After running the segmentation analysis, the results can be browsed and interpreted. Within the deployment stage, the second problem (analyze customer segments) is solved (cf. Figure 7).

During that phase, the segments are further inspected by means of OLAP. After interpretation, a report documenting the findings is generated. Again, deployment means to conduct another analysis project. To study cross-selling behavior within a certain segment, transactional data related to the customers from the respective segment have to be selected within the OLAP tool and transferred to the mining system.

Furthermore, additional warehouse data, such as product taxonomies and name mappings (assigning labels to article codes), may be supplied for generating association rules. After detecting cross-selling phenomena through dependency detection, actionable rules are interpreted and selected and a report suggesting deployment of the discovered knowledge in advertisements is generated. Having taken action, the complete project and its single parts have to be evaluated in order to determine possible improvements for subsequent projects.

CONCLUSION AND FUTURE WORK

Data analysis project planning may be supported by a comprehensive methodology, providing guidance to the user for selecting appropriate analytical problems and chaining single problems to investigate complex phenomena. The flexible combination of objectives, data and methods often points to interesting new analytical questions that would otherwise not have come to the analyst's mind.

Data analysis processes can be set up by combining tasks and arranging them in appropriate order. The tasks that finally have to be accomplished can be determined by stepwise refinement. Starting from high-level tasks inferred from analytical problems, these tasks are gradually broken down into executable process steps. Whenever a point is reached in an analysis project where general background knowledge or past experience can help decide how to carry on, this expertise may be used in whatever granularity. It is generally recommend that you document the experience gained during a project for later re-use, in order to make it easier for subsequent projects in a similar context to produce results. Processing tasks and steps and the specific experience associated with them can be arranged in a hierarchical structure, assigning each piece of knowledge to which context it applies.

Efficient user support for data analysis can only take place, if tools implementing the methodology are available. To that end, we suggest data analysis support environments (DASE) as an extension to knowledge discovery support environments as described by Brachman and Anand (1996). These may be enhanced by mechanisms for self-tuning processing steps, e.g., by employment of metalevel learning (Smyth, 2001; MetaL, 2001). We can also think of public repositories of data analysis experience, enabling interorganizational sharing of expertise. To accomplish that, standardized metamodels for case description have to be developed (cf. Vaduva, Kietz, Zücker, Dittrich, Morik, Botta & Portinale, 2001).

ACKNOWLEDGMENTS

In addition to my colleagues in Bamberg, I would like to say thanks to Liana for her invaluable and continuing support, and to Karina, who has inspired me so much.

ENDNOTES

[1]   It should be clear that the process of retrieval and summary can be sufficiently complex in some situations.

[2]   Compare how a preprocessing case has been defined by Kietz, et al., (2000, p. 4).

[3]   In the data mining context, results are often called models. However, as we take a much broader scope embracing any approach to data analysis, we use the more general term results here.

[4]   The statements made before in the data mining context apply to any approach to data analysis.

[5]   For an excellent reference to KDD terminology, cf. Klösgen and Zytkow (1996).

[6]   One example is the CRISP-DM (Chapman, et al., 2000).

[7]   Note that here, model is not meant in terms of data mining models.

[8]   SAP Business Information Warehouse (SAP BW) and IBM Intelligent Miner for Data (IBM IMD).

REFERENCES

Aamodt, A., & Plaza, E. (1994). Case-based reasoning: Foundational issues, method-ological variations, and system approaches. *AICom – Artificial Intelligence Communications, 7*(1), 39-59.

Adriaans, P., & Zantinge, D. (1996). *Data mining.* Harlow, UK: Addison-Wesley.

Berry, M. J. A., & Linoff, G. (1997). Data mining techniques – For marketing, sales, and customer support. New York: John Wiley & Sons.

Bigus, J. P. (1996). *Data mining with neural networks – Solving business problems from application development to decision support.* New York: McGraw-Hill.

Brachman, R., & Anand, T. (1996). The process of knowledge discovery in databases. In U. Fayyad, G. Piatetsky-Shapiro, P. Smyth & R. Uthurusamy (Eds.), *Advances in knowledge discovery and data mining* (pp. 37-57). Menlo Park, CA: AAAI Press.

Cabena, P., Hadjinian, P., Stadler, R., Verhees, J., & Zanasi, A. (1997). *Discovering data mining – From concept to implementation.* Upper Saddle River, NJ: Prentice Hall.

Chapman, P., Clinton, J., Kerner, R., Khabaza, T., Reinartz, T., Shearer, C., & Wirth, R. (2000). *CRISP-DM 1.0 – Step-by-step data mining guide.* Retrieved January 18, 2002 from http://www.crisp-dm.org/CRISPWP-0800.pdf.

Fayyad, U., Piatetsky-Shapiro, G., & Smyth, P. (1996). From data mining to knowledge discovery: An overview. In U. Fayyad, G. Piatetsky-Shapiro, P. Smyth & R. Uthurusamy (Eds.), *Advances in knowledge discovery and data mining* (pp. 1-34). Menlo Park, CA: AAAI Press.

Ferstl, O. K. (1979). *Konstruktion und Analyse von Simulationsmodellen.* Königstein/Ts., Germany: Hain.

Ferstl, O. K., & Sinz, E. J. (2001). *Grundlagen der Wirtschaftsinformatik, Band 1* (4th ed.). München, Germany: Oldenbourg.

Kietz, J. U., Zücker, R., & Vaduva, A. (2000, June). MINING MART: Combining case-based reasoning and multistrategy learning into a framework for reusing KDD applications. In R.S. Michalski & P. Brazdil (Eds.), *Proceedings of the 5th International Workshop on Multistrategy Learning (MSL 2000), Guimaraes, Portugal.* Print version n/a. Retrieved January 28, 2002 from http://www-ai.cs.uni-dortmund.de/DOKUMENTE/kietz_etal_2000a.pdf.

Klösgen, W., & Zytkow, J. M. (1996). Knowledge discovery in databases terminology. In U. Fayyad, G. Piatetsky-Shapiro, P. Smyth & R. Uthurusamy (Eds.), *Advances in knowledge discovery and data mining* (pp. 574-592). Menlo Park, CA: AAAI Press.

Knobloch, B. (2001). Der Data-Mining-Ansatz zur Analyse betriebswirtschaftlicher Daten. *Informationssystem-Architekturen, 8*(1), 59-115.

Knobloch, B., & Weidner, J. (2000, November). Eine kritische Betrachtung von Data Mining-Prozessen – Ablauf, Effizienz und Unterstützungspotenziale. In R. Jung & R. Winter (Eds.), *Proceedings of Data Warehousing 2000. Methoden, Anwendungen, Strategien, Friedrichshafen, Germany* (pp. 345-365). Heidelberg, Germany: Physica-Verlag.

Krahl, D., Windheuser, U., & Zick, F.-K. (1998). *Data Mining – Einsatz in der Praxis.* Bonn, Germany: Addison-Wesley.

MetaL: A Meta-Learning Assistant for Providing User Support in Machine Learning and Data Mining (2001). *ESPRIT METAL project* (26.357), Dec. 1998-Nov. 2001. Retrieved February 6, 2002 from http://www.metal-kdd.org/.

Mining Mart: Enabling End-User Data Warehouse Mining (2002). *IST Project* (IST-11993). Retrieved January 28, 2002 from http://www-ai.cs.uni-dortmund.de/FORSCHUNG/PROJEKTE/MININGMART/index.eng.html.

Pyle, D. (1999). *Data preparation for data mining.* San Francisco, CA: Morgan Kaufman.

Saarenvirta, G. (1998). Mining customer data – A step-by-step look at a powerful clustering and segmentation methodology. *DB2 Magazine online.* Electronic version of journal. Print version n/a. Retrieved June 14, 1999 from http://www.db2mag.com/98fsaar.html.

Skalak, D. B. (2001, May). Speed-up mining or Why is data mining iterative? *Proceedings of Workshop on Research Issues in Data Mining and Knowledge Discovery (DMKD'01), May 2001 Santa Barbara, CA.* Retrieved January 25, 2002 from http://www.cs.cornell.edu/johannes/dmkd2001-papers/p6_skalak.pdf.

Smyth, P. (2001, May). Breaking out of the black-box: Research challenges in data mining. *Proceedings of Workshop on Research Issues in Data Mining and Knowledge Discovery (DMKD'01), May 2001 Santa Barbara, CA.* Retrieved January 25, 2002 from http://www.cs.cornell.edu/johannes/dmkd2001-papers/p2_smythe.pdf.

Vaduva, A., Kietz, J.-U., Zücker, R., Dittrich, K. R., Morik, K., Botta, M., & Portinale, L. (2001). *M⁴ – The mining mart meta model* (Deliverables D8, D9). Retrieved January 16, 2002 from http://www-ai.cs.uni-dortmund.de/forschung/projekte/miningmart/deliverables/D89/MoM4.pdf.

About the Authors

Hamid R. Nemati is an associate professor of information systems in the Information Systems and Operations Management Department of the University of North Carolina at Greensboro (UNCG), USA. He holds a doctorate degree in management sciences and information technology from the University of Georgia and a Master of Business Administration from The University of Massachusetts. He has extensive professional information technology (IT) experience as an analyst and has consulted with a number of major corporations. Before coming to UNCG, he was on the faculty of J. Mack Robinson College of Business Administration at Georgia State University. His research specializations are in the areas of organizational data mining, decision support systems, data warehousing and knowledge management. He has presented nationally and internationally on a wide range of topics relating to his research interests. His research has been published in numerous top tier scholarly journals.

Christopher D. Barko is an information technology professional at Laboratory Corporation of America. His IT industry experience spans many years in various consulting, business intelligence, software engineering and analyst positions for a number of Fortune 500 organizations. He received his BBA in computer information systems from James Madison University and MBA from the University of North Carolina at Greensboro, where he specialized in decision support systems. His current research interests include organizational data mining, business intelligence and customer relationship management and how these technologies can enhance the organizational decision-making process to optimize resource allocation and improve profitability. His research has been published in several leading journals, such as the *Journal of Data Warehousing, Journal of Computer Information Systems* and others. He is also president of Customer Analytics Inc., a consultancy that leverages data mining and advanced analytics to deliver profit-enhancing marketing solutions.

*   *   *

Cheryl Aasheim was born in Miami, Fla. In August 2002, she received her Doctor of Philosophy in decision and information sciences from the University of Florida. She is currently an assistant professor at Georgia Southern University in the College of Information Technology, USA. Her current research interests are in the areas of information retrieval and data mining.

Riad A. Ajami is currently Charles A. Hayes distinguished professor of business and director of the Center for Global Business Education and Research at the University of North Carolina at Greensboro, USA. Ajami previously held the position of professor of international business and strategy and chair at the Ohio State University. He has had appointments as the Dr. M. Lee Pearce distinguished professor of international business and economic cooperation at the University of Miami; the School of Business Administration at the University of California, Berkeley; the Wharton School, University of Pennsylvania, and the Harvard Center for International Affairs at Harvard University. Ajami received his PhD from Pennsylvania State University in international business, strategic management and oil economics. He is an editorial board member of the *Journal of Global Information Technology Management, Competitiveness Review, Journal of Global Marketing, Journal of Transnational Management Development*, among others. Ajami is the author of *International Business: Theory and Applications*, among others. He has had articles published on international business in the *Journal of International Business Studies, Management International Review, Strategic Management Journal, International Journal of Management, Journal of Global Marketing, International Journal of Commerce and Management, International Journal of Technology Management, Multinational Business Review*, among others.

Pervaiz Alam is a professor of accounting at Kent State University, USA. He holds his PhD from the University of Houston. He is also a certified public accountant. His area of research is auditing, information systems and financial accounting. His recent publications have appeared in the *Journal of Accounting, Auditing, and Finance, Journal of Business Finance and Accounting, Journal of Managerial Issues* and *Expert Systems with Applications*. He has also published in several other journals.

Chandra S. Amaravadi is the State Farm professor of information systems at Western Illinois University, USA, and recipient of the £5,000 best paper prize from the National Computer Center, UK, for predicting the World and Business Computing in 2051. He holds a PhD from the University of Arizona and an MBA from the University of Minnesota. During his career, he served as a consultant with Wellspring Computer Services in Minneapolis and with Dun & Bradstreet in Madras, India. His research interests include data mining, executive support, knowledge management, office information systems and workflow models.

Pierre A. Balthazard is associate professor of information systems in the School of Management at Arizona State University West, USA. He received the PhD degree in IS and systems and industrial engineering from the University of Arizona. His current research interests include the design and investigation of collaborative and decision technologies to support teamwork across time and distance. His past research has been presented in numerous scientific publications and professional conferences around the world, and has been supported by the National Science Foundation. Balthazard is also a research associate for Human Synergistics Center for Applied Research and is president of Knowledge Instruments LLC, a Phoenix, Arizona-based consultancy on organization development.

Marca Marie Bear is currently an associate professor of management and international business, chair of the Department of Management and the associate director of the Center of Associate Professor of International Business and director of the Center for International Business and Economic Growth at the Rochester Institute of Technology, USA. Bear also served as a visiting assistant professor of international business at The Paul H. Nitze School of Advanced International Studies of Johns Hopkins University in 1996. Bear received her PhD in business administration, with a field concentration in international business and strategy policy from the Ohio State University. While at Ohio State, Bear earned a U.S. Department of Education Graduate Fellowship and the Bob Bartels PhD Fellowship in International Business. She is a member of Beta Gamma Sigma, the national honor society for business, and appears in the highly regarded reference book, Marquis Who's Who in America. She is also an editorial review board member for the Journal of Teaching in International Development. Bear has refereed articles and book chapters published in *Long Management and Development, International Journal of Management, Journal of Transnational Management and Development, Business & the Contemporary World*, among others. Bear is also a frequent contributor to national media and has appeared in the *Journal of Commerce* — published by the Economist Group, *USA Today*. She oversees teaching experience in executive MBA program at the Prague School of Economics, among others.

Charmion Brathwaite is a graduate student at the University of North Carolina at Greensboro (USA), pursuing a Master of Science degree in information technology and management. She graduated with a Bachelor of Science degree in computer science and mathematics in 1997 from the University of the West Indies (UWI), Trinidad and Tobago, and worked for several years as a software developer.

João Álvaro Carvalho has a degree in informatics and systems engineering from University of Minho, Portugal (1983), and a PhD in information systems from the University of Manchester Institute of Science and technology (UMIST), UK (1991). He is an associate professor at University of Minho, Portugal, and head of the Department of Information Systems. His research interests include the foundations of information systems, information systems development and knowledge management.

Ye-Sho Chen is a professor of management information systems in the Department of Information Systems and Decision Sciences, E. J. Ourso College of Business Administration, Louisiana State University (LSU)(USA). He is the associate director of the International Franchise Forum at LSU. He currently teaches and conducts research in the fields of knowledge management, business intelligence and electronic commerce in franchising and small business.

P. Pete Chong is currently the Martel Corp. professor of CIS, Department of Finance, Accounting, and CIS, University of Houston-Downtown, USA. His primary research interests have been in the area of information usage analysis and its application in business.

Mark S. Dale is a master's graduate and PhD student in the School of Business Systems at Monash University, Australia, and a member of the Data Mining Research Group in the Faculty of Information Technology at that institution. His research area is the strategic application of data mining within the Australian financial services industry. He teaches in the masters of information technology program within the Department of Information Systems at the University of Melbourne, and works as a private consultant within the Australian financial services industry in the areas of information technology strategy, process, control and security.

Farhad Daneshgar is a senior lecturer of information systems at the University of New South Wales, Australia. Prior to joining academia in 1994, he was an information technology (IT) consultant in the building and telecommunications industries in Australia. He received his PhD in computer science from the University of Technology, Sydney. His research interests include data mining, design of collaborative systems and collaboration patterns in organizational processes. More recently he has been the chief architect in the design and commercialization of a new generation of an Internet server appliance for SMEs that is based on a virtually infinite word-length processor.

Henry Dillon is a data mining consultant currently based in London. He completed a Bachelor of Commerce and Administration Honors degree at the Victoria University of Wellington, New Zealand. He has consulted on a number of data mining projects for organizations around the globe. His primary focus is the application of data mining and business intelligence initiatives within modern business. He has also presented and published at conferences in Europe and New Zealand.

Stephen D. Durbin received a PhD in physics (1984) from the University of California, Berkeley, and spent his formative years as a biophysicist and materials scientist at the University of California at San Diego, Carleton College and the Materials Research Institute of Tohoku University, Japan. The allure of artificial intelligence (AI) converted him to computer science, and he recently joined the Applied Research group at RightNow Technologies, USA. His particular interests include natural language processing, neural networks, cognitive science and knowledge management.

Ahmed Emam is assistant professor of computer science and engineering at Western Kentucky University, USA. He earned his PhD degree in computer science and engineering from the University of Louisville. Emam is currently researching trends in data mining and enterprise resource planning with Dr. Min.

Zuzana Gedeon is a member of technical staff at RightNow Technologies, USA. She received her MS in applied mathematics (1993) from Georgia Institute of Technology, and is currently working on her PhD in computer science at Montana State University. Her professional interests include clustering and data mining techniques.

Dale L. Goodhue is a professor of management information systems (MIS) at the University of Georgia's Terry College of Business, USA. He is an associate editor for both *Management Science* and *MIS Quarterly*, and has published in *Management Science, MIS Quarterly, Decision Sciences, Sloan Management Review* and other journals. His most cited works pertain to understanding the performance impact of matching technology functionality with task requirements, both at the individual and the organizational level, and techniques of data integration and their impacts in organizations. His current research interests include implementation issues and impacts of two such data integration techniques: data warehousing and enterprise resource planning systems.

Kara Harrington is a candidate for a master's in information technology management at the University of North Carolina at Greensboro, USA. She received a Bachelor of Arts degree in history and political science from the University of Massachusetts at Amherst in 1990. She has over 10 years experience in the real estate field and as a mortgage-banking auditor. She lives in Greensboro, North Carolina, with her husband and son.

Beverley Hope is a teacher in information systems within the School of Information Management at Victoria University of Wellington, New Zealand. She completed a Bachelor of Science and MBA at the University of Kansas and a PhD at the University of Hawaii at Manoa. During her PhD studies, she was supported by a scholarship from the East-West Centre. Her research focuses on information needs for quality initiatives, performance measurement, quality of online service delivery, electronic commerce and IS education. In her work, she takes a holistic or system view of organizations and the issues that face them. She has presented and published at many regional and international conferences in information systems, decision sciences and evaluation, and acted as referee for several international conferences and journals.

Robert Justis is the director of the International Franchise Forum at Louisiana State University, USA. He is a professor in the Management Department and the Entrepreneurship Institute, E. J. Ourso College of Business Administration, Louisiana State University. He specializes in the development and start up of franchising and entrepreneurial organizations. In addition, Justis has developed and presented franchising programs in Brazil, Mexico, China, Australia, Japan, Korea, Singapore, Philippines, Malaysia, France, Finland and Switzerland. He is recognized as an expert in franchising and entrepreneurship around the world and has served on the National Steering Committee of the Small Business Administration for five years. He was also a founder of the Society of Franchising and the Small Business Institute Directors' Association (SBIDA). He is the author of *Managing Your Small Business, Dynamics of American Business, Strategic Management* and *Policy and Basics of Franchising*. His most recent textbook, *Franchising* (co-authored with Richard Judd) is published by South-Western Publishing Co. and is the best-selling textbook in the field.

Bernd Knobloch is research and teaching assistant (Wissenschaftlicher Mitarbeiter) and PhD candidate at the Department of Information Systems – Systems Engineering at University of Bamberg, Germany. He holds a diploma degree of Diplom-Wirtschaftsinformatiker Univ. from the same university. He has broad data mining and data analysis experience from a number of projects, especially in the retail industry, and worked as a data miner with SAP AG. His current research concentrates on improving data analysis process efficiency and on integrating complementary approaches to data analysis.

Gary J. Koehler has held academic positions at Northwestern University, Purdue University and at the University of Florida, where he is the John B. Higdon Eminent scholar and professor of Decision and Information Sciences in the Warrington School of Business at the University of Florida, USA. He has published in *Decision Support Systems, Management Science, the Journal on Computing, Evolutionary Computation, Operations Research, Decision Sciences* and others. He is on the editorial boards of *Decision Science, Decision Support Systems, Information Technology and Management* and several other journals. His current research interests are e-commerce related.

Mary Jane Lenard is an assistant professor of accounting at the University of North Carolina at Greensboro (USA). Her PhD is from Kent State University and she is a certified management accountant. She is a member of the American Accounting Association, the Decision Sciences Institute, the Institute of Management Accountants and the Association of Certified Fraud Examiners. Her areas of research include auditing and the use of emerging technologies for business decision making and education. Her recent publications have appeared in *Decision Sciences, Journal of Management Information Systems* and *International Journal of Intelligent Systems in Accounting, Finance and Management.*

Hokey Min is professor of Supply Chain Management, Distinguished University Scholar and director of the UPS Center for World-wide Supply Chain Management at the University of Louisville, USA. He earned his PhD degree in management sciences and logistics from the Ohio State University. His research interests include global logistics strategy, e-synchronized supply chain, benchmarking and supply chain modeling. He has published more than 70 articles in various refereed journals including *European Journal of Operational Research, Journal of Business Logistics, Journal of the Operational Research Society, Information and Management* and *Transportation Research.*

Scott Nicholson is an assistant professor at Syracuse University's School of Information Studies, USA. Nicholson has an extensive background both in data mining and library and information science, and has worked to combine librarianship with statistical and artificial intelligence methods from decision science in order to improve library management.

Hanne Norreklit, MSc, PhD, is a professor of international management and control at the Aarhus School of Business, Denmark. She has served at various universities, including the International Center for Education and Research in Accounting, University of Illinois at Urbana-Champaign, UNSA and HEC Graduate School of Management, Paris, France. She has published a number of articles and books on the balanced scorecard, performance evaluation and transfer pricing in multinational companies.

Parviz Partow-Navid has been at California State University, Los Angeles (CSLA) in the Department of Information Systems since 1983. He is currently department chair of information systems. He earned his MBA and PhD from the University of Texas at Austin in operations research and mathematical programming. His publications in the information systems area can be found in several journals: the *Computers and Operations Research, Journal of Applied Business Research, Journal of Systems Management, Journal of Information Technology Management, Software Engineering* and *Technological Horizons in Education Journal.* Partow's interests are in decision support systems, intelligent systems, e-commerce, Internet security and distance learning.

Richard E. Potter is assistant professor of information and decision sciences in the School of Business Administration at the University of Illinois at Chicago, USA. He received the PhD degree in management and management information systems from the University of Arizona. His current research interest is cognition and behavior in the electronic environment, with emphasis on motivation and performance assessment and intervention with electronically supported groups. He has published in a number of leading scientific journals, and has presented his work in academic conferences around the world. Potter is also a research associate for Human Synergistics Center for Applied Research and consulting scientist for Knowledge Instruments LLC, a Phoenix, Arizona-based consultancy on organization development.

Isabel Ramos has a degree in informatics/applied mathematics from Portucalense University Portugal (1988), a master's degree in informatics for management and a PhD in Technology and Information Systems, both from University of Minho, Portugal (1994 and 2001, respectively). He is an invited assistant professor at University of Minho. Her research interests include the role of emotions in the adoption and use of computer-based systems, the way technologies can improve human learning capabilities, knowledge management, the impact of beliefs and values in requirements engineering and the multidimensionality of work and its impact on the adoption and use of computer-based systems.

Richard T. Redmond is chairman and associate professor at the Department of Information Systems, School of Business at Virginia Commonwealth University (VCU), USA. He specializes in software engineering, database systems, expert systems and applications of artificial intelligence (AI) to business. His research and publications have been in the areas of software productivity, expert systems, application of AI to business, database and image base design theory and compression theory. Redmond joined the faculty at VCU in the fall of 1983. He served as acting chairman from January of 1994 until fall of 1996; director of technology, Department of Information Systems from 1996 until summer of 2000, and acting chairman from summer of 2000 to July 1, 2001, when he was named chair.

J. Neal Richter is an applied artificial intelligence (AI) researcher at RightNow Technologies (USA). He has an MS in computer science (2002) from Utah State University and is a PhD student at Montana State University. Current interests include machine learning, natural language processing, fuzzy logic, dynamic systems, cellular automata, evolutionary computation and theoretical evolutionary computation models.

Rahul Singh is an assistant professor in the information systems and operations management Department at the University of North Carolina at Greensboro, USA. He obtained his PhD in business administration from Virginia Commonwealth University. His research interests are in the area of the design of systems that apply intelligent technologies to business decision systems. Specific interests include intelligent agents, knowledge management systems, data mining and machine learning systems. His research work has appeared in the *International Journal of Production Engineering, Journal of Decision Systems, Socio-Economic Planning Sciences* and *The Encyclopedia of Information Systems*.

Ludwig Slusky, PhD, is a professor of information systems at California State University, Los Angeles, USA. He was also an e-learning provider practitioner in administering international distance learning program over the Internet. Slusky is the author of a book on cases for database design, the author of various articles published by Software Engineering, Information and Software Technology, Data Management, Idea Group Publishing, etc., and papers presented at diverse conferences. Slusky's interests are in databases, e-development, e-commerce and distance learning.

Kate A. Smith is an associate professor, where she is deputy head of School and Director of Research. She holds a BSc(Hons) in mathematics and a PhD in electrical engineering, both from the University of Melbourne, Australia. She is also director of the Data Mining Research Group in the Faculty of Information Technology at Monash University, Australia. Smith has published two books on neural networks in business, and more than 100 journal and international conference papers in the areas of neural networks, combinatorial optimization and data mining. She is a member of the organizing committee for several international data mining and neural network conferences, and regularly acts as a consultant to industry in these areas.

Jeffrey Stanton is an assistant professor at Syracuse University's School of Information Studies (USA). Stanton is an organizational psychologist with two decades of professional and consulting experience putting technology to work in organizational settings. Stanton has published more than 20 peer reviewed journal articles and book chapters, about half of which pertain to research methods and statistics.

David M. Steiger is an associate professor of management information systems at the University of Maine, USA. He received his BS in electrical engineering, an MBA from the University of Texas at Austin and a PhD in management science/information systems from Oklahoma State University. Between his MBA and PhD degrees, he spent 15 years in various analysis and managerial positions in industry, applying the concepts of information systems and management science. Steiger's research interests include knowledge management, decision support systems and inductive artificial intelligence technologies. His articles have appeared in *Information Systems Research, Management Science, Journal of Management Information Systems, Interfaces, INFORMS Journal on Computing, European Journal of Operational Research, Decision Support Systems, Journal of Knowledge Management* and *Journal of Data Warehousing*.

Natalie M. Steiger received a BS and an MS in mathematics from the University of Southern Mississippi and a PhD in industrial engineering from North Carolina State University. From 1975 to 1986, she was an engineering economic analyst and manager of petroleum-reserve information systems for Cities Service Oil and Gas Company and Occidental Petroleum Company in Tulsa, Okla. She held a position as visiting assistant professor in the Information Systems and Operations Management Department of the Bryan School of Business at the University of North Carolina at Greensboro for the 1999-2000 academic year. Steiger is currently assistant professor of production and operations management in the Maine Business School at the University of Maine (USA) in Orono. She has published in *Management Science* and *INFORMS Journal on Computing*, and is a member of IIE, INFORMS and the INFORMS College on Simulation.

William L. Tullar is an associate professor of management in the Joseph M. Bryan School of Business and Economics at University of North Carolina at Greensboro, USA. He teaches courses in organizational behavior, organizational theory, personnel/human resources, marketing research, multivariate statistics and consumer behavior. Tullar is developing course work integrating SAP into the human resources course offerings, and is offering courses in Moldova via distance learning. He was a visiting fellow at the International Research Institute for Management Science in Moscow, USSR (1990, 1991), a visiting professor at the Fachhochschule Rheinland-Pfalz, Worms (1993-4), a 1999 Fulbright German Studies Scholar and an adjunct professor at the International Institute of Management in Chisinau, Moldova (2000-present). His current research interests include virtual teams and groups, selection interviewing via the Internet and reengineering.

Rustam Vahidov is an assistant professor of management information systems (MIS) in the Department of Decision Sciences and MIS at John Molson School of Business, Concordia University, Montreal, Quebec, Canada. He earned his PhD from Georgia State University, Atlanta. Vahidov's research interests include decision support systems, multi-agent systems, genetic algorithms, fuzzy logic, neural networks and electronic commerce. He has published in the *Journal of Management Information Systems, Journal of Decision Support Systems, Information & Management, International Journal of Intelligent Systems, Fuzzy Sets and Systems* and other journals and conference proceedings.

Doug Warner is head of applied research at RightNow Technologies (USA), where he has worked since 1999. He received a BS in computer science and psychology (1991) from the New Mexico Institute of Mining and Technology and an MS in psychology (1994) from the University of New Mexico. His current research interests include collaborative filtering and visualization of complex information.

Hugh J. Watson is a professor of management information systems (MIS) and a holder of a C. Herman and Mary Virginia Terry Chair of Business Administration at the University of Georgia, USA. He is the author of 22 books and more than 100 journal articles. Throughout his career, he has focused on the use of information technology to support decision making. Most recently, he has concentrated on data warehousing. Watson is the senior editor of the *Journal of Data Warehousing* and a fellow of The Data

Warehousing Institute. He is the senior director of the Teradata University Network (www.teradatauniversitynetwork.com), a free portal for the academic community. He serves the consulting series editor for John Wiley & Sons' Computing and Information Processing series.

Barbara H. Wixom is an assistant professor of commerce at the University of Virginia's McIntire School of Commerce, USA. She received her PhD in management information systems (MIS) from the University of Georgia, completing a large-scale study on data warehousing success as her dissertation. She is an associate editor for the *Journal of Data Warehousing*, has published in journals that include *MIS Quarterly, Information Systems Research, Journal of Data Warehousing* and *Communications of the ACM*, and has presented her work at national and international conferences. In 1998, Wixom was named a fellow by The Data Warehousing Institute for her research in data warehousing. She has co-authored two systems analysis and design textbooks for John Wiley & Sons.

Victoria Yoon is an associate professor in the Department of Information Systems at University of Maryland, Baltimore County, USA. Before that, she was an associate professor at the Department of Information Systems at Virginia Commonwealth University. She received her MS from the University of Pittsburgh and her PhD from the University of Texas at Arlington. She has published more than 30 articles in leading journals such as *MIS Quarterly, Decision Support Systems, Journal of Management Information Systems, Information and Management, Journal of Operation Research Society* and others.

Jeff Zeanah is president of Z Solutions, Inc. (USA). The company has been an industry leader in the application of adaptive learning and statistical methods for knowledge discovery. Clients have come from several industries, including computer manufacturers, automobile manufacturers, financial services, energy providers, risk management and public health. Zeanah has developed a reputation as a leading expert in the application of neural networks, predictive modeling and adaptive learning for data investigation, and is a frequent instructor on those topics. He specializes in working with all levels within an organization to achieve analytical success.

Index

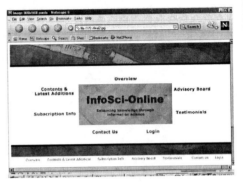